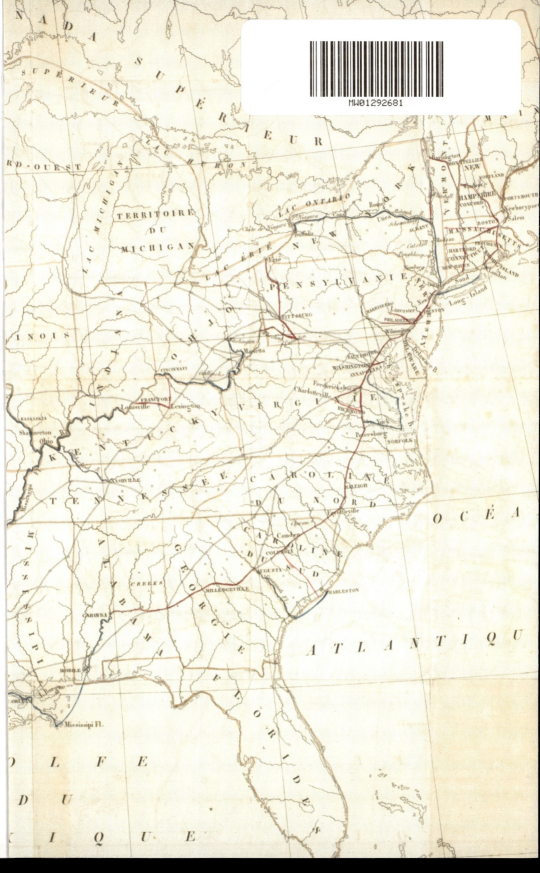

THE
LAST
ADIEU

Lafayette's Triumphant Return,
the Echoes of Revolution, and
the Gratitude of the Republic

RYAN L. COLE

HARPER HORIZON

The Last Adieu
© 2025 by Ryan L. Cole

Published by Harper Horizon,
an imprint of HarperCollins Focus LLC.

Any internet addresses, phone numbers, or company or product information printed in this book are offered as a resource and are not intended in any way to be or to imply an endorsement by Harper Horizon, nor does Harper Horizon vouch for the existence, content, or services of these sites, phone numbers, companies, or products beyond the life of this book.

ISBN 978-1-4002-5132-2 (ePub)
ISBN 978-1-4002-5131-5 (HC)

Library of Congress Control Number: 2025934844

Interior Design: Neuwirth & Associates, Inc.

Printed in the United States of America
25 26 27 28 29 LBC 5 4 3 2 1

*This book is dedicated to the memory and,
I hope, captures the spirit of my father,
Bruce M. Cole.*

CONTENTS

PART THREE

THE GRAND VOYAGE

PART FOUR

THE LAST ADIEU

PRELUDE

An Episode That Belongs to the Poetry of History

At sunrise on April 29, 1825, John Reynolds heard the salute of thirteen cannons from his home near St. Louis. At once he recognized what and *who* the sound signified. Thirty years later, Reynolds could hear the cannon still and remembered well that morning when he was transported to a revolution fought half a century before, to the times that tried men's souls.[1]

Fifty years after the fact, Ebenezer Stedman still recollected fishing with his brother under the shade of an oak tree on a Kentucky eve near their home in Georgetown, when a bugle's call announced a stage rider hurtling down the road with incredible information: *He* was at Frankfort and would soon be on his way. Stedman quickly lost interest in angling altogether.

Josiah Quincy Jr. was milling about Boston's city line when the barouche carrying the hero approached from the south. It was a sight so dazzling, he could not even find the words to describe it half a century later.

Though decades passed, for Harriet Johnson the day never faded. There she stood in the doorway of her family's homestead in the Vermont village of Royalton, holding her mother's hand: They watched as a carriage, pulled by six white horses, passed by, and an old man inside stood and bowed to cheering crowds. "Of all the pictures that hang on memory's walls, none is more vivid to me today," she reminisced.[2]

On a sun-drenched Fourth of July, he stepped from the carriage into a crowd on Brooklyn Heights, gently lifted a child in his arms. As an old man, that boy, Walt Whitman, could still remember the hero's kind face, the kiss he placed on his cheek.[3]

At midnight, well-wishers crowded the illuminated banks of the Ohio River and ships congested its port. As martial music floated in the air, competing with the boom of cannons, his steamboat pulled away from Cincinnati, never to return. Long after it had vanished upstream, John D. Caldwell wrote that the spectacle "seems to me, after a lapse of 50 years, the most brilliant sight of my life."[4]

What manner of event could burn so vividly, so long after it had passed, in the minds of men and women who had only participated in it peripherally?

In the words of Massachusetts senator Charles Sumner, it was "an episode which belongs to the poetry of history."[5] It remains one of time's most beautiful reunions: In 1824, after an absence of forty years—nearly equidistant from the ratification of the American Constitution and the beginning of the country's Civil War—the Marquis de Lafayette, the last living major general of America's revolutionary army, reappeared on its shores. A discouraged old soldier returned to his adopted home, where a hero's welcome awaited. Fate had afforded the warrior a final chance to embrace his brothers-in-arms who still lived and to shake the hands of the children of those who had gone to their graves.

On the eve of the fiftieth anniversary of their independence, as they celebrated Lafayette, Americans rallied together to express gratitude to the men who had fought for and won it. Catching the reflection of their prosperous republic in his happy eyes, they found affirmation in the progress made possible by the first patriots' sacrifices.

Ebenezer Stedman, who saw the Frenchman in Kentucky, shared this story with his daughter, part of a series of letters that doubled as a memoir of his life and times. "I cannot give you any idea of the feeling amongst the people. It seemed to pervade all classes, women and children from the first day he landed in the United States. Lafayette was on every tongue and in short time the patriotism and love for the companion of Washington ran so like some epidemic that everything was *Lafayette*," Stedman explained, lest the magnitude of his reminiscence be misunderstood.[6]

"He was proclaimed by the popular voice, the guest of the nation & his presence everywhere was the signal for festivals and rejoicing," Stedman recalled. "He passed though the 24 states of the Union in a sort of triumphant procession, in which all parties joined to forget their dissentions, in which the veterans of the war renewed their youth & the young were carried back to the doings & sufferings of their fathers."[7]

It was the greatest joy the young republic ever experienced, the grandest celebration it would ever stage, a heartfelt profusion of gratitude and an illumination of liberty, ignited by its great apostle around memories of the American Revolution, blazing from the coast of the Atlantic Ocean to the banks of the Mississippi River.

"As there never was such a guest," Sumner wrote, "so was there never such a host."[8] After a separation so long, in the summer of 1824, they met again, perhaps as fate had intended, when both needed each other most.

THE
LAST
ADIEU

PART ONE

The Walking Monument

1

The Shrine
of Sainted Excellence

"It is an old house, not at all ruinous, but *tres historique*," one sojourner remembered.[1] The voyage there took would-be pilgrims east from Paris, over primitive roads or no roads at all: Their carriages forded brooks, cut through forests, and across farms until, at last, its five spires rising in the sky, La Grange appeared.

Then the wilderness gave way to a twisting avenue lined with pear and apple trees. It crossed a moat, filled with fish, fed by a stream from a nearby pond, and wrapped around the castle, before passing through an arched entrance and coming to a stop in the château's courtyard. Visitors paused to admire the verdant park, the scars of cannon blast on the freestone walls, and the ivy crawling up one of the towers. Though it was a deeply romantic setting, like a dwelling conjured from a medieval fairy tale, the idealists who flocked to this remote castle in Seine-et-Marne in the early 1820s came not for the stunning milieu but for the old man at its center, whose life story was far greater than any work of fiction.

There they found him, the patriarch surrounded by his children and their children; the soldier returned to his plow. The chiming of the castle's bell summoned guests from their quarters to the dining room, where meals, "sumptuous, in the French style," were served. Conversation and coffee, "strong without cream," followed in the drawing room while his grandchildren played piano and sang. Afternoons were spent inspecting his farm, whose stalls were filled with every manner of livestock, though a special point of pride were the flock of merino sheep. There was even an enclosed aviary filled with "rare and curious birds."[2]

"We undertook our journey to La Grange with the same pleasure," Lady Morgan wrote, "as the pilgrim begins his first unwearied steps to the shrine of sainted excellence."[3] The relics in this shrine were works of art, trophies, gifts, and mementos, reminders of friends and family now gone, rewards for heroic deeds long ago rendered. On occasion, he would welcome visitors to his library, high in one of the towers, and present these curios, all carefully placed and organized, like the curator of a museum dedicated to the story of his tumultuous life. The precious collection, spread throughout La Grange, comforted its owner with warm memories as he neared the twilight of his life. Morgan observed that conversation with him opened "a splendid page in the history of man."[4] These objets d'art provided the illustrations.

There was a portrait of his parents: Michel Louis Christophe Roch Gilbert du Motier, a colonel in the French Grenadiers and the son of a cadet branch of a noble family, and Marie Louise Jolie de La Rivière, daughter of a far wealthier noble line. When Michel's head was blown off during the Battle of Minden in 1759, their only child, a boy born two years prior, on September 6, 1757, in rural Auvergne at the family château, Chavaniac, was left heir to the family title. His name was Marie-Joseph Paul Yves Roch Gilbert. At the age of two, he became the Marquis de Lafayette. When his mother died in 1770, followed soon after by her father, the young marquis was, at twelve, among the wealthiest men in France.[5]

A gold medallion, suspended around his neck, held another portrait. Lafayette had wed Adrienne de Noailles, the daughter of an eminent and well-connected noble family, on April 11, 1774. He was sixteen; she was fourteen. The union had been arranged by his uncle and her parents, but their love was genuine and, despite his indiscretions, long-lasting.

Marriage brought Lafayette a place among the young aristocrats at Versailles, in the court of King Louis XVI. A rustic by comparison to the urbane company gathered at Versailles, he felt out of place among the nobility. Reserved in nature, Lafayette had, by his own account, "an observing disposition."[6] Other nobles with whom he socialized were less charitable: He was "left-handed in all manners," the Comte de La Mark recalled, and "he danced without grace, rode badly on horse-back."[7] The former shortcoming even became a source of amusement for Queen Marie Antionette.

Also on La Grange's walls hung a portrait of the Duke de Noailles, Adrienne's father. In his memoirs, Lafayette recalled that from a tender age, he had been "burning with the desire to have a uniform," inspired by the desire to emulate and avenge his father. Studying Greek and Roman history at Paris's Collège du Plessis stirred in him notions of heroism, honor, and virtue. But Lafayette's earliest military appointment, at thirteen, required little more than galloping from Paris to Versailles to inquire whether King Louis XV had any orders for the company's commander—only to return with the news that he did not. Joining the Noailles offered somewhat better prospects: The duke secured Lafayette a commission as a lieutenant and then captain of a company in the Noailles Dragoons. In 1775, however, a new minister of war, the Comte de Saint-Germain, sought to install a merit-based system in France's army, precluding further advancement.

Over a door in one of La Grange's receiving rooms was a painting of a frigate, the American flag flying from its mast, the French flag at its stern, sailing toward a new world. As a young man, Lafayette harbored early dreams of "travelling over the world to acquire fame" with "glorious deeds."[8] But he was a stranger at court, uninterested in the hedonistic life of a listless aristocrat, a soldier who had achieved nothing on his own in a peacetime army. Chances were slender of realizing his aspirations.

In August 1776, Lafayette attended a dinner while stationed in Metz near the German border. The guest of honor was King George III's younger brother, the Duke of Gloucester, who shared correspondence he'd recently received from England regarding their colonies, now in revolt. Before the evening was over, Lafayette had determined he would go to America.

In Paris, Silas Deane, a Connecticut merchant dispatched by the Continental Congress to acquire supplies and recruit engineers to aid the American army, was overwhelmed: Frenchmen eager to join *les insurgents*, including Lafayette, besieged him for military commissions. The teenager had never seen battle; he spoke no English. His connections, though, intrigued the American agent hoping to advance an alliance with France. The marquis's title and wealth sweetened the pot: Lafayette, keenly aware of the power of imagery, correctly predicted the jolt of excitement a French nobleman joining the rebel army would create. On December 7, Lafayette and Deane signed a contract making him a major general. On April 20, 1777, when he left behind a pregnant wife and disapproving father-in-law and sailed for America from the Bay of Biscay, it was on *La Victoire*, a ship he had paid for himself, at the cost of 112,000 livres, the rendering of which years later hung in his home.

Another adornment on the walls of La Grange's receiving room was an engraving of America's Declaration of Independence, passed by the Continental Congress on July 2, 1776. Nearly a year later, Lafayette stood outside the Pennsylvania State House in Philadelphia, where the new nation had avowed its freedom. He was ready to risk his life and spend his fortune to secure it. The journey there, from Charleston, South Carolina—*La Victoire* dropped anchor off North Island, on June 13, 1777—began in coaches, which soon broke down, continued on horses, which then died, and finished on foot, a grueling march through sweltering heat, beset by insects and dysentery.

Lafayette, who began to learn English during the voyage to America, was enthralled with this new country. His letters to Adrienne were full of idealistic impressions of its people. Their manners, he wrote, were simple and polite, their society free of class distinctions, and their landscape a collection of "vast forests and immense rivers" that created an appearance "of youth and majesty."[9] The contrast to his more jaded companions highlighted Lafayette's enthusiastic disposition—a quality that would endear him to America's leaders and people. In his journal, Charles Louis, Vicomte de Mauroy, a lieutenant colonel in the French grenadiers whom Silas Deane had commissioned as a general, expressed disdain for the colonies. He was appalled by the slovenly women, drunken men, and amateur army, concluding "the Americans are disunited regarding their common cause and I don't think they will ever do anything remarkable."[10]

The cynicism traveled in both directions. When the Frenchmen reached the seat of the Continental Congress, they were presented to James Lovell, a congressman and former schoolteacher who spoke French fluently. Standing outside the State House, where the Continental Congress met, Lovell lectured the weary travelers: Congress was frustrated at Deane, whose generous offers of commissions had sent French soldiers descending on Congress, some of whom were inept on the battlefield and whose arrogance off it had stirred resentment among American politicians and officers alike. The army had no need for the services of these "adventurers" and no intention of recognizing their contracts, Lovell told his stunned audience. Too rashly: Lafayette quickly appealed to Congress, whose members took note of his useful wealth, connections, and title. An apologetic Lovell, accompanied by a fellow congressman, the more tactful and also French-speaking William Duer, tracked down the boy and eventually tendered a new commission as a major general, dated July 31, so as not to supersede the seniority of other officers. It was offered on the conditions that Lafayette himself would stipulate in a letter to Congress: "After the sacrifices I have made, I have the right to exact two favors: one is, to serve at my own expense—the other is, to serve at first as volunteer."[11]

At last, he could take his place in America's army. Nearly half a century later, reminders of its leader and Lafayette's adopted father, were spread across La Grange: busts and portraits, a pair of ivory-handled glasses, a faded parasol, and even a piece of fabric sewn by his wife, Martha.

They first met at a dinner held at Philadelphia's City Tavern on August 5. Lafayette spotted him from across the room: The stature and bearing were unmistakable. Here was George Washington. After they were introduced and the dinner ended, the commander in chief of the Continental Army pulled the young soldier aside and encouraged him to feel welcome at his headquarters.

Three days later, on August 8, at Germantown, outside Philadelphia, Lafayette first viewed the American army: just under eleven thousand soldiers, poorly armed and attired, some barely clothed. And for the first time, they saw him: an elegantly outfitted major general, not yet twenty, thin and tall—he stood just under six feet—with broad shoulders, an aquiline nose, hazel eyes under a prominent brow, a high forehead, and reddish hair. "We must feel embarrassed to an exhibit before an officer who has just quitted French troops," Washington confessed to Lafayette. The Frenchman did not judge, reminding his new friend that he had come "to learn, and not to teach."[12] Such humility, Lafayette recalled, was "unusual for a European"—and charming to Americans. "There has been an addition to the General's family lately—the Marquis Lafayette of one of the first families in France, a young gentleman of modest manners," wrote Timothy Pickering, adjutant general of the army.[13]

In a room on La Grange's first floor, a space was dedicated almost entirely to objects from America, including weapons pulled from the battlefield where Lafayette first tasted the military glory he had come from France to acquire. On the morning of September 11, 1777, Washington's army waited along the eastern banks of Brandywine Creek; General Sir William Howe's army of British regulars and Hessians approached from the west, attempting to cross the river at Chadds Ford on its way to take Philadelphia, twenty-six miles to the north. While the two forces exchanged fire across the river, another British column under Lord Cornwallis crossed the river farther north, intending to swing south and attack the American's right flank.

When a division under General John Sullivan rushed to meet them, Lafayette followed. As the American soldiers began to fall back in the face of British fire, he dismounted and rallied the men, even pushing their shoulders until they steadied and fought, retreating only when the enemy was within twenty yards. During the chaos, Lafayette's aide-de-camp alerted him to the blood pouring out from the boot on his left leg; a musket ball had shot straight through it beneath the calf. After nearly fainting from blood loss, Lafayette was carried off the field and attended to by Washington's personal doctor, John Cochran.

The injury was ultimately minor, though its symbolic impact was considerable. The night of the battle, when Washington dictated a report to Congress, he made special mention of the young Frenchman's wound. Colonial newspapers reprinted Washington's message and heaped praise of their own on the new hero: "The Marquis de la Fayette, that most accomplish'd Youth, behaved with a Bravery equal to his noble Birth and amiable Character," the *Independent Chronicle* of Boston celebrated. Here, to the colonists' astonishment, was a young nobleman who had disinterestedly come to their aid, not only bleeding for America at Brandywine, but by his presence on the battlefield, affirming the righteousness of their cause.

To Adrienne, Lafayette claimed to be "loved by all parties, both foreigners and Americans." "All the foreigners who are in the army," he explained, "they do not understand why I am the only stranger beloved in America, and cannot understand why they are so much hated."[14] Among those who now grew fond of Lafayette was Washington himself. "I am established in his house, and we live together like two attached brothers," Lafayette wrote to Adrienne, with perhaps a touch of embellishment. The esteem, though, was mutual. "I do most devoutly wish that we had not a single Foreigner among us," Washington later wrote, "except the Marquis de la Fayette, who acts upon very different principles than those which govern the rest."[15]

Half a century later, visitors to La Grange saw a beautiful present Congress gave to Lafayette for his services, "a small mark of their grateful acknowledgments," as Benjamin Franklin, America's ambassador to France, described it.[16]

In the fall of 1778, as Lafayette prepared to take furlough and return to France, Congress commissioned a sword to be forged by his Parisian cutler and delivered by Franklin's grandson William Temple Franklin to Lafayette when he reached Le Havre. On one side of the knob under its golden handle was his adopted motto, *Cur Non*; on the other, an engraved half-moon shining on the sea; in the foreground, France, and in the distance, America. Between them, the words *CRESCAM UT PROSIM*—"I will grow so that I can do good." On each side of the handle were medallions: One pictured Lafayette, sword in hand, standing over the English lion; the other, a female figure of America, broken chains in her left hand, offering laurels to the Frenchman with her right. The scenes that provoked this gratitude were carved across the sword's curved guard. In one, Lafayette—his injury not yet fully healed—returned to the army on November 25, 1777, attacked the Hessian pickets, and sent them retreating during the Battle of Gloucester in New Jersey; the successful reconnaissance mission further enhanced Lafayette's standing within the army and with Congress. On December 1, 1777, at Washington's urging, Congress awarded Lafayette command of his own division. In a second relief on the sword's guard, after the miserable winter at Valley Forge, Lafayette led the skillful escape from the British army outside Philadelphia at Barren Hill. In a third, he appeared on horseback, sword in hand, at Monmouth Court House, helping salvage symbolic victory from near defeat. In the final relief, Lafayette commanded the rearguard as the Americans safely retreated from Newport.

"The idol of congress, of the army, and of the American people," Lafayette returned to France in February 1779, after a two-year absence. A redeemed hero's welcome waited. His reunion with Adrienne was both anguished and joyful: Their first child, a daughter named Henriette, died in 1777, while he was in America. But another daughter, Anastasie, was born in his absence on July 1, 1777. On Christmas Eve 1779, his only son was born. "The Boy shall be Call'd *George*," Lafayette informed Franklin, "and you will easily Guess that he bears that Name as a tribute of Respect and Love for my dear friend Gnl. Washington."[17] Evidence that the admiration was reciprocal came during Lafayette's absence, when François, Marquis de Barbé-Marbois, secretary to the French minister La Luzerne, noted in his diary that Washington, when speaking of Lafayette, was overcome with emotion. "Tears fell from his eyes," Barbé-Marbois wrote. "He clasped my hand, and could hardly utter the words: 'I do not know a nobler, finer soul, and I love him as my own son.'"[18]

Working with Franklin, Lafayette used his furlough to secure funds and supplies for the American army and to convince the French government to send an expeditionary force to aid its fight against England. Lafayette hoped he would be placed at its head. When the command was instead given to the more senior and seasoned Comte de Rochambeau, he left for America ahead of the force, assigned to bring Washington word of the reinforcements and a frigate full of supplies. But not before leaving with a characteristic flourish, registering his disappointment. "He took leave of the King a few days ago," John Adams wrote his wife, Abigail, "in the Uniform of American Major General, and attracted the Eyes of the whole Court more than ever." Adams, in Paris as the American envoy, took note of the sword at Lafayette's side. "He had on no doubt his American sword which is indeed a Beauty, and which he shews with great Pleasure, upon proper Occasions."[19]

Congress's gift was among the objects in the collection most prized by Lafayette, but pride of placement suggested an even more treasured work: a painting of the high command at Yorktown, hung above his bed. By the winter of 1780, the infant nation's fortunes were at a nadir. Congress was divided; its currency was worthless. The army camped at Morristown endured a winter even crueler than the one in Valley Forge; soldiers were starved, half-clothed, and deserting. A British blockade of the Hudson River choked off supplies; the previous fall, General Benedict Arnold, the hero of Saratoga, defected to the British; and in March, the port of Charleston fell. "There never has been a stage of the War in which the dissatisfaction has been so general or alarming," Washington wrote in April 1780. "It has lately in particular instances worn features of a very dangerous complexion."[20]

It was no wonder, then, that when Lafayette landed at Boston on April 28, 1780, his arrival was a hopeful sign to desperate citizens. Cannons boomed and bands played during the afternoon. Fireworks and bonfires blazed in the evening. Similar receptions guided his path to Morristown, where he was reunited with Washington and shared the happy news of the coming French army.

Word of French aid and Lafayette's lobbying of states for additional matériel prodded Congress, reenergized the war effort, and resulted in much-needed aid for the army. When an attack on New York City proved impractical, Washington dispatched Lafayette southward at the head of a corps of twelve hundred soldiers—uniformed at his own expense—to stop Arnold's raids on American supply depots in Virginia. When British Lord Cornwallis, after costly fights with Major General Nathanael Greene's army in the Carolinas, moved north to Virginia, Lafayette's outnumbered troops followed, feinting, attacking, and retreating, eventually trapping Cornwallis at his base on the York River. Meanwhile, a French fleet led by Comte de Grasse blocked the Chesapeake Bay after the Battle of the Capes. Washington and Rochambeau's combined forces marched to Virginia, rendezvoused with Lafayette, trapped Cornwallis, and laid siege to Yorktown, climactically storming two forward redoubts on the British left under the cover of night on October 19, 1781. Two days later, the British general surrendered. The war was not yet formally over, but America's independence was won.

Four years earlier, the colonial government had viewed the boy as a well-connected adornment for their cause, one who would play soldier and then return home. Lafayette, on the other hand, had come in search of glory and fame. And he earned both in battle. But in the process, he had fallen in love not only with America but also with its cause, beginning a lifelong campaign for the rights of men.

In December 1781, Lafayette returned home to a hero's welcome in France. Shortly after Adrienne gave birth to another daughter, Virginie, he proudly announced to Washington, "I took the liberty to Call Her By The Name of <u>Virginia</u>."[21] Guided by "Principles of Public and American Utility," over the next three years he zealously represented the fledgling nation's interests abroad and founded the French chapter of the Society of the Cincinnati, the organization established in 1783 by officers who had served under George Washington to perpetuate their bonds. Its name, inspired by the Roman general Lucius Quinctius Cincinnatus, who refused lifelong power and returned to his plow, was itself a tribute to Washington.

Lafayette, however, was restless. "Both duty and Inclination Lead me to America," he wrote to his general in 1782.[22] Departures were set but delayed: America's peace commissioners maintained he would be of more value in Paris during their negotiations with England than at Washington's headquarters in Princeton during a nearly concluded war. The absence ate at his heart. "Every Mention, Every Remembrance of America makes me Sigh for the Moment When I May Enjoy the Sight of our free and Independent Shores," he wrote to Washington.[23]

Friends and admirers across the Atlantic Ocean longed for a reunion too. Washington, in what he presumed would be his "last bow," surrendered his commission in December 1783. In his words, now "a private citizen on the banks of the Potomac, & under the shadow of my own Vine & my own Fig tree, free from the bustle of a camp & the busy scenes of public life,"[24] he explained to Lafayette that after nearly nine years' absence from his Virginia plantation, Mount Vernon, he was in no position to visit France. "This not being the case with you," he reasoned, "come . . . view me in my domestic walks—I have often told you, & I repeat it again, that no man could receive you in them with more friendship & affection than I should do."[25]

Persuasion was unnecessary. After securing American access to four French ports, Lafayette set sail in the spring of 1784. Traveling aboard the *Courier de New York*, a French packet ship, Lafayette reached New York on August 4, 1784, and wasted no time setting out for Mount Vernon, where he arrived on August 17, providing the most welcome interruption to Washington's morning rounds on his plantation. The joyful reunion of a father and adopted son after a separation of nearly three years followed. The meeting, Lafayette wrote, "was very tender and our satisfaction completely mutual."[26]

"After having thoroughly discussed the past, the present, and the future," Lafayette recounted, "he withdraws to take care of his affairs and gives me things to read that have been written during my absence. Then we come down for dinner and find Mrs. Washington with visitors from the neighborhood. The conversation at table turns to the events of the war or to anecdotes that we are fond of recalling. After tea we resume our private conversations and pass the rest of the evening with the family."[27]

From Virginia, Lafayette embarked upon a five-month journey through ten states. Along his path, he was received with grand receptions, toasted at elaborate banquets, saluted with artillery, and celebrated by fireworks. He was embraced by his fellow veterans and offered tokens of gratitude for his service: a degree at Harvard, the freedom of New York City in a golden box, the promise of a marble bust of his likeness from the state of Virginia, and honorary American citizenship from Congress. "He has been much caressed here as well as every where else in his Tour," James Madison, who met with Lafayette in Baltimore and accompanied him on his journey north, reported.[28] In a letter to Thomas Jefferson, Madison claimed to possess "a pretty thorough insight into his character." Lafayette's talents were great, his temper frank, but he had "a strong thirst of praise and popularity."[29]

Beyond the happy reunions with old friends, during his travels Lafayette saw America and its people in a spring of sorts—a fragile beginning of a newly sovereign nation, equal with promise and challenges. Thirteen independent states were now tenuously connected into a confederacy by a threadbare government. Citizens were gazing toward prosperity in western territories: At the time of Lafayette's visit, Washington was busy promoting a possible linkage of the Ohio and Potomac Rivers.

Lafayette was present in upstate New York during the council between the United States and the Iroquois' Six Nations, which yielded tribal lands in the Ohio Valley and upper New York. Keenly interested in abolitionist movements and already conceiving plans to address American slavery, Lafayette proposed to Washington a plan to purchase land on which to gradually free slaves. During his visit to Richmond in November 1784, he spoke in favor of universal liberty for "all humanity, in its entirety," addressing Virginia's House of Delegates. He also supported the emancipation of James Armistead, who had carried out reconnaissance work for Lafayette during the 1781 campaign. Armistead's application for manumission was based on his important services during the Revolution.

Lafayette had left America at the end of 1781 a soldier; he returned in 1784 something else entirely: The independence he had helped secure was no guarantee of union between states. Indeed, the threadbare government that had won the former struggled to hold the latter together. Lafayette returned at a time when Articles of Confederation—the agreement of states that had held during the war—surrendered to the self-interest of its parties, debilitating the government's ability to carry out basic functions of commerce and defense. Amid this tension, Lafayette, disinterested in his service to the nation and unattached to any part of it or any party within, was once again a unifying presence—and this was not merely symbolic.

After returning to Mount Vernon, where he and Washington spent nearly two weeks together, the pair set off for Annapolis, arriving on November 30, 1784. The following day was filled with celebration. Maryland's legislature assembled and offered tributes, followed by an elaborate ball. "The evening," a reporter noted, "was crowned with the utmost joy and festivity, the whole company being made by the presence of two most amiable and all-accomplished men, to whom America is so deeply indebted for her preservation from tyranny and oppression."[30]

The next morning, December 1, Washington accompanied Lafayette part of the way on the road toward Baltimore. Then the adopted father and son exchanged goodbyes and embraces, stepped into their carriages, and were pulled in opposite directions—Washington toward Mount Vernon, the young Frenchman on his way to New York, the point of departure for a return to France.

Despite terrible weather, Washington was home once more on December 2. In his carriage, he grew melancholy. "In the moment of our separation upon the road as I travelled, & every hour since," he wrote to Lafayette a week later, "I often asked myself, as our Carriages distended, whether that was the last sight, I ever should have of you? And tho' I wished to say no—my fears answered yes."[31]

Lafayette made his way east, pausing in Trenton, the temporary home of the nation's Congress, where delegates from twelve of the thirteen states assembled to receive him. "May this immense temple of freedom ever stand a lesson to oppressors, and example to the oppressed, a sanctuary for the rights of mankind!" he encouraged the assembled representatives. "And may these happy United States attain that complete splendor and prosperity which will illustrate the blessings of their government, and for ages to come rejoice the departed souls of its founders."[32]

On December 21, well-wishers and friends crowded New York Harbor as La Fayette walked across the Whitehall steps, extending off the Battery, and onto the frigate *Nymphe*. A delayed departure gave him time to compose a response to Washington's gloomy letter.

Ever optimistic, Lafayette foresaw many future reunions with his adopted father and second home. "No, my Beloved General, our late parting was Not By Any Means a last interview," he reassured Washington. "My whole Soul Revolts at the idea—and Could I Harbour it an instant, indeed, my dear General, it would make me Miserable . . . to You, I shall Return."[33]

In a vestibule near Lafayette's chambers on the second floor of La Grange, a carefully placed collection of flags was displayed. Among them was a faded standard of the Parisian National Guard. If visitors to La Grange had inquired, they might have learned that the blade on the ceremonial sword gifted to Lafayette by the American Congress—the piece of pride in his collection—was not original to the hilt but rather a replacement. The original blade had rusted, buried underground, as his family fled their home when the tide of another revolution turned against him. The replacement was a reminder of a heroic turn in another revolution, though, as he would later explain, contrasting the American to the French, "the scene of the one action was in Heaven, the other in Hell."[34]

In the years following his peacetime trip to America, Lafayette settled into the domestic routine of a young nobleman blessed with adulation and fortune. Neither was destined to last. He had always spent freely: tailoring, an opera box, servants for his home, a governess for his children, and the purchase and furnishing of a home on the Rue de Bourbon in 1782.[35] He financed the medals for the French Society of the Cincinnati members, designed by Pierre Charles L'Enfant. And his trips to America and Germany, and the promised experiment with emancipation—in 1785 he purchased a plantation on Cayenne with the intention of educating and freeing the slaves there—added to the tab.

Lafayette was now the "benefactor of two worlds," as his friend the Marquis de Condorcet described him in a dedication about the American Revolution's influence in Europe. An emissary for America in France, he assisted with securing commercial ties between the two nations, working with and developing a warm friendship with America's minister, Thomas Jefferson, who was soon an intimate in Paris. Not only Jefferson, but John Adams and his wife, Abigail, were regulars at American dinners at Lafayette's house in the rue de Bourbon. During those occasions, the two elder children, who had learned some English, sang to the delight of their American guests. Adrienne, too, was very much admired by their American visitors. Abigail Adams described her as "sprightly and agreeable" and "strongly attached to Americans."[36] So great was Lafayette's ongoing admiration of his adopted country and compatriots there that, in 1787, he took in the son of Nathanael Greene, Lafayette's old compatriot, who had died two years prior. He arranged that the boy, named George Washington Greene, study alongside his own son in Paris. During this interlude in Lafayette's life, Jefferson observed to James Madison, "He has a great deal of sounder genius [and] is well remarked by the king & rising in popularity. He has nothing against him but the suspicion of republican principles. His foible is a canine appetite for popularity and fame."[37]

In 1788, when the Philadelphia Convention created a Constitution to replace the unworkable Articles of Confederation, Lafayette was enthused. "I May Rejoice in the Happy Prospects that oppen [sic] Before My adoptive Country. Accounts from America Give me Every Reason to Hope the New Constitution will Be Adopted."[38] The new government it proposed was imperfect, however, unless a "guardian angel" could guide its initial steps. "Permit me once More, My Beloved General, to insist on Your Acceptance of the Presidency," Lafayette wrote Washington. Though prospects, properly guided by his old general, were bright in America, storm clouds gathered at home. "The affairs of france [sic] are Come to a Crisis," he wrote Washington, "the More difficult to Manage as the people in General Have no inclination to Go to Extremities—liberty or death is Not the Motto on this Side of the Atlantic."[39] Here, he would be proven incorrect.

When Lafayette wrote of a coming crisis, France was so desperately bankrupt that its debt was impossible to estimate. Allegations of extreme spending by the royal family were widespread among the populace and not inaccurate. Assisting America's revolution had only put the nation further in arrears. Its king, Louis XVI, though well-intentioned, was crippled by indecision; Queen Marie Antoinette's rejection of royal decorum was construed as debauchery. A series of devastating harvests at the end of the decade—drought, hailstorms, frost—led to widespread poverty among the lower classes.

When proposed reforms, adjustments to the nation's system of taxation, divided unequally among its three classes—the clergy, nobility, and commoners (the First, Second, and Third Estates)—proved impossible, Louis XVI called for a meeting of the Assembly of the Notables. Beginning in May of 1787, representatives of each class gathered to consent to a series of remedies to France's fiscal woes. These proved unworkable, did not go far enough in addressing the imbalances, or were inoperable. Lafayette's participation as a member of the Second Estate provided a formal entry into French politics as an advocate for the same freedoms he had fought for in America.

Representatives of the estates gathered again in May of 1789 at Versailles as the Estates General, called by the king to address the ongoing fiscal disorder. The convocation quickly came to an impasse over the matter of representation, with each estate, regardless of population, receiving equal votes in the deliberations. The Third Estate, the most populous, rebelled, refashioned itself as a National Assembly, and, finding the meeting hall locked on the morning of July 12, adjourned to an unlocked tennis court near the royal palace. There, they swore not to dissolve until they had written a new constitution. Members of the clergy and some nobles soon joined, forcing the king to recognize the body, which began work on a charter. The streets of Paris were soon filled with angry and armed mobs, and coffee shops were ablaze with the talk of revolution.

Lafayette now saw his opportunity to introduce a proclamation of rights, establishing guiding principles for the reforms pending in France in the manner the Declaration of Independence had for

America's Revolution. With the input, if not outright approval, of the author of that document, Thomas Jefferson, Lafayette introduced his Declaration of the Rights of Man on July 11, 1789, in a speech, which was printed and met with much applause in America. A self-fulfilling prophecy—he had hung on his wall a framed copy of the Declaration of Independence, with enough space within its frame for a corresponding French document. Conforming, in Lafayette's words, "to the principles of the American era," it was "no concession or petition for rights,—but the first declaration of rights that had been proclaimed in Europe."[40]

The effect of his declaration was blunted when, on the following day, the popular finance minister Jacques Necker was dismissed by the king. By now, thousands of royal troops had amassed outside Paris. The city neared the brink of anarchy. Hoping to restore calm, its electors created a citizen militia to defend the streets. The following day, July 14, a mob crossed the lowered drawbridge, breached the Bastille—the stone fortress and prison where the government was accumulating gunpowder and arms, a symbol of tyranny, and a target of Parisian rage—and, after a battle with its guards, which left eighty-three dead and dozens wounded, liberated seven prisoners. The mob left with its arms and the warden, whose head was shortly lopped off. The building was slated for demolition, but the effect was electric nonetheless.

The following day, the king announced to the National Assembly that he had ordered royal troops to quit Paris. With an imminent attack still rumored, the Marquis de La Salle, who had been appointed to lead the city militia, vacated his post. During deliberations on who should assume control in his place at the Hôtel de Ville, one of the electors pointed to a bust of Lafayette on a fireplace mantel, sculpted by Jean-Antoine Houdon; the room erupted in applause and nominated Lafayette. He was to maintain order at the head of the Parisian National Guard and to unify discordant factions, all while the process of winning liberties commenced.

Paintings on opposite sides of one of the castle's receiving rooms continued the story of Lafayette's heroic turn in the early chapters of France's revolution: A painting of the Bastille's demolition showed clouds of dust and smoke rising above the fortress, with rubble scattered below. The destruction had commenced immediately after its siege. Lafayette shipped the keys to the fortress, along with a sketch of its demolition, to George Washington, who displayed these tokens in his presidential residences in New York and Philadelphia, eventually bringing them home to Mount Vernon. The gift was, Lafayette wrote, "a tribute Which I owe as A Son to My Adoptive father, as an aid de Camp to My General, as a Missionary of liberty to its patriarch."[41]

On the other side of the door hung a painting of the Fête de la Fédération, or French Federation, the high point of Lafayette's influence. On July 14, 1790, the one-year anniversary of the storming of the Bastille, citizens and nobles alike toiled to turn the Champs de Mars—a large field used for military exercises—into a giant outdoor amphitheater. There, the country would celebrate its unity and affirm its nationhood. Though he was in attendance, the hero of the day was not King Louis XVI.

The previous October, Lafayette had ridden through a rainstorm, following thousands of market women who marched to Versailles demanding food and promises of reform. In August, the assembly had begun to dismantle the ancient regime, ending feudalism, leveling the burden of taxation, and approving a new draft of the Rights of Man. The king resisted. When the protesters surrounded the château at Versailles, Lafayette diffused the tension with his flair for dramatic symbolism. He handed a tricolor cockade to one of the king's guards, bowed to the queen, and kissed her hand on a balcony before the angry crowd. Cries of "Long live the general!" and "Long live the Queen!" erupted. "Peace was from that moment made," he wrote.[42] Louis XVI was persuaded to leave Versailles for Paris, where he was little more than a captive in the Tuileries Palace. On July 14, 1790, it was Lafayette, appearing on his white horse, who scaled the steps of the altar at the center of the spectacle at Champs de Mars and led three hundred thousand of his countrymen in an oath of allegiance to their nation, laws, and king. He was, an English traveler wrote, "so justly the idol of the French nation."[43]

But not for long. Control of the National Guard slipped from his grasp as both radicals and monarchists accused him of disloyalty and of using the National Guard to advance his own fame. When the king and queen, rebelling against the rebellion, slipped away from the Tuileries, bound for Varennes, only to be intercepted and eventually returned to Paris by Lafayette, he was blamed for allowing the near escape. When the National Guard opened fire on a crowd of protesters on the Champ de Mars, nearly a year after the Fête de la Fédération, his standing eroded further. Rumors of indiscretions with the queen abounded. To the radical Jacobins, their power growing in the government, he was a "criminal or imbecile."[44] Royalists attacked his "servile manner in front of the mob."[45]

In October 1791, Lafayette resigned from the National Guard and retreated to Auvergne. Months later, as war with Austria loomed, he was appointed to lead one of three newly formed armies and stationed in Metz. In July 1792, when another mob entered the Tuileries and threatened the king, Lafayette unwisely abandoned his army to ride off to Paris and deliver a pointed rebuke of the Jacobins in front of the Legislative Assembly. Upon returning to his soldiers, Lafayette was stripped of his command and bidden back to Paris, where he would likely be killed. On August 19, 1792, Lafayette fled toward the Belgian border, seeking "asylum in neutral country." From there, he planned to travel to Holland, then to England, where he would gather his family and flee to America. "He has spent his fortune on a revolution and is now crushed by the wheel he put in motion," Gouverneur Morris wrote to Thomas Jefferson from France in August 1792, just as Lafayette slipped across the Austrian border.[46]

Another work of art at La Grange, displayed on the doorway outside the main bedroom, depicted Lafayette's fate. It showed a rather ordinary-looking man, his face illuminated by a lantern in one hand, turning the key in the lock of a large prison door. The subject was Colomba, the warden at Olmütz, where Lafayette was imprisoned for three dreadful years. The artist was his daughter Anastasie, who, along with her mother and sister, had shared his misery in a dank cell on the German border.

Near Rochefort, Lafayette was arrested by Austrian authorities and passed between prisons—first Magdeburg, then Neisse—before being handed back to the Austrians and locked away from the world in a chamber in Olmütz Castle with little else than a single change of clothes. Lafayette, an émigré, had his lands and possessions seized and sold by the French government. At Chavaniac, Adrienne looked on while government authorities inventoried and looted all of their belongings. In September 1792, she and Anastasie were arrested; Georges was absent, Virginie in hiding.

George Washington was reluctant to intervene on Lafayette's behalf, wary of compromising American neutrality in the conflict among European nations. But American officials—first Gouverneur Morris and later his successor as minister, James Monroe—stepped in to rescue Adrienne from the fate that had befallen her mother, sister, and grandmother, all of whom had been executed. Monroe, a Virginian and fellow Revolutionary soldier, arranged for a fine carriage and sent his wife, Elizabeth, accompanied by servants, to the Paris prison where Adrienne was being held, emphasizing American interest in the fate of the marquise. Adrienne was freed and settled briefly at Monroe's home before the minister helped her obtain passports. She gathered her daughters—Georges was secreted off to America—and, in an act of devotion and bravery equal to any of her husband's, journeyed to Olmütz to join him in captivity.

When the doors of his cell swung open, the man inside was hardly recognizable: Gaunt, bald, wheezing, and coughing, he appeared much older than his thirty-eight years. For the next two years they lived in seclusion—Lafayette and Adrienne in one cell, their daughters in an adjoining one. Food was "indescribably filthy," and the only available doctor spoke no French.[47] Adrienne suffered from constant headaches. The score to this confinement was the sound of soldiers being whipped in the courtyard. Their jailer, Colomba, a comically unpleasant figure, was immortalized in a sketch by Anastasie—the same drawing that later hung at La Grange.

Lafayette's imprisonment sparked outrage among Americans, British liberals, and even his compatriots in France where the bloody excesses of the Reign of Terror had given way to a more moderate government helmed by a five-man Directory. Poems and prints commemorated the plight of the Hero of Two Worlds in his miserable prison. Even George Washington, writing as a private citizen, appealed to Emperor Francis II for Lafayette's release. It was ultimately another general, Napoleon Bonaparte, who made this possible. After defeating the Austrians in Italy and threatening Vienna, Napoleon forced Austria to negotiate peace, which included the liberation of French prisoners. On September 19, 1797, Lafayette and his family were freed, escorted to Hamburg, and placed in the care of the American consul.

"I long to be in America," Lafayette wrote to Washington a year and a half later.[48] Indeed, Lafayette had shared with William Vans Murray, the American ambassador to the Netherlands, a plan to relocate to Virginia and settle near Washington. "I found him still much bent upon going—Leaving his lady & daughter in France & his plan, if he go, is to settle for life," Vans Murray informed Washington. "To buy a farm near Mount Vernon—To land in the Chesepeak & hasten to present himself to his paternal house."[49] A world transformed during his imprisonment rendered this impractical. A quasi-war between America and France, and the resulting factional antagonisms raging across the former nation, made it unlikely, Washington explained, that Lafayette would be greeted warmly should he reappear. In typical fashion, to an astonished Vans Murray, Lafayette asked if his return might not unify squabbling Americans. "I told him no!" Vans Murray reported to Washington.[50]

Instead, in 1799, Lafayette returned to France using a forged passport obtained by Adrienne. Bonaparte, wary of a potential rival, permitted it only on the condition that Lafayette would find purpose beyond politics and at a distance from Paris. He accomplished this at La Grange, the ancient castle in the Seine-et-Marne, part of Adrienne's inheritance from her mother, which she had reclaimed after their release from Olmütz.

As the century turned—in 1800, Bonaparte had struck Lafayette's name from the list of émigrés and restored his status—Lafayette, emulating his mentor's retreat at Mount Vernon, threw himself into farming. He filled the stalls and planted apple and pear trees along the path to the home. Washington's prophecy, that after their adieu outside

Annapolis in the winter of 1784 the two men would not meet again, was proven true with his death in December 1799. "My mind is so used to introduce him every thought, every sentiment, every concern of mine, that I hardly can believe that while I am living, he has left us," Lafayette wrote to Martha Washington in an emotional letter of condolence. The time was nearing, he told the widow, when he would have been reunited with his adopted father in America. "But alas, in this world we can no more meet!"[51] When Washington was honored posthumously at a ceremony in Paris, Lafayette was conspicuously uninvited, a sign of his estrangement from public life.

Lafayette had opportunities to return to America, including offers from President Jefferson of the French ambassadorship and the governorship of the Louisiana Territory. But Lafayette declined. A planned visit to America in 1805 was scuttled for fear that British warships, as authorized by the Jay Treaty, would seize him on the high seas as enemy property. So, he remained at La Grange, tending to his farm, surrounded by his growing family: Georges married Émilie de Tracy, the daughter of the liberal political theorist Antoine Destutt de Tracy, much to his parents' approval. Anastasie was wed to Juste-Charles de Fay de La Tour-Maubourg, and Virginie to Louis de Lasteyrie du Saillant. These were blessed additions.

There was a terrible farewell too. Adrienne's release from Olmütz did not save her life but only prolonged it. Never fully recovering from her ordeal, she took ill in the fall of 1807, was rushed to Paris, and fell into a delirium. She died surrounded by her family on Christmas Eve, 1807. "Before this Blow, I Confess I did not know What it was to Be Unhappy," Lafayette wrote Jefferson after her death.[52]

In his mourning, Lafayette composed his memoirs, traded correspondence with old American friends—Jefferson, Madison, Monroe—and tended to his farm, always welcoming reverent visitors. After Napoleon's abdication and exile to Elba in 1814, the Bourbon monarchy was restored under the Comte D'artois—the younger brother of Louis XVI—who fashioned himself Louis XVIII. He granted Lafayette a cordial but wary audience. A year later, when Napoleon escaped exile, rallied his disaffected supporters from the French army, and returned to Paris, the king fled to Ghent and Lafayette was lured out of retirement. He won a seat in the Chamber of Representatives, the lower house of parliament created during Napoleon's Hundred Days. There, Lafayette and fellow liberals convinced Napoleon to abdicate again after he was vanquished at Waterloo.

Louis XVIII was restored to the throne, the Chamber dissolved, and Lafayette returned to La Grange, away from public life and politics. "The marquis Lafayette, retired on his farm, waits patiently a better state of things," William Eustis, a fellow veteran of the Revolution and America's minister to the Netherlands, wrote to James Madison in 1815.[53] Certainly, Eustis referred to a changed political climate, but perhaps also to Lafayette's long-deferred dream of returning to America, a hope he had carried since sailing away from New York in the winter of 1784. The desire no doubt remained, but time and circumstances appeared to preclude it. Still, through memories and mementos, Lafayette could imagine himself in America once more. "You are now in America," he told a Virginian visitor, gesturing to the portraits of Washington and Benjamin Franklin.[54]

There was another curious item in the collection at La Grange. It was not a portrait of a family member or friend, nor a glorious historical scene, but rather a simple depiction of a few buildings set in a clearing surrounded by the American wilderness. In 1783, the residents of a community in south-central North Carolina, along the Cape Fear River, christened their new town Fayetteville in honor of the young hero—the first to do so. A French artist, Horace Say—son of the economist Jean-Baptiste Say—traveling in America, passed through and sketched the town. On his return to France, he framed the drawing and sent it to Lafayette. Later, Say accepted an invitation to La Grange.

During his visit, Say awoke one morning and was about to depart for a walk on the grounds when a servant informed him that his presence was requested in the château. Directed to Lafayette's cabinet, he found the general, who invited him to sit in a chair beside him. Then, he pointed to the sketch of Fayetteville, perhaps a symbol for an America that had transformed fantastically since his last visit in 1784. "There is your drawing, which I have kept near me," Lafayette said. "I shall probably never see the place itself, but you have at least given me an idea of it."[55]

2

An Eagle of Glorious Omen
or a Turkey Buzzard?

Viewed from across First Street, the United States Capitol was little more than a shell. Its sandstone wings were charred, the columns that once adorned its north wing now absent, scars from an August evening three years prior when British soldiers marched through Washington, DC, and set the building ablaze. On this particularly brilliant spring day, though, there were signs of renewal. Scattered across the yard in front of the structure lay piles of stone and marble, evidence of the restoration underway.[1] While the construction went on, Congress was forced to temporarily gather in a hastily constructed brick building directly east of the burned Capitol.[2] At noon, March 4, 1817, James Monroe emerged from its door.

The president-elect walked into the sunlight and across a raised wooden portico. Below, thousands of onlookers spread out across the crest of Jenkins Hill, many sitting in open carriages. For the first time since the office's creation, the quadrennial ritual of presidential inauguration was conducted outdoors. The elements cooperated beautifully: It was as if the "fourth of March was ushered in by the handmaids of June," wrote Sally Foster Otis, the wife of Massachusetts senator

Harrison Gray Otis. "Not an unruly breeze ruffled the plaits of the best handkerchief or disturbed the locks of the best powdered Beau."[3]

After affirming the oath of office, Monroe began his address, mentioning the recently ended war, the peace now at hand, the necessity of strengthening the nation's defenses, and, where the Constitution allowed, the construction of roads, bridges, and canals to hasten its economic growth. "During a period fraught with difficulties and marked by very extraordinary events the United States have flourished beyond example. Their citizens individually have been happy and the nation prosperous," he said.[4] As the president drew near his conclusion, an appeal for the continued blessings of the Almighty, he struck a note of rapprochement. The nation, so bitterly divided by faction in the years leading up to and during the War of 1812, was at last, he believed, healing. "The American people have encountered together great dangers and sustained severe trials with success," he recalled. "They constitute one great family with a common interest."[5]

Nature's acoustics, Monroe's own oratorical limitations, and the size of the crowd ensured that, as Otis told her father, "few if any heard" the president-elect's optimism. After the ceremonies concluded, a large bird soared over the leisurely departing crowd. "Some imagined an eagle of glorious omen," wrote Otis, unimpressed with the entire spectacle. "I am to say that I could make nothing more nor less than an old Carolina acquaintance a Turkey buzzard."[6]

If Monroe's speech was largely inaudible to his audience in Washington, its most hopeful passages attracted attention elsewhere, some of it skeptical. "Mr. Monroe makes many pleasing promises and professions; but those are easily made," observed a Federalist newspaper.[7]

But the new president spoke sincerely of union and common felicity. He was a living link to America's Revolution, bearing a scar on his left shoulder where a musket ball had severed an artery and nearly killed him as an eighteen-year-old first lieutenant in the Third Virginia Regiment during the Battle of Trenton in 1776. He was not only a veteran of America's War of Independence, but also a voice in the political debates that led to the formation of its government. At fifty-nine, James Monroe had dedicated the majority of his life to serving America in one high office or another, with varying success—as a diplomat, senator, secretary of war, and secretary of state. The years and cares of his public service had whitened his hair and creased his face. His dated dress—a preference for knee britches in an age when fashionable men wore pants—and knotted, powdered hair in a queue were reminders of an earlier era.

Months after taking office, in the summer of 1817, the president embarked on a trip that took him from Washington, DC, across the mid-Atlantic, and north through New England. The stated purpose of the voyage, as well as tours in 1818 and 1819, was to inspect the nation's defenses. But the president had another motive.

Among the profound changes wrought by the War of 1812 was the diminishment of the two-party system of the early republic. The war, fought against England for American territorial and maritime sovereignty, was agitated for in Congress by Democratic-Republican legislators and waged by their president, James Madison. Federalists, whose strongholds were northern states along the Eastern Seaboard and whose economies benefited from trade with Great Britain, intensely opposed the war.

This followed the Embargo Act and Non-Intercourse Act, defensive economic policies against England that had chilled commerce in New England. Resistance came to a head in the winter of 1814, when twenty-six Federalist leaders covertly gathered in Hartford, Connecticut, in an attempt to formulate strategies to revive their party's sagging fortunes. During the debates, more radical attendees raised the possibility of secession from the Union, but their moderate counterparts did not embrace this idea. The secret nature of the meeting and the whispers of disunion coincided with the formal ending of the war and its symbolic conclusion with Andrew Jackson's rout of the British in New Orleans. This mixture of impressions and events further damaged an already reeling political party.

That Monroe's visit, undertaken as a private citizen and at his own expense, included stops in New England, particularly in Boston, where much of the remaining Federalist power was concentrated, was evidence of the new president's desire to promote a form of factional harmony across the country and present himself as a catalyst of unity.

Visiting states that neither of his predecessors, Jefferson or James Madison, had set foot in while president, Monroe proposed a return to republican virtues. He conjured memories of George Washington's own tours in 1789 and 1791, echoing the first president's parting warning to the American people about the dangers of faction and evoking memories of the Revolution. In a particularly poignant example, in Vermont, Monroe was reunited with Maria Wheelock (formerly Shum), who had tended to his wounds at Trenton.

The tour was well received by Federalists, who saw in the olive branch a means to salvage their party by collaborating with Monroe, or even to earn appointments in his administration. They welcomed him warmly with carefully choreographed parades and dinners across his tour. Citizens, regardless of political affiliation, turned out to catch a glimpse of their new president and feel a connection to their past.

During Monroe's tour, Benjamin Russell, publisher of the arch-Federalist paper the *Columbian Centinel*, wrote a paragraph heralding the arrival of "An Era of Good Feelings." "During the late presidential jubilee many persons have met at festive boards, in pleasant converse, whom part politics had long severed. We recur with pleasure to all the circumstances which attended the demonstrations of good feelings."[8] It is unlikely that Russell was looking into the future or even beyond the limits of Boston, but the term "Era of Good Feelings" was widely reprinted and in time became a sobriquet for the period in the country's history coinciding with Monroe's presidency.

The Federalists' standing further eroded. As it did, many of the policy-based distinctions between the parties disappeared, as some Democratic-Republicans embraced, for example, internal improvements funded by public expenditure—measures championed by their Federalist rivals.

Still, events ultimately conspired against Monroe's best intentions. The "good feelings" of party consolidation did not mean the end of factional animosities. Rather, the years following his inauguration in 1817 saw a reordering of American politics, sowing intense divisions based on class, region, and ideology—all, for a time, under the banner of the Democratic-Republican banner.

Two years into Monroe's presidency, the nation suffered its first great economic collapse and recession. At the onset of the War of 1812, America was largely rural and agrarian, its economy supported primarily by the exportation of cotton, wheat, and tobacco. America's neutrality in the wars between France and England provided a market for these exports. Manufacturing, on the other hand, was scarce and confined to a few large cities, such as New York, Philadelphia, and Boston. What passed for an organized monetary system was loosely regulated and lacked a common currency. Banks were few and far between.

A second war with England dramatically restricted trade, denying America's farmers the primary venue to sell their crops and American consumers the manufactured goods they desired from abroad. The loss of the latter, coupled with a federal government ill-prepared to fight a second war with England, forced the upscaling of domestic manufacturing. While the government was also compelled to borrow heavily to fund the war effort, another means of generating capital was the sale of public land, most of it in the West, at discounted rates, as low as $2 an acre.[9] The availability of land encouraged an increase in the chartering of banks in the South, mid-Atlantic, and West to provide loans for the rush or settlers as new states—Louisiana, Indiana, Mississippi, and Illinois, between 1812 and 1818—joined the Union.

After the Treaty of Ghent was ratified, and the war ended in 1815, states continued to give out charters like sweets; often, the legislators presiding over these charters and the officials overseeing the new banks were one and the same. The banks themselves printed and passed out massive amounts of paper money, sometimes with little to no specie in reserve. A second Bank of the United States—Congress allowed the original to expire in 1811—was chartered in 1816 and began operations the following year with the purpose of imposing order on the nation's monetary system. Instead, it encouraged the debt and speculation boom by waiving requirements that banks back their notes with hard currency—a policy endorsed by the U.S. Treasury to facilitate the purchase and settlement of western lands, which were often paid for with depreciated banknotes.

The twin availability of inexpensive land and easy credit fanned a boom in speculation and a rise in the value of land. Americans in the West and South took on debt in order to acquire new land or finance improvements on farms or properties to keep pace with a thriving export market as demand for American crops remained strong. European yields were especially poor in the years immediately following the war, particularly in 1816 when the eruption of Mount Tambora in Indonesia sent a cloud of volcanic particles into the atmosphere, reducing global temperatures, depriving much of the Western world of summer, devastating crops and further increasing the price of American grain, flour, cotton, and wheat. The rise in prices for American produce fueled the mad dash to acquire land on credit. More banks were created—there were nearly four hundred banks in the nation by 1818. There had been fifty in 1811. "The whole of our population are either stockholders of bank or in debt to them," lamented Condy Raguet, a Philadelphia-based politician and economist.[10]

Among those in hock was Jefferson, who, long in debt, borrowed money from the Virginia branch of the Bank of the United States as well as other Virginia banks. Still, he was well aware of the inevitable contraction. "Like a dropsical man calling out for water, water, our deluded citizens are clamoring for more banks, more banks," he wrote in 1816.[11] Others predicted a reckoning. Hezekiah Niles, a confirmed nationalist and the Baltimore-based editor of the *Weekly Register*, one of the nation's first nationally circulated magazines, saw only disaster ahead. In an early 1818 editorial, he decried "the demoralizing and pernicious business of banking; which we seriously believe is the Pandora's box that is to fill the republic with all sorts of moral and political diseases."[12]

Sure enough, the good times ended. The resumption of European imports, which flooded the market with the arrival of peace, leveled newly established American manufacturing. In 1817, European crops rebounded, curtailing demand for American cotton and wheat, the latter of which England banned from importation. Prices for American crops sank. And then, in the summer of 1818, the Second Bank of the United States, faced with shrinking specie in its reserves and the reduced value of its own notes, forced its branches to redeem the debt it was owed by state banks. The banks, in turn, called in the loans made to land-hungry customers, a commitment many of the borrowers were unable to fulfill.

The confluence of economic pressures crashed America's economy, bringing misery not before seen and equally suffered by its citizens. Banks disappeared. Factories shuttered. Their workers drifted across the landscape in search of employment. Millions of men were left unemployed. Others, unable to repay their loans, ended up in prison. The land they had bought with easy credit was reclaimed by the government. Homes and farms were foreclosed. Cities were deserted. Pauperism spread widely. Houses of industry and soup kitchens became regular fixtures in cities, where citizens relied on donations—beef, cords of wood, boxes of smoked herring.

The ruin in Cincinnati, the economic capital of the West, was emblematic. Building stopped; businesses closed. Families fled the city in an attempt to find work. Bricklayers sold watermelons. In the absence of money, townspeople turned to barter: Farmers exchanged butter with carpenters for a table or a bureau. Coffee, now unaffordable, was replaced by rye coffee. Staples such as corn, beef, eggs, and flour were nearly worthless, yet most citizens still could not afford them. Speculators began "to scatter like rats from a submerged flour barrel."[13]

Gorham A. Worth, a cashier at the U.S. Bank branch in Cincinnati, looked on in despair from the "glorious but now crestfaln city." "All things are changed," he wrote. "The rich have become poor, and the poor distrust, one universal state of embarrassment exits; tis want, and fear and prosecution and suspicion and terror and dismay and bankruptcy and pauperism on all sides and on all hands . . . The wealthiest are considered ruined . . . It is 'save himself who can.'"[14]

The economy, after much debt liquidation, began its slow recovery by 1821, though unevenly as states in the Northeast sprang back to life sooner than those elsewhere. The Americans who were caught up in the land bonanza, who took advantage of the lax credit and then suffered most for it, many of them farmers in the western states, held banks—particularly the Bank of the United States and, by extension, the federal government—responsible for their pain. "Dam the Banks and the Witch that begat them!" cried Worth, speaking for many of his countrymen.[15]

Politicians and religious leaders lectured in turn about the nation's drift from industry and frugality. Potential remedies or preventative measures created their own political antagonisms. Farmers in the West and parts of the South called for government-funded internal improvements to provide employment and a means of transporting their nearly worthless crops to markets on the East Coast. They were joined by northern voices in calling for tariffs to protect fledgling industries; some Southerners saw these remedies as unleashing federal power and destructive to their economy.

Looking on worriedly from Monticello, Jefferson saw far worse on the horizon. "The banks, bankrupt law, manufactures, Spanish treaty are nothing," he wrote to John Adams in 1819. "These are occurrences which like waves in a storm will pass under the ship. But the Missouri question is a breaker on which we lose the Missouri country by revolt, & what more, God only knows. From the battle of Bunker's hill to the treaty of Paris we never had so ominous a question."[16]

In 1803, Monroe, dispatched by Jefferson, joined U.S. Minister to France Robert Livingston in successfully negotiating the purchase of 828,000 square miles of land west of the Mississippi River for $15 million. The acquisition from France accommodated America's westward-moving population and secured vital navigation rights of the Mississippi River as well as its port in New Orleans. The land was split in two administrative districts along the thirty-third parallel, with the portion to its north forming the Territory of Louisiana, later renamed the Missouri Territory, and the southern part constituting the Territory of Orleans, the majority of which was incorporated into the Union in 1812 as the state of Louisiana.

After the Louisiana Purchase, slave owners departed agriculturally exhausted southern states, such as Virginia, North Carolina, and Georgia, and set out for Missouri in search of fertile lands. By the time the territory petitioned Congress for statehood in 1818, there were over

10,200 enslaved people in Missouri. The Union was then evenly divided, with eleven slave states and eleven free states.

As Congress debated a bill fulfilling the request, New York congressman James Tallmadge Jr. introduced an amendment he aptly described as a much-loved but "ill-fated offspring."[17] Tallmadge, whose motivation was likely equal parts well-intentioned ideology and ambition for glory, proposed that slavery be prohibited in Missouri and that slaves born in the future state would be freed at the age of twenty-five. The House, with a northern majority, narrowly passed the amendment. The Senate, where the balance of power tilted to the South, rejected it just as the Fifteenth Congress ended in March 1819. When the Sixteenth Congress took its seats in December, the debate was revisited, and the nation was thrown into agony.

The argument that so riled the nation rested on whether Missouri would enter the Union as a slave state or free state. Northerners who opposed the former were motivated not simply by a moral revulsion to slavery but also by an objection to the power balance its spread would upend in the southern states' favor: A tragically flawed but life-giving bargain, the Constitution's three-fifths compromise stipulated that three out of every five slaves counted toward a state's population when determining representation in Congress. Southern passions were violently inflamed by the prospect that the federal legislature could dictate the nature of a state's institutions or policies, in this case stipulating the prohibition of the institution upon which the region's economy depended. This would restrict the growing Black population to its existing confines within the slave states, a prospect that denied their owners new avenues to sell their human chattel and portended a day when they would be outnumbered by their slaves and threatened with insurrection.

The debate over Missouri consumed the country: Newspaper editorials fulminated, public demonstrations were staged, committees of correspondence formed. Through their representatives, state legislatures transmitted dueling resolutions to Congress, alternately opposing Missouri entering the Union as a slave state or any restrictions on its doing so. New Jersey's legislature declared slavery in Missouri a danger to equal representation in Congress. Kentucky's condemned its prohibition as "perpetual vassalage."[18]

Members of Congress gave violent speeches that lasted upwards of four hours. The most agitated voices raised the specter of disunion. Perhaps most shrill among them was that of Virginia aristocrat John Randolph of Roanoke. Once a spokesperson for Jefferson in the House, he strode into the chamber accompanied by his hunting dogs and razed foes with a cruel wit and silver tongue for sport. Gangly—his head was described as small, his torso short, and his legs long—Randolph spoke in falsetto tones, and there was not a hair on his wrinkled, pallid face, both traits possibly the result of childhood tuberculosis. "God has given us the Missouri and the devil shall not take it from us!" he shrieked during one of his hours-long speeches on the Missouri question.[19] Northern leaders spoke in no less dramatic terms. "Now, sir, is to be tested whether this grand and hitherto successful experiment of free government is to continue," predicted New Jersey's Charles Kinsey.[20]

"Some prudent and discreet men (in other aspects) in Congress have brought themselves to this awful alternative, 'to dissolve the union, rather than submit to the establishment of slave states over the Mississippi,'" Abner Lacock shared with an exasperated Monroe. "This is met in temper equally fixt & determined on the other hand, these men Mutually throw firebrands arrows & death."[21] Speaker of the House Henry Clay lamented that in Congress all other matters had yielded to the Missouri question. "It is a most unhappy question awakening sectional feelings, and exasperating them to the highest degree . . . The words civil war, and disunion, are uttered almost without emotion."[22]

Disaster was ultimately averted when Clay and Virginian senator James Barbour attached the admission of the Maine Territory of Massachusetts, which had petitioned Congress for statehood, as a free state paired with the admission of Missouri as a slave state. This, after much debate, was then combined with an amendment offered by Illinois senator Jesse B. Thomas, which stipulated that slavery would be prohibited west of the 36°30' parallel of the Louisiana Purchase. A year later, when Congress gathered to count the states' electoral votes, another fierce dispute erupted over language in Missouri's constitution prohibiting the migration of free Blacks. Once again, Clay brokered a compromise before Missouri was formally admitted into the Union and the votes were tallied. The first compromise brought Jefferson, so alarmed by the debate, little comfort. To Maine senator John Holmes, who had supported the bargain, he wrote that the conflict "like a fire bell in the night, awakened and filled me with terror." It was, Jefferson continued, "the knell of the Union. It is hushed indeed for the moment. But this is a reprieve only, not a final sentence."[23]

When Monroe ran for reelection in 1820, he was unopposed, winning all but one electoral vote. The amalgamation was nearly complete. Instead of a great rush toward unity, Randolph attributed Monroe's victory to apathy. The public mind, he claimed, was "torpid," and "the unanimity, about which we hear so much, is the unanimity of indifference, & not of approbation."[24]

The Federalists cast candidates for the vice presidency and continued to hold statewide office, but when the Seventeenth Congress convened in March 1821, Democratic-Republicans outnumbered Federalists by 39 seats to 4 in the Senate, and 150 to 31 in the House of Representatives. The party was isolated to Massachusetts and Delaware and was effectively dead by the end of the decade. "You are told indeed that there are no longer parties among us. That they are all now amalgamated, the lion & the lamb lie down together in peace," Jefferson warned his old ally Albert Gallatin, then serving as America's minister to France, in 1822. "Do not believe a word of it. The same parties exist now as ever did. No longer indeed under the name of Republicans and Federalists."[25]

Political discord lived on. On the heels of society-wide economic collapse, widespread suffering, and a passionate debate over the fate of slavery, new factions influenced by the tumult of the preceding years formed within the Democratic-Republican Party. As Monroe's second term began, these factions found life in what was destined to be an unruly contest to succeed him in the presidency. The election of 1824 would be unlike any presidential contest in the nation's history—chaotic and bitter, a clash of personalities and regional interests, heralding a new era in electioneering.

The Panic of 1819 hastened the democratization of America. Farmers and laborers, particularly in the western states, began to take a more active role in politics out of necessity, advocating for relief bills and debt forgiveness in parts of the nation most devastated by the depression. At the same time, more and more Americans were directly participating in the selection of their presidents.

Most states in the early nineteenth century selected presidential electors through their state legislatures. Recognizing the increasing demand for voters to directly pick electors, new states entering the Union established popular voting for presidential electors. This had the happy effect of making those new states attractive to settlers; in order to compete with their western counterparts, established states now followed suit.

By 1824, eighteen of the twenty-four states chose presidential electors by popular vote. The traditional method among political parties for selecting their candidates was a caucus of their members in Congress. In the years of Democratic-Republican dominance, when the nomination nearly guaranteed the presidency, Congress selecting a chief executive in a closed convocation was distinctly undemocratic.

The positioning to succeed Monroe in the presidency began as soon as Monroe began his second term. Early speculation focused on his treasury secretary, William Harris Crawford. A formidable suitor to the office, physically imposing, coarsely charming, and a public man of considerable distinction, Crawford had served as a senator from his home state of Georgia, minister to France during the War of 1812, and secretary of war under both James Madison and Monroe. When his friends had suggested him for the presidency in 1816, Crawford had checked his ambitions rather than contest the nomination of the anointed Monroe. But his position in the outgoing cabinet made his place within the Democratic-Republican Party somewhat awkward: Crawford had made no case against the policies accompanying party amalgamation, federal improvements, the rechartering of the Bank of the United States, or tariffs. Now, as he sought the presidency, Crawford presented himself as a return to old Jeffersonian Republicanism, fiscal rectitude, and states' rights. Indeed, the treasury secretary, a slave-owning

Virginian by birth who had left for Georgia early in life with his family, was Jefferson's as well as Madison's preferred candidate and eventually won the support of the old Republicans, such as Randolph and the arch-conservative Nathaniel Macon.

A usurper emerged from among Crawford's colleagues. John C. Calhoun, Monroe's secretary of war, was brilliant, cold, and at this stage in his career a passionate nationalist. He was among the hawks who had so eloquently argued the case for a second American war with Britain in Congress. The course of the conflict had convinced Calhoun of the justification for federally financed improvements to enhance national defenses and modernize America's economy; he had supported the chartering of the Second National Bank and the Tariff of 1816. A South Carolina planter, educated in the East—Yale University, Litchfield Law School—Calhoun was, in theory, a candidate with cross-sectional appeal. Noting this promise, a band of congressmen from the crucial state of Pennsylvania, where Calhoun had already worked to cultivate support in Philadelphia, successfully requested he stand for the presidency in 1821.[26] He was, at the time, all of forty-two years old.

Creating additional awkwardness was the candidacy of a third member of Monroe's cabinet, John Quincy Adams. The son of the second president, Adams was a man of great accomplishment in his own right: minister to Russia, senator, co-negotiator of peace with Great Britain at Ghent, and the current president's chief diplomat—the draftsman of the doctrine of American sovereignty over the Western Hemisphere. "Of the public history of Mr. Monroe's administration, all that will be worth telling to posterity has been transacted through the Department of State," he boasted to his wife, Louisa Catherine.[27] Though his own man apart from his father, Adams shared many hereditary similarities with him. Like his father, the younger Adams was rigid; his genius was accompanied by a foreboding, puritanical personality and detached manner. "I am a man of reserved, cold, austere, and forbidding manners," Adams confessed, "my political adversaries say a gloomy misanthropist, and my personal enemies, an unsocial savage."[28] Politically, Adams had an independent streak: He began his career as a Federalist but defected to the Democratic-Republican Party in 1807. After a lengthy career of service to the country, Adams conceived of himself as a national, not regional, candidate. But Northerners, after considering other possibilities, such as former New York governor DeWitt Clinton, eventually consolidated around the Massachusetts-born Adams. This support, energized in part by agitation caused by the Missouri question and fear of further expansion of slavery across the continent, left Adams—the lone Northerner against four slave owners—as a regional candidate.

During the negotiations with British ministers in Ghent that concluded the War of 1812, Adams rose early one morning to prepare for the day ahead, only to hear a night of gambling concluding in the rooms of his co-commissioner, Henry Clay, at 4:00 a.m.[29] Clay was a drinker, gambler, dancer, and, the whispers alleged, a philanderer. A gangly man with sandy hair and a broad smile, immense talent, and unusual charm, he could carouse late into the night and preside effectively over the House of Representatives the following day. Clay was a Virginian who had migrated to Kentucky in 1797. As Adams was a candidate of the East, Clay was a star of the West. His candidacy was balanced on his American System, a program of national tariffs and federally funded infrastructure projects—roads, canals, and bridges—designed to bind the country's regions and interests and nurse its manufacturers to maturity.

"Electioneering begins to 'wax hot,'" Hezekiah Niles wrote, warily, two years away from the contest. "It cannot be supposed that Messrs. Adams, Crawford, or Calhoun, Mr. Clay and others spoken of to succeed to the chief magistracy of the United States, are cold enemies of their country, destitute of talents, or without moral principle."[30]

There was one more candidate whom Niles had not mentioned. In July 1822, Tennessee's legislature nominated a favorite son, Andrew Jackson, for president. "Let the people do as it seemth good unto them," he responded when allies asked permission to present his name for the presidency.[31] And they did. The hero of the Battle of New Orleans instantly gained national fame after his ragtag band of militia defeated the British army in 1815 and proved immensely popular with voters. Not because of any program—he remained vague on policy—but because of celebrity and timing; as American politics became the dominion of the masses, no politician better appealed to the public. Jackson was a self-made man of action, a frontier aristocrat, and personally magnetic military hero. Though he had served briefly in the House of Representatives and the Senate and would be elected to the latter body in 1823, Jackson, unlike any of the other would-be presidents, could claim to be untainted by Washington's political squabbles and corrupt elite. His confidant, Tennessee senator John Eaton, in a series of letters pseudonymously written by "Wyoming" and published in the *Columbian Observer*, a Philadelphia newspaper, articulated a case for Jackson as a representative of the people's interests versus a corrupt ruling class in a far-off national capital where the elites "maneuvered after power" and "intrigue passes for talent."[32]

The contest unfolded in a most unfortunate way for the first two candidates: Calhoun's national strategy rested on winning Pennsylvania as well as North Carolina. When Jackson's popularity soared in both states, the secretary of war abandoned his pursuit of the presidency and instead became a candidate for the vice presidency. In September 1823, Crawford left Washington for Virginia, where he had planned to visit with Jefferson and Madison, when he was stricken by a terrible case of what he called "inflammatory rheumatism." For eight weeks, he was bedridden at the home of Virginia senator James Barbour. It is likely that Crawford suffered from a stroke: His vision was impaired, his hands and feet immobilized, his speech became inaudible mumbles. A series of medical interventions—twenty bleedings and then the constant application of leeches—on his return to Washington further weakened Crawford. Nevertheless, when Republican-Democrat members of Congress met in February 1824 to nominate a candidate, they settled on Crawford. But only 66 of the 240 participated. By the time the caucus had made its decision, 12 state legislatures had already nominated candidates themselves. "King Caucus," as its detractors called it, was finished. Crawford's hopes for the presidency, like the man himself, were in sorry shape.

What followed was, as a New York paper called it, "very warm and continued warfare" between friends of the candidates.[33] The campaigns were a clash of factions and personalities, waged through vituperative newspaper editorials, rallies, militia musters, public meetings, and straw polls organized by the candidates' supporters in crucial states. "It is a disgrace to the nation that men of such standing should be spoken of as more fitting for the cells of a penitentiary than to mix in the society of decent men," Niles commented on the acrimony.[34] Policy debates were downwind of the economic collapse and Missouri controversy: the expansion or prohibition of slavery, the institution of tariffs, the approval of government-funded internal improvements, and the role of the Second Bank of the United States.

"The Present is a most interesting period in the history of our republic. A contest must shortly take place that may severely test the durability of our free institutions; one that may shake the union to its center," members of a Pennsylvania nominating convention threatened after endorsing Jackson.[35] Northerners and Westerners alike chafed at the prospect of another Southern president—all but one man to hold the office since its creation had come from Virginia; the last three of these men—Jefferson, Madison, Monroe—had won with Northern votes; now was the time for Southerners to support a Northern man: Adams. Southerners saw a Northern or Western president as a threat to their interests: slavery in the case of the former, and tariffs in the latter. "We have everything to distrust in a Northern president . . . the whole mass of the people of New England entertain notions very inadequate to our merits," wrote a Tennessee newspaper.[36]

The Union's newcomers in the West demanded a larger role in its control. "Instead of bowing and cringing to our elders . . . we now have the right to command, and should we remain united, the question of the next president must be left to us," exclaimed an Indiana newspaper in 1822. "The seat of empire will be moved this side of the Allegahanies. The election of a Western president is but an entering wedge of Western Power."[37]

"Common feeling which operated alike on a democrat and federalist of Maine and of Georgia no longer exists; its place has, in my opinion, unhappily been supplied by others of a sectional character, and these must and will have an effect on the election by the people," Niles predicted.[38] "In this part of the country thus far it is very evident that the sectional had prevailed over the national feeling," a Boston newspaper fretted.[39] In Georgia, an observer predicted that the new political tensions "will bury our free governments in irretrievable ruin." A Maine editor commented that the citizens "piping themselves out of breath to the tune of the North and the South . . . sounds too much like the knell of liberty to suit our ears."[40] So worrisome was the release of sectional animosity that some editors even suggested a third term for Monroe to forestall the feared disunion.

An apt metaphor for the contest took place on May 15, 1823, on the track at the Union Course in Queens, New York. In front of a vast crowd, including Clay and Jackson, Eclipse, who had defeated the South's finest horses, and was owned by Cornelius Van Ranst, a wealthy hippophile from New York, raced Sir Henry, owned by William Ransom Johnson, a Virginian breeder. It was the greatest sporting event in the young nation's history, rich with symbolism. A $20,000 prize. Sixty thousand spectators. The Great Match Race. The pride of the North against a Southern avenger.

Sir Henry dominated the first heat; Eclipse, the second. By the third and decisive heat, the crowd had grown so large that the race was started with spectators mingling on the track. After the crash of the starter's drum, Eclipse quickly assumed and never relinquished the lead. "There was never a contest more exciting," one spectator recalled. "Sectional feeling and heavy pecuniary stakes were both involved."[41] Despite its excitement, the race was not without its critics. A New York newspaper lamented that the contest amplified troubling dynamics across America and portended that they could develop into something far more dangerous than a horse race. "Besides," the *National Advocate* opined, "these contests of North against South, lay the foundation of sectional jealousies, and create a spirit of rivalry when there should be union."[42]

But there was another subtext to this acrimonious election beyond personalities, policies, and sectional interests. On the surface, it was best represented by Monroe's pending departure from public life. He, like every previous president, had participated in the Revolution, either as a soldier or as a statesman. "Hitherto, revolutionary services have given a few men preponderating claims to the presidency; but the small remnant of this class being precluded by weight of years, if by nothing else, the time has now come when the nation must select for this exalted station, one among several, who are equal in talents, services and virtues," wrote a Virginia newspaper in 1823.[43] Whoever succeeded Monroe would be the first of a second generation of Americans to lead the nation—a passing of the torch from the founding generation to its children. This transition discomfited Americans, who were anxious about sustaining their inheritance.

As Monroe's generation departed, they did so from an America transformed by the fruit of their labors: The nation's borders had broadened; the thirteen original colonies were now twenty-four states. The population, which stood at three million in 1790, reached nine million by 1820. Citizens were spreading across the continent and spilling beyond the Mississippi River. Domestic ingenuity such as Robert Fulton's commercial steamboat eased and sped the movement of goods upriver and into the West. Thomas Gilpin's continuous papermaking machine proliferated newspaper production, disseminating information across the country. Newspapers were carried on stagecoaches via an extensive postal system, which delivered six hundred different publications daily, semi-weekly, and weekly nationwide. The designers of the republican institutions which enabled much of this transformation, the revolutionary generation, like parents in their twilight years, could take comfort in the nation their children were inheriting. And the grateful children could be optimistic about the boundless promise of their birthright.

Accompanying the changes, technological as well as political, were anxieties. Americans worried whether material progress and the relentless pursuit of wealth were compatible with the republican virtues of the Revolution. Did the leisure it afforded a new generation encourage vice or the ingratitude cynical European nations associated with republics? Did the spread of the population into areas so far removed from the original thirteen colonies portend a change of American character? A second generation of Americans wrestled with these questions, fearful that they might spoil all that their dying fathers and mothers had built.

As Americans moved toward the future, they glanced back to their past with a sense of painful nostalgia, a sense of historic homesickness.[44]

When Monroe was inaugurated for the second time, it was not in the brick building on First Street, but in the House Chambers of the newly rebuilt Capitol. During his address, which mentioned "powerful causes" drawing the American people together, Monroe took note that forty-four years had now passed since the Declaration of Independence. The math was simple enough: In six more, the Declaration and America would turn fifty.

The approach of the anniversary and the angst over the passing of generations were accompanied by a growing fascination in the nation's founding. Engraved copies of the Declaration of Independence were published; so too were lives of its signers and other Revolutionary-era figures. In 1817, Congress commissioned John Trumbull to paint scenes from the Revolution, including the Declaration of Independence, to be installed in the rotunda of the resurrected Capitol with its planned copper dome.

Other histories of the era were published, including Niles's *Principles and Acts of the Revolution in America*, which reprinted Revolutionary-era speeches and documents. In its preface, he wrote that so few men who had participated in the war for independence remained, and the chance to compose a history of the era with their input was "transient." It was a reminder that time had claimed many of the founding generation; those who remained were in the twilight of their days.[45] By 1824, only four signers of the Declaration lived: the elder Adams, Jefferson, Charles Carroll of Carrollton, and Charles Thomson.

"Another Revolutionary Hero gone!" regularly appeared at the top of columns announcing the passing of yet another aged veteran. Ruben Hopkins.[46] Alexander Murray.[47] Michael Will.[48] Constant Freeman.[49] Henry Graybill.[50] Their deaths marked a countdown to the day when the remaining connections to the nation's first generation would be severed. Only a few thousand of the generation now remained.

Capitalizing on the nostalgia and angst, supporters of the presidential candidates sought to associate their man with the earlier era. In most cases, this required considerable stretches. Supporters of Calhoun, the youngest candidate and the one furthest removed from the Revolution, pointed out that he was nearly the same age as Washington when he assumed leadership of the Continental Army. Clay and Crawford had to settle for suggesting themselves as worthy heirs. Adams had come of age during the Revolution, in the shadow of Bunker Hill. But detractors could argue that these connections were merely coincidental. In their effort to envelop their candidate in the glow of revolutionary nostalgia, Jackson's supporters had an undeniable advantage: the ties to the war visible on his face and lingering in his heart. On the former was a scar from a soldier's saber, inflicted when Jackson refused to shine his boots. In the latter burned a still-smoldering hatred for the British, fueled by the loss of his mother and two brothers during the war.

It was Jackson, his supporters argued, who would form a bridge between the generations. "In him we behold a golden link between generations. He connects us with our venerated sires of the days of *Seventy-Six*," a pro-Jackson club declared late in 1823.[51] Wyoming portrayed Jackson as a form of redemption against the corrupted leaders who had strayed from the founders' virtues. "Look to the city of Washington, and let the virtuous patriots weep at the spectacle."[52] In a clever bit of propaganda, they argued that not only was he the man of the people, but he had also defended their rights in 1780 and then again in 1815. Some partisans even suggested that Jackson was the second coming of Washington.

In January 1824, a pair of congressmen, Charles F. Mercer and Stephen Van Rensselaer, met with Jackson in Washington, DC, carrying a gift: a pair of elegant pistols once owned by the first president. A distant heir of America's original general-hero had inherited the pistols and now wished to give them to the military idol of the hour. Jackson's victory at the Battle of New Orleans in 1815 was still a source of national pride and gave him a halo of celebrity. Eaton, writing as Wyoming, encouraged his readers to think of Jackson and to "Remember he was of the Revolution!"[53]

In a published note of acceptance of the pistols, Jackson, happy to float comparisons between himself and Washington, wrote, "no present, I assure you, could be more acceptable to me, or better prized" than the gift. The present, Jackson explained, had additional value because of the man who had originally given them "to our illustrious Chieftain; a man who lives, as he merits to live, in the hearts and affections of the people of this country."[54]

Here Jackson placed himself near another man who was not merely a link to but an actual vestige of the Revolution. One who still lived, remaining an object of fascination and reverence for Americans, though he was no longer in their midst and had not been seen on their shores in nearly four decades. Newspapers published his speeches, celebrated his triumphs, mourned his defeats. Americans eagerly read sketches of his glorious former life, when as a boy he had come to their aid and helped win their freedom. He was, a Washington paper wrote, the "truly noble friend of America," one "who from a strict adherence to the principles of Washington, has become the most distinguished and admired patriot living in the two hemispheres."[55] In a period characterized by intense sectional differences straining the Union, but also a growing fascination with the men who had formed it, he was a rare figure: No section could claim him as their own, no political faction could claim his allegiance; he was an object of the entire nation's admiration. "The impressions which your services in our revolution, made on every patriotic breast of our country, cannot be erased, and it will be handed down to our descendants, by a faithful preservation of the merits of that important epoch," Monroe assured this fellow veteran, whom he had befriended in the summer of 1777.[56]

In April 1823, at the president's direction, a fire-beacon of sorts was lit: A newly finished fort, made of granite, sitting atop the reef one hundred yards from the Long Island shore below New York, was dedicated to this "revered foreigner." During the dedication ceremony the American flag was raised, a salute was fired, and he was cheered by the observing crowd repeatedly. Waves crashed upon the citadel, and gusts of wind carried the name *Lafayette* to the sea.

3

———— ≈ ————

Disappointments and Disgusts

In his youth, Lafayette was enchanted by tales of great men from antiquity. By the early 1820s, he had become one himself. To the novelist Stendhal, he was "quite simply a hero by Plutarch,"[1] one with evident patina. He entered the salons of Paris leaning on a cane; a slip on an ice patch in 1803 had broken his femur, and the experimental brace used to set the bone left him with a limp in his left leg. His height was now matched by an expanding figure, and he dressed shabbily in a gray coat over a white vest and blue pantaloons, finished off by a poorly tied cravat. The reddish hair was replaced by a short brown wig that sat unconvincingly on his large head. His aquiline nose had grown fleshy and his brows bushy. Only the hazel eyes under the latter betrayed the passing of years, alternately "flashing with the fire of intelligence, or softening into the mild expression of kindness."[2]

"He lived from day to day," Stendhal observed, "quite simply doing great deeds as the opportunities arose."[3] One such opportunity surfaced on the afternoon of March 4, 1823, when officers of the National Guard entered the assembly room in the Palais Bourbon. The Chamber of Deputies, then in session, had expelled Jacques-Antoine Manuel the day before as punishment for a speech he had given criticizing the

French government's pending military expedition into Spain, even alluding to the execution of King Louis XVI. When he returned the following day in defiance of the order, promising he would be removed only by force, the Chamber's president requested the National Guard remove Manuel from the building.

As cries of "Not the National Guard!" erupted in the hall, one deputy rose from his chair and caught the attention of the officer leading the battalion. Then, this man, as an onlooker in the gallery recalled, "with a paternal air, beckoned him to stand down."[4] The officer, overcome with doubt, went to receive his orders, returned, stammered, and then turned to his sergeant, who abandoned their mission. The guardsmen, observing this scene, "remained still and as though seized with respect; their faces displayed the most lively emotions," as reported by a correspondent for the *Constitutional*. Reproached by General Lafayette, they abandoned their orders, left Manuel where they had found him, and departed the hall. Shouts of "Long live the National Guard!" erupted.[5]

"I must insist," Lafayette wrote to Lady Morgan later, "that the conduct of the national guard at the critical moment on March 4th, reminded me of the sensations of 89."[6] After the National Guard exited the assembly room, however, the gendarmerie escorted Manuel from the Palais. Heartening as the Guard's conduct was to its old commander—in a letter to the *Constitutional* he described it as "one of the most vivid joys of my lifetime"—the incident's value was nostalgic.[7] The white horse he rode at the height of his powers during the French Revolution was gone. In fact, due to lameness in his leg, Lafayette could no longer sit in the saddle; he was plagued by recurring flareups of gout; his pecuniary situation was precarious, and the "angel" who had "blessed his life for thirty years" was no more.[8] By 1823, Lafayette, now sixty-five, was an aging hero with good reason to dwell on distant memories.

Formally returned to politics in the fall of 1818, Lafayette was among a wave of liberals who won twenty-two out of the fifty-seven seats in the Chamber of Deputies that season. The Charter constitution from 1814 bridged the gap between the freedoms created during the French Revolution and the restored monarchy. Candidates were eligible for office if their taxes reached 300 francs and were selected by electoral colleges of eligible voters in the country's departments. Lafayette had stood for office in the Seine-et-Marne, where La Grange was located. But his candidacy was undercut by the government, whose agents pressured voters and whose funds paid for pamphlets reminding them, depending on the audience, of Lafayette's revolutionary past or opposition to Napoleon. Defeated, he then stood successfully for the Chamber in a delayed election in the western department of Sarthe, further from Paris and government mischief. The return to office was most unwelcome to the government: King Louis XVIII had worried over the election of "that animal Lafayette."[9]

Élie Decazes, the king's trusted advisor, who assumed the prime ministership in 1819, saw Lafayette and his fellow liberals in a more strategic light. The government had worked to elect "ministerial" candidates, moderates sympathetic to the king, over the conservative Ultra-royalists, who were often critical of Louis XVIII. With the former's numbers dwindling, Decazes formed an alliance with the liberals in hopes of charting a middle course, reconciling royalists to the progress of the Revolution and winning support for the king among subjects with warm memories of it.

In 1819, additional liberals won seats. Among them was Henri Grégoire, a priest who had supported the regicide of Louis XVI. For the Bourbons, this was too far. That former—and perhaps future—revolutionaries, including Lafayette, were gaining power was an alarming prospect to the royal retinue. Then, in February 1820, the king's nephew and third in line to the throne, the duc de Berry, was fatally stabbed in the back by a stablehand outside of the Paris Opéra.

The assassin was a madman, but Ultras and their propagandists hung the blame for his act on their liberal rivals. Decazes's ministry collapsed. Liberal gains were quickly reversed. Ultras sought to restrict the franchise and roll back press freedoms. Police scrutinized the business of would-be radicals. And, in the spring of 1820, after much passionate debate, the Chamber passed an amendment altering France's electoral system, creating 175 new seats in the Chamber, to be elected in newly made departments. Only those whose taxes were in the top 25 percent were eligible to vote in these contests, though these same men could also vote in the regular elections as well, hence the amendment's nickname, the Law of the Double Vote. The newly restricted franchise ensured Ultra victories in the elections and majorities in governing. The brief interlude of liberal advances had come to an end.

The French government's worries about revolution were enflamed because when they looked south, revolution was all they saw. Lafayette, in contrast, saw a great battle underway, a contest between "rights and privilege" that would sweep the continent, with France the central player.

On the first day of 1820, Spanish soldiers, led by General Rafael del Riego, mutinied. They had been on the verge of departing for South America, where King Ferdinand's colonies were in revolt, but instead marched to Madrid, forcing the king to reinstate the 1812 constitution. Then, in the Kingdom of the Two Sicilies, revolutionaries led by General Guglielmo Pepe and organized in part by the Carbonari—meaning "charcoal burners" in Italian, a shadowy revolutionary society originating in southern Italy—pressured their own monarch, King Ferdinand I, to adopt a government modeled on the Spanish constitution. A short-lived revolt in Piedmont followed in 1821. In Portugal, revolutionaries successfully demanded King John VI return from Brazil, where he had ruled since fleeing during the Napoleonic Wars. He too agreed to a constitutional government.

The following year, Greeks began their own rebellion, which soon turned into a bloody war of independence against the Ottoman Empire. This last conflict was an especially romantic cause among European liberals, Lafayette included, who viewed the Greek rebels as direct descendants of antiquity battling to liberate themselves from Muslim oppression.

Lafayette envisioned these revolutions as theaters in a larger contest of liberty. To his dismay, though, most of their gains across the continent were brief. "Happier would I be to inform you that the rights of mankind are amicably settled on this side of the Atlantic. It is far from being the case," Lafayette wrote in one of his regular updates to President James Monroe on the state of freedom across the continent.[10]

Alarmed by the revolutionary advances, in 1821, Austria stamped out the rebellion in Naples, crushing an army led by Pepe outside the walls of Rieti. Two years later, in the spring of 1823, with approval from the Quintuple Alliance at the Congress of Verona, France sent its military over the Pyrenees, ending the rebellion in Spain and reestablishing King Ferdinand's absolute rule in Madrid. The Portuguese revolution collapsed soon after.

"The peninsula south of the pyrenes is tormented with counter revolutionary intrigues and disguised attempts to overthrow their constitution. Italy has been submitted to a leaden yoke tainted with blood. Conspiracies against the rights of man by the Holy Alliance at Verona,"[11] Lafayette lamented to Monroe. After the reestablishment of Spain's monarchy, Riego was convicted of treason and hanged. His wife, Maria Teresa, sent the black silk cravat he had untied while standing on the scaffold, along with a lock of his hair, to Lafayette. Preserved in a crystal box, they were placed among the relics at La Grange.

Whether there or in Paris, Lafayette was seldom far from his son, Georges Washington; elected a member of the Chamber in 1821, the younger Lafayette was devoted to and deeply revered his father. A far less romantic figure, no hero from Plutarch, but gallant in his own modest way, he had, as the historian Achille de Vaulabelle wrote, a "calm and sweet disposition, an honest and upright heart, a firm conscience."[12] Like his father, Georges could rightfully claim America as a second home and his namesake as a second father. At fifteen, with Lafayette imprisoned, Adrienne arranged for her son to escape from France, sent to America, and find safe harbor in the Washington home. "After many troubles and crossings, it is in America, it is with you, that I come to seek an ancestor, and my father," young Lafayette wrote to Washington after reaching Boston in the fall of 1795. "Will you be so kind as to allow the unfortunate son of a man, whom you have honored with some friendship, and who with good luck learned from him to look upon you as his father, to come to offer you the expression of his gratitude, and the homage of a respect as deep as tender. Dare I say filial?"[13]

The answer was, of course, yes, though matters of state held Washington back for the moment: Rather than welcoming the child of an émigré into the president's home, Washington directed Georges to New York, where he passed a summer in the home of Alexander Hamilton before finding his way to Philadelphia. When Washington, finally retired from the presidency, returned to his farm, traveling from Philadelphia to Mount Vernon in the spring of 1797, his French namesake was at his side.[14]

For the next two years, he lived among Washington's family and with new siblings: Martha Washington's two youngest grandchildren, Eleanor "Nelly" Parke Custis and George Washington Parke Custis. They had joined the Washington household after their father, John Parke Custis, an aide to Washington, succumbed to yellow fever in 1781.

When the architect Benjamin Latrobe visited Mount Vernon in 1788, he observed as Georges Washington de Lafayette descended the stairs before dinner was served. "He is a young man about seventeen, of a mild, pleasant countenance, favorably impressing one at first sight. His figure is rather awkward. His manners are easy, and he has very little of the usual French air about him." Latrobe recorded in his journal that Georges spoke English passably, and mostly with Nelly. Most tellingly though, was the interaction between the head of the household and his young charge: "A few jokes passed between the president and young Lafayette, whom he treated more as a child than as a guest."[15]

During his exile from public life, Lafayette lived vicariously through the exploits of his son, who by 1800 had enlisted in the French army, serving with distinction as an aide to General Grouchy, whose life he twice saved in battle. "Papa, I think has seldom been so proud and happy," Virginie noted after her brother was wounded during the French crossing of the Mincio River in 1800.[16] Along with his sisters Virginie and Anastasia and their own families, thirteen grandchildren, and, by the end of 1823, two great-grandchildren, surrounded their beloved patriarch at La Grange.

The home's matriarch remained in spirit. Adrienne's quarters were walled off, converted into a mausoleum of sorts, which only the family were to enter. Every Christmas Eve, on the anniversary of her death, they gathered to honor her memory. Lafayette also performed a daily tribute to his late wife: Every morning at five, his loyal valet Sebastian "Bastien" Wagner would wake him and he would spend the next hour in bed, reading, writing, and lost in thought, forbidding all interruptions. He'd conclude this ritual by clutching a gold medallion with the words *I am yours* surrounding Adrienne's portrait, fixing his gaze on her likeness, and holding it to his lips.[17]

He was not entirely lonely though. Nearer the end of Lafayette's life, Stendhal observed his fondness for women young enough to be his granddaughter, and found the way his eyes came alive as "soon as they are within a foot of a pretty chest" humanizing. Recalling his fondness for a young Portuguese woman, Stendhal wrote, Lafayette "imagines that he is signaled out for special attention, he only thinks of her, and what is amusing is that often he is right in his imaginings."[18] But at La Grange, he welcomed and mentored numerous women, taking a sincere interest in their careers. These included not only Lady Morgan, but also the Spanish-born contralto-soprano Maria Malibran, whom he described as his "great pupil," and later, the Italian writer and revolutionary Cristina Belgiojoso.[19]

In September 1821, however, Lafayette met a young woman with whom he would develop a uniquely intense bond. In time, this relationship provoked unwelcome innuendo and threatened to divide his tightly knit family. The initial connection between the two was an object of mutual affection. "We held an earnest tete-a-tete, until after midnight," she wrote of their first meeting. "The main subject of our discourse was America."[20]

The day before they met, she had impulsively journeyed to La Grange without an invitation in hopes of finding him at home. Flattered by his gracious family, who expressed their regret that he was in Paris at the time, she at once set out to find him there. Frances "Fanny" Wright was not one to stand on ceremony or delay her dreams. In time, she would be regarded as "the advocate of opinions that make millions shudder."[21]

From an uncritical comparison of their early lives, Wright could claim, in some ways, to be a second coming of Lafayette. Beyond their shared birthday of September 6—separated by thirty-eight years—

they were both well-born, orphaned early, left with a fortune, and, uninterested in the life of the well-to-do, captivated and drawn, at a tender age, across an ocean by an idealistic portrait of America.

Wright was born in Dundee, on the Scottish coast. Her father, James, was a linen merchant with more interest in radical politics than business: He had earned the enmity of the British government for printing a budget edition of Thomas Paine's *Common Sense*. There was no time, however, for James or his wife, Camilla, to have an ideological influence over their oldest daughter. In 1798, when Fanny was not yet three, both her mother and father died within months of one another. She and her siblings—a brother named Richard and a younger sister, Camilla—were separated after their parents' death.

Fanny was sent to London where she lived with her grandfather. The sight of pleading mothers and hungry children on the city's streets kindled an early sense of outrage at inequality, human suffering, and the disruption brought by the Industrial Revolution. "I cannot see begging in our towns & villages and read of injustice in every paper I cast my eye upon & and witness political & religious hypocrisy wherever I turn without feeling pain, indignation or disgust," she wrote.

The death of a wealthy uncle in 1803 left Fanny and her siblings with half his considerable estate. Reunited with Camilla, who would be her loyal and steady companion in life, Fanny moved again, to the home of their aunt, Frances Campbell, in Dawlish, a picturesque town on the English coast. She grew to hate this woman and her bourgeois lifestyle. This resentment, coupled with the constant presence of death—her grandfather and brother both died by 1809—left Fanny with a coldness that she expressed in an early poem:

> *And now, the worst—a heart whose pulse is killed.*
> *And hath no more to give or to receive,*
> *Shrunk in itself, all passive, mute and chilled,*
> *That hopes not, cares not, joys not, nor can grieve.*[22]

This disposition, coupled with an urgent need to remedy society's injustices, inspired an independence irregular among women of the era;

she also rejected the limited callings available to them and the societal strictures placed on them in early nineteenth-century England. But her high ideals were paired with a seriousness and righteousness that precluded humor and, to her detriment, diplomacy.

Abandoning their aunt, Fanny and Camilla found a harbor at the home of their great-uncle James Mylne, a free-thinking professor of philosophy at the University of Glasgow. Life in the Mylne home exposed the Wrights to a new circle of acquaintances, as well as entry to a library full of enlightenment literature that inspired Fanny's own writing. It was the subject of another author that most fascinated her, however: the Italian historian Carlo Giuseppe Guglielmo Botta's account of the American Revolution, published in 1809. The book stirred interest in a new country dedicated to liberty, governed by its people. The growing fascination in America was furthered by her relationship with Robina Craig Millar, a surrogate mother for Fanny and Camilla who had lived for a time with her husband before his death in Pennsylvania.

By 1818, she was determined to cross the Atlantic and discover whether her romantic image of the nation on the other side of the ocean matched reality. In August of that year, with Camilla at her side, and much to their great-uncle's dismay, she embarked from Liverpool bound for New York. For nearly two years the Wright sisters remained in America, visiting its cities and frontier. Two young women traveling alone across the country and into Canada itself was noteworthy; the elder Wright, who was unusually tall, nearly six feet, likely was a singular figure wherever they ventured. Later, travelers in America recalled that she "is of tall stature and masculine manner"[23]—the latter description likely a reference to her willingness to challenge any man on any subject.

In a series of letters to Millar, Fanny shared her reflections on the country, its people, and its customs. Her rosy observations were not unlike Lafayette's own in the letters he wrote to Adrienne upon arriving in South Carolina fifty years before. Fanny was struck by the "republican simplicity" of the Americans she encountered. She saw little in the way of class—there were no poor or uneducated as far as she could tell.

New York, she wrote, was "as civil as any City in England and perhaps a little more honest."

She was convinced that the citizenry was deeply connected to the actions of their representatives and the function of its institutions. Fanny was impressed that Americans used the word *our* when discussing the president, and *we* in the context of the actions of Congress; every man was a "politician and a philosopher." Regarding women, she found Americans quite attractive, "as if no rude wind had ever fanned them." But she commented upon how early marriage and preoccupation with domestic matters were limiting. America's progress, she hoped, "may yet be doubly accelerated when the education of women shall equally be a national concern with that of the other sex." Returning to England in 1820—she and Camilla applied for citizenship in New York during their visit—Fanny contemplated settling in America, "the only country to which I acknowledge an attachment." But her admiration for the republic was tainted by the southern states, where one would cast their eyes and "see liberty mocked & outraged."

"When my thoughts turn to America," she wrote to Harriet and Julia Garnett, sisters whom she had met in America, who later relocated to France, "the crying sin of her slavery weights upon my heart; there are moments when this foul blot so defaces to my mind's eye all the beauty of her character that I turn with disgust from her & in her from the last & only nation on the globe to which my soul clings with affection, pride & hope."

Here though she clung to optimism: By 1820, many of the Northern states had outlawed slavery; other states, she was certain, would follow their example. "Many I see at present that operate in your southern States to delay the annihilation of Slavery; but this I rely on—that they can only delay it . . . already he feels the chain, & and he who feels will soon snap it, especially in a country such as yours where are all that meets the eye or the ear breathes freedom."[24]

Fanny edited and published the letters to Millar as *Views of Society and Manners in America.* The travelogue was an almost entirely positive examination of American society and the benefits of representative government. Accordingly, it was savaged as a work of near fiction by conservative reviewers in Britain. The book did have defenders at home. Among Fanny's new admirers was the author Jeremy Bentham, an occasional visitor at La Grange. Fanny had sent a copy of her book to Lafayette, and in July 1821, he forwarded a complimentary note of thanks for the gift. Overjoyed, Fanny wrote back, raising the possibility of a meeting. "I anticipate the moment which will give to me one of the earliest and fondest wishes of my youth."[25]

That moment came in September 1821, when the Wright sisters visited Paris. After her disappointment of not finding him at La Grange, Fanny returned to Paris, where she sent a note to Lafayette the next morning. He soon appeared at her door. "Our meeting was scarcely without tears, (at least on my side,) and whether it was that thus venerable friend of human liberty saw in me what recalled to him some of the most pleasing recollections of his youth, (I mean those connected with America,) or whether it was only that he was touched by the sensibility which appeared at the moment in me, he evidently shared my emotion," she confided to Bentham after the meeting.[26]

Weeks later, Wright was at La Grange, where she and Camilla were soon regulars, among the "inmates of that consecrated dwelling," as she described it.[27] From the first late-night conversation in the fall of 1821, Fanny and Lafayette's friendship grew extraordinarily warm. He served as a paternal figure, nurturing her career and bolstering her confidence. Lafayette helped secure a French translation of *Views,* which was published in 1822, and promoted its virtues among the same network of friends, intellectuals, activists, and politicians that gathered at La Grange and now welcomed Fanny into their midst. She, in turn, provided Lafayette with an adoring understudy, whose praise, often verging into idolatry, no doubt cheered the aging widower enduring personal and political disappointment. This role spread to her literary pursuits: In the spring of 1822, she began a lengthy stay at La Grange to begin work on a never realized biography of her host. As he ushered her into his circle of friends, Wright's own friends became his: Harriet and Julia Garnett also developed lasting friendships with Lafayette.

The relationship between the storied revolutionary and young radical transcended mere friendship but almost certainly stopped short of romance. "General L is to me a father," she explained to a correspondent a year after they had met.[28] Indeed, he adopted a paternal posture toward her, referring to both Wright sisters as his daughters. Her letters to him were characterized by profuse outpourings of affection. They began with salutations to "an angel of goodness & my beloved friend."[29] They closed with promises of devotion, to be her correspondent's "most fondly & devotedly till death."[30] It was, in Wright's telling years later, a "friendship of no ordinary character."[31] Their correspondence bears this out.

Increasingly, a note of possessiveness crept into her communications. "I like to think of you at La Grange my excellent friend although it deprives me of your society," she wrote him just months after their initial meeting. "I am indeed unreasonable enough to lament that I do not pass them with you and to envy those who enjoy the satisfaction that is denied to me."[32]

"You know I am your child—the child of your affection the child of your adoption. You have given me the title and I will never part with it. To possess this title was the highest of my wishes—to deserve it is my proudest ambition." Her pretensions on his paternal love, however, grew ever more immodest. "I love you dearly, you never had a child that loved you more tenderly, never a friend who felt your interests to be more her own," she wrote him.[33] The expressions, if indicative of her behavior when they were together or in the company of his family, were harbingers of strains to come.

Wright's arrival in Lafayette's life coincided with his abandonment of electoral politics for ill-wrought conspiracies to topple the French government. After the conclusion of his assignment as American minister to France in 1823, Albert Gallatin recalled that Lafayette "was very ungovernable in all that related to petty plots during my residence in Paris as minister."[34] Jacques Laffitte, a Parisian banker and fellow liberal deputy, reflected on Lafayette's preoccupations during this period with an endearing story.

On a day when Lafayette had come to visit his house, a stockbroker friend of Laffitte's had stopped by to inform them of a crashed cabriolet in rue Saint-Denis, where thirty curious onlookers had gathered to gawk at the accident.

After the stockbroker departed, Lafayette drew his chair near his host's. "My good friend, what if we made use of this event?" he asked. "What event?" Laffitte questioned. "The one in the rue Saint-Denis." At this point Laffitte recognized that his friend had hatched from an overturned carriage a means to overthrow the Bourbons.

"You're joking, right?" asked Laffitte.

"My good friend, it's a gathering!" replied Lafayette.

"A gathering? Of twenty or so people?"

"My good friend, they are thirty!"[35]

Lafayette described La Grange as an "asylum for the condemned."[36] He was not entirely exaggerating. Some who found refuge inside its walls were involved in schemes that risked a trip to the gallows, including Lafayette himself. In the early 1820s, cells of the Carbonari, the clandestine organization that had fomented revolution in Italy, began to sprout in France. Active members of these groups were often among his guests, such as Dutch-born painter Ary Scheffer, who began a portrait of Lafayette in 1818 and gave lessons to his grandchildren in La Grange's drawing room, and his historian brother, Arnold, who researched in its library. These radicals sought patronage for their plots, which Lafayette provided, while his involvement with another generation of insurgents allowed the old revolutionary to relive the glory of his earlier days. His involvement with another generation of insurgents allowed Lafayette to relive the glory of his earlier days.

In the winter of 1821, Lafayette, accompanied by his son Georges and valet Bastien, was en route to the town of Belfort in eastern France, where Carbonari cells, financed by members of the Chamber of Deputies, were in place, preparing to seize control of a military garrison. Lafayette's arrival in Belfort would activate the cell; he would then serve as part of a quickly established provisional government. Soldiers from across the country would then join the revolt and topple the Bourbon regime. Before he reached Belfort, another carriage intercepted Lafayette's, warning him off with word that the local authorities had discovered the conspiracy and foiled the plan. He escaped arrest or direct implication, though evidence later surfaced linking him and six other deputies to the Belfort affair. The entire proposition was a fool's errand, vastly overestimating the French opposition to the Bourbons; Lafayette had misjudged its political impact.[37]

"Is he crazy, then?" asked the liberal monarchist member of the chamber, Pierre Paul Royer-Collard following the Belfort conspiracy.

"On the contrary, he is one of the wisest, most reasonable, and most spiritual men you could know," Laffitte replied, explaining that to Lafayette, "insurrection is the most sacred of duties."

"So what does he want exactly?" Royer-Collard wondered.

"I'm not entirely sure," Laffitte answered. "Lafayette is a walking monument in search of his pedestal. Whether his path leads him to the scaffolds or to the chair of the President of the Republic, he wouldn't give a dime for the choice," he concluded.

Lafayette, observing the conversation, asked Laffitte what had been discussed. After he heard the bit about the scaffold or the presidency, Lafayette, laughing, exclaimed, "It's true!"[38]

The Belfort scheme, as well as the foiling of another Carbonari plot led by Jean-Baptiste Berton in western France, only strengthened the counterreaction Lafayette so loathed. Military trials of the alleged conspirators underscored the violent nature of the Carbonari's ambitions. Disturbed French voters punished liberal candidates at the polls, even those who had no connection to the plots. The government seized the opportunity to purge their opponents' names from the electoral rolls and attempted to render their candidates, including Lafayette, ineligible to seek office.

In the aftermath of his involvement in the Belfort conspiracy, police surveilled the flow of traffic in and out of La Grange. "We are living under the pressure of criminal law, investigations by the King's attorneys, judicial infamies of every kind," Georges wrote.[39] Victor de Broglie, an occasional visitor to La Grange whose mother-in-law, Madame de Staël, was one of Lafayette's oldest friends, lamented the marquis's involvement with the conspirators and their schemes to liberate Europe. "All his fine fortune, so nobly earned, offered and received, was squandered by the hands of spies and adventurers."[40]

The diminishment of his finances began long before the Second Restoration. Lafayette left for America in 1777 a wealthy man, but experimenting in freedom came at a cost. The purchase of *La Victoire*, which was uninsured and later lost at sea; money drawn for his companions on the initial journey to America; and the swords, pistols, tents, saddles, and belts packed aboard *L'Hermione* when it carried the young general back to Boston in 1780—collectively, these expenditures amounted to a significant sum. Jacques-Philippe Grattepain-Morizot, who oversaw Lafayette's accounts, estimated the total cost at $200,000.[41]

Returned from his exile in 1799, Lafayette found his remaining possessions in disrepair, his coffers bare, and his needs great. The American government was not unsympathetic. In 1794, Congress provided $24,424 in back pay for Lafayette's services as a major general. In February 1803, in the House of Representatives, John "Beau" Dawson, a Virginian member, attached an amendment to a bill granting Lafayette 15,000 acres of land, commensurate with the grants given to other major generals of the revolutionary army. "I have spent two days with this adopted child of America on his little farm. I saw him surrounded by an amiable family, but not with wealth," Dawson shared in a speech on the House floor. Both chambers passed the bill, though the Senate reduced the size of the grant to 11,520 acres north of the Ohio River.[42]

Lafayette wished to use the land to repay debts and establish income as quickly as possible. Acreage in the newly acquired territory of Louisiana, with access to the port in New Orleans, held greater promise of a rapid increase in value than land in the Northwest Territory. In 1804, with Jefferson's approval, Congress relocated Lafayette's grant to Louisiana.[43] Lafayette transferred power of attorney to a quickly overwhelmed James Madison, tasking him with locating the land both near New Orleans and at Point Coupée along the Mississippi River. He intended to use the New Orleans land to pay down $100,000 in debt owed to the British financiers Baring Brothers and Daniel Parker, while using the remainder to generate income from farm leases. Additionally, he planned to establish his own plantation and leave behind an inheritance for his children.

The gift never produced the income stream Lafayette had hoped for. Titles for the land were contested by other claimants. Years passed, and Lafayette waited, his optimism waning and his finances still in tatters. The value of the land, impacted by wars in Europe, never rose to meet his expectations. It was not until 1810 that Lafayette took title to parts of the Pointe Coupée land. Five thousand acres were given to the Barring Brothers to relieve his debt. The rest was sold to the Englishmen John Coghill and Henry Seymour. However, possession of the New Orleans land—which had also been sold to Coghill before it was properly located and deeded—drew both Lafayette and Coghill's heirs into a protracted dispute over the location of the acreage. This wrangle continued to torment Lafayette into the 1820s, by which time he was once again in debt. In 1824, his expenses, totaling 19,724 francs, exceeded his revenues of 19,427.[44]

Through his discontent, Lafayette looked toward America for consolation—and there he found it, both political and personal. Liberal ranks had thinned in the Chamber of Deputies, and democratic reforms were being reversed across Europe. But in America, government by consensus thrived. "Every Account I receive from the U.S. is a Compensation for European disappointments and disgusts, there our Revolutionary Hopes Have Been fulfilled," he wrote to Jefferson.[45]

Revolutionary movements across Europe had been mostly extinguished by the Holy Alliance, the coalition of monarchical powers, but in December 1823, in his annual message to Congress, Monroe warned the great powers against future colonial adventures and military interventions to restore their former possessions in the Western Hemisphere. "It has been hailed by every friend of liberty," Lafayette congratulated Monroe, "and by none, of course, more than by your old brother soldier who in every concern of the United States feels a patriotic interest and patriotic pride."[46]

"Our country is in a very prosperous state, in all of its official concerns, The government is successful, in all its branches, & the movement of the two govts, state & national, is in the highest degree harmonious," Monroe happily informed Lafayette. "Our population has augmented beyond all former example."[47]

It was not simply America's representative government that lifted Lafayette's spirits, but details of the progress it had wrought. In the fall of 1823, John Trumbull, the revolutionary soldier turned painter of the Revolution, wrote to Lafayette describing the construction of an ambitious canal linking the Great Lakes to the Atlantic Ocean, now underway in the same once-wild region in New York he had known as a soldier. "In these wonders of virtuous freedoms, national sense, and unshackled industry," Lafayette responded to Trumbull, "my mind seeks a refuge from too many disquiets and disappointments on this side of the Atlantic."[48]

The distant past occupied his thoughts and lifted his spirits as well. Trumbull sent Lafayette a print of his rendering of the presentation of the Declaration of Independence, commissioned by the U.S. government for the rotunda of the Capitol, which was gradually being restored after its burning in 1814. The likenesses of old acquaintances—John Adams, Benjamin Franklin, and Charles Thomson—stirred old memories. James Thatcher, a surgeon in the Continental Army who published a journal written during the Revolution, mailed him a copy of the book, complete with impressions of a youthful Lafayette. "Old dear recollections, happy years, and beloved friends, have, at once, reappeared before me," he told Thatcher in a letter of thanks.[49]

Some of those beloved friends still lived: Lafayette carried on a particularly tender correspondence with Marinus Willett, who had joined Washington's army shortly before the Battle of Monmouth, where his detachment was placed under Lafayette's command. Willett still recalled, half a century later, the image of the Frenchman galloping toward his light infantry company with orders to march against the British grenadiers, shortly before the chaotic American retreat.[50]

"We remain but too few survivors of that glorious epoch in which the fate of two Hemispheres has been decided; it is an additional motive to think more and more the ties of brotherly friendship which united us," Lafayette wrote to Willett in the summer of 1822.[51] But the passing years thinned the ranks of survivors, as Lafayette was regularly reminded. Not long after receiving a letter of reminiscences from

Joseph Bloomfield, who had also been wounded at Brandywine, he learned that the old soldier had died. If Lafayette wished to embrace his brother once again, the time to do so was not unlimited.

Increasingly he thought of setting out one final time for the New World, to which he had assured Washington—now almost forty years ago—he would return. "Mr. Gallatin and family are going to the U.S. I wish I might accompany them," he mused to a friend, with almost an air of desperation, in the spring of 1823 upon the American minister's departure.[52] There was no shortage of invitations. In correspondence, his old friends, aware of his political straits, urged Lafayette to seek refuge and spend his remaining years in his adopted country. "Recollect Venerable Sir what an asylum you have here," William Lee, a Virginian friend of Monroe, reminded Lafayette. "Here you will be received with open arms as the friend of Washington the early defender of our rights and liberties and the proud chief & and head of the liberal party of all countries."[53] Lafayette was not at all shy about his desire to accept these invitations. "You invite me, my dear doctor, to the happy shores where so many unutterable emotions await me. Far am I from giving up the delightful hope," he wrote to Thatcher.[54]

During the summer of 1823, inspired by the publication of his correspondences—particularly his letter to Willett—in American newspapers, rumors began to circulate that Lafayette indeed was prepared to embark for friendlier shores. It was an exhilarating prospect. "The rumor is revived" the *Pittsfield Sun* excitedly reported, with assurance that there was no man across the Atlantic who "might expect to receive so cordial and hearty a reception among us." Editors were already offering advice to the government. "Should the marquis, in his old age, really design to visit the United States we trust that he will not, as before, be permitted to come at his own expense," a gesture that would not only "evince to crowned heads, that republics are not always ungrateful" but also honor Lafayette's contributions.[55]

The editor Paul Allen imagined a possible visit by Lafayette as a series of beautiful vignettes. He would gather once more with the four living signers of the Declaration of Independence: "What respect and veneration would an interview between Lafayette, Thomas Jefferson, John Adams, Charles Carroll, and Charles Thomson inspire! What memories would such a reunion conjure up!"

He would revisit the site of American and French victory at Yorktown: "What emotion Lafayette would feel, trampling underfoot the same places where he once retreated before Cornwallis!"

And then, inevitably, he would pay his last homage to a departed father: "How he would like to wander among the graves of Mount Vernon, and, above all, how many times would he go meditate before the one containing the ashes of Washington."[56]

But leaving France was as complicated as reaching America would be sweet. To do so, despite his desires, would be to cut and run. His absence, even for a time, would signal to the forces of reaction a battle abandoned. Even the rumor of it provided a political cudgel for his opponents: At the end of 1823, the French government dissolved the Chamber of Deputies, necessitating elections early the next year. The rumor that Lafayette was readying to run off to America once more was used to undermine his candidacy. The "ebb of freedom in France is just now very low," he reminded Lee. "I know what you and my other friends will say. But as long as duty or even honor point over the field of action, can an old herald of the charge now sound the retreat!"[57]

In private conversations, even with strangers—though no American was a stranger—it was clear where his heart lay. During the winter of 1824, John Ambler, a twenty-two-year-old Virginian, arrived in Paris, where he would spend a year before traveling across Europe. On his arrival, Ambler was welcomed and often socialized with Isaac Cox Barnet, the American consul. In January, Barnet proposed that he and Ambler visit Lafayette's apartment in Paris, a rite of passage for Americans visiting France. They arrived at his home only to learn that he was visiting Wright. Undeterred, Barnet and Ambler trekked to her lodgings, where they found Lafayette, who warmly greeted them.

During the visit—at one point, Wright spoke about America for nearly thirty minutes without interruption—Lafayette requested that Ambler sit by his side, inquiring if the young man spoke French, which he did not. Lafayette cheerfully observed that he had been in the same predicament in 1777 when he arrived in South Carolina unable to speak English. He then asked numerous questions about America and shared stories of George Washington and the Revolution. Before the meeting drew to an end, and Lafayette stood, with some difficulty, and walked out the door, he made a confession to his new friend. On the subject of America, he said to Ambler, with a romantic flourish, that he was indeed "extremely anxious to return to her, to pass the last years of his life and bury his bones there."[58]

4

—≈—

His Heart Is Fixed
Upon a Voyage to America

O n the evening of February 21, 1824, the Stars and Stripes and the
white flag of France hung on the walls of a banquet room in
Le Cadran Bleu, on boulevard du Temple in Paris. On this night, the
restaurant—a venue for revolutionary fervor in 1789—was reserved
for a particularly American celebration. Led by Isaac Cox Barnet, the
American consul, a clique of his countrymen, including young John
Ambler and Lieutenant Uriah P. Levy, who would decades later rescue Monticello from ruin, gathered to celebrate George Washington's
birthday. The actual anniversary fell on the 22nd, but since that was a
Sunday, the event was instead held the night before.

There was an obvious addition to the Americans' invitation list. As
guests entered through the folding doors of the banquet room, they
were greeted by two names surrounded by laurels: the first, *Washington*,
the cause of the gathering; the second, *Lafayette*, its guest of honor.[1]

As the evening progressed, following a multicourse meal—the
last of which incorporated American flags on every dish—the party,
which also included Georges Washington de Lafayette, concluded with
toasts. One for Washington. Another for King Louis XVIII. A third for
President James Monroe. And then, at last, a tribute to Lafayette, whose

fate in the Chamber of Deputies would be decided by the electors of Meaux days later.

When it came time for him to speak, Lafayette showered praise on Monroe's recent message to Congress, restated his own role in the battle between rights and privilege, and ended with a fond wish: "There exist for me motives of duty and honor which must dictate the period when I shall have again the happiness to see again the shore of liberty. But this happiness will be the most delightful that I shall ever be able to experience."[2]

While Lafayette and his friends raised glasses on one side of the Atlantic Ocean, James Brown waited expectantly on the other. A fifty-seven-year-old Southerner "of large fortune, respectable talents, handsome person, polished manners, and elegant deportment," Brown had been appointed America's minister to France the previous fall by James Monroe. Now, he was destined for Paris but delayed in New York. Detained with him was a letter from the president to an old friend, one Brown assured Monroe "shall be carefully kept and delivered immediately after my arrival."[3]

Brown was a member of a minor political dynasty with Virginian roots. He was born in the Shenandoah Valley, educated there by his father, John, a Presbyterian minister who founded what would eventually become Washington and Lee University, before immigrating to Kentucky. At the close of the nineteenth century, the exodus of land-hungry Virginians to Kentucky was so great that the elder Brown remarked the emigrants must have believed they were destined for "a new found paradise." His sons, first John Jr., who had served in Congress from Virginia, and then James, joined the diaspora. If they did not find paradise, they did indeed prosper; the elder brother became one of Kentucky's preeminent politicians; the younger received a number of appointments—district attorney for the Kentucky District, and, after it entered the Union, secretary of state for the commonwealth.[4]

A description from a contemporary Kentuckian captures Brown's bearing: "a gentleman of high literary and legal attainments, a good speaker but not eloquent . . . a man of towering and majestic person, very proud, austere and haughty in fact repulsive in his manner, and was exceedingly unpopular." These last two descriptors were perhaps not widely shared, as Brown was successful in politics, though outshone by his elder brother. A far greater shadow was that of his brother-in-law: His wife Nancy's sister Lucretia was wed to Henry Clay, the Speaker of the House at the time of Brown's departure for France.[5]

Brown had less enthusiasm for elected office than for the pursuit of wealth. After the U.S. government purchased the Louisiana Territory from France, he pulled up stakes in Kentucky and headed southward. There, he was offered public assignments by President Thomas Jefferson. Because he was insufficiently fluent in French and because the pay was not commensurate with his needs, Brown declined the offer of a judgeship and instead opened a lucrative law practice and purchased a farm above New Orleans. He was not immune to other public assignments: In 1805, Brown helped write the territory's civil code and later Louisiana's constitution, and he was twice—in 1812 and 1819—elected to the U.S. Senate.

In between these two nonconsecutive terms, Brown and his wife traveled to France, where he met Lafayette and would join the ranks of Americans enlisted to help the Frenchman untangle the matter of his Louisiana lands.

Monroe had floated other ministerial appointments to Brown during his administration: Mexican society was far too crude for Mrs. Brown; Spain was a more appealing post, but at the time, Brown's rheumatism prevented it.[6] Undeterred, the president thought of another appointment for a pressing need. In early 1824, American relations with France were in crisis. The U.S. government objected to France's intervention in Spain—Monroe included a mild rebuke in his message to Congress. The French government had rejected American rights to a fishery in the Strait of Belle Isle, off Newfoundland, while a frigate carrying the American minister was prevented by French ships from entering Cádiz.

Now, the French government plotted to link the matter of spoilage claims—appeals for compensation for freight stolen from American ships—with acceptance of Article VIII of the Louisiana Purchase, which extended most-favored-nation status to France's ships. The previous October, Monroe had beseeched Gallatin, who had happily returned home to Pennsylvania, to once again assume his role as minister, without success.[7] He then turned to Brown, whose wealth, abilities, and connection to New Orleans, with its French population, made him a suitable replacement.

In November 1823, Monroe announced his intention to nominate Brown as minister to France at a meeting of his cabinet, to the surprise of most of its members.[8] The president's secretaries, respectively, found Brown brilliant but timid, worried about his rheumatism, and they remarked upon his "showy wife."[9] But there was little time for deliberation. Secretary of State John Quincy Adams offered Brown the French ministry in December, and he accepted.

Before the year ended, Brown's colleagues in Congress confirmed the appointment, he resigned his seat, arranged his affairs, and, before departing, received his orders. "Besides the objects of interest in the particular relations between the United States and France, herein recommend to your attention," Adams wrote, "the general state of our relations with her, and with the other European powers, will form, perhaps, the most important part of the duties of your mission."[10]

As it turned out, another critical duty would fall to Brown on his arrival in Paris, the discharge of which would be among his most important public endeavors. The letter Brown safeguarded on the eve of his departure contained an invitation for Lafayette to visit America. And he had reason to believe Lafayette was likely to accept it: "From the dispending tone of several letters I have lately seen written by him to friends in the U States," he wrote Monroe, "I shall not be surprised should he visit us in the Course of the present year."[11]

The fates seemed to conspire against Brown reaching Paris, however. The *Cayne*, the frigate designated to carry the new minister to France, was unable to set sail; its captain, John Orde Creighton, was struck with an eye infection, and his orders were overdue. While Brown lingered in New York with Monroe's letter of invitation to Lafayette, Congress extended its own.

In January 1824, amid its debates over the generosity of pensions for Revolutionary War veterans, federal support for the surveying of potential canals, and the construction of a long-delayed monument to George Washington, a physician-turned-congressman from Maryland named George Edward Mitchell proposed a national invitation for the old hero.

Emboldened by correspondence made public or shared by its recipients, the preamble to a resolution introduced on January 12 noted that Lafayette, "distinguished champion of freedom, and hero of our Revolution, the friend and associate of Washington," had expressed "an anxious desire to visit this country." It then resolved that the president communicate to Lafayette and "assure him that the execution of his wish and intention to visit this country, will be hailed by the people and Government with patriotic pride and joy."[12] Additionally, when the date for such a visit was set according to Lafayette's wishes, a national ship would be dispatched to retrieve him.

Subsequent debate concerned Lafayette's actual wishes. Lewis Williams, a representative from North Carolina, raised the possibility that Congress, in passing the resolution, was casting rather than fulfilling a wish. After all, Lafayette had expressed a hope—one achievable only at some point in the future—not any concrete plans to visit; it was Americans who had aired their desire for him to reappear among them.

But a congressman from Louisiana, William Brent, claimed to have seen a letter written by Lafayette to Auguste Davezac of New Orleans, expressing his wish for a last visit to America; his brother-in-law, Edward Livingston, had also received a letter expressing the same sentiment. Now, Brent argued on the House floor, was the time for the American people, through their representatives in Congress, to vote unanimously to extend a national invitation to their old benefactor; doing so would cost nothing nor establish any troublesome precedent. Charles Rich of Vermont proposed a solution: striking out "expressed an anxious wish" for "announced his intention" in the resolution's language.[13]

On Monday, January 18, 1824, Mitchell reintroduced an amended version of the resolution with an altered preamble. Then, in an emotional turn, Livingston, who represented New Orleans, rose to plead with the House to pass the resolution unanimously. He recounted how, as a student at Princeton, he had visited Lafayette's headquarters during the Revolution and witnessed the general leading two thousand men, all attired and equipped by him, all yielding to the leadership of the young stranger. It would be, Livingston argued, "an imputation on the American character" if the House of Representatives was unable to pass the resolution extending an invitation to Lafayette unanimously. "Surely sir, it is fit, it is becoming, if such be his wish, that he should be wafted to our shores beneath that flag which he once planted on the breastworks of our enemy."[14]

At this point in the discourse, Mitchell passed to the Clerk of the House letters from Lafayette, including the one addressed to Marinus Willett, which had appeared in American newspapers, to be read aloud as confirmation of Lafayette's aspiration to visit. Finally, Andrew Stevenson stood to read a portion of another letter from Lafayette in his possession expressing the same desire and concluding with the wish that "I more and more look forward to the day when, with a safe conscience, it shall be my happy lot to find myself on American ground."[15] Stevenson mentioned that the letter was dated November 25 of the previous year but did not name a recipient. The communication was, in fact, the same one Lafayette had sent to Monroe the previous fall. Stevenson, a fellow Virginian, had omitted a portion of the original letter in which Lafayette had expressed his unwillingness to leave France due to political responsibilities. All this suggested the hidden hand of the president in extending the congressional invitation to his old friend. The House then passed the resolution unanimously; five days later, the Senate did the same. Through their representatives, the American people had officially invited Lafayette, after an absence of forty years, to return at last to his adopted home. As the debate concluded and the resolution passed, Brown was still waiting to depart for France. The delay allowed for a dispatch from Washington, carrying the congressional resolution and a new letter of invitation from Monroe, to arrive before the *Cayne* at last sailed for France in late February.

By then, Lafayette had met his political fate. At the end of the previous year, the French government had dissolved the Chamber of Deputies, necessitating elections beginning on February 26. Lafayette, standing for reelection in Meaux, faced an onslaught of government manipulation undermining his candidacy. After police apprehended the wife of François Cheavet, one of the conspirators in the dashed Carbonari plot in Saumur, a letter of introduction to Lafayette was found on her person. Upon its discovery, he was forced to testify at her trial, the timing of which—February 7—was scheduled to impact his viability in the elections. Other underhanded means, such as denying liberal voters their ballots, removing them from the rolls while adding others with government sympathies, coupled with the lingering impact of the Carbonari trials and the government's increased popularity due to its successful military intervention in Spain, stacked the deck significantly against him.

"The Elections are over . . . promises, threats, chicanes of all kinds . . . at no time had the abuse of power been brought to such a high degree," the liberal *Le Constitutionnel* lamented after the voting had concluded.[16] The results were a manufactured triumph for the Bourbons and the Ultra-royalist candidates and a calamity for their liberal opponents. In the Chamber of Deputies, forty-five liberal members were swept from office. Among the names, the delegate representing Meaux. Lafayette had received 152 votes. His opponent, François Pinteville-Cernon, received 184.

This electoral defeat, as fate would have it, was a blessing. By February, Lafayette was keeping watch for the arrival of Brown—and along with him, a better explanation of Congress's invitation. "I know only what I read in the newspapers," he admitted about the overture.[17] Apparently, the little he could discern was enough to inform a decision. In March, Ambler paid a visit to Lafayette at his rooms at 35 rue d'Anjou, where he found the American consul, Barnet. The party was eventually joined by Maximilien-Sébastien Foy, a storied veteran of the Revolution and Napoleonic wars and now an especially eloquent liberal member of the Chamber of Deputies. During the conversation, when Foy inquired if Lafayette intended to accept Congress's invitation, Lafayette offered only that "he would see about it." Later, though, after Foy departed, Lafayette was more forthright with his American friends. As Ambler recorded in his diary, "he had determined to go and only waited for the arrival of Mr. Brown our new minister to give him the time of his departure."[18] The interval was anxious. "We are every day expecting Mr. Brown. I hope he will be here before the departure of the April packet and have many public and personal motives to wish for his speedy arrival," Lafayette wrote to Monroe in March.[19]

The *Cyane* docked at Cherbourg on March 21. Brown reached Paris nine days later.[20] He had scarcely settled in the Hotel Le Prince, presented his credentials to King Louis XVIII—whose failing health constrained the frequency of his receiving the diplomatic corps—and conferred with the French minister, Chateaubriand, before a seemingly rejuvenated Lafayette appeared at his door.[21] "I had the pleasure of delivering your letters to Genl. Lafayette, whose health and spirits appear to be renovated by the marks of respect which he has received from the American people," Brown informed Monroe in his first letter from Paris.[22] There were whispers around the capital, the minister reported, that the invitation of Congress was meant as a slight to the Bourbons. These opinions, however, were in the minority, as most observers viewed the invitation to Lafayette as a sign of honor upon France. And, besides, prior to the loss of his seat in the Chamber of Deputies, the government would likely have applauded a gesture by its American counterpart that lured Lafayette, a political nuisance, away from France.

By March, an invitation was already on its way from Josiah Quincy, mayor of Boston, for Lafayette to visit the city. "I joyfully anticipate the day, not very remote, thank God, when I may revisit the glorious cradle of American, and in future, I hope, of universal liberty," Lafayette replied.[23] And yet he remained coy about committing to the trip. "General Lafayette has been with me very frequently since my arrival, but has not informed me what he intends to do in consequence of the invitation," Brown wrote Monroe. But only days after Brown had written to Monroe, Lafayette had informed Richard Peters by letter, another fellow Revolutionary veteran, politician, and jurist, of his "intended visit" to the United States. The indecision was not a matter of desire but of means. "I fear he wants money as it has been intimated to me that he wished to borrow a few thousand dollars," Brown told the president. "He has never intimated anything of that nature to me and I hope my informant may be mistaken."[24]

Of course, the informant was not wrong. In subsequent conversations, Brown discovered the state of Lafayette's finances was in such a state of disarray—his debts nearly as great as his desire to set sail—that they prohibited any possible departure. Brown vented to the president that the money necessary to send a federal ship to fetch Lafayette (though Congress had not actually appropriated any funds for the gesture) would be much better spent as financial assistance to Lafayette.[25] This was no surprise to his friends in America, some of whom were already, weeks after Congress had passed its resolution of invitation, conceiving the contours of his visit. "I shall be among those most rejoiced at seeing La Fayette again," Thomas Jefferson wrote to Monroe, "but I hope Congress is prepared to go through with their compliment worthily: that they do not mean to invite him merely to dine; that provision will be made for his expenses here, which you know he cannot afford, and that they will not send him back empty handed." Gifts of townships in newly created states would, Jefferson hoped, "restore his family to the opulence which his virtues have lost to them."[26]

For the time being, though, there was the matter of simply gathering the money that would allow Lafayette to even leave. To Brown, Lafayette now confided how desperately he wished to depart. "He is willing to raise money at any sacrifice for the purpose of embarking," Brown wrote Monroe, "and looks forward to the honor of landing on our shores as the happiest one in his life."[27] By late spring, Lafayette wrote to Monroe accepting the invitation, announcing his "determination to embark in the course of the summer."[28]

What followed, from spring to summer of 1824, was a hurried effort by Lafayette to raise enough money to realize that honor. He sold off livestock from La Grange—rams at 60 francs a head, sheep at 20—to chip away at his debts.[29] He consulted with Vincent Nolte, an Italian-born cotton merchant who had migrated to Louisiana and then to France, about other solutions: He mused about taking out a mortgage on La Grange but refused to do so, hoping to leave it for his children. Perhaps, Lafayette suggested to Nolte, the Baring family, who had extended him a lifeline in the years after his return to France after his imprisonment, would be willing to help once again. In his retelling, Nolte broached the matter with the Barings, who politely declined to become financially entangled with Lafayette once again. Upon hearing this news, Lafayette was crestfallen, sensing the long-awaited opportunity to return to America slipping away.

As late as June 11, Brown remained pessimistic about the entire enterprise. "I saw Genl Lafayette yesterday and find his heart is fixed upon a voyage to America," began the minister's regular updates to Monroe. "I greatly fear however that he will not be able so to arrange his affairs as to enjoy that gratification . . . and I apprehend he will find some difficulty in obtaining a sufficient sum to enable him to arrange his affairs for an absence so protracted from his country and property."[30] His desire to leave for America now well known in Paris, the failure to do so would be another in a string of recent embarrassments.

Nolte, in a memoir written decades later, recalled that Lafayette charmed him so, "as he did every one who knew him well," that he was unable to let the matter rest.[31] In search of a remedy, Nolte called on Brown, whom he had known in New Orleans. "Cool and serious as this gentleman was in all his dealings, yet he took hold of this affair right heartily, and with a fire that much encouraged me," Nolte recalled.[32] With little time to spare, Brown, along with the American consul Barnet, sought and obtained the philanthropy of sympathetic expatriates. Among them were Jacob Gerhard Koch, who had grown rich as an underwriter of marine insurance in the States before relocating to France, and Jean François Girod, who had immigrated to New Orleans, earned a fortune, and then retired to Europe to spend it. He extended a loan of 10,000 francs, with interest at 6 percent.[33]

As a plan to relieve Lafayette's debt materialized and the possibility of his departure for America increased, there was also the matter of his conveyance there. The offer of a public ship, extended by Congress, still stood. But Lafayette preferred a private vessel and gently communicated this desire to Monroe. Writing to tell the president that the invitation and resolutions of the government "prompt me to go over as soon as I can," he added, "I hope nobody will find it amiss or disrespectful that I am so positive in declining the honor intended to me of a national ship."[34] Despite his finances, Lafayette hoped to avoid any cost to the American government.

In meetings during the summer, both Monroe and his cabinet debated the possible consequences of sending a government ship to fetch Lafayette. The president, after learning of Lafayette's wish to sail on a private vessel, wondered if the government should still send a ship, to meet the public's wishes. But he also worried that it would be seen as an insult to the Bourbons, with Brown naturally becoming the target of retaliation. Adams perceptively thought that Lafayette was aware of the cost of sending a ship to the U.S. government and, as a result, was trying to delicately decline the offer without giving offense to its people. Of course, the symbolism and nostalgia could not be missed: As he had sailed for America for the first time on a private ship, he would return on one as well.

In 1777, Lafayette could use his fortune to purchase *La Victoire*. In 1824, no such resources were at hand. Numerous American captains, however, had offered him free passage on one of the packet ships that sailed between the port of Le Havre in northwestern France and New York. Lafayette accepted passage first on the *Bayard*, set to sail on June 1, and then the *Stephania*, which was scheduled to sail on July 1. But he was unable to settle his affairs by either date, and the captain of the former ship was unwilling to postpone its departure. Again, the trip was thrown into uncertainty. Only two suitable ships remained at Le Havre, one of which, the *Don Quixote*, Lafayette was apprehensive of taking because of the impractical implication of its name. The other vessel, named for a mythological Greek adventurer, founder of Thebes, and slayer of dragons, was more appropriate.

At the end of June, the captain of this ship, the *Cadmus*, happened to be in Paris. Francis Allyn was a Connecticut-born sailor who had served as an artillery captain during the War of 1812 and whose father, Robert Allyn, was a veteran of the Revolution. His ship, one of the Havre-Whitlock Line, was owned by New York shipping magnate William Whitlock and his family; the owner's sister had named the boat, which weighed 306 tons and could accommodate thirty passengers. It was built in 1818 and made its first passage to Europe five years later.

Allyn was in Paris to gather any mail before the *Cadmus* made its regular journey to the States; he had already purchased a ticket on the stagecoach back to Le Havre. The night before he was to leave, Allyn visited both Brown and Barnet to inquire if they had any dispatches. He also stopped by Lafayette's home on the rue d'Anjou for the same purpose, only to find the general away. When Allyn returned to his lodgings that night, a note was waiting. Lafayette had stopped by his rooms three times and requested that he come to his house the following day. The next morning after rising, Allyn abandoned his trip to Le Havre and instead went to 35 rue d'Anjou.

There Allyn found Lafayette nervous about the fate of his much-hoped-for trip. Then Allyn, with no way of earning approval from the owner of the *Cadmus*, told Lafayette that, if he wished, the ship was at his disposal. It would leave when he was ready. Overjoyed, Lafayette accepted the offer. This was a rash gesture that necessitated considerable work and risk on Allyn's part: The freight, totaling over $4,000 on board the *Cadmus*, would have to be unloaded and placed on another ship to take them to America. Now committed, the captain rushed back to Le Havre and arranged for the cargo to sail on another packet ship, the *Spartan*, an arrangement that also meant forfeiting the profit from the *Cadmus*'s scheduled trip to New York. Shouldering the loss, Allyn believed was a form of national duty. "Considering the age of General Lafayette, and that he was preparing himself for the voyage, and if he were disappointed in a passage at this time . . . and therefore, that the citizens of the United States might never have the gratification of seeing the only remaining general of the Revolution, I think I have only anticipated the wishes of our government and citizens in offering him free passage," he rationalized.[35]

Allyn, aware that the *Cadmus* would now play a central part in an important national event, carrying an honored guest, beautified the boat with a fresh coat of lacquer and stocked it with French wines, poultry, cattle, and sheep, all at his own expense. Before the *Cadmus* departed Le Havre on July 10, 1824, he boasted that the ship had "never looked half as well as she now does, thoroughly painted, varnished."[36]

Two young Americans from Boston, Joshua Henshaw Hayward, a doctor, and Jonathan Mason Jr., a portrait painter, tiring of their European travels, had obtained passage on the *Cadmus* before Allyn offered it to Lafayette. They would make the voyage, but the captain decided to take on no additional travelers other than Lafayette and his retinue.[37] Despite receiving over a hundred letters with requests to accompany him, Lafayette would travel only with his son Georges, who had not seen American soil since his abrupt departure from Mount Vernon in 1797, and his valet, Bastien. In the spring, Lafayette met Friedrich List, a liberal economist, professor, and politician who had fled Württemberg in order to avoid a prison sentence for his activism. Reasoning that in America he could begin a new life, Lafayette asked List to join him on the journey and received a tentative yes from the German.

Apart from the nostalgic value of the voyage, Lafayette's desire to see old friends once more, and his wish to view with his own eyes the growth of a nation he had helped create, there was the matter of European politics. At the ebb of revolutionary movements across the continent, Lafayette's voyage to America provided a useful means of reviving moribund liberal spirits in France.

Lafayette and Jean-Pierre Pagès, a writer for the liberal *Constitutionnel*, envisioned his visit to America as a means to promote republican ideals back home and demonstrate to European governments and people the progress created through representative government. This plan necessitated a correspondent to document Lafayette's travels for eventual publication, as well as a personal secretary to help him with letters and speeches. For this assignment, Lafayette hired a twenty-eight-year-old former French officer named Auguste Levasseur. Born in Thionville in the northeastern department of Moselle and educated at Versailles, he had entered the French army at a young age and was a member of the Twenty-Ninth Regiment of the French army—the same unit that had been implicated in the Belfort conspiracy in 1820, which ended his military career.[38]

Hiring Levasseur as a personal secretary and propagandist—as his letters and journals would prove—was a brilliant decision; the young Frenchman was a keen observer and eloquent author, whose political sensibilities naturally aligned with Lafayette's own, though Levasseur had the advantage of never before having visited America, and what awaited him across the Atlantic was entirely new.

Another obstacle appeared in the form of George W. Erving. The former American minister to Spain was at the time in Paris and doing all in his power to prevent Lafayette from embarking on his trip. An excitable gossip, Erving wrote to Monroe in the spring, reasoning with the president that if Lafayette were to leave his home and family in search of the compliments and celebrations waiting for him in the States, it would be construed in Europe as staggering vanity, and that the cost of this exercise would fall upon the American government and people.[39]

Though he prefaced his worries with the perfunctory admiration of Lafayette, Erving was not entirely acting out of public spiritedness. A doctrinaire Republican, angered by the party's amalgamation of Federalism, he chafed at the president's "revolutionary reminiscences" and believed Monroe had "unwittingly done as much as it was possible for him to do to demoralize the republican party, & hence the confusion which we are now in about the election."[40]

A supporter of William H. Crawford, Erving was convinced that the invitation to Lafayette was another blunder, that the old hero's return to America in the middle of a presidential contest would likely give one of the rival candidates an advantage. "I sincerely hope on his own account that he may not go, for I esteem him myself in a considerable degree & again I fear that electioneering use is to be made of him," Erving told Crawford. This would manifest, he predicted, in "Jackson's handing once to him Washington's sword, or spy glass," reinforcing his connection to the first president and the Revolution.[41]

As Lafayette's plans were formed, Erving attempted to enlist Brown to delay his departure from France. When this failed, he secured a meeting with Lafayette himself. Lafayette had already made clear his plan to visit Boston first after landing, "this falling as directly as possible into the focus of the Adams interests!"[42] Erving complained. To the arguments, that he would quickly be made a prop of rival candidates, Lafayette was not insensitive; nor would he let it alter his plans. "He said that having received this invitation from a whole people through the organ of their government, besides special invitation from leading men he could not defer his departure," Erving reported to Crawford.[43]

Lafayette reminded Erving at this point that he was a friend of two of the candidates; he had known Crawford during his own ministry in Paris and Adams during his in St. Petersburg. Though he had never met Jackson, he held him in high regard as well. Lafayette gently countered Erving's dire predictions that "those who meant to turn his popularity to account would not hesitate at the means of doing so" and further inflame partisan passions. He thought his return to America could have the opposite effect. Indeed, Lafayette made a pledge to Erving: "That he would keep himself neutral & do every thing possible to conciliate the parties & assuage their asperity, by showing to them the necessity of union."[44]

The conversation concluded with Erving unconvinced. "He goes I am sure in the very best dispositions to do good, & to abstain from doing injury to any one," he wrote to Crawford, "to be the man of the publick in general, & to hold himself aloof from partialities;—yet considering the temper of his mind, & in my estimate of his judgment, I cannot see that good can be done."[45]

Then there was the vexing matter of another would-be companion. In the winter of 1823, Fanny Wright was absent from the Lafayette home, a sign of emerging tensions between the author and the actual children of her "father."

By the time she returned to France in the spring, Lafayette was arranging his return to America. Wright believed that she would accompany him. But when she was once again at La Grange, his family's attitudes toward her and her sister Camilla had visibly turned. The Wrights were at first apparently unaware. Their friend in the family, Madame Charles de Lasteyrie, sister-in-law of Virgine, in a letter to Fanny, quoted her own husband's shock at their terrible treatment: "I assure you that when I was in the house, my remark was to my husband, 'if I experienced anywhere, even for one hour what I saw them endure for one week, I would have left the house in an instant.'"[46] Then came a letter from Julia Garnett warning Wright that rumors were circulating that her relationship with Lafayette was more than filial. Stung by the gossip, she returned to England, only to hear the same innuendos in her social circles. She had left without informing Lafayette of her plans or sending him word of her whereabouts. Already dealing with an ailing sister-in-law, he was thrown into anxiety; he sent her letters pleading for updates on her whereabouts or plans.

When Wright again heard from Madame de Lasteyrie, it was with information that after reading her letter, Lafayette had been thrown into a two-day long fit, "which after depriving him for sometime of sense, was followed by vomiting to an alarming degree of violence."[47] In late May, she boarded a train from London, rushed to Dover, and from there returned to France, where she was greeted by a wan Lafayette in Paris.

Now the acrimony between Wright and his family came to a head. She traveled to La Grange to meet with them to press for her participation in his intended trip to America and establish the purity of their relationship. To do this, she presented the family with two options: Lafayette could take her for his wife or adopt her as her daughter. Madame Charles quickly poured water on the second scheme. "Having heard my proposal," Wright wrote to Camilla, "her countenance saddened. 'Alas! You know not France or you know not yet that family.'"[48] Pages, Fanny's only other ally in the Lafayette orbit, dismissed the rumors of romance as fantastical.

The journalist also assured Wright that legal adoption was not unheard of in France; it would have to be and certainly would never be approved of by Lafayette's children, however. A marriage, too, was an impossibility. Lafayette explained to Wright that he had made a promise to Adrienne on her deathbed to never wed again. Wright later wrote that the vow only pertained to one woman, his mistress,

Diane-Adélaïde de Damas d'Antigny, comtesse de Simiane, and if not for the undue attention it would bring upon his family, he would have considered marrying her.

As the object of so much desire—a return to America—was in view, Lafayette was now in a tormented state. "His countenance and complexion still retain the evidence of the force of his late seizures," Wright wrote, "and in all our conversation I have constantly to watch the effect of every word, to soothe the mind and conscience, for he is ever reproaching himself either for what has been done or what not done, so that I must always represent as lighter than the reality the difficulties that surround us."[49]

Wright's estimation of her own importance in his life grated on his friends and family; she in turn resented their interventions. "Mischief-makers and busy-bodies work of whom I knew little or nothing. Meddling politicians jealous of my supposed influence, who had asserted to the son that nothing was done or said without my approbation and that his father was held in leading strings! Silly and ill-natured women, who supposed intentions of another nature, and the Lord knows what. All this is operating upon little minds and petty jealousies," she fulminated.[50]

Strung through Wright's correspondence from this period is not only a striking hostility toward Lafayette's children but an oversized sense of importance in his heart that, in her mind, far outweighed their own. She was his only conversation partner, the only remedy for his weakened state, which, she wrote, "only appears evidence to me, that a separation, however much delicacy and generosity would urge his consent to it, would shorten his existence."[51] Wright was even harboring improbable hopes that he would possibly chose to remain and live out the remainder of his life in America with her at his side.

At an impasse, in early June, Wright was at Le Havre, visiting with the Garnett family, while he and his children held a conference at La Grange. There, they at last reached a compromise. She was brought back to La Grange and told by the family of a "warmly expressed desire that we should be with our father in America." There was a condition: "Our friends and counselors in Paris also urge our making the voyage to

America," she wrote Camilla, "but to humor the folly of those who are supposed to misinterpret things, suggest that we make it separately."[52] Was, she wondered to her sister, traveling apart not a tacit admission of the impropriety of their relationship? The idea, she believed, could not have originated from Lafayette but was rather a means of placating his children. "I must observe that the proposal made by my father does not originate with him and that I doubt secretly whether he concurs with it."[53]

"As regards me, I care not to imagine what their feelings may be, but none good, doubtless. They desire sincerely our going to America, but perhaps have real or pretend scruples as to our accompanying him," she wrote to Camilla.[54] The sincerity of any words of conciliation from his family she doubted greatly; they remained a thorn in her side that she hoped to pluck once across the Atlantic. "So far as I can yet judge of the feelings of that ill-fated family," she told her sister, "I see no hope that it can ever cease to be an obstacle and annoyance, except in the one unforeseen, or at least doubtful alternative of his remaining in America."[55]

The arrangement was agreed upon—Lafayette at this point had planned on a July 1 departure; the sisters would follow him a month later. But it was still a defeat for Wright: "There was but to choose between me and his family. The courage for this was wanting."[56]

This family agony settled, his debts sufficiently met to leave France, and a fine boat at his disposal, the hour for farewells approached. Allyn had hoped to depart by July 10 from Le Havre, where Allyn and his two passengers, Hayward and Mason, waited. On the 4th, in a symbolic farewell, Lafayette, joined by Brown and other Americans in Paris, attended an Independence Day celebration, an event electrified by the pending voyage. When Lafayette rose, he spoke happily of "the prospect I have of finding myself in a few days on my way to America under the old flag of our Revolution and independence."[57]

Even with all the hurdles cleared, with *the Cadmus* waiting, Lafayette was once again struck with sickness in Paris and tormented by ailing family members: not only his sister-in-law Madame de Montague but two nieces, a grand-nephew, and one of his granddaughters as well.

When, finally, his carriage departed from Paris on the 11th and made its way to sea, he was in an enfeebled state.[58]

On July 12, as Lafayette arrived in the town of Bolbec, he was greeted by a large crowd: The Merchants of Le Havre rode out on horseback and in carriages to meet and escort him to the city's gates. From there they rode together to Harfleur, six miles from Le Havre, where the entourage multiplied in size and congested the road but slowed in pace as afternoon passed to night. Reaching Le Havre, Lafayette was met by a quiet crowd of thousands. "A religious silence reigned over these brave citizens!"[59] *Le Constitutionnel* reported. The solemnity was interrupted by Swiss mercenaries, their bayonets drawn, aided by gendarmes, who pushed the crowd back, as the carriage rode alone into Le Havre where it was greeted by repeated shouts of "Longue vie Lafayette!" and guided by the glow of lamps placed at intersections, to the home of a local businessman named Philippon where the men dined and rested for the night.

The next morning, crowds reassembled only to be again discouraged by irritated local authorities. Georges and Levasseur rose early to have their passports stamped but discovered the office was not yet open. A police commissary, who had no idea whom he was speaking with, assured them there was no need to rush or worry: If they were leaving on the *Cadmus*, the boat was delayed a day. Both men had just talked with Allyn, who was planning to depart in two hours, and knew this was a lie calibrated to discourage crowds from forming to wish Lafayette bon voyage.

"You are mistaken," Georges challenged the commissary.

"Sir, I can assure you that the *Cadmus* will not depart today," he shot back, smugly.

"But—" the younger Lafayette began but was quickly cut off.

"There are no *buts* about it, besides your own; I tell you the *Cadmus* will not leave today, and I should know something about it." Lafayette, the officer explained, was attending a dinner that evening in Le Havre.

With voices now raised, Georges told the officer that Lafayette had no such plans.

"I am telling you that Mr. de Lafayette is having dinner here," the officer shouted back. "I am sure of it. I, of all people, ought to know something about it."

This was enough. "And I as well, I, who am his son," Georges said, ending the ruse.

"Ah! That's different . . ." the embarrassed officer replied.[60] The attempt to create a rumor that Lafayette's departure was delayed failed, clearly: The immense crowds congesting the roads of Le Havre were proof and a great irritation to the local authorities.

Hours later, Lafayette stood on the crowded wharf, with his son, secretary, and valet. They were joined by Haywood, Mason, and two additional passengers the general had permitted to join: John Pendleton King of Georgia and John Milhan, from Baltimore. Friedrich List, whom Lafayette had hoped would also be on board, had decided to return to Württemberg rather than flee to America.[61] The entourage assembled and boarded a steamboat, and were carried out to the *Cadmus* under a clear sky; as they left, the gendarmerie shut the gates to the pier to discourage spectators.

When the steamboat pulled alongside and Lafayette stepped aboard the *Cadmus* and under the American flag, the boat's crew erupted in cheers; the same sound came from the ships floating nearby and a small crowd watching a few miles from the pier. Shortly, a gust carried the *Cadmus* to sea. From on board, as the French coast grew smaller and smaller and then disappeared, feelings of uncertainty developed. "One loves to recall the last sounds of the shore of one's country," Lafayette sighed in the middle of sea, between worlds once again.[62]

———≈———

The Nation's Guest

"MORE SHIP NEWS," announced the *Painesville Telegraph* in July 1824.

"The good ship *Adams* is still under way," the Ohio paper reported, "Her ship's crew are chiefly of experienced Aristocrats of the old times."

Then there was the "ship *Crawford*," which had sprung a leak.

"The *Jackson*," meanwhile, had met with "a very serious disaster sailing around Tariff Island." This was, after all, originally a "War ship, and not calculated to carry merchandize of any description."

And then there was the ship *Clay*: "Her rigging is entirely of American manufacture—her load consisted entirely of instruments for constructing roads and canals."[1]

In the summer of 1824, Americans were preoccupied with the presidential question: A dispute had erupted between Adams and Washington's oldest paper, the *Daily National Intelligencer*, when the publication, whose editors supported Crawford, printed documents unfavorable to the secretary of state. Adams canceled the State Department's advertisements in the paper—government agencies paid for notices in publications—and instead gave them to a newly founded but sympathetic paper, the *National Journal*. The behavior, another capital paper, the *Washington Gazette*, commented, was worthy of the "Holy Alliance of the Sovereigns of Europe."[2]

Another controversy surrounded a series of letters written anonymously by "A.B." alleging Crawford had mismanaged public funds. The matter came to a head when Illinois senator, newly appointed minister to Mexico, and Adams supporter Ninian Edwards was revealed as the author and forced to resign his diplomatic post.

"It is the opinion of many, and certainly mine, that there is a greater amount of political intrigue now existing in the United States than there ever was before," Hezekiah Niles wrote earlier, while surveying the "ship race."[3]

But increasingly, Americans were on watch for a ship of another sort. "The shores of our country, from Louisiana to Maine, are about to ring with shouts at the arrival of La Fayette," wrote a correspondent for the *New-York Statesman*.[4]

A returned captain started a rumor that Lafayette had booked passage across the Atlantic on the *Bayard*, set to sail June 1. Accordingly, by July, his arrival was likely imminent. These hopes were dashed when the *Bayard* arrived without Lafayette on board. Its captain, Henry Robinson, speculated that Lafayette might leave from Le Havre on another boat. By this time, the English papers were already reporting he was at sea on board the *Cadmus*.

News, whatever its reliability, that Lafayette was on his way spurred a flurry of activity. Boston was a trendsetter, sending its invitation in the spring. Now, New York and Baltimore's governments considered how best to welcome him, prepared to draw from their treasuries whatever was necessary. If a long-absent family member was en route for a reunion, Americans would not be accused of being ungracious hosts.

A sense of competition immediately emerged. Looking on from the South, citizens of Richmond, Virginia, were anxious, lest they be outdone by their Northern countrymen. After all, the climactic scene of Lafayette's service to America transpired in their state. "And shall Richmond suffer Boston, New York, Philadelphia, and Washington, to outstrip her in her expression of gratitude?" a Richmond paper asked.[5] Soon enough, in July, the city's planning was underway. In Yorktown, volunteers met to begin organizing a giant celebration on the anniversary of the American victory; locals offered up housing for Lafayette at no cost; Secretary of War John C. Calhoun pledged enough tents to be brought from Washington to temporarily house more than two thousand people; one hundred muttons were promised by the community of Gloucester.[6]

Civic associations sprang into action. The Societies of the Cincinnati, their memberships declining since the turn of the century, were especially energized by the return of their fellow member. State societies in New York—led by Lafayette's old friend Marinus Willett—and Maryland gathered to map out in what manner they would honor their brother soldier. New Jersey's Society of the Cincinnati, whose ranks had dwindled from over one hundred members to barely twenty, resolved to "bid him hail and welcome."[7] South Carolina's chapter had a special interest in seeing him once again in their state, where he had first set foot on American soil. "We shall kindle again the brightest flame which ever warmed our citizens. We shall revive, as it were, the spark of '76, and the patriotism which it kindled," promised one Virginia editor.[8]

Volunteer military companies were formed. The Lafayette Guards in New York drilled and practiced during Fourth of July parades in New York. The La Fayette Legion in Washington designed their uniforms: long blue coats, red cuffs and collars, thirteen buttons emblazoned with a likeness of Lafayette. West Point's cadets were placed on standby and readied to leave for New York upon Lafayette's arrival, while the academy's band rehearsed Handel's "See, the Conqu'ring Hero Comes!"

Poets flattered him. One published composition compared him favorably to the ancients:

> *Let Greece tell her story of patriots bright*
> *Like stars in the firmament set*
> *Yet they fade in the beams of purer light*
> *When placed by the side of Fayette*[9]

Newspapers printed columns recounting his past deeds; Americans were full of curiosity: How old was he—sixty-six, sixty-seven, or sixty-eight? When did he first arrive in their nation—was it 1776 or 1777? "No wonder, then, that our countrymen are so anxious to pour out their feelings before him—*no wonder then that Lafayette guards are voluntarily springing up*," one editor wrote after reviewing his past heroism on behalf of the American people.[10]

Hezekiah Niles helpfully replaced *Marquis* with *General* before his name, "seeing that he himself has disavowed the title, it is to be hoped that the republicans of the United States will not offend him by heaping the senseless things upon him."[11] There was some mystery regarding his status as America's last living revolutionary general. When the Continental Army's engineer Rufus Putnam died in May, papers reported that Lafayette was indeed the last general. This, as it turned out, was not true: Thomas Sumter still lived. Lafayette was, however, the last remaining major general.

There was even a plea: While turning over revolutionary history, editors discovered the fate of another old soldier. William Barton, a lieutenant colonel in a Rhode Island regiment, had led the capture of British Major General Richard Prescott in 1777, earning a congressional commendation and the gift of a sword, one only of fifteen awarded during the war, made in France, notable for its silver hilt and enameled in golden laurel. After Barton took a bullet to his thigh battling a British raid in Rhode Island, Lafayette visited him during his convalescence. Later major-general of Rhode Island's state militia, Barton was embroiled in a legal dispute in Vermont where he had sold the same land to two different parties and was eventually sentenced to fourteen years in debtors' prison, where he now languished. "Forbid it our country!" "Forbid it La Fayette!" editorials entreated. "Is there no redeeming spirit to intercede? Lafayette, listen to my humble voice, and to the invaluable services which you heretofore rendered to our country, add this one more of restoring one of your brother officers of '77 to liberty, and to his family."[12]

On Independence Day, Americans, no matter the region, raised a glass in his honor, in anticipation of his return. "His name almost everywhere remembered on the 5th," wrote the *Washington Gazette*, "he was hailed as the friend of liberty, the benefactor of America, 'the nation's guest.'"[13]

While Americans anticipated the arrival of a conquering hero, the reality on board the *Cadmus* was far less glorious. "I don't know if I should blame the shriveling up of old age or the bad preparations of sorrows that preceded our departure," he wrote to his daughters while on board, "but in having everything one could possibly desire to avoid maritime disagreements, I've suffered more and more constantly than at any other time."[14]

Lafayette had been stricken by seasickness during his first expedition to America in 1777 on board the *Victoire*; he was once again on his final journey there. The trials and anxieties leading up to his departure had likely left him in a weakened state. The health of his granddaughter Mathilde was a source of continuing distress. "I think these worries have left me less able to contend against the physical ills of seasickness," he wrote to Lady Morgan. Georges fared even worse. So sick was he that his ailing father pitied him. Every passenger was ill other than Jonathan Mason Jr.

The voyage began portentously: Two days after leaving Le Havre, a violent squall tore off two of the boat's topmasts. Then the sickness. Then the boredom. Passengers fought the ennui by reading (Lafayette brought the Carlo Botta book on the American Revolution that so captivated Fanny Wright), playing chess, or listening to Lafayette's stories of George Washington, the capture of Major André, and his own exploits during the American Revolution. Or the passengers on the *Cadmus* contemplated the vastness of the sea or the majesty of the boat itself. The roped, suspended wooden pegs, the intricacies of its navigation, Lafayette observed, resembled the operation of a large harpsichord, "except for the sounds of its maneuvers which aren't exactly as similarly pleasing."[15]

He occupied himself with letters to his children and friends; the secretary Levasseur began a chain of wonderfully descriptive letters, which once they reached land were full of keen and candid observations of America and its people. "We applaud ourselves all the more for our association with Levasseur, who is really excellent and full of merits, and who has a very joyful disposition," Lafayette reported.[16] Meals with Captain Allyn and First Mate Daniel Chadwick were some consolation. Near Grand Banks, Lafayette declared to his companions a desire for a chowder. Seated under an awning on deck, he watched as the *Cadmus* crew cast unsuccessfully into the ocean. Disappointed, he asked Allyn if there was a "Cape Cod man" onboard. Indeed there was, the captain answered before summoning a man from below deck who then promptly reeled in a giant haddock.[17]

The greatest excitement of the voyage came on August 1. At the close of a particularly brilliant day, a cloudless sky above, a still sea, the *Cadmus* rested on the Grand Banks, off the Newfoundland coast, sails gently flapping against its masts, the calm providing a reprieve from seasickness. Near dusk, the peaceful scene was interrupted by the boat's crew shouting from the main-top that another vessel was in the distance and approaching.

The passengers gathered on deck and fixed their weary eyes on a minute black dot in the far distance that moved in the *Cadmus*'s direction. This mysterious object on the horizon was a reprieve from the inexorable boredom. Several passengers conjectured it was a whale, but as it grew nearer, this was disproven: The mysterious object, identifiable by its movement, was a boat. Anticipation spread across the deck. Was it, perhaps, a longboat dispatched from a larger ship visible far off on the horizon, sent to retrieve potable water from the *Cadmus*? Then, a happier possibility: It was sent from another American packet ship, the *Don Quixote* perhaps. And, as it came closer, the white clothing of the passengers could be seen. Maybe there were women aboard. "They are coming to visit us, they are coming to dance with us. . . . Dancing with ladies in the middle of the ocean!" Levasseur hoped.[18]

Then the cruel truth: The white was the sleeves of a British soldier's uniform. "But, oh lord! What disappointment!" Levasseur recalled.[19] The skiff skimmed across the water and pulled up parallel to the *Cadmus*. Looking up at the boat were seven English officers, hostile expressions on their faces, and in the hands of one, a rifle. They were detached from a transport on its way to the garrison at Halifax. The visit to the *Cadmus* was their own attempt to escape boredom. Its captain demanded, in a supercilious tone with a British accent, that the steps be dropped in order that he and members of his regiment may board. A rope ladder was thrown down, and the soldiers cavalierly climbed on board the larger boat.

Allyn welcomed them, and the American crew paid them no notice; judging from the anger in their eyes, Levasseur claimed, the American passengers' thoughts dwelled on the burning of their Capitol a decade prior. While the soldiers pestered Allyn with questions about the nature of his voyage, he coolly informed them that the older man among the party was General Lafayette. Stunned, they doffed their hats and took him by the hand—the hand, Levasseur wrote, "that he offers them with the goodness that a generous man always loves to display with old enemies over whom he has triumphed."[20] The group was invited below deck for food and drink, though they were unable to concentrate on either, distracted by the presence of Lafayette.

With night approaching, the guests, carrying with them bottles of Bordeaux and Madeira, gifts from Allyn, reboarded their skiff and rowed away. The boat was still in sight when Lafayette, betraying his usual ebullience, revealed old animosities, personal and national, sneering at the departed officers. During conversation, the soldiers had bragged of the luxury of their transport to the Americans. But Lafayette's valet, Bastien, had gone on board the skiff and been told by the sailor who remained on board that they were, in fact terribly short on supplies. "What a set of liars these English are," he told Mason, as they walked on the *Cadmus*'s deck.[21] Later, one of the Americans on board explained that Frenchmen would have been a far warmer reception. "I admit that I was quite sensitive to this expression of esteem, from a free man, for my compatriots," Levasseur wrote to Émilie.[22]

On August 11, after twenty days at sea, Lafayette shared an itinerary with his daughters. After landing, "our plan will probably be to go, not by water—we've had enough of that—but by land to Boston as quickly as we can leave New York." The path there would be through Connecticut, along Long Island Sound, and take them through

Providence. "All of this country is charming," he shared, relying on decades-old memories.[23] From Boston to Hartford and Albany, and then back to New York by steamboat, stopping along the way at West Point. Then, on to Washington, Philadelphia, and Baltimore. The invitation from Boston conveniently delayed Lafayette's arrival in the capital. He would purposely not rush to Washington, suggesting to the French government that the tour was taken by a private citizen wishing to revisit the country of his youth, independent of the American government. Though, as he wrote General Pepe, he planned to be there when Congress came into session in December and travel to Virginia as well. His hope, he told the Italian, was to return to France by the beginning of May. "I am already experiencing a great desire to breathe in the air at the Grange, and I can see that the calculated time of our American visit will be more than sufficient," Lafayette wrote to his daughters.[24]

Other children also ran through his mind at sea. "There is another boat in which I am more interested," Lafayette wrote to their mutual friend Julie Garnett as the voyage neared its end. He hoped Fanny and Camilla Wright, who were to sail for New York on August 11, would be waiting there once he returned from Boston. "What happiness to receive these two dear friends," he exclaimed. Once reunited, he planned to show them New England, and then together in the spring they would all return to La Grange together.[25]

By the second week of August, the *Cadmus* had made its way south from Newfoundland toward New York. On August 12, with a lull in the wind, the ship was eighty leagues away. Two days later, they had reached port. Lafayette sat anxiously on board the *Cadmus*. After forty years, he had returned to America. The interval—the glory turned wreckage of another revolution, the five long years in miserable confinement, and the wilderness that followed—had been transformative. The loss of Adrienne, the infirmities of age, and the "disappointments and disgusts" of his return to public life may well have been forty lifetimes. He returned to a nation equally changed, where many of his

dearest friends were long in the grave. Who and what would be waiting once he stepped off the *Cadmus* and once again onto American
soil?

"We see Long Island, my dear friends," he wrote to his family at
La Grange. "It is not without emotion that I have dreamed of this
shoreline."[26]

PART TWO

See,
the Conqu'ring
Hero Comes!

5

Happy Omens

After thirty-three days at sea, on the morning of Sunday, August 15, 1824, the *Cadmus* glided into New York Harbor and past the green hills of Staten Island, dotted with white cottages. The families inside, spotting the white flag of France on its fore, the Stars and Stripes flying from its main-top, emerged and hurried to the shore. Longboats bobbed, waiting expectantly on the water.

"Great perpetrations are making in New-York to receive this distinguished hero and national guest, who is now hourly expected," one of the state's journals reported, scarcely a week prior.[1] During the summer, American newspapers carried word from France of Lafayette's travel plans, reprinting his letters, hoping to discern the date of his arrival. Hopes rose and then were disappointed. By the end of July, reports from France confirmed that Lafayette had set sail for America, with an initial destination of New York. But the precise date of his arrival was unknown, dependent on the wind and sea. The city sat on edge.

One of the boats floating off Staten Island approached, slowed, and then pulled alongside the *Cadmus*. "Is Lafayette onboard?" its sailors called out apprehensively. When *the Cadmus*'s crew answered affirmatively, cheers rang out and embraces were exchanged on board the smaller ship. Concerned questions about Lafayette's journey and his health followed the merriment.

Weeks prior, President James Monroe had ordered all military posts that might lie in Lafayette's route to afford him honors fitting his "highest military rank." Accordingly, across the Narrows, the strait separating Staten Island from Brooklyn, thirteen cannons boomed from a diamond-shaped fort two hundred feet from the shore. The cannon fire from Fort Lafayette was as much a salute to its namesake as an announcement that he had arrived—the wait had ended.

A signal was given from nearby Fort Tompkins. Shortly, a ferry named the *Nautilus* approached the *Cadmus*. On board were the sons of the boat's owner, Griffin and Minthorne Tompkins. Their father, the vice president of the United States, Daniel D. Tompkins, had dispatched them to receive Lafayette and his party and invite them to spend the day at his home on Staten Island.

It was the Sabbath, and though New York City officials had made elaborate plans to welcome the nation's guest, given his unannounced arrival, time was required to set them into action. Lafayette agreed to remain at Tompkins's house and travel into the city the following morning. The vice president's invitation accepted, Lafayette, along with his party—Georges, Levasseur, Bastien, and Francis Allyn—boarded the *Nautilus* as it towed the *Cadmus* to anchorage at the Quarantine Grounds.

Sitting on thirty acres on the southeast side of Staten Island, the Quarantine Grounds was a collection of medical buildings, offices, and dormitories, surrounded by a brick wall and reached by a long wooden pier. The federal government had claimed the land in 1799 and designated it as a way station for sick passengers aboard arriving ships. Periodic outbreaks of yellow fever terrified the residents of Staten Island, who grew to loath the Quarantine's presence; decades later, they burned it to the ground. It was here, a perhaps inauspicious spot, that Lafayette once again touched his "beloved land," with dramatic accompaniment by the sound of further cannon salutes, this time from the *Importer*, a ship owned by Thomas H. Smith, a wealthy tea merchant. Even after his long journey, Lafayette was described as in "excellent health, full of conversation and rejoiced beyond measure, in having his foot upon American ground."[2]

It was a short distance from the Quarantine Grounds to the vice president's estate. When Lafayette and his companions arrived at Tompkins's home, they were greeted by a prematurely aged man dressed plainly in a peaked cap and casual jacket. Levasseur, accustomed to the formality of European monarchs and statesmen, was surprised by the casual appearance of America's second-highest-ranking public official. Apart from the nature of his attire, Tompkins cut a sad figure.

Scarsdale-born and Columbia-educated, Tompkins had progressed from New York's state legislature to Congress and from there to a decade as the state's governor before his election to the vice presidency in 1816. Tompkins was a congenial politician and a capable administrator who had fortified, often at his own expense, New York City against British attack during the War of 1812.

During his surveys of the defenses around the harbor, Tompkins devised a plan to purchase and develop the land near the Staten Island shore. He acquired seven hundred acres, laid out the town of Tompkinsville, named the streets for his children, built a road across the island, and developed a series of stages that for years was the primary route between New York and Philadelphia.

These exertions drained his finances. By the time of Lafayette's arrival, Tompkins was deep in debt; he turned to alcohol for relief and was often inebriated when he presided over the Senate—a rare occasion, as he spent most of his time as vice president in New York attempting to right his finances. In an era where the vice president was little seen or heard, Tompkins was a ghost. His physical and financial state precluded any serious consideration as a candidate in the presidential contest currently underway.

"Our friend on Staten Island is unfortunately sick in body and mind," Tompkins's ally-turned-rival DeWitt Clinton acknowledged.[3] The vice president was an ailing man with less than a year to live; welcoming Lafayette to America was the final act in a distinguished public life coming to an inglorious end. He had confided to John

Quincy Adams that he "wished for nothing hereafter but quiet and retirement."[4]

At the vice president's home, Tompkins's two daughters, holding each other by the arm, graciously welcomed Lafayette. Watching the charming little spectacle, Levasseur noticed Georges overcome with emotion. By the time Lafayette had stepped into Tompkins's house, word of his arrival was spreading across New York. American flags were raised across the city and citizens, unable to wait a moment longer, made their way to Staten Island, filling the harbor with boats. Members of the city's Common Council, which had organized the imminent celebrations, boarded a steamship, the *Bellona*, and traveled to Tompkins's house to formally welcome Lafayette and brief him on their plans. A crowd spread around the house, voices raised from within for Lafayette to appear. Answering the calls, he stepped out on the balcony that wrapped around the vice president's estate. New York could be seen on the horizon, masts rising from its port; in the distance was Fort Lafayette, and beyond that the ocean. Lafayette was soon surrounded, "women, old men, children, squeeze his hands with transportations of joy and give him the most tender names—imagine this, and you will have barely an idea of this enchanting picture," Levasseur observed in a letter to Georges's wife, Émilie.[5]

That morning, a tremendous thunderstorm had moved over Staten Island, but then with the *Cadmus*'s arrival, it had wondrously disappeared, the black clouds leaving behind what Jonathan Mason Jr., the young American who had sailed from Le Havre with Lafayette, described as the most "magnificent rainbow" he had ever seen.[6] Its ends spanned from the Narrows to Fort Lafayette. "This appearance was not lost on the multitudes, who immediately exclaimed that heaven agreed with the Americans in celebration of the arrival of their friend," Levasseur wrote.[7] Standing in the newly emerged sun on the piazza of Tompkins's home, Lafayette took note of the meteorological coincidence. "This day has been full of happy omens to me," he remarked, "arriving among those who have treated me with such unmerited kindness."[8]

The following morning was unseasonably cool and mild for late summer. Across New York, stores and businesses were closed. Citizens rose early, put on their finest clothes, and lined the sidewalks. Carriages were forbidden south of Chambers Street in Broadway, Marketfield Street, or Whitehall Street. Bells across the city were to be rung between noon and two. It was as if the Fourth of July had appeared for an encore in August, though with perhaps even greater reverence.

"We have avoided all unmeaning pomp or parade. Vain and ostentatious ceremonies would be equally unacceptable to our illustrious guest, as opposed to our republican habits," a resolution from the Common Council explained prior to Lafayette's arrival. "There are occasions, however," its members continued, "where the American people choose to pour forth their feelings in acts of unrestrained hospitality, munificence, and profusion. Such will be the case when the Marquis arrives in our City."[9] The stage was set.

Around 10:00 a.m., a procession formed on the North River and departed for Staten Island. At its head was the *Robert Fulton*, appropriately named in honor of the late inventor of the commercial steamboat. Several other boats took up the rear, but neither these nor the *Fulton* were to carry Lafayette to New York: That mission was reserved for the *Chancellor Livingston*.

The vessel, regarded as the finest riverboat in America, was completed in 1816 at a reputed cost of $110,000. Named for Fulton's patron and partner, Robert Livingston, a patriot politician and diplomat, the boat was Fulton's last and finest work, though he died the year before its completion. It weighed five hundred tons, with three towering smokestacks at its bow, three masts, and a 150-foot keel. Novelties included boxed paddle wheels to avoid splashing and an engine that burned coal rather than wood. Space for passengers was commodious: a dining saloon to the aft, surrounded by two tiers of curtained sleeping berths below a cabin designated for ladies.

On Staten Island, a smaller procession of just two carriages formed and departed the vice president's home. In one sat Lafayette, his son, and Tompkins, joined by Aaron Ogden, who had led a company of light infantry under Lafayette. A former governor of New Jersey, Ogden, at the order of Washington and under the supervision of Lafayette, had ridden to British lines in September 1780 and extended an offer to

General Henry Clinton: a trade, the traitor Benedict Arnold for Major John André, the spy who had facilitated his defection. The offer was rebuffed; Ogden was told by the British his horse would be waiting for him the following evening. André was hanged a month later.

In the other carriage were Levasseur, the vice president's sons, and Allyn. As they passed through Tompkins's front gate, it was under a blazing transparency—the painting of an eagle on paper, illuminated from behind by candles. Over its head was an arch carrying the words *Welcome Fayette*, with the Stars and Stripes and French tricolor crossed. Beneath its talons, *American Independence 1776*.

The carriages made the short trip to Nautilus Hall, a resort that often hosted political confabs, with its tree-shaded yard that stretched out to the water. There they rendezvoused with the procession of boats arriving from Manhattan, amid loud huzzas along the path. After a reception, Lafayette, with Tompkins to his right and Ogden to his left, made his way toward the *Chancellor Livingston*. Two rows of spectators lined his path.

They saw a man, aged sixty-six, standing nearly six feet tall, dressed plainly in a dark coat. He carried his hat in his right hand and leaned on a cane with his left. The brown wig sat low on his forehead, covering his wrinkles and slightly obscuring his advancing age, as did his evident energy after a long voyage from France. As he stepped under another arch of American and French flags and aboard, the West Point Military Band waiting on the *Chancellor* struck up "See, the Conqu'ring Hero Comes!" then "Marseilles Hymn" and then "Hail Columbia." A twenty-four-gun salute boomed overhead, and the boat departed. Behind it, the steamboats *Connecticut* and *Nautilus*, and to their rear the *Bellona* and *Olive Branch*, together towing the *Cadmus*, only a day after its journey ended, seemingly a revered relic of history.

As they sailed toward Manhattan, the collection of ships formed a ribbon of colors upon the water, each adorned with flags, flowers, and banners, crowded with passengers and musicians. The *New York Evening Post* described it as "a spectacle of beauty which can scarcely be surpassed in imagination; and which in former times might have been portrayed in a work of fancy."[10]

On the shores, in the perches of forts and in front of homes, citizens stood watching, screaming, and crying. Scores of other boats darted around the procession with those on board shouting cheers. Periodically, when one would pull aside the *Livingston*, Lafayette walked to the railing and bowed. As the fleet cut across the water, an emotional reunion began. Waiting on board the *Livingston* were a handful of Lafayette's old brothers-in-arms, faces he had last seen half a century ago but recognized instantly.

There was Philip Van Cortlandt. In 1781, Washington took Van Cortlandt, a colonel of the Second New York Regiment, by his arm, walked him down the road from the ferry at Stoney Point on the Hudson River, and charged him with bringing up the American army's rear as it marched to Virginia. The journey took him to Williamsburg, where, as Van Cortlandt recalled, he "was made exceedingly happy to meet my General Lafayette."[11] Now, at seventy-four, he "marched" once more to be with Lafayette: The night before, an express was sent to his home in Westchester County, where he had retired to tend to his orchards. There it had fetched the veteran, who traveled overland under the moon until reaching Manhattan.

They were joined by the seventy-one-year-old Richard Varick. An aide of Benedict Arnold, Varick was arrested, court-martialed, and declared innocent in the wake of his superior's treason. As a consolation of sorts, at Washington's behest, Congress employed Varick as the official recorder of the American army's papers and correspondence, resulting in forty-four books' worth of material, spanning the formation of the republic to the aftermath of its Revolution.

The men embraced repeatedly. They relived the Revolution as if it were not five decades ago, but days past. They shed tears, a contagion that soon spread across the boat as the passengers, struck with emotion, watched the joyous interaction of the old soldiers. "It was a reunion of a long separated family," recorded the New York's *Evening Post*.[12]

And then there was Marinus Willett, who as a teen won an appointment to a New York regiment during the French and Indian Wars. His return to civilian life was interrupted with the unrest in the colonies, which he helped foment with gusto. Willett went from raiding British arsenals in New York as a leader of the rabble-rousing Sons of Liberty, to helping secure and then, through a daring midnight escape to summon reinforcements, fend off a British siege of Fort Stanwix.

Willett joined Washington's army shortly before the Battle of Monmouth, where he met and grew close to Lafayette. Just two years prior, in 1822, Lafayette had penned a tender note, reminiscing about the "ties of brotherly friendship" that bound the two men. "May it be in my power before I join our departed companions," he closed, ". . . to tell you personally my dear Willett, how affectionally I am your sincere friend."

Now, at last, the two old men were reunited. They sat down next to one another as their boat approached the city. "Do you remember me at the Battle of Monmouth?" Willett, now eighty-four, asked. "I saw you in the heat of battle, you were but a boy. Aye, I remember." Lafayette struggled to hold back tears.[13] Purposely, one of their companions intruded on the scene announcing the boat's arrival at the Battery.

It was nearing two in the afternoon when the maritime parade reached the southern tip of Manhattan, where the boats that had accompanied it from Staten Island merged with those waiting in the harbor, multiplying the procession greatly in size. Once the *Chancellor* docked, Lafayette stepped off and onto a barge, disembarking for Castle Garden. The circular fortress, sitting on Battery Park, was built to fortify the city in the years before the War of 1812; it was known, during its military lifetime, as Castle Clinton, for DeWitt Clinton. By the 1820s, its wartime life had ceased and the federal government had ceded the fort to New York City. In July 1824, with newly installed gaslights, it began a second life as a leasable social venue, a setting for parties and celebrations.

Stepping onto land and scaling a set of carpeted stairs, passing under a wreathed arch, Lafayette made his way toward the Castle. Its ramparts were covered with onlookers, so too were nearby wharves and forts, across the bay every home and building was covered with people, jostling for any vantage to view the pageant. Levasseur estimated the number at two hundred thousand. The New York newspapers counted the crowd on and around the Battery at fifty thousand.

He was greeted by the Lafayette Guards, the volunteer militia organized for the occasion of their namesake's arrival and outfitted with great flair, a portrait of Lafayette on their breasts, on their heads elegant military caps made by local saddlers, Crosby and Prebble's. They surrounded and escorted him to the head of a long battle line of militias. As he passed, each tilted its flag downward, revealing the words *Welcome Lafayette* stitched over their standards.

Pressing through the crowd, Lafayette stepped into Castle Garden, and was ushered off into a receiving room for a pause and refreshment. When the crowd inside the building, itself estimated to be three thousand, grew impatient, he reemerged, walked to the heart of the structure, eliciting an incredible chorus of cheers. Amid the swelling noise, Lafayette climbed into an open-topped carriage harnessed to four white horses, and was drawn away from the Castle up Broadway to City Hall. In the vanguard and the rear were the Lafayette Guard.

The way was clogged with spectators. The mile journey was prolonged because of the difficulty of moving through the crowds. Every building and house along the path was draped with bunting and densely packed. Men shouted and huzzaed, women waved and tossed their white handkerchiefs, which twirled and fluttered in the air before descending to the ground, all as bells pealed, cannons thundered, and American flags fluttered. At each intersection flowers and wreaths flew through the air, landing by the carriage. An eyewitness wrote that it was "impossible to describe the enthusiasm and joy expressed by the multitude."[14] As Lafayette slowly made his way north from Castle Garden, a near frenzy set in among some of the spectators along his path. Men rushed toward the carriage, attempting to unhook its horses and carry its passenger the remainder of the way to City Hall themselves.

"In all truth, madame, I no longer know how I can tell you what I have seen," Levasseur wrote to Émilie, struggling to describe the spectacle. "An entire people at the feet of a man, calling him their father, their benefactor, letting fall on his hands and on his clothes the sweetest tears of gratitude, and then passing into the most lively and joyful delirium. No, never has man had such a triumph!"[15]

When Lafayette reached the front of City Hall, a crowd waited for him on the long flight of steps inclining to a columned portico at the center of its white marble façade. Among them were women who offered their hand, and young children who repeated his name, trance-like, time and time again.

Inside City Hall, where New York's civic authorities, its Corporation, and its mayor, Stephen Allen, offered the first formal welcome to Lafayette. "Your contemporary in arms, of whom few indeed remain, have not forgot, and their posterity will never forget the young and gallant Frenchman . . . The people of the united states look up to you as one of their most honored parents."

"I hope and trust, sir," he said, "that not only the present, but the future conduct of my countrymen, the latest period of time, will, among other slanders, refute the unjust imputation, that republics are always ungrateful to their benefactors."[16]

Lafayette, giving the first of what would be many responses and expressions of gratitude over the following year, responded in kind. "The sight of the American shore, after so long an absence," he said with a pleasing French accent, "the recollection of the many respected friends and dear companions, no more to be found on this land; the pleasure to recognize those who have survived; the immense concourse of a free republican population, who so kindly welcome me . . . have excited sentiments to which no human language can be adequate."[17]

With the formal welcome concluded, Lafayette was led onto the colonnade of the City Hall. Below, militias marched by. After they passed, he retreated inside to the Governor's Office, a room designated for the state's chief executive's use. On its walls were portraits of men Lafayette called friends: Washington, Hamilton. Under their gaze, he received any New Yorker who cared to shake his hand. In they came, rich and poor, Black and white, mothers who presented their children for some sort of civic benediction, old veterans, young soldiers. Some walked toward Lafayette, but overcome with emotion, turned away, unable to speak. Instead, they turned to embrace Georges, a more approachable surrogate for his father.

Levasseur watched in disbelief, observing the men and women who "come to touch the clothes of the General like a superstitious people would go to touch a relic," and was moved when "colored men remind him with emotion of his philanthropic efforts to lift them to the rank that is still refused to them in certain countries with horrendous prejudice." Another man stepped forward to take Lafayette by the hand; he was aged, and by the condition of the clothes, a laborer. "Me too, General," he said. "I am one of those 10 million individuals who owe to you the happiness of liberty."[18]

A fellow Frenchman attending the reception shared the secretary's astonishment. "This is quite peculiar!" he told Levasseur. "These so serious, so reflective people are unrecognizable. Man, woman, child alike, everyone leaps!" One of the *Cadmus*'s sailors, hearing the conversation, interjected. "Oh! It's not only that. If you had been with us, you would have seen during the journey all the fish around his vessel."[19]

At 5:00 p.m., his availability ended for the day, his energy taxed, Lafayette departed for his room at City Hotel, a five-story, seventy-eight-room lodging on Broadway, complete with barroom and coffee house. The nearly block-long building was a landmark in early American hospitality, one of the young nation's first luxury hotels. Elegantly furnished, the setting for soirees and people watching, it had "no equal in the United States" thanks to proprietor Chester Jennings, who was rarely seen outside of the hotel.[20] It was the perfect accommodation for the Nation's Guest.

During the early evening, Lafayette emerged from inside to shake hands with hundreds of young people calling for him from outside. Later, the hotel hosted a dinner in his honor. Toasts went up to Lafayette and New York City, naturally, and the bodies and organizations who had planned the events of the day, the liberty of France. But it was a New York doctor, J. H. Hayward, who stood, raised his glass, and captured the spirit of the moment, saluting "those who so nobly won for us our independence, and those who have so nobly shown today that we know how to value it."[21]

Over dinner, the fates and families of the old companions were discussed. When Alexander Hamilton's name was mentioned, it came to Lafayette's attention that his widow, Elizabeth, still lived. Later, he slipped away to pay her a visit.

As the day ended, the atmosphere was electric. At Castle Garden, the showmen Stuhl and Gunther released a giant balloon into the sky. Painted across it was the racehorse Eclipse, a knight in armor, plumed helmet on his head, unsheathed sword clenched in his right hand. A glowing transparency was lit in front of the recently opened Chatham Garden Theatre, the work of Hugh Reinagle, a scene and landscape painter who was an inaugural member of the National Academy of Design. Other buildings across the city were alight, transparencies burned, fireworks streaked in the sky. A joyful ending to a day, which, according to another New York newspaper, the *Commercial Advertiser,* "shines proudly in the annals of our country—proceedings which were more brilliant than any that have ever been witnessed in America."[22]

On Tuesday the 17th, the *New York Daily Advertiser* regretfully reported, "We are sorry to learn that it is the intention of the general to leave as soon as Thursday or Friday, on a visit to Boston, and that he will not return here until September."[23] Lafayette had agreed to attend Harvard's commencement on August 25.

"Here I am again, at last, on the beloved shore of America, where at the moment of my landing, I find myself honored with new testimonies of your kindness," Lafayette wrote to Monroe in a moment of quiet from New York. "The reception I met in this city I dare not dwell upon as it looks like vanity, while I would like to express the feelings of gratitude, and all the delightful emotions that overwhelm my heart. You will particularly sympathize in my sentiments at the meeting with our surviving brother soldiers."[24] Delays in the post and demands on his time had prevented Lafayette from sharing his travel plans with the president, and it was much to his regret that the trip to Boston would delay their reunion.

In the time remaining in New York, he steamed across the East River to approvingly inspect the Navy Yard on Long Island. Back in the city, he was besieged with visitors, the city's clergy, members of the Bar and the Society of the Cincinnati. Delegations from Philadelphia and Baltimore arrived, extending their own invitations. When New

York's French expatriates feted him, Lafayette, characteristically optimistic, offered words of encouragement. "Do not let us despair, gentlemen, of the cause of liberty," he told them. "It is still dear to the hearts of Frenchmen and we shall one day have the felicity of seeing it established in our beloved country."[25] On the 19th, when he and his son were inducted into New York's Historical Society, the city's first museum, Lafayette sat in a chair once belonging to King Louis XVI in front of a crowd of one thousand under a portrait of himself as a young man, painted in 1784. Over the course of the next three days, he regularly received visitors at City Hall, many who traveled from other towns and states, fearing they may not otherwise meet him, while the Common Council passed a resolution agreeing to seek a painter to capture Lafayette's likeness so that his portrait could hang alongside Washington and Hamilton in the same room he welcomed the public.

The honors were so many that the Frenchmen hardly had time to record what they had seen or felt, or answer the letters and requests already arriving from other parts of America. "Since my last letter the triumphs of the General have multiplied with such rapidity that I find myself well behind on the events and I don't know how I'll catch up to them," Levasseur explained to Émilie. "I am not strong enough to traverse the fields, to admire, to weep with tenderness, and to write at the same time."[26]

At seven in the morning of the 20th, the Lafayette Guard strutted in front of the City Hotel. After a breakfast with Philip Hone, a member of New York's Common Council, Lafayette emerged, took his place once again in a carriage provided by the city, and began to move north up Broadway. To its sides, cavalry trotted and soldiers marched, civilians followed too on foot and horse, or stood on the streets cheering. The enthusiasm had not dimmed and the crowds had not diminished. They watched, like children following the departure of a beloved elderly parent, fearful to let him out of their sights, despite their reassurance of his return, as Lafayette's carriage made its way up Bond Street, to Third Avenue, and eventually faded from sight.

Four days had passed with little else than joy and harmony. The only thing resembling discord or conflict was the jostling to catch a glimpse of Lafayette or the occasional pickpocketing. "Every paper teems with his praises, every lip seems to delight in uttering his name. Gentlemen are ready to throw by their business to shake him by the hand and ladies forget their lovers to dream of him. If a man asks, 'have you seen him?' You know *who* he means," wrote a reporter for the *New York Mirror*.[27]

The sight of the old hero struck a nerve. It awoke memories in those old enough to remember the young nobleman who had risked his life and fortune for the freedom of a nation he barely knew. It stirred a romantic sense of history in those who had only read his saga.

In many ways the reaction to Lafayette's reappearance was the result of a perfect confluence of feeling, history, and time. When the West Point band struck up "See, the Conqu'ring Hero Comes!" aboard the *Chancellor Livingston*, it was serenading Lafayette. But the euphoria erupting as he made his way to Manhattan was enhanced by a supporting cast of heroes: the elderly men who appeared along-side Lafayette—Van Cortlandt, Varick, Willett, Ogden, and the other silver-haired soldiers who had rushed to embrace him—and, of course, the ghost of departed fathers, none so prominently as Lafayette's own adopted father, George Washington. With Lafayette, the revolution Americans had looked back on so longingly had returned.

The happy news soon spread across the Union, as many newspapers carried word of his safe arrival. Others printed poems written in his honor: *"Hail, Patriot, Statesman, Hero, Sage! Hail Freedom's friend, hail, Gallia's son!"*[28]

Upon reading these columns, citizens far beyond New York left their homes and gathered in public spaces to celebrate and light illuminations of their own. "Separated, as we are, by our brethren of the great Atlantic Cities, by a territory of one thousand miles, and living, as it were, in a wilderness," wrote a correspondent in Missouri, "we could make no splendid display of anything—but could only give vent to the effusions of our hearts."[29]

Reflecting on the excitement and reverence, a newspaper editor, only days after Lafayette's arrival, celebrated its impact. "The papers are very barren of news, and in this respect the arrival of La Fayette has been most timely and fortunate," the *New York Commercial Advertiser* wrote. "Our party editors were getting too angry upon the presidential question; and we had become so wearied with these squabbles, and with seeing the names of Crawford, Adams, Clay and Jackson, staring us in the face in every print, and on all occasions, that we were right glad for a moments relief. The name of Fayette, however, is endeared to us by so many and various recollections, that we shall not soon wish to have it give place to those of Crawford or Gallatin."[30]

Little remarked on during the excitement, though, was another omen. During the Revolution, Charles Thomson was the secretary of the Continental Congress, dutifully keeping record of the debates and decisions of that body for the duration of its existence. Later, when the colonies became a country, he designed the Great Seal of the United States.

In his retirement, the bookish Thomson penned a comprehensive and lengthy history of the American Revolution, only to eventually destroy the manuscript. His accountings of the era and its actors were too flesh and blood. Sensing the unifying power they could have on later generations, he believed that for the sake of posterity, even mankind, it was better to let their memories remain unblemished. "Perhaps they may adopt the qualities that have been ascribed to them, and thus good may be done," he wrote.[31]

By the summer of 1824, those memories were long lost. Addled by dementia and confined to a settee in his Philadelphia parlor, Thomson, who had believed he would live to one hundred, died at the age of ninety-four. It was August 16—the day of Lafayette's arrival in New York City.

6

Memories of the Revolution
Have Come Back to Life

In March 1824, Boston's mayor Josiah Quincy wrote to Lafayette expressing a hope that he would include his city on any itinerary should he visit the United States.[1] "I joyfully anticipate the day, not very remote, thank God," he replied, "when I may revisit the glorious cradle of American, and in future, I hope, of universal liberty."[2] As the summer of 1824 came to a close, that day arrived.

He had promised Quincy that "whatever port I first attain, I shall . . . hasten to Boston."[3] The urgency was natural. Massachusetts's capital was one of the great stages of America's Revolution, one that Lafayette had strode across, perhaps most dramatically in April of 1780, when the *Hermione* docked at Marblehead and he sailed on to Boston. His reappearance was greeted with great fanfare and a sense of relief: In the patriotic doldrums of that terrible winter just passed, the general brought with him reassurance of the ongoing French support of America's cause at a time when its survival seemed particularly uncertain.

That celebration, though, would greatly pale in comparison to what the citizens of Boston, forty-four years on, had planned for Lafayette. But this would have to wait a spell. Despite his eagerness to reach the

Cradle of Liberty and a promise to attend Harvard's commencement on August 25, his path to Massachusetts was impeded: The two-hundred-mile trek turned into a five-day odyssey of adoration. In each town and village between New York and Boston, no matter its size, citizens awaited or hurried hither from the countryside to catch a glimpse of Lafayette as he passed by, a memory that would be recollected decades hence when the Nation's Guest was, for a moment, *their* guest.

On August 20, Lafayette left Manhattan, joined by his son, secretary, and valet, as well as David Cadwallader Colden, son of New York's former mayor, a delegation from the city of New York, as well as a military escort provided by the state. This suite turned into a cavalcade, as it was augmented by citizens in their carriages or following it on horseback at each town. Together they followed the Lower Post Road, along the Long Island Sound, then swept northward to Providence before reaching Boston.

Lafayette rose early in the morning and rode often until midnight. During the day, the blue Atlantic Ocean flittingly came into view to his right; at night, bonfires glowed atop the hills to his left. The anxious residents of villages were alerted that their wait had ended by the blast of cannon, the echo of bugle, and the approaching orange flames atop torches held aloft by the horsemen who buttressed the carriages. Then the bells rang, cannons boomed, well-wishers gathered and pleaded that he step out of his carriage, while their civic leaders cleared their throats and read from the carefully prepared tributes clutched in their trembling hands and white-haired veterans emerged from the crowds to exchange memories with a compatriot they had not seen in nearly half a century.

When Lafayette exited New York, after celebrations in New Rochelle and Rye, and entered Connecticut at Byram, the military escort assigned by the former state refused to surrender their charge, instead joining forces with their peers from the latter state, marching together toward Greenwich. Once there, Lafayette left his carriage, with the population of the town in tow, and walked to view the slope where American general Israel Putnam had escaped the British army in 1779.

Across the road cutting through the slope was an arch, made of pine and decorated with roses, the beauty of which betrayed its hasty construction. At the center of the arch was a shield carrying an inscription composed by Rev. Isaac Lewis, who had led the resistance to the British landing at Norwalk, also in 1779, when he gathered his flock in a distant house while their town smoldered.[4]

Now he chaperoned Lafayette around Putnam's Hill, pointing to the arch and its inscription, which paid tribute to Lafayette, "the early and distinguished Champion of American Liberty, and the tired friend of Washington."[5] As Lafayette began his walk back to the hotel where his carriage waited, Lewis called out, "General, America loves you!" To which Lafayette replied, "And I sir, truly love America."[6]

Along the road to Boston, businesses were closed in anticipation of Lafayette's arrival. If his route did not run through their communities, New Englanders rushed to ones where it did, traveling great distances in the process. If he had departed before they arrived, these travelers embarked for the next town in pursuit. Schools were dismissed. The roads were filled with young boys, "little rascals, completely covered with dust and sweat," many without shoes on their feet or hats on their heads, hoping to catch up with the procession. Along one Connecticut road, a reporter spotted a boy sprinting to the next town in hope of, he explained, arriving before the "Markis La Fayette" left.[7] Meanwhile, the line of admirers following the "Markis'" grew so large that the cloud of dust it kicked into the air could be seen for miles on the horizon and choked all those in its wake. As the cloud moved east, honors awaited in towns such as Saugatuck and Norwalk, where militia paraded, French and American flags mingled, and bridges were spanned by arches inscribed "Welcome Lafayette."

In Fairfield, where he arrived late at night, at Mrs. Knapp's Washington Hotel, a dinner awaited upon a table decorated with flowers, wreaths, cranberries, and wintergreens. It was, a reporter commented, "like the bed of some fairy's enchanted garden."[8] When a member of the New York delegation traveling with Lafayette inquired after a bill for the banquet, a local informed him that there was no charge, joking that Connecticut's roads had to prove they were as inexpensive to travel as New York's canals. The truth was, though, that along Lafayette's path tolls for roads, bridges, and gates were waived. The reporter following the spectacle struck up a conversation with a woman minding a turnpike gate on the route. When he asked her if she had made a fortune that day, she brushed him off. There was no toll for Lafayette or those who joined his procession, she chastised. "I should like to have him pass a thousand times!" Other travelers, she warned her interlocutor, who were unattached to the general's cavalcade, had to pay up. The reporter promptly handed over a shilling.[9]

The tributes offered by the local politicians at each stop sounded common themes and contrasted ages. In Fairfield, where Lafayette passed through in 1778, Samuel Rowland compared the current joyous reunion to the tragic winter of 1779, when the town was razed by the British army. Lafayette's name was constantly paired with George Washington's. Through the adopted son, Americans communed with the spirit of their departed father. And, of course, there was the matter of debt: Americans were, a speaker in New London testified, "filled with gratitude for the great and eminent services rendered their country."[10] They were not unaware of his strained finances. "I have heard that the General is poor; but I hope and trust he won't die so," one Yankee was heard to say, adding that, if need be, he would happily take the general into his own home, meager as it might be. And he was not alone in this generous urge. When a reporter questioned if others in Connecticut would be willing to help Lafayette, the man said certainly, "more'n ten thousand of 'em."[11]

After resting at Bridgeport on the morning of the 21st, the procession reached New Haven, whose citizens waited for his delayed arrival, which was announced with a twenty-four-gun salute. The crowd was still and silent until the point Lafayette stepped out of his carriage, then it erupted in a deafening roar. "Such a shout here was never heard before," another reporter estimated.[12] Meetings with New Haven's mayor and Connecticut's governor followed; speeches were delivered, all harmonizing on the debt of gratitude long due to the Frenchman by "millions of freeman, yet unborn, who will soon overspread this great continent."[13]

Then the old soldiers arrived. Benjamin Tallmadge, the dashing Continental officer who collaborated with Washington on the creation of the Culper spy ring, one of the Continental Army's central intelligence operations in the British nerve center of New York City. With him in New Haven, Aeneas Munson, who joined the army as a surgeon's mate, at the time of his graduation from Yale, and was present during the siege of Yorktown, part of a battalion commanded by Alexander Hamilton. Lafayette needed no introduction to either man. They embraced, they exchanged memories, and all those watching were overcome with emotion. "The effect was electric," claimed the *Connecticut Journal.*[14]

There were introductions to Yale's faculty and New Haven's civil authorities. Citizens pressed around him, sharing stories of their father or uncle who had served under him. Military parades, and more artillery salutes followed by the marching of three hundred students. When his carriage made its way to the Green, the town's outdoor meeting space, it was hauled there by men, not horses, replaying the rather unrepublican scene that had almost unfolded in Manhattan upon his arrival. In the campus library, he beheld John Trumbull's full-length portrait of Washington at the Battle of Trenton.

The march to Boston went on, only pausing momentarily in the town of New London, in deference to the Sabbath. Both the Congregationalist and Episcopal churches invited him to worship among their flock. In order to offend neither, he attended both. Levasseur observed admiringly how the pews of each were filled with men and women of different denominations, and the sermons contemplated morality instead of preaching dogma.

The Lord's Day provided only a temporary respite from the traveling: Breaking Connecticut's blue laws, which frowned on travel on Sunday, the trek resumed. Lafayette left France in August ailing; the voyage aboard the *Cadmus* had not improved matters. But now, he was rejuvenated. Reporters studied his appearance, noted his inability to bend his left knee, simple dress—a blue coat, nankeen pantaloons, the hat, a gift from a New York merchant, which he rarely wore. They were surprised by how he looked not a day over sixty. When a curious American, in Providence, asked if the voyage had wearied him, Lafayette reportedly claimed he was experiencing too much pleasure to be tired. One Yankee complimented Lafayette on how he spoke English. "And why should I not," was his reply, "being an American just returned from a long visit to Europe."[15]

The pace was possible because of relays of fresh carriages and horses along the road; the drivers, singular by the silk ribbons on their breasts, tasked with conveying such precious cargo, were figures of distinction themselves. Even their horses were reminded of the weight and honor of their task. While a new carriage was being equipped in a Connecticut town, its driver was heard to admonish one of his horses. "Behave pretty now, Charley—you are going to carry the greatest man in the world."[16]

On the morning of the 24th, Charley and his four-legged colleagues continued across the Rhode Island line and into Providence, where the by-now familiar but still affecting routine played out: Local politicians orated, militias marched, salutes were fired, spectators crowded around his carriage to grasp his hand. In front of the state house, he stepped out of his carriage and walked toward its entrance, when columns of young women dressed in white scattered flowers in his path. When he reached the building, another reunion: Stephen Olney, a veteran of Yorktown, ran to embrace and kiss Lafayette. More tears followed. Once ushered inside the state's seat of government, a local orator, and future congressman, Tristam Burges, struck a welcome note of contrast between worlds old and new, that would be oft-repeated and most pleasing to Lafayette, if not the Bourbons and their allies:

"Might the Potentates of Europe but behold this Republican spectacle in America! They would then feel that the blaze of loyalty cannot warm like the ardor of patriotism; and realize how much less dear to the heart is the exacted homage of subjects, than the spontaneous gratitude of freemen."[17]

After nearly a week of constant travel, on the evening of the 23rd, Lafayette crossed the Massachusetts border, where he was received by a military escort. From there he was led to Roxbury, two miles from Boston, where the voyage terminated, at 3:00 a.m., at the mansion of the state's governor and Lafayette's friend, William Eustis. A Revolutionary

War veteran, Eustis had served as a surgeon in the Continental Army, a former secretary of war, and America's minister to the Hague. Upon their reunion, which began with an embrace of several minutes, Eustis reportedly exclaimed, "I am the happiest man that ever lived!"[18]

A few hours later, Lafayette's brief rest was disturbed by the sound of music outside his room. When he walked to the window and looked below, he was transfixed and transported back five decades; outside Eustis's home a light infantry performed maneuvers, clad in the same uniforms his own light infantry wore during the Revolution, part of a cavalcade seven hundred strong sent to escort him into the city.

While the Nation's Guest was led into Boston, at the city boundary thousands of dragoons and light infantry milled about, occasionally eating the bread and cheese or drinking the punch provided by the city while they waited on Lafayette. Among their number was twenty-four-year-old Josiah Quincy Jr. (actually the fourth of that name). Absent was his cousin Charles Francis Adams. The two young men were both of revolutionary stock and Massachusetts political royalty: Quincy's great-grandfather and namesake was an early patriot; his father was the current mayor of Boston. Adams was the grandson of John Adams, the son of John Quincy Adams. Quincy had graduated from Harvard in 1821 and now was pursuing his master's degree; Adams was studying there. Their two families were united by marriage, and two decades later the two men traveled to the American West together. But on the occasion of Lafayette's visit to Boston, their attitudes diverged somewhat.

When Quincy, a member of the Massachusetts Artillery, at last saw Lafayette come into view, resplendently seated in an open barouche pulled by four white horses, the scene, as he wrote in his memoir decades later, "awakened an enthusiasm which I shall not attempt to describe."[19] For Charles Francis Adams, who remained in Cambridge reading Walter Scott's *Waverly*, the production held less appeal. "Great preparations have been made and it is expected every thing will be very splendid. For my part I have seen many such shows and have ever disliked them," he jotted in his diary.[20]

Original visions for the preparations had been even greater: While in New York, Boston's assistant city marshal, John Rouleston, had informed Lafayette that the city hoped that he would mount a horse and cut a grand figure riding through the city's streets. But it was no longer 1780. Lafayette, due to the lameness of his left leg, was unable to sit in the saddle. After receiving the idea with good humor, he sent a note to the elder Quincy, stating that a barouche would suffice.[21]

Once that barouche, carrying Lafayette along—Georges Washington and Levasseur followed in another—had arrived in Boston, its mayor, the elder Quincy, gave the required tribute and climbed in next to his guest. Accompanied by light infantry, dragoons, marching band, city officials, as well as thousands of citizens on horseback—carters and wood wharfingers, dressed in white frocks, which Josiah Quincy Jr. wrote "had the effect of mounted priests."[22] They rode through immense crowds, by a grand arch across Washington Street, near the remains of a British breastwork. The inscription at its base read 1776: WASHINGTON AND LAFAYETTE, A NATION NOT UN-GRATEFUL.

People sat atop balconies, on fences, trees, or perched in windows, shouting as Lafayette passed by, a badge stamped with his likeness affixed to a blue ribbon on their chests. John Graham, a naval officer who was in town on his way to Norfolk, wrote to this father in St. Louis that "there was not less than 70,000 people to welcome the venerable old general in the city of Boston, the windows were filled with ladies who shook their white handkerchiefs as the general passed there."[23] Not even the coolest Bostonian was immune from the excitement. Nathaniel Bowditch, famed mathematician and father of naval navigation, sought to take in the parade from some distance at his office. His walk there was obstructed by the procession on Washington Street, which he unsuccessfully attempted to cross. He then climbed a flight of stairs to watch the spectacle. Moments later, he had fallen into some sort of trance. When he regained his senses, Bowditch found himself cheering till he was hoarse, in the middle of the surging crowd clinging to Lafayette's carriage.[24]

When the cavalcade reached Boston Common, two thousand young girls arranged in two columns waited to greet the Nation's Guest. In a moment of incredible theater, one, the daughter of the physician John Ware, broke ranks and stepped to Lafayette's carriage, where Mayor

Quincy lifted her and held her aloft. Then she slipped a crown of laurels over Lafayette's head or placed it on his hand. Reaching the statehouse, Lafayette was led to the Senate Chamber, where Eustis took his turn in the ongoing national oration in the general's honor. "Under our illustrious Washington you were instrumental in establishing the liberties of our country," he said, a superfluous reminder at this point.[25] "Sir, I am delighted with what I see; I am oppressed with what I feel," was Lafayette's response.[26] Another surreal moment occurred when his carriage rolled slowly through Tremont Street past the homes on Colonnade Row. When Quincy pointed out a woman on one of the balconies—John Hancock's widow, Dorothy Quincy Hancock Scott, who had hosted Lafayette under her roof so long ago—Lafayette asked that the carriage stop. He stood, caught her eye, and placed his hand over his heart. In turn, she sobbed and said, "I have lived long enough."[27]

Asked by a friend for a contribution to an album, a woman named Elizabeth Crosby attempted an objective description of the events in Boston. "You have doubtless seen much in the papers about the gratitude done to this distinguished stranger," she wrote after Lafayette's visit. "But this is all and in my opinion quite ridiculous." Lafayette, like many a young soldier, had come to America in search of fame, for the love of honor. True, he was genuinely attached to the American people and their government, she allowed. But the debt owed to him was no greater than that owed to any other general.

And still, she could not look upon the spectacle on the Common without awe. "We go out to gaze on the hero, patriot and sage as he passes, more from curiosity, than from gratitude. But when once our eyes are fixed upon this hero of our revolution—this living Washington, it must be allowed that our breasts are filled with mingled emotions, which I will not disgrace by attempting to describe," she explained. "Could you look on the old remains of our revolutionary army, as they totter on their crutches, to shake hands with their commander—with the man who in his youth, led them through danger, and suffering, to liberty and happiness?" She went on: "Could you behold the wives of our revolutionary heroes, as they look on the companion of their husband's toil and labor—the alleviator of the pains and agonies of those most dear to them, without experiencing something of an indescribable emotion rising in your heart?"

The revolutionary widows and daughters, little Miss Ware placing a wreath around Lafayette's head—how could one see or read of these scenes and be unmoved?[28] "In short, stoical as I may have felt, when reading the news-papers, on beholding the hero, as he passed, I could not help joining in the general feeling of the people. My heart responded to the sentiments contained in the inscription on the triumphal arch, through which he entered the city, and I as well as others was ready to say,

> We bend not the neck,
> We bend not the knee,
> But our hearts, La Fayette,
> We surrender to thee.[29]

Lafayette and his companions ended the night at the Amory-Ticknor House on the corner of Beacon and Park Streets. Without consulting the city's leaders, one of Massachusetts's senators, James Lloyd, had invited them to lodge at his home in Sommerset. Boston's leaders discouraged the plan: Lafayette was not the guest of any one individual, but the Nation's Guest. Setting a precedent for much of the remainder of his trip, his accommodation would be paid for by state and local governments.

When Mayor Quincy showed the Frenchmen to their temporary accommodations, he encouraged them to feel at home, apologizing for any luxuries that might be lacking. "We are giving you the republican treatment; we are not familiar with superfluity," he explained.[30] The quarters were lavishly furnished, with crimson upholstery, claret-colored carpets, muslin curtains, silk drapes, and porcelain vases. The city had contracted carpenter Isaac Vose & Son to provide new lamps and mirrors, rosewood tables, and couches, and Gilbert Stuart's portraits of the five presidents adorned the walls. Contemplating their rooms, not to mention the fine coaches and horses provided at the city's expense, the Frenchmen were puzzled. Quincy's speech, Levasseur wrote to Émilie Lafayette, "made me think that for the republicans of Boston, the limits of the necessary are much far advanced, because the richness of our apartments, the sumptuousness of our table, the perfumes placed in our toilets, were such that we could have believed ourselves to be in the court of the king of Persia." The prohibition on Lafayette or his party paying their own way for anything was so extensive that the following morning, Georges and Levasseur, unwilling to have others pick up the tab for their bath, were forced to throw money at the counter and sprint out of a bathhouse.[31]

John Graham, the naval officer who was one of the thousands who took Lafayette by the hand, wrote to his father that "the general is a fine looking man for one his age and stands the fatigue remarkably well for they keeping moving all the time."[32] Sure enough, during the days that followed the general's arrival in Boston, he traveled from there to Cambridge and back, on the 25th to attend Harvard's commencement ceremony, and on the 26th to join a meeting of the Phi Betta Kappa Society. On the first occasion, Charles Francis Adams walked onto the piazza at the front of the school and watched Lafayette's approach with his gimlet eye and no little wonder. "The enthusiasm of the people with respect to him is astonishing, he was almost prevented from moving yesterday and today there was nothing but a sea of heads to be seen," he recorded.[33] In front of another arch, Harvard's president delivered his welcome address before the procession moved on to the meetinghouse for a ceremony unlike any other in Harvard's history. "To describe the enthusiasm that greeted the guest of the day is simply impossible," Quincy recalled. "Those who felt it—those who were lifted up by it—knew that I was a unique experience of which nothing adequate could be said."[34]

"The appearance of the General in the hall excited, among the ladies, the most extraordinary transportations," Levasseur wrote. "It was an enchanting picture: something more that 400 young people, almost all of them very pretty, heads crowned in flowers, waving their handkerchiefs in the air to greet him."[35] The galleries were full; the men and women seated in them dressed in their finest. On the stage below sat Lafayette. When each speaker—and they all did—referenced him, the room exploded. Mere mention of his name caused "the repressed rapture to burst forth."[36] The constant cheering and handkerchief waving caused the ceremony to drag on until the late afternoon, only ending at 5:00 p.m. "It was," Quincy wrote, "as if one of the great heroes of history had been permitted to return to earth."[37]

The mayor's son was obligated to deliver the day's valedictory; he had spent much of the previous evening composing and revising the address, at the expense of interacting with Lafayette during dinner. The final product, by his own admission, was a series of rather uninspiring Latin phrases that provoked little response from its listeners. When he reached his close, though, with its mandatory mention of Lafayette, the galleries came alive, the spectators jumped to their feet, and Quincy's conclusion was rendered inaudible with approbation. His cousin Charles Francis Adams was not among those cheering. After one attempt to enter the meetinghouse failed—the crowds were simply too large—he wandered around campus taking note of the spectacle outside, archly "observing the passions of men." "It was a singular scene," he wrote in his diary, "and for a quantity of rogues, knaves and whores matched almost any in the world. Most deficient however in the last mentioned article."[38]

The following day, when Lafayette attended a meeting of the Phi Betta Kappa Society, the scene was much the same, and the size of the crowd gathered in Cambridge to see him was undiminished. Adams listened to a number of the society's speakers but determined that "there were none worth hearing."[39] Irritated by insipid rhetoric and the lack of seating for students, he left the chapel to visit with a friend; when he returned, the quality of the discourse had improved.

In 1824, Edward Everett was at the outset of his career as America's preeminent orator of the nineteenth century. Born in the Boston neighborhood of Dorchester, he developed a particularly florid speaking style studying for the ministry at Harvard, where he had already earned a bachelor's degree at the age of seventeen. After a sojourn in Europe, where he became the first American to study at the University of Göttingen in Germany, he returned to Harvard as a member of the faculty. By 1824, he was an in-demand speaker, delivering a sermon at the U.S. Capitol two years before. In the years to come, he would hold numerous political offices and, in 1864, deliver a two-hour speech at the dedication of a cemetery in Gettysburg, Pennsylvania—one that would be overshadowed in history by the two-minute address that followed it. On this day, though, Everett delivered.

His speech was preceded by a poem read by the Unitarian theologian Henry Ware, pastor of Boston's Second Church, who had not originally been scheduled to speak. In the days leading up to the event, Ware's father had shared stories of a man and a woman who, in 1794, had dreamt of Lafayette. Inspired by Lafayette's visit, the pastor transformed these tales into a poem that cast its subject in quasi-religious terms. When the originally scheduled speaker failed to appear at the meeting, Ware volunteered to read his poem. In it, a man spots a magnificent temple and walks toward its entrance, only to be interrupted by the ringing of a bell. When he looks up, he sees, shining in gold, the words "that all mankind might read—thy honored name, Fayette!"[40]

Everett's address lasted nearly two hours. Its finale, naturally a tribute to Lafayette, awed the audience. Echoing themes already voiced along the route that had brought the general to Boston, Everett framed Lafayette as a link between generations—the founding and the present. Most of the former were no more: "You have looked round in vain for the faces of many who would have lived years of pleasure on a day like this with their old companion-in-arms and brother in perlil," he declared.[41] Among them, Hamilton, Greene, and Knox were gone. And Washington, in eternal repose on the banks of the Potomac River, was unable to welcome his adopted son home once more.

But a new generation of Americans, standing before Lafayette now, could. Everett noted the nearing of the fiftieth anniversary of the beginning of the Revolution and how the years since had "laid down in the dust" many of the men who had participated in it. But one had returned "to receive the gratitude of the nation," for the sacrifices he had made—abandoning the comfort of home, the life of a nobleman, all to fight for America.[42] Quincy, quoting from the journal of a friend who heard the speech, claimed, "Every man in the assembly was in tears," and he verified this in his own memory of the day.[43] Ware wrote that "it shook the whole audience and bathed every face in tears . . . Luckily

I had spoken first."[44] Even Charles Francis Adams, who listened to twenty minutes of the address and then exited, annoyed at the size of the crowd, confessed his regret, "as the passages I heard were really fine and I had understood since, his final close was quite effecting."[45] At a dinner of the society, attended by more than two hundred and lasting over two hours, there was more clapping than conversation; among the numerous toasts was one offered by the diplomat Alexander Hill Everett: "May America grow old, and Europe young."[46]

But the first generation of Americans, like Lafayette, *had* grown old. On August 28, he arrived at the site of the Battle of Bunker Hill, trailing a procession, greeting by cheering crowds everywhere in Boston. There, he was met by a few aged veterans of the battle. Abram Thompson explained to Lafayette that, in 1823, a parcel of land encompassing the battlefield had been put up for auction. Determined to protect the site, an informal association of Bostonians banded together and purchased the acreage. After incorporation by Massachusetts government as the Bunker Hill Monument Association, they were now raising money by subscription to build a monument to the heroes of Bunker Hill. Lafayette happily pledged his name to the list of subscribers. He should also know, said Thompson, that the following June, on the fiftieth anniversary of the battle, a ceremony was scheduled at Bunker Hill. On his trip from France, Lafayette had expressed hope to return home by the following spring. Already wavering from that intent, he promised that if he was still in America during the summer, he would be present.

The next morning, a Sunday, Lafayette attended services at the Brattle Street Church, sitting in John Hancock's pew. Then, dispensing with the usual escort and pageantry, he exchanged his carriage drawn by four horses for one pulled by two and quietly rode to Quincy, Massachusetts, where an old friend awaited.

Nearly forty years earlier, while in Paris negotiating peace with Great Britain, John Adams, though initially fond of Lafayette upon his arrival in America in 1777, seethed that his popularity paired with "an unbounded ambition which it concerns us to watch."[47] John Adams's brilliance, which helped give life to an independent America at numerous junctures, was matched by his vanity and tendency toward self-righteousness.

He was skeptical of America's alliance with France, felt overshadowed by fellow envoy Benjamin Franklin and marginalized by the French minister Comte de Vergennes, and resented Lafayette's involvement in the diplomatic process. He was deeply suspicious of the Society of the Cincinnati, believing it an effort to establish a heraldry in the republic. "I see in that youth the seeds of mischief to our country if we do not take care. He was taken early in our service and placed in a high command, in which he has behaved well, but he has gained more applause than human nature at twenty-five can bear," Adams wrote in 1783.[48] But by the turn of the century, with Lafayette returned to France from his imprisonment and Adams turned out of the presidency, the rigid New Englander, commiserating on their mutual fate of isolation in a "rural Solitary place of retirement," hoped for the opportunity to host him at Peacefield, the Adamses' farmhouse in Quincy, Massachusetts. "Your Country of Adoption has grown and prospered since you saw it. You would scarcely know it, if you should make a Visit," Adams wrote Lafayette in 1801.[49]

Though he had once been unnerved by Lafayette's popularity, in 1824 it overjoyed him. "There is not a man in America who more sincerely rejoices in your happiness and in the burst of joy which your presence has diffused through this whole continent than myself," Adams wrote to Lafayette, shortly after the latter's landing in New York. The reunion, though, was a difficult proposition, due to Adams's infirmity. "I would wait upon you in person but the total decrepitude and imbecility of eighty nine years has rendered it impossible for me to ride even so far as Governor Eustis's to enjoy that happiness."[50] Charles Francis Adams, who returned home to Peacefield after the conclusion of the festivities at Cambridge, recorded that his grandfather was "exceedingly weak, he is evidently departing, I think."[51] Lafayette, unwilling to leave Boston without a reunion, determined he would come to Adams.

After a morning of bustling preparation at Peacefield, at two thirty in the afternoon on Sunday, Lafayette, accompanied by his son and secretary, as well as Eustis, Quincy, and David Cadwallader Colden, arrived at the Adams estate. Levasseur was in disbelief that a former head of state would live in such a humble home. Lafayette entered the house and came face-to-face with a man considerably altered by time. "The Marquis met my grandfather with pleasure and I thought with some surprise, because really, I do not think he expected to see him quite so feeble as he is," wrote Charles Francis Adams.[52]

But the presence of Lafayette had a temporarily restorative effect: Adams came alive and commanded the room. "Grandfather exerted himself more than usual and, as to conversation, appeared exactly as he ever has," his grandson wrote. "I think he is more striking now than ever, certainly more agreeable, as the asperity of his temper is worn away."[53] Levasseur noted as well how Adams was energized by the meeting. "We found this esteemed old man surrounded by his family. He received us and embraced us with a very touching kindness. The sight of his old friend did him a pleasure and a good that seemed to rejuvenate him."[54]

Charles Francis Adams, whose father, John Quincy Adams, had hoped to join the visit but had not yet arrived at Peacefield from Washington, jotted down his usual frank assessment of the guest of honor. "He is a mincing man in his manners, he has much ease and grace and knows the proper side of men," he observed of Lafayette. "His lot is an enviable one, on the whole, as without being an extremely great man, he has received honors which are the lot of only a few."[55] Over dinner, Lafayette and Adams reminisced about the Revolution. Before departing, Lafayette said his farewells, meeting and shaking hands with much of the town's population, which had gathered outside the house to see him off. Adams, deeply moved by the experience, moved away from the dinner table and retired; "my grandfather appeared considerably affected and soon rose after dinner was over," Charles Francis recorded.[56] "During the entire dinner," Levasseur wrote of the elder Adams, "he led the conversation with such an ease and freshness of memory that one forgot his 80 and some odd years."[57]

Charles Francis, who griped about where he was seated at the table, confessed that he too was overcome by the sight of his grandfather and Lafayette reunited. "I would wish to recollect the scene of this day, as the actors will soon depart from this busy scene and memory only will bring life to their looks, their tones, their language," he wrote in his diary, expressing the feeling of many of his countrymen who had viewed Lafayette only from afar the past two weeks. "All these things in illustrious men are worth recollecting, and it is one of the most desirable things in great distinction, to be sat up in this way to the observation of the world. There being no body to converse with, I went to bed early."[58]

A fitting coda for Lafayette's time in Boston though it might have been, his departure back to New York was delayed by a review of Massachusetts militia on August 30 and a trip to see the naval installation in Portsmouth, New Hampshire. Along the way were the towns of Lexington and Concord, where the first shots of the American Revolution were fired and the first patriots fell. Standing on a hill in the former, he listened as aged veterans of that fight recounted, then named, their lost friends and gestured down toward the graveyard where they rested. At the moment of their departure from Lexington, Lafayette and his companions were approached by a man who presented them a rusted gun, explaining that his father had carried it during the battle. The Frenchman held the relic before returning it to its owner and encouraging him to inscribe "April 19," the date of the battles, on its handle and placing it in a box for safekeeping.[59]

In Concord, punch and cake were served in a tent on the town's common; one of the couples who attended returned home with a candy likeness of Lafayette for their daughter. She kept it for the remainder of her life.[60] Not everything was so saccharine in Concord, however. Attendance for Lafayette's reception was exclusive: Only the local officials who planned the reception, a few old soldiers, and the young women with crowns of flowers in their hair, moving around the tent offering refreshments, were allowed in. Many of the townspeople of lower social standing were not. Instead, they gathered beyond the tent, pressing against the ropes that cordoned it off, and were shooed away at bayonet point by the soldiers standing guard. This exclusion sparked outrage: After all, many of those denied entrance to the soirée were the children of soldiers who had fought in the Revolution. Were they not as entitled to shake Lafayette's hand as the town's "great people"? The bitter memory of their exclusion on the day of Lafayette's visit lasted for decades among the people of Concord.[61]

On the afternoon of September 2, Lafayette departed Boston, taking the upper Post Road, passing back into Connecticut where the revolutionary nostalgia did not relent. In Hartford, Daniel Wadsworth presented Lafayette with a pair of epaulets he had worn during the war and the bloodstained crimson sash used to bind his wound at Brandywine. He gave these items to Heman Swift, who was standing nearby during the battle and had reportedly draped his own sash around Lafayette's waist before he was carried off the field. Swift died in 1814, but his family had preserved the relics. One hundred revolutionary veterans escorted Lafayette to the steamboat *Oliver Ellsworth*, which headed down the Connecticut River as the day ended. A band played continuously on the bridge; the 150 passengers on board exchanged roars with the people who raced along the shore to cheer Lafayette or fire their muskets in his honor. "We could have conducted ten years' worth of war in Europe with the amount of powder lit since the General's arrival in the land of liberty," Levasseur estimated.[62]

Three weeks into the journey, the Frenchmen were exhausted—with one exception. "Since our arrival in New York on August 16th until today we have not had one single moment of rest," Levasseur wrote Émilie. "We have barely been able to get 3–4 hours of sleep each day. It's a continuous triumph. I am all in a daze. M. George is tired and Bastien is sick. Only the General can stand up to everything as though he were a young 20."[63]

When morning arrived, the boat steamed along Long Island Sound, and by noon, it had reached the port of New York, where the city's population had reassembled to welcome Lafayette once more. "During a two-hundred-mile tour, we have experienced everything that can flatter and touch the human heart," Lafayette wrote to his daughters. "I have found more old soldiers of the Revolution than I could have ever hoped for, and it has touched me so deeply to hear of the memories I left in their hearts."[64]

On September 2, as Lafayette was making his way back to New York, one of that state's newspapers, thrilled with the wealth of stories he had created, opined that "nothing else is talked of or heard of—even our hot-headed politicians seem to have caught the general enthusiasm and have thrown aside their inky weapons and forgotten their animosities that they may extend the hand of fellowship and congratulations to the noble General."[65] "The presidential question is at a stand," the newspaper reported.[66] And if he could provide a pacifying distraction, it was only additional happiness to Lafayette.

"I have the satisfaction of thinking that my presence has had a great reconciliatory effect between the two parties: men who have not spoken to each other for over twenty years are brought together and mutually invited to celebrate us," he wrote home to La Grange. "Memories of the Revolution have come back to life."[67]

On the afternoon of September 6, 1824, a line of old men, "vestiges of the War of Independence," walking in pairs, unsteadily marched their way past reverently silent crowds and into Washington Hall. "What a touching picture! More than two hundred old soldiers, glorious remainder of the war for independence, as worn down with glory as with age," Levasseur observed. "I barely dared to raise my eyes toward these men."[68]

The building, which sat at the intersection of Reade and Broadway Streets, had seen its share of grand celebrations, including the occasion of peace between America and Britain in February, 1815.[69] On this evening, New York's Society of the Cincinnati planned to outdo them all in celebration of Lafayette's sixty-seventh birthday.

Here another arch was built of evergreens and laurels, and under it an eagle clenching a scroll in its beak with the dates of both Brandywine and Yorktown on opposite ends. To the left of the guest of honor's seat was a shield with an image of a rising sun; to the right, one with New York State's coat of arms and a scene of the sun rising over the Hudson River, supported by Liberty and Justice.[70] Around the room were not only American flags, but banners carrying the names of soldiers lost in the Revolution.

Though she had no invitation, Anna J. H. Fitch was in town from her home in Albany that day and determined this was her chance to meet Lafayette. At four in the afternoon, she and some friends slipped into Washington Hall and waited in the reception room, where refreshments were laid out for Lafayette, who had yet to appear.

As soon as a constable spotted the women, they were informed that all spectators were required to leave the room. "I remonstrated on the inexpediency of the measure, but my arguments were overruled by hearing that there would not be sufficient room," she related to her sister, Sarah. As the women turned to leave the room, Marinus Willett, walking with the aid of two other men, entered. Fitch and her friends informed the old colonel of their plight. "Let the ladies stay, oh! Let the ladies stay—there will be room enough, plenty of room," he insisted to the constable, who obliged the old hero.[71] Minutes after this was settled, in Lafayette walked, surrounded by members of the Society of the Cincinnati and escorted by the guard named in his honor: "The generous, the disinterred La Fayette," as Fitch styled him. After he had shaken the hand of each member of the Society, he "then turned to the ladies who eagerly extended the hand of friendship to the ally, the companion of Washington."

"This world is even in extremes—and every one now is La Fayette mad," Fitch observed. "But surely this is a subject on which the highest degree of enthusiasm is not only excusable but praiseworthy—it is but the express of heartfelt gratitude, for past services, of incalculable value."[72]

After the uninvited guests had at last left the hall, members of the Cincinnati sat down for a multicourse birthday meal; the feast was followed by a series of toasts, including a tearful offering from Lafayette to Alexander Hamilton Jr.—"My friend and associate, your father!"[73]

A giant transparency of Liberty was set ablaze. Nearby was a column decorated with forty muskets, pistols, and swords. As the dinner ended, the old men were reduced to tears. Those among them who were seated too far away to reach for Lafayette found comfort instead in his overwhelmed son. Then, one by one, the soldiers of the Revolution marched out into the dark. "The advanced hour of the night, and the emptying of our bottles," Levasseur wrote, "finally forced the veterans to return to their lodgings, a trek that, I believe, was not very easy for certain among them."[74]

7

It Surpasses My Imagination, I Know

On August 30, 1824, Jacob Morton and Charles King presented a petition to New York's Common Council at city hall. Their appeal asked that the laws prohibiting carriages on the Battery leading to the bridge of Castle Garden be lifted for a night.[1] The committee invested with authority over public lands acquiesced. More than that, the city yielded entirely to the group of citizen planners in their ambition to transform the structure—where Lafayette had first landed in Manhattan two weeks prior—from a purposeless old fort into a coliseum, a "fairy zone," in which to stage the grandest ball not simply in New York's history, but in America's.[2] And it would be in Lafayette's honor.

The project was fitting symbolism for the American artisanship and industry unfurling before Lafayette's eyes. The most ostentatious flowering of this rising prowess may have orbited the grand fête at Castle Garden, but additional evidence was found in New York and during a trip up the Hudson River, where education, arts, and ambitious civic projects left Lafayette happily stunned by the transformation made possible, in part, by the services Americans now thanked him for.

King and Morton were members of a committee of citizens overseeing the immense project at Castle Garden, the realization of which required its own small army of artisans and laborers. The artist Hugh Reinagle, famed for his stage settings, was placed in charge of painting. Henry Ritter, an upholsterer who owned a shop on Broadway, handled furnishings. A member of the Brinnell family of shipping magnates oversaw logistics, and the carpenter Martin E. Thompson supervised design.[3] One hundred sailors from the navy yard were volunteered to assist in the construction.[4] They converted the wooden bridge connecting the castle to the shore into an elegant, carpeted colonnade with a stretched canvas serving as a roof, decorated with pine and cedar branches. Inside, workers sealed off Castle Garden's open top with over one thousand feet of sail, stretched by cords connecting to columns at the center of the floor and adorned with flags of many nations. Hanging galleries with seats were suspended, and thirteen columns were erected, each featuring medallions bearing the states' flags. For the guest of honor himself, a tent of blue and white muslin was constructed and placed above the castle's entrance, decorated with busts—including one of Alexander Hamilton—paintings, and artillery pieces.[5]

In early September, notices appeared in the local papers: A limited number of tickets were available at $5 each. This included admission for one man and two women. A large police presence was promised and a strict system of traffic was to be enforced: All carriages dropping off passengers were to form a line through a gate across from Greenwich Street. Attendees who arrived on foot were to enter through another entrance across Bridge Street. Anyone not wearing proper attire would be refused admission. And those without the correct gown, suit, or top hat were likely out of luck: New York's tailors and milliners had received so many commissions they were unable to take on any additional orders. But there were other options.[6]

Across the city, businessmen sold fashionable Lafayette garments and accessories guaranteed to help their wearer cut a most elegant form at Castle Garden. James Campfield at 303 Broadway offered gloves and belts with Lafayette's likeness, engraved by Asher B. Durand, "the *only correct one* offered to the public." The likeness was so striking, an advert claimed, a customer ordered a set for Lafayette's family in France.[7] Doremus and Suydam, at 171 Broadway, sold silk and satin belts and handkerchiefs emblazoned with their own likeness of the general.[8] Chesterman, Son and Paddock sold waist ribbons and sashes with a miniature likeness of Lafayette. Robert Lovett offered a Lafayette medal of gold and silver, perfect for the ball and "the only good likeness yet executed in medallion."[9] Under the heading of "Honor to the Brave," Samuel Valentine offered miniature likenesses of Lafayette on "items of every description."[10] H. W. Taylor advertised his top hats with a portrait of Lafayette stamped on the lining, "which for elegance of shape &c, surpass anything of the kind heretofore offered."[11] T. W. Dyott sold Lafayette flasks and pint bottles, blown at the Kensington Glass Works. "There is a fine market for all these things, and those who want to buy these things must do so quickly," one newspaper warned.[12]

And it was not just in New York. Ambitious entrepreneurs in all parts of the Union sought to capitalize on Lafayette mania, launching one of the first nationwide commercializations of a national event or phenomenon on such a scale. Lafayette badges, uniforms, and canes were available in Virginia, umbrellas in Baltimore and Philadelphia, leghorn hats in Georgia. With Americans eager for souvenirs of a national sensation, a market quickly developed for all things Lafayette. Entrepreneurs in all parts of the Union were happy to flood it with their wares.

Some Americans frowned on the commercial component of the Lafayette excitement. The *Catskill Recorder*, taking note of the Lafayette gold rush, mockingly wrote, "Little fruit boys run around our streets with their Lafayette peaches and Lafayette pears," a "La Fayette's barber's shop," and butchers with their "Lafayette ox," concluding, "it is amusing in what ways our countryman (and women) contrive to get our money."[13]

But the mania fired artistic impulses as well. Before he had even reached Staten Island, the aged poet of the Revolution and Jefferson propagandist Philip Freneau composed a poem dedicated to Lafayette:

> *Of the great actors on our stage,*
> *Of warrior, patriot, statesman, sage,*

How few remain, how few remain!
Among the first, you claim esteem,
The historian's and the poet's theme.[14]

And he became the musicians' and playwrights' theme too. "The Hero's Welcome," a piano forte composed by Charles Thibault, was performed at the Park Theatre. "Welcome Lafayette" by J. C. Taws was available at Dubois & Stodart on Broadway.[15] The Italian émigré Lorenzo Da Ponte, who wrote librettos for Mozart's *The Marriage of Figaro* and *Don Giovanni* and later relocated to America, penned a few verses for the Nation's Guest:

> Never did loquacious Fame carry a more dear name on velocious wings, and never did the wish of thousands of thousands of hearts appear more satisfied with the beloved object it obtained.
>
> Already every one flies towards the blessed sails that have carried to this land the One he loves. Every one, exulting, cries "He comes, he comes!" and calls him deliverer and father.[16]

At the Park Theatre, Lafayette was treated to a performance of the comedy *Laugh When You Can,* melded with a new composition, "The Siege of Yorktown," the story of a girl named Kate who related the landing of the French troops to her jealous beau, Zekiel. It was received with wild applause.[17]

Soon after Lafayette's arrival, New York's Common Council had opened a competition for a commission to paint a portrait for City Hall. Numerous painters—John Vanderlyn, John Wesley Jarvis, James Herring—now made their case to the council for the commission. Among those who would soon arrive in New York and pursue the assignment was a frustrated painter from New Haven named Samuel Morse. Meanwhile, the sculptor Nicholas Gevelot created a plaster of Paris bust of the Nation's Guest, which the city displayed in a "conspicuous situation" in the gallery of paintings.[18]

If Lafayette's return proved an inspirational (and lucrative) opportunity for some Americans, he was inspired in return by the nation's budding artistic prowess and the growth of institutions dedicated to the general diffusion of knowledge as well as the betterment of its citizens.

In early nineteenth-century America, schooling was the domain of the church or, for affluent families, under the purview of private instructors. This left children from poor families without access to education. New York, led by its farsighted mayor DeWitt Clinton, established a chain of free schools, chartered by the state but supported by private donations and public assistance, enrolling over four thousand students. On September 10, Lafayette toured several of these schools, listened to recitations, was addressed by their students, and admired their crafts, such as needlework and knitting. What was of particular interest to Lafayette was a school he visited that afternoon on Mulberry Street.

Three years after its 1785 founding, the New York Manumission Society, its members aware of his ambitions to ameliorate slavery, appointed Lafayette a member. Nearly forty years later, his desire to see the institution eased out of existence had not diminished. His return to America coincided with a vote in Illinois to assemble a constitutional convention to strike down a statute prohibiting slavery. When the state's citizens rejected the initiative, Lafayette was heartened; he too was supportive of the immigration of free Blacks to Haiti and planned to promote the idea when he reached Washington.[19] The moment of national jubilee in his honor was no time for Lafayette to criticize his hosts, but he could, in subtle and diplomatic ways, encourage his American friends on the subjects of racism and slavery. One such way was a visit to New York's African Free School. The original schoolhouse, established in 1787, was the first institution in America dedicated to the education of Black students. It proved so successful, and enrollment grew so great, that a second school was established on Mulberry Street and by 1824 had enrolled more than seven hundred students. Lafayette arrived in the afternoon and was greeted by a young pupil. "Here, sir, you behold hundreds of the poor children of Africa sharing with those of a lighter hue in the blessings of education," he said, "while it will be our pleasure to remember the great deeds you have done for America, it will be our delight to cherish the memory of General Lafayette as a friend to the African emancipation, and as a member of this institution."[20] That boy, James McCune Smith, the son of a self-emancipated slave, would be the first Black American to earn a medical degree, though he was denied admission to American colleges and was forced to obtain it in Scotland.[21]

On the evening of September 11, the anniversary of the Battle of Brandywine, Lafayette returned to Washington Hall for a dinner held by New York's French residents. This time, however, mementos evoking memories of the Revolution were replaced by a model projecting the American future. In the banquet hall sat a seventy-foot-long table, carved with a lead-lined model of the Great Canal, flanked by miniature cities, factories, and forests. Water flowed through the carved canal, while a sun suspended above it rotated continuously.[22] The model's effect was aspirational, but the canal it replicated was not imaginary. The completion of the long-mooted—though never realized—project was now drawing near in upstate New York.

From the free schools, to the Historical Society, to even Castle Garden—which had once been known as Castle Clinton—wherever Lafayette went in New York City, the shadow of its former mayor, DeWitt Clinton, loomed. These and other institutions Clinton had promoted and helped build. In part, Clinton was a grandly ambitious politician, and indeed these ambitions were aided by his position in one of New York's first political families: His father, James Clinton, was a major general in Washington's army. His uncle George Clinton was governor of New York before and after the Revolution.

DeWitt himself served ten terms as mayor and had once been and would soon be again governor of New York. In 1812, he had run, unsuccessfully, for president. He was a rumored candidate for that office once again in 1824. There was a brief spell as New York's senator too. Clinton was an early American renaissance man, visionary administrator, naturalist, philanthropist, and public intellectual; these qualities helped build New York. He described Lafayette as "the most popular man in America—likely in the world."[23] But as the New Yorker recorded in his diary, Jefferson had supposedly described Clinton as "the greatest man in America."[24]

His paramount exertion and great accomplishment was captured in the impressive wooden model Lafayette stared at in wonder at

Washington Hall. The idea of a passage linking the American interior to the Atlantic Ocean was ancient, contemplated by Indian tribes and studied by the area's white settlers in the early eighteenth century. The project inched toward reality in 1792, when New York charted the Western Inland Lock Navigation Company. When this enterprise, aided by some public funds, proved incapable of determining a route for the canal—falls between Albany and Schenectady were among the intractable obstacles—and incapable of sustaining itself, in 1810 New York's legislature commissioned a survey, conducted by both Federalists and Democratic-Republicans, to determine a suitable route. Clinton joined fellow commissioners on a trip to the western reaches of the state, memorializing the voyage and its many inconveniences and unpleasantries—bedbugs, drunken celebrations on the Fourth of July, foul lodging, fly-covered foods—in his journal.

The trip's revelation, submitted in a report to New York's government, was that the ideal route for the canal, though the longest, was from the Hudson River to Lake Erie. The project, they added, was impractical without public funding. The federal government would not be lending aid: When Clinton and fellow commissioner Gouverneur Morris approached President James Madison in 1811, he was intrigued by the canal but saw no permission in the Constitution for federal participation in the project. Three years before, Jefferson had allegedly declared the scheme "little short of madness."[25]

The prospect of a canal traversing New York faced political opposition as well: Other regions of the country, eyeing the state's growth, were loath to see money go to a project that would exponentially further its development. Clinton then turned to New York's government for help, which, in 1812, passed a law permitting the commissioners to borrow money to conduct additional surveys. The War of 1812 stalled progress on the canal but ultimately boosted interest in it as well: The conflict reminded lawmakers of the vulnerability—and, in some cases, decrepitude—of America's roads and waterways, creating urgency for the creation of internal improvements.

In 1815, Clinton composed a manifesto coinciding with a public meeting at City Hotel to discuss the canal. He also prepared a memo for the state government, expressing a vision that went beyond mere commerce: Great civilizations, such as Egypt and China, were made prosperous by inland navigation; so too would America, where new cities were already emerging on the frontier. But the flow of goods inland along the canal would not only enrich the communities along its path but also strengthen their ties, so that, as Clinton predicted, "the inhabitants of the same country should be bound together by a community of interests and a reciprocation of benefits."[26] The case made, political currents shifted, and Clinton's fortunes rose. In 1817 alone, a bill passed New York's legislature authorizing the construction of the canal, Clinton was elected governor, and, in July, ground was broken in the town of Rome. A handful of laborers began digging in opposite directions along a 363-mile route.

In 1817 there were no true native-born civic engineers in America; there were no canals of this size, only much smaller and unprofitable waterways in South Carolina and Boston. The construction of the Erie Canal proved to be an education for the handful of novices—lawyers, land surveyors, teachers—who were selected to oversee the project. In real time they innovated around many obstacles: cutting through forests, over mountains, across waterfalls, and through the earth. Aided by an army of Irish immigrant laborers, as well as local contractors along the project's path, they improvised means of removing trees with cables strung between the trunk and a crank-turned apparatus. Massive stone culverts were built and held aloft by dirt. To cross valleys, a giant stone aqueduct was constructed. Hydraulic locks lifted boats over escarpments, plows with iron plates dredged up the earth, powerful drill bits were developed to carve trenches, and a waterproof cement for the construction of locks was created by crushing local cement rock.

The first segment, from Rome to Utica, the canal's middle section, was completed by 1819 and then extended west to Syracuse by 1820. An eastern leg, reaching Albany, was finished the following year, along with a separate canal linking Lake Champlain to the Hudson River. To the west, a 802-foot-long stone aqueduct crossing the Genesee River at Rochester was also completed in 1823; a 1,320 embankment over the Irondequoit Creek was built the year before.

The last major challenge—raising the canal sixty feet to meet the Niagara Escarpment—was now underway, as well as a sloping channel from Lockport to Buffalo, scheduled for completion in 1825. In time, New York's leaders hoped, Lafayette would see firsthand not just a wooden model, impressive though it may be, but America's greatest civic achievement of the nineteenth century. Its chief advocate, Clinton, notably remained in Albany for Lafayette's arrival. The Nation's Guest would come to America's Greatest Man, as Jefferson had supposedly called him.

Eleanor Parke Custis Lewis, for her part, happily made her way to New York. Martha Washington's granddaughter and George Washington's "Beautiful Nelly" traveled from Virginia to see Lafayette and reunite with Georges, her "beloved brother," whom she had last seen in 1797, when he left Mount Vernon. At the time, Nelly was one of the most privileged and remarkable young women in America. She was intelligent, fluent in multiple languages, and talented—and she was not unaccustomed, from behind the piano, to providing music at congressional parties, though she thought little of the politicians themselves.

She was witty, beautiful, and curious, even sharing her step-grandfather's passion for agriculture. It was Nelly who left one of the most striking impressions on visitors to the Washington home.[27] After the architect Benjamin Latrobe visited Mount Vernon in 1788, he wrote that Nelly "has more perfection of form, of expression, of color, of softness, and firmness of mind than I have ever seen before or conceived consistent with mortality."[28] While she grew close and fond of young Lafayette, she also left no doubt of the parameters of that relationship. "I shall ever feel an interest & sincere regard for my young adopted Brother—but as to being in love with him it is entirely out of the question."[29]

Since they had said farewell, they had not lost touch, trading letters, entertaining the hope they might one day meet again. "The time we passed together as allowed at Mount Vernon and in Phila, under the care of my lamented grandparents is indelibly impressed on my memory," she wrote him in 1821. Their French lessons and rides around Mount Vernon, she wrote, were "Frequently recalled to my memory, as though as if they had just now passed before me—nothing would give me more pleasure than to see you again."[30]

But when the two did reunite, the gay and brilliant young woman whom Georges had known was no more. A year after the younger Lafayette returned to France, she married Lawrence Lewis, one of Washington's nephews, a decade her senior. The turn of the century brought a string of losses, beginning with Washington in 1799, then her beloved grandmother, and, over the course of her life, seven of her eight children. "I look back with sorrow & and to the future with no hope," she wrote to Elizabeth Bordley Gibson, with whom she carried on an intimate correspondence for much of her life.[31] Gibson's father, John Beale Bordley, a Maryland planter, was an associate of Washington's.

The marriage to Lewis was cold; his mismanagement of their finances left the family impoverished and Nelly isolated on their plantation, Woodlawn, built near Mount Vernon on land Washington had given to the couple as a wedding gift. Nelly was now an embittered woman in middle age, who had lost interest in most of the things that had so captivated her as a girl. "I have forgotten my small stock of knowledge, and my music very much. Indeed I am a very humdrum character," she confessed to Bordley.[32] She was often sick—or imagined herself sick—suffering from headaches that she attempted to treat by dosing herself with Seidlitz powders while fixating on ever-distant memories of her past.

The return of the Lafayettes provided a moment of incredible excitement for Nelly. Perhaps even more than seeing the general again, whom she had met as a child when he had visited Mount Vernon in 1784, Nelly looked forward to the return of his son. "I should have the additional pleasure of seeing one who almost idolized the Gen'l & Grandmama, & the friend & brother of my happy days—George."[33] But this reunion coincided with another rendezvous that inevitably led to discord with another in the Lafayettes' ambit.

As the final preparations at Castle Garden were completed, several days of rain necessitated postponement—the event had originally been planned for September 10, then rescheduled for the 13th, and finally for the 14th. Two travelers recently arrived in New York believed there was another motivation for the rescheduling. On September 11, after forty days at sea following their departure from Le Havre, Frances and Camilla Wright arrived in New York. Late that evening, Lafayette welcomed them at the home of former mayor Cadwallader D. Colden, where they lodged in the city. To her cousin James Mylne, Camilla Wright claimed Lafayette "had anxiously been awaiting our arrival for some days that we might be present at the grand festivity given in his honor by the city, and he had thro' various ways procured its delay and thus afforded us one of the most splendid and gratifying sights I ever before witnessed."[34]

This assertion—that Lafayette had conspired to delay such an intricately planned event—was fanciful, though perhaps Lafayette, whose very first letters upon reaching the American shore expressed his anticipation of reuniting with the Wrights, led them to believe that was the case. Camilla's claim, on the other hand, that the fête at Castle Garden was one of the most stupendous events she had ever seen, was no doubt true. On the day of the ball, September 14, Lafayette wrote to his daughter-in-law, Émilie, at La Grange, "The Americans' kindnesses have not let up one day, even one hour, since our arrival. And everything that's in store heralds the most touching and honorable continuation of these kindnesses."[35] This, though, when it came to the ball at Castle Garden, at least, was an understatement. He might have added "extravagant."

"To give an adequate description, at any time, would be impossible," wrote a New York reporter, "and, at present, a very feeble sketch indeed must serve to convey an idea of a festival, which realizes all that we read of in the Persian Tales or Arabian Nights, which dazzled the eye and bewildered the imagination, and which produced so many powerful combinations, by magnificent preparations, as to set description almost at defiance."[36]

Outside the fortress, two passageways, one built to accommodate carriages, the other for foot traffic, were filled. On a terrace wrapping around the building, hundreds more stepped off steamboats. "We never saw ladies more brilliantly dressed" wrote the *New-York Evening Post*.[37] They wore headdresses of flowers and ostrich feathers, gowns of lace, gloves embossed with Lafayette's image, sashes with his likeness around their waists, and, hung from chains around their necks, medallions engraved with his bust; men brandished the medals as well, only from a chain slipped through the button hole of their coats.[38]

After guests surrendered their ticket to the officer waiting on the bridge, they were guided by gas lamps, throwing off only enough light to create an air of mystery, to the castle's entrance. Somewhere beyond the entrance, the faint sound of a band playing provided the score. Inside was a giant wood-framed, illuminated pyramid with a glowing star on its peak and an arch supporting a statue of George Washington. The rush of guests in front of it created a bottleneck leading to the entrance. The author James Fenimore Cooper, who had secured a ticket to the event and recorded his experiences for the American newspaper the morning after, feared the rush portended a smothering crowd inside the castle. "But though so many poured along the approaches, like water gushing though some narrow passage," he wrote, "the rush, the crowd, and the inconvenience ceased as you entered the principal space, like the tumult of that element subsiding as it merges into a broad basin."[39]

Thousands of revelers were inside, dancing quadrilles, looking down from the seats suspended on the ledge, or leaning over the fort's belvedere. Cooper, digesting this image, halted for a minute, "gazing around us and upwards with wonder." Then he looked around to see so many others stunned by the transformation of the fortress. "When first we stepped within the magic limits of the circle—where we had often before placed our chair upon the green grass and smoked our segar beneath the moonlight sky," wrote one correspondent, "the light that burst upon us caused a thrill through our system, and we started back in absolute surprise."[40] Overcoming their awe, partygoers wandered the circle as the West Point band played, while servants in livery provided refreshments in a brick building near the castle's portal. Near its own entrance was displayed a giant painting of Lady Liberty. Treats included a giant-pyramid-shaped cake, *Ever Welcome La Fayette* inscribed on in sugar plums.

When Lafayette arrived at 10:00 p.m., the commotion in Castle Garden froze. The dances concluded, and the crowd formed in two long columns. Between them passed Lafayette, greeting each man and woman. "He was literally like a father among his children," Cooper wrote.[41] At this moment, the curtains draped around the side of the castle opened, revealing the spectacle beyond its walls: thousands of boats gathered on the moonlit Hudson to observe the scene from afar. Once Lafayette had reached the canopy built as a station for his suite, the painting of Liberty was retracted and replaced with a brilliant illumination of La Grange, with the words *HIS HOME*.

He remained there for several hours, often at the center of spontaneous dances that followed him around the castle. Then, at two in the morning, he broke away, exited the castle, and boarded the *James Kent*, provided by its owners, the North River Steamboat Company, who had also offered free admission for members of the Cincinnati to join Lafayette on his trip north to visit West Point. They were joined by numerous other guests, including Alexander Hamilton Jr. and his mother, Elizabeth; the Wright sisters; and Nelly Lewis. The boat, which one observer resembled "an enchanted castle upon the waters," lifted anchor and steamed away; a crush of partygoers pressed against the battlement to bid it farewell with cheers. Back inside the castle, dancing continued. "We hazard nothing in saying," the *New York Evening Post* wrote the following day, "that it was the most magnificent fete, given under cover, in the world."[42]

"The 14th was the famous ball of Castle Garden, which will still be spoken about in New York after four generations as though a miracle," Levasseur wrote.[43] For the younger Frenchmen, it was all too much, the attention exhausting. When the transparency of La Grange was revealed, Lafayette's secretary found himself oddly depressed. "I don't know why, but the view of these good old towers, for which we have sometimes let out deep sighs, did not contribute to developing my gaiety; and I would have been quite happy if, instead of walking as though I were some curiosity in front of the groups of women, I had been permitted to go daydream a little in a small corner. It seemed to me that good Georges was more or less of the same disposition."[44]

To his daughter Anastasie, Lafayette described the *James Kent* as a boat "where one feels like one is in a floating hotel."[45] Still, he, his son, and secretary shared a cabin with ten women, with only five beds between and a tricolor petition separating them. While the passengers on the other side of the divide conversed loudly into the early morning, Levasseur and Georges left to find quiet outside. This proved impossible, as the merriment of Castle Garden had followed them up the river. The boat was full of drunk revelers, still in their ball costumes on deck, where they "wander like shadows and murmur for beds." The band, also inebriated, "seem to find pleasure in awakening the echoes of the Hudson." Cannon blasts periodically announced the passing of a town on the river. The partiers awoke in the morning, hungover and stranded. The pilot drove the boat into a sandbank in the wee hours and it was only dislodged by the tide after a three-hour delay. When the *James Kent* was again on its way, it was against the current, going six miles an hour.[46]

Day broke with Levasseur contemplating the Hudson Highlands, the mountain range framing the Hudson River. "Nothing is more imposing, in a word," he wrote, "as the sight of the high mountains, by turns wooded and rocky, which embanks the river in nearly its whole length."[47] This country was stunning to his secretary but was not new to Lafayette, who had passed through the Hudson Valley during the Revolution and visited West Point, then in disrepair, with Washington in the autumn of 1780. More than four decades later, he recognized the mansion across the Hudson: the home of Benedict Arnold and his wife, Peggy, where he had double-crossed the American army. Memories returned of the moment Lafayette had seen tears fall down Washington's cheek upon learning of the general's treason. No passage of time could ease the pain of betrayal. Lafayette and the other old veterans stood on the deck of the *James Kent* and cursed Arnold's name once more.

When Lafayette had inspected West Point in 1780, it was, much to Washington's irritation, a dilapidated fort. In 1824, it was home to a military academy with an enrollment of two hundred cadets. When the boat arrived at noon, a reporter on board wrote that there was "more bustle and confusion than there had been before witnesses on the Point, since the army of the revolution."[48] Lafayette disembarked, followed by the aged veterans and the rest of his party, and was greeted by cadets. He observed their drills, visited their library, and, after dining with them in their mess, was gone again. On the *James Kent*'s way north up the Hudson, men and women lined both banks as the sun set; villages fired cannon salutes and citizens fashioned their own salutes with gunpowder. "There, General, I give you the best I can!" one man yelled after blasting a shot from his musket from the riverbank.[49]

The delay on the sandbank, plus an overlong visit to West Point, had greatly slowed Lafayette's progress up the Hudson. He was expected in Newburgh by 4:00 p.m. The townspeople, who had prepared a banquet—at the center of the table was a thirty-pound loaf of bread, prepared by the local baker—grew impatient. "The tables were set, the wine barrels were drilled, the sun had gone down, and the General had not appeared," Levasseur wrote. As the hours passed with no sign of Lafayette, food and wine eased the people of Newburgh's anxiety. "First a small bite was eaten, then a small sip to help the bite go down, then a second sip and a third sip, until finally so many sips one lost count." By the time the *James Kent* arrived, "the mayor, the citizens, the militia, and the ladies were in the Lord's vineyards."[50]

Lafayette arrived late to a scene of celebratory pandemonium. So wild was the ride from the water to the town center, Levasseur thought the horses pulling their carriages, distressed by the boom of welcoming cannons, were perhaps also inebriated. One hundred mounted militia rushed them to the local hotel where the town's mayor waited to deliver a speech. Only he could not remember its words, "his tongue and his memory denied each other the mutual support that they both needed," Levasseur wrote. "The poor man could scratch at his ears and rummage in his pockets as he much as he wanted, but his speech was gone for good." Lafayette was then forced to deliver an impromptu response to an address the mayor was unable to deliver. No matter: Lafayette's speech was then drowned out by wild applause and booming cannons, which in turn rendered most of the remarks inaudible. As they cheered wildly, the people of Newburgh turned to one another and whispered, "What is he saying? I can't hear anything."[51]

Inside the hotel, Lafayette was directed to the giant banquet table and beckoned to join his hosts' intoxicated revelry. Absolutely not, insisted the committee of New Yorkers who accompanied him on the trip upriver. The party, all sober, would board the *James Kent* once more and depart for their next destination rather than join the debauchery. The offended (and drunk) citizens of Newburgh protested loudly. A shouting match erupted with Lafayette's travel companions. "He is ours!" a man yelled. "He is national property!" roared another. "He will bless our children!" yelled the next. "The sun needs to see him in Newburgh!" one pleaded. Several men then dashed out of the hotel and began to scream, "They want to take the General from us, our brother, our friend!"[52]

The militia, alarmed, appeared at the hotel door, preparing to draw their sabers, swearing Lafayette would not be taken from them. Then the citizens of Newburgh appeared behind them, determined to break into the hotel to prevent Lafayette from leaving. Now, the militia, previously determined to detain him, was forced instead to protect him. In a bizarre drunken reenactment of the October Days, when Lafayette stood on a balcony at Versailles with Marie Antoinette before the angry crowd of Parisians, the mayor stumbled his way onto a balcony of the hotel with the Nation's Guest and shined a torch in his face. "Your conduct distresses him!" he screamed at the mob. The crowd grew silent and repentant. Representatives from the rabble were sent to apologize to the mayor. All consented to release Lafayette, though only on the condition that on his way back to the river, the townspeople be allowed to array themselves in his path and touch his hand.[53]

"We descend to the bank, but what a touching picture along our route!" wrote Levasseur. "The whole dismayed population bows before him whom they tremble at having offended, they ask him pardon, and passionately kiss his hands or his clothes."[54] It was not until midnight that the *James Kent* was back on its way up the Hudson. Its passengers were now quite weary. "Four hours of agitation among the good folk of Newburgh had given us great need of rest," Levasseur admitted. At Newburgh many of the passengers who had traveled up the Hudson, including the Wrights and Lewis, returned to New York aboard the

Chancellor Livingston, which had arrived from Albany, which Lafayette reached on the evening of the 17th after stops at Poughkeepsie and Hudson.[55]

In New York's capital, where the party arrived on September 17, Clinton waited with an honorary membership to the Literary and Philosophical Society—of which he was, of course, the president—and an invitation to travel six miles from Albany to Troy on the Erie Canal. The former governor, Levasseur observed, looked like a future president: "It is difficult to have at the same time a more imposing stature and more noble character."[56]

They boarded several galleys, one with Lafayette and local dignitaries, another with a handful of adoring citizens, and a third with a band, whose music was the only sound audible. Men and women lined both sides of the canal, and carriages filled the streets in the distance. The first two boats were each drawn by six horses, their riders outfitted in blue jackets and white trousers. Passing by the arsenal in Gibbonsville, where a salute was fired from cannons appropriated from the British at Yorktown, the procession then moved through the side cut, connecting the canal with the Hudson. From there, it was towed across to the eastern bank of the river to Troy.

In 1778, when Lafayette had last ridden through Troy, it was little more than a collection of cottages; one could scarcely find a "cup of milk or piece of cornbread," as he recalled to his fellow passengers. Now it was a town populated by some eight thousand people and a growing commercial hub of the state, home to shipyards, paper mills, and soap makers, as well as libraries, schools, a printing press, and newspapers. "Is this City one which has just sprung from the ground by magic?" Lafayette asked as he reached Troy. "No," one of his traveling companions answered, "but it was created and populated in a few years by industry protected by liberty."[57]

Especially interesting to Lafayette in Troy, though, was a two-story schoolhouse where young women were taught languages, painting, mathematics, history, and philosophy—subjects widely considered by American society unsuited to the "fairer sex." Not only did the young women at the Troy Female Seminary study these subjects, but they were also taught by female teachers. The founder of this academy was Emma Willard, a self-schooled intellectual well-versed in the works of Euclid, who rejected the idea that women were limited in their endeavors or in what their education could entail. The academy was her brainchild and mission.

In her book *A Plan for Improving Female Education*, Willard argued that women were by nature "not the satellites of men."[58] To support her assertion, she opened an all-female academy in Waterford, Connecticut. The local government provided little assistance, and she relocated the academy to Troy in 1821. Clinton, who was governor at the time, encouraged Willard's endeavor with his usual farsightedness. The town's corporation raised money through taxes and subscriptions, helping fund the school and raise a brick building to house it. By 1824, nearly two hundred women—the daughters of well-to-do families—were enrolled. For Lafayette's arrival, the students had constructed a wooden arbor, decorated it with evergreens and flowers, and placed it in the front of the building. Lafayette, unaccompanied by any members of his party, passed through it and up a flight of stairs leading to the school, where Willard was waiting to greet him. Then, the students, accompanied by their music instructor on piano, performed a song written by their principal for the occasion. Its chorus proclaimed:

> *Then deep and dear they welcome be;*
> *Not think thy daughters far from thee:*
> *Columbia's daughters, lo! We bend,*
> *And claim to call thee Father, Friend!*[59]

When Lafayette descended the stairs and departed, the students—all wearing white—walked him to the school's gate. In his hands, he held copies of the song for his daughters as well as Willard's book, and tears glittered in his eyes.

Levasseur, to whom all the signs of American enlightenment were astonishing and novel, believed these institutions could serve as a model. Should Europeans replicate them, they too would be free and virtuous, he foresaw. "I am so convinced of this truth that if I ever marry, and if I have a son, and if liberty has still not been established in my unfortunate country, I vow to send him to spend some time in this country," he wrote to Émilie. "I am persuaded that so long as he has this disposition to goodness, he will return a true man."[60]

After returning to Albany late on the night of September 18, the *James Kent* began its journey back down the Hudson, arriving in New York on the 20th. The next day, Lafayette penned a letter to Mathieu Dumas, once Rochambeau's aide during the American Revolution and ally during France's, reflecting on what he had seen after a month in America. "You cannot imagine how I was struck by the miracle wrought here by forty-eight years of independence, instruction in government, and liberty," he wrote from New York. "It surpasses my imagination, I know. What would France be today, if our revolution of '89 had kept its original direction!"[61]

When at last he departed New York—whose parties, banquets, parades, and demonstrations had delayed an already compressed schedule (celebrations were also planned in Philadelphia, Baltimore, and Washington)—Lafayette left tearful New Yorkers behind. He crossed the Hudson, was received by jubilant New Jerseyans, passed through Newark, reached Trenton, and sojourned in Bordertown on the Delaware River, on Sunday, September 25.

There, on the banks of the Delaware River, in an opulent home filled with treasures—including statues by Antonio Canova and paintings by Jacques Louis David—connected to its many outbuildings by a system of tunnels, buttressed by a large park and man-made lake, lived Joseph Bonaparte, brother of the fallen emperor, in his melancholy exile. Though Joseph, the oldest of the six Bonaparte children, had more interest in gardening and collecting art than statesmanship, he had served as a diplomat for his brother Napoleon and later as the commander of the Army of Naples.

When Napoleon's army vacated the throne of the Two Sicilies, he placed his brother atop it, who in turn proved a popular and effective monarch. When victories on the battlefield brought more territory, Napoleon moved Joseph to another throne, this one in Spain. There,

Spaniards resenting the rule of a Corsican outsider rendered his reign disastrous. With Napoleon's defeat at Waterloo in 1815, Joseph, now disguised as the fictional Comte de Survilliers, escaped to America. He eventually settled in Bordentown because of its location between Philadelphia and New York and built his mansion, Point Breeze. The estate became a gathering place for French soldiers who had also fled after the Bourbon restoration. Americans, initially wary of the brother of the loathed Bonaparte, came to admire Joseph and his mansion.

Though gracious and pleased to see Lafayette, Bonaparte was a sad figure. "His fortune is considerable, his family cherishes him; however, he does not seem happy," wrote Levasseur. During Lafayette's visit, Joseph opened the doors of Point Breeze, welcoming the locals—whom Levasseur described as "rustics." In they streamed, paying little notice to the gallery of fine art, instead fixating on the Nation's Guest and leaving most happily after shaking his hand or introducing him to their children.[62]

"We made a little visit the day before yesterday to Joseph Bonaparte, who was very pleasant, but whose ego might have suffered a bit because as soon as the General entered his home the house was invaded by a large number of inhabitants from the neighboring countryside," Levasseur wrote to Émilie.[63] "These good people were so occupied with the joy of seeing the object of their veneration that they seemed not at all to suspect they were in a royal house. I saw the moment when the prince was knocked off his feet by the crowd who wanted to see and touch the General."[64]

At various times during his exile in America, which lasted nearly two decades, Bonaparte was offered opportunities by visiting emissaries to assume to the kingship of Mexico. This he had little interest in; instead, he preferred to remain in America, admiring its republican institutions—the same ones responsible for the transformation that so stunned Lafayette.

The arrival of his French guests left Bonaparte torn between maintaining a reserve befitting a king and readily engaging with his countrymen. When he introduced Lafayette and his companions to his daughter and son-in-law, Bonaparte did so hesitatingly, wanting to call them the princess and prince but resisting for fear of being derided. "Finally, fatigued with his position, he offered his arm to the General and led him, full of vivacity, to a neighboring room."[65] Georges and Levasseur waited outside for an hour while Lafayette and Bonaparte commiserated over the fate of France and wondered how popular rights may be won there and work the wonders they had in America.[66]

8

—— ≈ ——

Where Independence Was Declared

On the evening of March 24, 1824, while Lafayette was planning his visit to America, four men broke into the old State House on Chestnut Street in Philadelphia. They entered through a room on the first floor of the redbrick Georgian building, where the Mayor's Court announced verdicts in civil cases. Once inside, they stacked benches and chairs against the wooden walls and lit the pile ablaze.[1]

It was only by good fortune that a man walking home from the theater spotted the fire and alerted the city's authorities. The flames were doused, and the structure was saved. For the old building, it was another chapter in a long story of defying destruction.

When the $300 reward for information leading to the arrest of the arsonists was published, it reported that the fire was set by "some incendiary or incendiaries for the purpose of destroying that most ancient and useful building (the State House)."[2] As evidence, it mentioned the museum housed on its second floor but not the room on its first.

It was in front of this building, after a weeks-long journey from South Carolina in the summer of 1777, that Lafayette came to pledge his fortune and risk his life to secure the American independence declared inside its walls the year before. Lafayette had wondered if he would ever return to America; there was reason to believe that if he did and found his way once more to Philadelphia, the old State House would no longer be standing.

In the summer of 1776, America's independence was declared here in a room leased from Pennsylvania's colonial government. Fifteen years later, the Constitutional Convention designed the architecture of a new government within the same walls. But in the years before 1824, it was mostly just walls that remained.

For decades, demolitions were planned, but reprieves always came. The building remained, purposeless, its past storied, its future uncertain. Viewed from Chestnut Street, it had changed little over the years. Extensions were added, subtracted, and added again over the decades. The wooden steeple, rotting for years, was gone. New trees were planted, and benches were placed in the yard to its south.

As a measure of the success of the experiment launched in this building nearly fifty years before, a population had grown up and spread west. A rising nation had little interest in nostalgia and priorities greater than preserving its history.

Philadelphia's spell as the center of American political life ended when the federal government decamped for a new site on the Potomac River in 1800. The city's time as a state capital concluded the year before. As its population drifted toward the Allegheny Mountains, Pennsylvania's government searched for more central locations, moving to new homes: first to Lancaster and then to Harrisburg.

Over the years, new residents came to and went from the building. State and local courts sat in the first-floor room from whose walls militiamen had ripped and then burned King George's coat of arms after hearing the Declaration of Independence. Artist and entrepreneur Charles Willson Peale set up his museum of wonders in the long gallery on the second floor. Where wounded soldiers had once convalesced during the Revolution now stood a stuffed grizzly, the skeleton of a woolly mammoth, and an extensive collection of insects and birds, along with portraits of notable Americans.

Other parts of the complex were converted to accommodate records storage, requiring modernization and fireproofing: In 1812,

Philadelphia, with the state's approval, demolished and replaced the fifty-foot wings and colonnaded arcades that connected them to the main building. Collateral damage included the small room on the southeast corner of the building, which housed a library of history, literature, and English statutes, as well as a towering clock case built into the west wall.

Four years later, searching for $150,000 to finance construction of its new statehouse on the Susquehanna River, Pennsylvania's legislature approved of a plan to demolish its old one. The land under and around it would then be divided into parcels and auctioned off for commercial development. Whatever was left standing inside—lumber, and even the copper bell presumed to have rung during reading of the Declaration of Independence—would be auctioned off.

William Duane, editor of the *Philadelphia Aurora*, unhappily took note of what was about to be lost. "In the spirit of ancient times, or of that virtue which ought to govern at all times," he wrote, "the building in which the Declaration of Independence was deliberated and determined, would obtain veneration the most sensible and endearing, as a monument of that splendid event."[3]

Others agreed. Financier Nicholas Biddle, a Pennsylvania state senator and the scion of a storied Philadelphia family, future president of the Second Bank of the United States, slipped a stay of execution into the bill sealing the State House's fate: For $70,000, Philadelphia could buy the decaying old building.

Confronted with the prospect of losing the landmark and encouraged by Duane, the city launched a subscription and raised the necessary funds. In 1818, Philadelphia took ownership of the Old State House. The cradle of American liberty would live on. But salvation and preservation were two different matters.

While the transaction was being completed, a city commissioner, providing a family member employment, authorized a virtual dismantling of the Assembly Room. The intricate cornices were sawed off, the planked floors ripped up, the pine walls and paneling stripped. The room where America was born became unrecognizable and useless.

In the summer of 1824, it found purpose once more.

"What is occurring here seems to me a dream," Auguste Levasseur wrote to Émilie Lafayette from the Frankfort Armory, north of Philadelphia. "Can you imagine," he asked, "that an entire population, without excepting a single individual, be so struck with such a profound feeling of gratitude for the services rendered by a man that it has never seen, and who is for it ancient history? That its enthusiasm is forever growing? That the most active and hardworking people all of a sudden abandon their occupations to follow, across roads of very long distance, the one whom everyone calls with pride the father of the country, the guest of the nation? It's something stated up to this day, and I don't think one could find anywhere in history anything like it."[4]

Even so, he could not have imagined what awaited Lafayette in Philadelphia. If New York had aspired to host the greatest fête in American history, Philadelphia, not to be outdone, would reach back into history—both recent and ancient—to fashion its own celebration, so powerful it would soon be emulated elsewhere along Lafayette's journey and recalled long after it had concluded.

On August 21, while Lafayette made his way toward Boston, a crowd gathered in a yard outside the old State House. Responding to a notice in the papers, Philadelphia's citizens met to determine an appropriate means of welcoming Lafayette to their city. Their government had already passed a resolution of invitation, sent to Lafayette by its mayor, Joseph Watson, in July, in anticipation of his arrival. Three days after he reached New York, Lafayette accepted, declaring his desire to return to "the illustrious city, where so glorious scenes of the Revolution have taken place, and where I have passed so many happy days," promising a mid-September arrival. This was delayed by the excursions into New England and up the Hudson.[5]

The invitation from the mayor was not quite enough. When Philadelphians met in the old State House yard, it was to plan a welcoming celebration for Lafayette arranged not by a civil authority but by Philadelphia's citizens, to better correspond with his republican feelings. A celebration "as may become a Free People to offer, and a distinguished Friend of the Rights of Man to *accept*."[6] A committee of twenty-one citizens was formed, led by Thomas Leiper, a Revolutionary

War veteran and businessman who had constructed the first experimental railway in Pennsylvania. The publisher Mathew Carey and Thomas Biddle—younger brother of Nicholas, hero of the War of 1812, and explorer of the West—also participated. Their first proposals were to illuminate the city on the evening before Lafayette's arrival and to encourage citizens to wear revolutionary cockades or Lafayette badges on the occasion.

For their chapter of the national celebration, Philadelphia chose to cite its own history: On July 4, 1788, shortly after the Constitution was ratified by the requisite ten states, Philadelphia staged a procession to celebrate the new beginning for the republic as well as the anniversary of its independence. Artisans and laborers—fifty-eight separate guilds representing the city's manufacturers—paraded through the city streets in a procession rich with symbolism. At its vanguard marched a flank of men clutching axes, a reminder of the now forever severed relationship with Great Britain. Farther back in the ranks, ten men joined arms, symbolizing the linkage of the Union and the first ten states to ratify the Constitution, while an enormous bald eagle was carried on a float.[7]

Additional inspiration echoed the self-comparison common in the early decades of the fledgling republic to its predecessors in Greece and Rome. This manifested in the names of towns and the Grecian designs of the buildings on their streets. Though the national capital had removed to a new location on the Potomac, and New York was the rising industrial center of the nation, Philadelphia—often identified as the "the Athens of America"—could still lay claim to be its cultural center, home to artisans, institutions, and flourishing neighborhoods.[8]

Philadelphia's planners merged the earlier parade and inspiration from the ancients to create a celebration for their city and the era. They purposely evoked the Roman military procession, the *triumphus*: At war's end, the victorious general was escorted into the city, drawn by a chariot, trailing along the spoils of war, prisoners, and treasure, terminating at the Temple of Jupiter on the Capitoline Hill.

Philadelphia would create a republican, civic variant of this ritual (given the area's Quaker population, martial aspects were downplayed) with Lafayette in the role of the conquering hero. Instead of bringing the spoils of war into Philadelphia, he would be accompanied by the free citizens of Philadelphia—its artisans and laborers, members of its civic associations, and surviving veterans of the Revolution—through its prospering neighborhoods, concluding in front of a temple of a distinctly American sort: the one in whose shadows the planners had sat.

As the Committee of Arrangements laid out its plan to prepare Philadelphia for Lafayette's arrival, they conceived the idea of using the east room of the old State House as the space to welcome Lafayette. Once installed in the room, any citizen who wished to meet him could do so in the very place where independence was declared. The job of refurbishing the east room was given to one of the committee members, William Strickland, a native Philadelphian. His early career included a tempestuous internship with Benjamin Latrobe; the assignment ended when Strickland abandoned work for a fishing trip. Unreliable though he may have been, the boy, Latrobe recognized, was a gifted artist. For a time, he painted theater scenery alongside Hugh Reinagle, who had helped prepare Castle Garden for Lafayette's great ball in New York, before returning to Philadelphia, where he earned several high-profile commissions—none more prestigious than the Greek Revival Second Bank of the United States, inspired by the Parthenon and completed prior to Lafayette's arrival.

On August 19, with little more than a month to execute the task, the Committee of Arrangements resolved that the east room of the State House be "fitted up as a hall of reception and audience" for Lafayette and directed Strickland to proceed immediately to prepare the space for its guest.[9] The ceilings were painted a stone shade and the windows covered with scarlet and blue drapery embroidered with stars. Elegant mahogany furniture was placed about the room.

The sculptor William Rush offered use of his statue of George Washington. The committee accepted, and Strickland placed it at the end of the room in an alcove once occupied by the Speaker of the first session of Congress. A blue star was hung behind it, hanging on with spears and wreaths. Around the room were placed portraits of revolutionaries—Jefferson, Adams, Robert Morris, Hancock, Madison, Monroe, and the late Charles Thomson. Above the entrance hung another likeliness of Washington, a portrait loaned by Rembrandt Peale, who had balked at the hanging of his painting anywhere else in the room—"it is of too much importance to me to have this Picture in a good situation and light when Lafayette shall see it, to suffer it to be placed in any secondary place where its appearance would be injured and its character undervalued."[10] From a vacant room to a shrine of independence—indeed, even the committee, in its minutes, soon referred to the room as the Hall of Independence. In the weeks preceding Lafayette's arrival, Philadelphians increasingly used this moniker when describing the building.[11] In truth, it resembled less the modest room in which independence was declared than a richly ornamented tribute to the men who had declared and won it.

Lafayette would walk into the building with appropriate pomp: The committee requested Strickland build a civic arch under which the Nation's Guest, at the completion of his triumphant procession, would pass. Collaborating with his assistant, Samuel Honeyman Kneass, Strickland looked to the ancients for guidance. He took inspiration from the Roman Arch of Septimius Severus, which commemorated the conquests of its namesake emperor. But here Strickland aimed not simply to copy but to surpass.

A wooden frame, forty-five feet across and twelve feet deep, was built. Then a canvas measuring nearly three thousand square feet was stretched over the structure and painted to resemble marble by the scene painters of Philadelphia's New Theatre. Spandrels on each side of the arch were filled with statues of Fame clutching wreaths. In niches as the center of the arch were the figures of Liberty, Independence, Plenty, and Victory. Atop the arch was placed a large entablature featuring the city's coat of arms, with Justice and Wisdom, sculpted by Rush, on each side. At its highest point, the arch was thirty-eight feet above the pavement on Chestnut Street, where it was placed in front of the State House.

The flurry of activity around the old building was only one movement of the symphony heard across Philadelphia. "Our streets resound with the notes of preparation," a local correspondent reported four days before Lafayette's arrival. "The noise of the hammer and the axe, and the sound of the trumpet and the drum. And the spirit-stirring fife, are the be heard on our streets."[12]

The Committee of Arrangements was besieged with requests and suggestions. A man who claimed to have served with Lafayette asserted that, as a Frenchman, only he was fluent in the dancing styles of Paris. Therefore, he argued, he should be given oversight of the ball planned for the night after Lafayette's arrival. "I can assure you, sir, that I feel myself fully capable and more than any other person in this place to direct this ball in the French style, which will no doubt please the General," he wrote. He also took the chance to advertise that he had composed a waltz and cotillion, both named in Lafayette's honor, of course.[13]

Another Philadelphian, revealing an increasing competition between cities in their reception of the Nation's Guest, pleaded with the committee to remove the sign advertising Peale's museum in front of the State House, lest "the New Yorkers and others will say that you put La Fayette in the Philadelphia Museum."[14] Franklin Peale, son of Charles, wrote to inform the committee that a plan to close their museum on the occasion of Lafayette's arrival at the State House would cost their enterprise $250, for which he requested compensation. If they were allowed to open after his arrival, he suggested, $50 could be deducted from the total.[15]

Would-be caterers offered refreshments—tea, coffee, chocolate, chicken salads, lobsters, and various jellies—for the ball.[16] After a meeting at the house of one John Miller, a number of Revolutionary officers and soldiers rejected the committee's offer of $25 to defray the cost of the music they arranged for Lafayette's arrival. They declared they "will procure such as they can for themselves although many of them unable to contribute any thing to defray the expense."[17]

There were suggestions on the proper route to take Lafayette to the State House and debates over the proper means of conveying him there. The matter of the carriage and horses designated to bring Lafayette into the city required detailed planning, right down to the livery of the drivers. There was anxiety among some of the planners that the postilions be American. Rumors circulated that the riders would be "Englishmen, and on that account objectionable."[18] There was even an anonymous request, inspired by a perceived lack of attention in the eastern cities, for a proper show of respect to Georges Washington de Lafayette. "Please to have him duly honored when he comes among us—he is the son of La Fayette and the namesake of Washington."[19]

Along the route designated for Lafayette to enter the city, bleachers were built, with seats on them offered for $5. Portraits, all dissimilar yet all claiming to be *the* likeness of the general, were sold. The engine of Lafayette entrepreneurship was fired: "His name was applied to ever thing; we had Lafayette hats, Lafayette coats, Lafayette birches, Lafayette gloves," a Philadelphian wrote. There were even, for especially daring women, garters available emblazoned with "*ne plus ultra.*"[20]

Mr. Bonnaffon rented out the Masonic Hall, installed gas lights and life-size illuminations of Washington and Lafayette, and charged $2 a head.[21] Loud & Brothers, instrument manufacturers, built and then donated a piano forte to the Committee of Arrangements for Lafayette's use, should he like to play the instrument. A series of quickly written biographies were available in stores across the city. One shop, Carey and Lea, offered *Lafayette in the Castle of Olmütz*, a melodrama in three acts.[22]

Food was in such demand for the balls and dinners planned for the occasion there was even Lafayette inflation: The price of butter jumped from 12 cents per pound to 33; eggs went from 10 to 20 cents. There were no rooms available in the city or its adjoining districts; never before had Philadelphia received such a sudden and immense influx of visitors. "You would not have recognized Philadelphia so extraordinary was the change. It was in fact more like an immense fair, and unlike anything that was ever seen here before," wrote a resident.[23]

Sunrise on the morning of September 28 brought with it a flurry of activity across the city and its northern suburbs, Kensington and the Liberties. Artillery battalions and militias gathered on Arch Street, the State House yard, or on the corner of Sixth and Vine Streets. The city's mechanics assembled at Maguires Hotel. Soldiers sprinted to their designed rendezvous; companies formed, veterans of the Revolution fixed cockades to their hats and badges to their breasts. Citizens, hours in advance, wearing their finest clothes, secured their spots atop balconies and on bleachers. One by one the companies departed on the march north to meet their guest at Rush Field, a fifty-four-acre parade ground a few miles above the city.

Upon their arrival, the troops formed a square and waited, along with the thousands of spectators beyond the field, for Lafayette's arrival from the federal arsenal at Frankford, where he had spent the previous night. This was announced minutes after 10:00 a.m. by the sound of trumpets and excited shouts. Then came a stunning entrance: The barouche carrying Lafayette was yellow with a cream cloth lining and azure trim; its horses were cream colored as well. The drivers, postilions, and outriders all wore blue jackets and buckskin trousers. When the vehicle came to a stop and Lafayette stepped to the ground, it was on a summit in the field, allowing a perspective of the troops arrayed before him and the thousands of civilians. There was the presentation of arms, and Lafayette, supported by Pennsylvania governor John A. Shulze and General Thomas Cadwalader, walked along reviewing the troops and bowing to the citizens who came forward to meet him. The crowd parted only when a single Revolutionary veteran emerged in their midst to clasp Lafayette's hand.

It was not until one in the afternoon that he climbed back into his barouche, seated next to Richard Peters, a member of the Continental Board of War as well as the Continental Congress, and U.S. judge for the District of Pennsylvania, and set out for Philadelphia, the triumphant general destined for the temple of liberty with his treasure. Before Lafayette in the procession were the various companies of militia in their brilliant uniforms, executing their maneuvers flawlessly. Following his path, behind the carriage carrying Georges and Levasseur, were three carriages carrying soldiers of the Revolution, *Defenders of our Country* and *The Survivors of '76* painted on their sides.

Then, joining the procession on a bridge near Kensington were the civic associations, the professional guilds, and the evidence of industry of free people and equality: Heads of state marched in line with laborers and farmers, old veterans and young soldiers, artists and priests. The printers carried a press atop a float—bearing the inscription "freedom of the press protects all other freedoms"—from which members of their association plucked out copies of an "Ode to Lafayette" ("A RESCUED COUNTRY hymns thy name; a WORLD that thou hast made rejoice, Rejoices in thy fame") and tossed them to the crowd. One landed in Levasseur's carriage. He kept it, later sending it to La Grange.[24] Interspersed were the civic societies—the La Fayette Association, the Young Men of the city. Then came the Cordwainers in their aprons, the weavers with their banners and badges, the rope makers in their blue jackets and white trousers, carrying a banner with a ship sitting atop stocks. The mechanics, painters, coopers, making casks atop their float, followed, along with the butchers, carpenters, and, finally, a long train of militia on white horses bringing up the rear.

The route, from the northern districts into the city, was a gauntlet of arches—a dozen, at least. The first, in Kensington, was itself bound by two smaller arches on the sidewalks. On one were inscriptions of welcome; on another, portraits of Washington and Franklin, alongside the flags of France and America. Near one arch were platforms on which stood twenty-four girls and twenty-four boys singing "See, the Conqu'ring Hero Comes!" As the procession crossed the Philadelphia city line, the USS *John Adams*, stationed at the wharf beyond Vine Street, fired its salute. The cannon boom competed with the sound of fife and drum and shouts of "Welcome, Lafayette!" The procession passed by the Chestnut Street home of the late Robert Morris, who had helped finance the Revolution and died in 1806. When Lafayette saw Morris's widow, Mary, standing in the window, he stood and bowed.

On Chestnut Street, Lafayette paused in front of the Bank of the United States, where another troop of Revolutionary veterans waited and saluted. Then the procession moved toward the State House, on its final leg, as women tossed wreaths from the sides of the street into his barouche. The vanguard turned and presented arms. Lafayette passed, then his carriage halted. He stepped down and stood again before the old State House.

Nearly half a century before, as an idealistic nineteen-year-old, he had arrived in Philadelphia a supplicant; now he returned a hero. Where he had once been dismissed by a peevish congressman, now he passed under Strickland's magnificent arch, over a carpeted platform, and into the Hall of Independence—resurrected in his honor and, in fact, preserved for generations to come because of his visit.

Georges and Levasseur were introduced first to the assembly; the former stood to the right of the mayor, Joseph Watson, the latter to his left. Minutes later, the boom of a cannon announced the entrance of Lafayette. He was shaken—overwhelmed by memories of his own past—as he saw the spot where the cause that had animated so much of his life had begun. "The feeling the General experienced upon first entering this hall, in which he met for the first time the magistrates of this rebellious people, was so intense that he could not hide it," Levasseur wrote.[25]

He was greeted by Mayor Watson, who, speaking at the feet of Rush's statue of Washington, offered a tribute, recalling that "Forty-eight years ago, in this City, in this very hall that one could justly call the cradle of independence," an assembly of Americans had altered history by choosing to govern their own destinies. Lafayette responded, remarking that it was "in this sacred enclosure that the independence of the United States was emphatically declared," before making a pointed wish that the liberty declared in the room where he now stood would reign over the entire "American hemisphere." There were happy reflections on the army formed in this room and the general appointed to lead it. "But these memories and a throng of others are mixed with the profound regret for the loss of men, great and good, for whom we have to mourn."[26]

At 6:15 p.m., the general illumination began. Nearly every public building and private home was ablaze with light; giant transparencies were lit, bonfires burned, and nearly two hundred thousand people—some who called Philadelphia home, others who had traveled far from their own to see Lafayette, if only for a moment—happily wandered into the streets, their faces illuminated by the glowing tribute.

"I can't end such a beautiful day without celebrating it with all my dear children. We arrived in Philadelphia today: we were received in the hall where independence was declared, which has been reserved for me and my receptions with the citizens of this beautiful and great city,"

Lafayette wrote his daughters that evening. "I have relived so many memories and felt such diverse emotions."[27]

Philadelphia surrendered the newly resurrected shrine to Lafayette for the remainder of his stay in their city; he, in turn, made himself available to its citizens. They made pilgrimages there to address him, hold his hand, or simply gaze at his face. The city's French residents, its clergy, its philosophical society, its veterans of the Revolution, and its young students—thousands of whom passed in review while Lafayette watched from the steps of Independence Hall—all came to pay their respects. Though they were forbidden from doing so, many of the young people defied the order and rushed up the steps to shake his hand.

"I had learned from the history of the revolution, to venerate the character of the youthful hero, who forsook the youthful delights of domestic enjoyment and the splendid and luxurious ease of a princely fortune, to share in the trials of a doubtful contest and risk his life in the sacred cause of liberty," one Philadelphian wrote after exiting Independence Hall, "but I never expected it was to fall to my lot to see the man, who had been so dear to our illustrious Washington, much less to grasp that hand which wielded the sword, so terrible to tyrants, yet I have enjoyed both."[28]

Fanny and Camilla Wright parted ways with their "father" during his trip up the Hudson River, then spent a week in Greenwich before leaving for Philadelphia and arriving in advance of Lafayette.[29] Though they traveled a discreet distance from him, Fanny did not go unnoticed. Sympathetic papers noted approvingly that the author of *Views of Society and Manners in America*, a book so flattering to the fledgling nation, was now again among Americans, in Lafayette's wake. The description of Wright as merely following Lafayette was inaccurate, however. She made her own impression in Philadelphia. "At a social gathering in that city Miss Wright stretched herself on a sofa, spoke little, and gave herself little or no trouble about anyone, now and then breaking out into detached sentences such as this, for example. 'I believe that bears have more value than men,'"[30] a later traveler across the states was told.

Fanny's second visit to America was not simply to shadow her adopted father. For example, Wright's return to America coincided with a visit from Jonathas Granville. A Haitian-born soldier who had fought for France in the Napoleonic Wars, Granville returned to Haiti during the Second Bourbon Restoration, where he assumed a diplomatic role, traveling to America to encourage free Blacks to immigrate to Port-au-Prince, with the aid of the Haitian government. Granville, who was mixed race, was dashing, eloquent, educated, handsome, and a persuasive advocate for his mission.

When Fanny heard he was in America, she invited Granville to come to Philadelphia and arranged a meeting with Lafayette in his quarters at the Mansion House. When their interview ended, Lafayette intentionally walked Granville through a crowded reception room to his hotel's stairs and gave him a warm farewell. This was a considerable gesture, as meeting publicly with a Black man defied prevailing prejudices. "The visit of this amiable man, whose character is peculiarly suited to the occasion, has I think already been of service," Fanny wrote. "A little more intercourse with men of his nation will I trust soon rub off (I speak of the Northern States) the degrading Prejudices against the color of their skin."[31]

John Quincy Adams, traveling east to Washington from Massachusetts after visiting his father, arrived in Philadelphia by the 2nd of October and immediately called on Lafayette at his lodgings at Mansion House. He recorded in his diary that during a dinner party he saw the "two Misses Wrights, maiden ladies, who have followed General Lafayette to this country."[32] While accompanying Adams to numerous dinners and receptions in Philadelphia, Lafayette maintained his strict avoidance of publicly discussing the presidential contest in which Adams was embroiled. "We are complete strangers to the national and electoral quarrels—there isn't a mention of them in front of us, and groups of people the most opposed to each other come together to celebrate us," he wrote to his daughter-in law, Émilie de Lafayette.[33]

But he could not entirely avoid politics. One of the early editorials, celebrating Lafayette's calming effect on a population so agitated by electioneering, suggested a proposal outlandish and yet indicative of the enraptured reaction to Lafayette's return: elect him to America's second-highest office. After all, one of the suggested candidates for the position was, for a time, the Swiss-born Albert Gallatin. "Indeed as to the latter," the commentary continued, mentioning the former treasury secretary, "if we should have to have a foreigner for Vice President, we should prefer putting La Fayette upon the ticket. HE has some claims. He fought his way to a clear title to American citizenship."[34]

The idea was not unpopular. "By the by, it has been said here that a feeling is prevailing in some of the Atlantic cities to make the Marquis Lafayette Vice-President," Henry Clay, who was not entirely uninterested in the office himself, wrote to his confidant Josiah S. Johnston. "Such a disposition of the office would be highly creditable to the national gratitude, if it could be made without any constitutional impediment."[35]

Such proposals—or even making Lafayette president—did not sit well with the general. "I was angered the other day by an article in a gazette that proposed to end discussions about the presidency by appointing the man who would win the most votes," he wrote his daughter-in-law. After all, "having come here for a visit, to gather the parties together around me, it would be very displeasing to me to have my name used against the diverse candidates . . . Thank god, the country is too well set up to require such a sacrifice from its old servants."[36]

Regardless of suggestions to install Lafayette in some high office, the populace was spellbound. "For the few days that the marquis remained here the most complete mental intoxication seized upon our community," a Philadelphian wrote. Some of this adoration found altruistic outlets: In Delaware, the women of Wilmington founded the Lafayette Asylum for Widows and Orphan Children. "This," one editor wrote, "is turning to good account the enthusiasm of the moment."[37]

To Levasseur, it was no longer a reunion of a long-separated son with his adopted country. "This is not the journey of a man, but the journey of a god for whose blessing everyone runs with alacrity. One need only touch his hands, his clothes. All the roads have been converted into triumphal arches draped with standards bearing the name of LF," he wrote to Émilie Lafayette.[38] "The women crown him with flowers, the men carry him in their arms, the soldiers pray for him to touch their hands. The mothers of families come to present their children to him, supplicating him for his blessing. Some call him their brother, others their father; all say 'He's the guest of the nation.' In the entire republic there is not a single individual who does not pay tribute of everything that he owns, proclaiming that 'we owe more than life to you, we owe you freedom.'"[39]

On the other hand, a few observers of the wild national celebration underway felt a sense of unease about the adulation afforded Lafayette and questioned whether, despite his worthy sacrifices long ago, it was entirely compatible with the spirit of a republican people. Perhaps this discomfort was provoked by the lavish display in the cradle of liberty, where the "most unbounded and lavish expense [was] incurred with universal consent and approbation."[40] There was a fine line between showing Lafayette gratitude and turning him into a god, some Americans reasoned. But quietly.

"The people are wild with joy," Hezekiah Niles wrote, "and the gratitude and the love of all persons, of every age, sex and condition, seems hardly to be restrained within the bounds of propriety—as if it would cause many to forget what was due to themselves and the general, whom they delight to honor." When Niles related stories of men attempting to pull Lafayette's carriage in New York, he was in disbelief that Americans had "failed so far in self-respect as to contend with *horses.*"

"It is to be hoped that the general will not be this insulted again— for insulted he must be, when he sees the sovereigns of this great and glorious country," Niles concluded disgustedly, "converted into assess or other beasts of burden. It is his desire to be treated like a man, not as a titled knave or brainless dandy."[41]

One local, writing anonymously to the *Philadelphia Inquirer,* wondered if the tenor of the extravagant preparations was entirely fitting for a republican people in the city where their republic began. The plan to illuminate the entire city for Lafayette's arrival, he wrote, would have been uncommon even in Europe and should be reserved for victory in war or a change of government, "not the private and friendly visit of a single individual, however meritorious or illustrious he may be, in his personal and political character, or however grateful or welcome his visit may be to [the] shores of his adopted country."[42] His suggestion, that private individuals light up their homes if they wished to do so, went ignored.

Days before the procession that carried Lafayette into Philadelphia, the Federalist Timothy Pickering, a fellow veteran, once quartermaster general of the Continental Army and secretary of war and state, griped privately to John Jay about the spectacle.

"What is our Nation in regard to La Fayette?" Pickering wondered. "He is entitled to the lasting gratitude and respect of Our Country, for his extraordinary zeal, bravery and sacrifice in our cause: He was a valuable officer. Greene, however, also a major general, was as much superior, for talents and important services, as can well be conceived.

"What, were he living, would he think of the current National celebrations?—The apotheoses of heroes in ancient times, when, too, idolatry was the public religion, must cease to excite our wonder. But all mankind seem prone to idolatry; only varying in its objects. Now the excess springs evidently from rival ambition in our great towns."[43]

The dissent of old revolutionaries was decidedly in the minority. "Thousands and thousands followed in his train as he passed from one place to another," a Philadelphian wrote, submitting to the prevailing sentiment inside the Hall of Independence and across the city. After all, he granted, "'when all are mad tis folly to be wise.'"[44]

9

A Cherished Father

During Lafayette's visit to Philadelphia, representatives of Montgomery, Chester, and Delaware Counties, in the southeastern region of Pennsylvania, made their way to Independence Hall with invitations for the general: Would he come to their communities and once more visit the hallowed sites of the Revolution to survey the landscape of his own history—Brandywine, Barren Hill, and Valley Forge?

With William Rush's statue of George Washington at one end of the room and Peale's portrait of him above the opposite door, Lafayette apologetically explained that time would not allow him to accept their invitation; he was expected in the national capital and had to reach Yorktown by October 19 to join the celebration planned for the anniversary of the siege. And there would be an additional stop on the journey. "I need not inform you I cannot pass Mount Vernon without stopping," he told the delegations. No reminder was necessary.[1]

One cause for the euphoria now spread across the Union since Lafayette's reappearance was the return, in spirit, of George Washington. The "adopted son of Washington," the "illustrious friend and companion of Washington"—however they chose to characterize the relationship—was how a citizenry in the grips of nostalgia for the Revolutionary era and its actors communed with their deceased father.

Visits to the rising centers of industry and population, returns to the cradles of the Revolution and liberty, none of these were preceded with the intense interest accompanying Lafayette's inevitable pilgrimage to Washington's tomb. The path there, though choreographed more by chance than by some committee's elaborate plan, was, in sheer symbolism, a spectacle rivaling any parade of his entire tour. It would begin in Baltimore, at Washington's "war house"; proceed to the federal city named for him; then to the vault overlooking the Potomac River, where his bones lay; and then conclude on the bluffs above the York River, among the remnants of the stage of his and Lafayette's great triumph.

The procession began to take shape weeks before. "On Saturday evening last our town was enlivened by the most novel and highly interesting spectacle that we have witnessed for many years,"[2] the *Alexandria Gazette* reported during the first week of September 1824.

While the people of the northeastern states rushed down roads or along riverbanks to cheer Lafayette's passing carriage or steamboat, the citizens of Alexandria, then part of the District of Columbia, beheld a somewhat less exciting but nonetheless interesting spectacle in their own streets: a flower-covered carriage rolling toward the Potomac River, accompanied by a stately band and four companies of volunteers.

But the convoy carried no distinguished personage; the citizens of Alexandria had not gathered to watch a passenger disembark and wave farewell before a river voyage. Instead, the spectators stood in hushed reverence for relics: The carriage rolling along the cobblestones bore two tents in which George Washington had slept and worked during the Revolution. The marquees were the property of George Washington Parke Custis, the custodian of the First Family's material legacy.

Custis and his older sister, Nelly, were raised by their grandmother Martha Washington and step-grandfather, George Washington. Like Nelly, Custis had, for a time, lived with de Lafayette when he took refuge in America. Two older siblings, Eliza and Martha, remained with their mother at the family's Virginia plantation, Abingdon.

Custis was spoiled by his grandmother; his lack of interest in academics a source of frustration for his step-grandfather who took a fatherly interest in his progress—he dropped out of St. John's college after a year. After Washington's death in 1799, Mount Vernon descended to his nephew, Bushrod. But upon his grandmother's death in 1802, Custis inherited many of the family's belongings—China, bedding, militaria, portraits, even a pair of mounted deer heads, which Washington had hunted himself. In 1803, on a hilltop plot in Alexandria County overlooking the infant capital city from across the Potomac River, he began construction on a Greek Revival mansion to serve as a repository for his "Washington treasury." To the items he inherited from his grandmother, he added his own amateur paintings of Revolutionary scenes and purchased numerous other items to supplement the collection. The duck canvas tents, purchased for $160 in Philadelphia in 1777, were among these acquired items.

For Lafayette's visit to Baltimore, Custis offered the tents to John Eager Howard, an officer admired for his composure and courage, who had received a silver medal from Congress for his heroism during the Battle of Cowpens and now served as president of Maryland's Society of the Cincinnati.[3] The tents—one used for dining, the other as an office and bedroom—reached Baltimore on September 14, where another crowd gathered to watch as members of the Maryland's Cincinnati reverently escorted them ashore to await Lafayette.

On the evening of October 5, Lafayette bid farewell to Philadelphia and departed for Chester; three cheers rang out from the wharf while the music of bands playing aboard the other boats on the Delaware River filled the air. The following morning the party crossed by carriage into Delaware and arrived at Frenchtown, a village on the Elk River in Cecil County, Maryland, and a junction for travelers passing back and forth by boat between Philadelphia and Baltimore. There Lafayette recognized a face from the far past: François-Augustin Dubois-Martin. When he made the bold gesture of buying his own boat to travel to America, the Frenchman had helped Lafayette negotiate the purchase of *La Victorie* and joined the band who sailed in it to the New World, where he remained after the war, and now, eighty-two, resided in Baltimore. Reunited, the two men drifted off, for a time, into memories of the Revolution.

John Quincy Adams also prepared to leave Philadelphia and return to Washington. When Baltimore's Committee of Arrangements learned the secretary of state would pass through their city, they sent a representative to Philadelphia with a request that he attend their reception for Lafayette. Not wishing to insult the planners, Adams accepted and traveled by steamboat—the same one that carried Fanny and Camilla Wright—to Newcastle, and then by stagecoach to Frenchtown.[4] There, a delegation from Baltimore, sent to accompany Lafayette to the city, asked Adams to join the general on the steamboat *United States*.

The boat set sail in a downpour, soaking many of its passengers but not stopping the celebrations and banquet on board. When the dinner was over, Georges and Levasseur were vexed to learn that Adams had taken a bed in the crowded sleeping cabin, where he was surrounded by other passengers with less elevated titles.

When the Frenchmen pleaded with him to take their spot in the ladies' cabin, which was specially furnished for Lafayette and his party, Adams refused. The matter was eventually settled when one of the Marylanders who had planned the trip arranged for an additional bed to be brought to Lafayette's cabin. To Levasseur, the member of the party still a stranger to America, this little drama—the son of a president, a ranking member of the government, and a candidate for its highest office sleeping on a cot among his fellow citizens—was a distinctly republican spectacle. "If aristocracy is in American mores, one must admit at least that the high officials of the Government enjoy its prerogatives but little," he later observed in his journals of the trip.[5]

Around eight in the morning, as the *United States* entered the Patapsco River, the rain ceased and the sun shone. The boat neared Baltimore Harbor, where four other vessels, their passengers and crew cheering, moving in the opposite direction, swung behind the *United States* and formed a line that slowed a few hundred yards from the shore. A troop of barges rowed out to retrieve the passengers. The one designated for Lafayette was carpeted, with an eagle at its stern. In its mouth a scroll read, *Welcome, Lafayette, to the home of the free and the land of the brave.*

Once it brought him ashore, Lafayette ascended a winding route leading to the star-shaped fort at the edge of the harbor. From New York to Philadelphia, Americans had offered material evidence of the success of the Revolution. Now he saw proof of its martial progress. When he passed under Fort McHenry's arched entrance, Lafayette stood where a second generation of Americans symbolically reasserted their independence from Britain.

The fortress stood as an unconquerable obstacle to the British army's ambitions of seizing the crucial port of Baltimore after they had set Washington ablaze. Yet the bombardment of mortar shells and Congreve rockets launched from Admiral Alexander Cochrane's fleet on September 13, 1814, failed to dislodge the garrison inside Fort McHenry. The following morning, Francis Scott Key, a lawyer detained on a British warship in the harbor, beheld the giant garrison flag flying above the fort—it had replaced the storm flag, which had been shredded during the attack. Overwhelmed with relief at the sight of the flag still waving over Fort McHenry, Key composed a poem that later generations of America would set to music: "Defence of Fort M'Henry."

For Lafayette's arrival, several of the soldiers who had manned the fort that night were reassembled and the flag that had flown during the siege—riddled with holes—was lofted once more, fluttering in the October breeze. As Lafayette walked into the fort, its garrison formed a line; when the order was given, the line broke in two. The soldiers swung to the left and right, revealing Washington's tents. George Washington Parke Custis stood nearby. While he and the Lafayettes embraced, it was obvious to onlookers that an absent father occupied their thoughts.

The general steadied himself as Maryland's governor, Samuel Stevens, read his speech. "Beneath this venerable canopy," he said, "many a time and oft have you grasped the friendly hand of our illustrious Washington, aided his counsel with your animating voice, or shared with him in the hardy soldier's meal."[6] When the governor finished and Lafayette offered his brief response, the tent's door opened and

Lafayette stepped through and into the past: Waiting inside were the aged members of the Maryland Society of the Cincinnati, "their brows," a reporter wrote, "whitened with the snows of age."[7] They were joined by Charles Carroll of Carrollton, one of the three remaining signers of the Declaration of Independence, who was now eighty. None of the men could summon a word; it was not necessary. "They fell into each other's arms at the memory of their old brotherhood, and they felt emotions of pain and of pleasure that they could only express by their tears," Levasseur said of the reunion. "Under this tent the General was received and emotionally embraced by all his old companions in arms. This fraternal reception lasted quite a while; they could not be separated, there was so much to be said! So much to remember!"[8]

One Baltimorian, Mannie Williams, writing to Jared Sparks, a theologian and later historian of George Washington and the Revolution, could hardly find the words to describe what transpired at Fort McHenry. The city's Committee of Arrangements, she explained, accepted the tents because "rejoining his old friends under such a revolutionary relic could not fail to be gratifying to him;—and truly it <u>did</u> make a '<u>speech</u>' such as one as words could not convey to any heart."[9]

In fact, the small gathering inside Washington's old "war house" made any future festivities in Baltimore irrelevant. All who beheld the weeping soldiers, Williams wrote, had "never witnessed anything like it, that their emotion was entirely beyond their control and that it exceeded in interest all the display of the town arrangements." A bit more economically, Adams, equally touched by the reunion, simply described the scene as "purely pathetic."[10]

"We are now in Baltimore. We were welcomed with the most touching of circumstances," Lafayette wrote his daughters. "We all cried hugging my old comrades under the tent of General Washington; every day there is a new way of displaying the most tender public affection." Among them was a train of cavalry, numbering over eight hundred, that formed in a line around Lafayette's barouche—pulled by four black horses—as it exited Fort McHenry and entered Baltimore, passing under a forty-foot-wide arch. A local reporter noted approvingly that, to the eye, its columns appeared to be made of cloudy marble mined from the Susquehanna River, rivaling the more famous Italian marble from Carrara.[11]

When Lafayette paused under a canopy on Eighth Street to watch the military review pass by, Williams sat in the window of a house across the street. "I presume that my feelings at the first sight of him, were common for all Americans who love their country and their country's friend," she wrote, "but they were exquisite & vivid in the recollection, nor can they ever pass away." As Lafayette bowed as the parade passed by, "my eyes dwelt upon his gracious countenance for an hour & a half, while his were bent upon those passing in review before him—occasionally he bowed to the ladies in our house always accompanying his with smiles almost unequalled in sweetness," Williams shared with Sparks.[12]

The procession brought Lafayette to the Merchants' Exchange Building, where the city officials waited with tributes, women sat in the balcony above, and veterans of the Revolution mustered. The old soldiers came forward to present the cockade worn at Monmouth, to remind him they had fought together at Brandywine, or simply uttered the word *Yorktown*.

As Lafayette traveled to his hotel, a military salute, made up of volunteer companies, passed by for nearly an hour. Each marshal of one company, the De Kalb Cadets, held a scroll, cinched with a blue ribbon, the word *gratitude* inscribed across it. One by one they placed the scroll at Lafayette's feet. As they came and went, he spread and then drew back his arms, imitating an embrace for each soldier; when the salute ended, no longer able to hold back his tears, he turned away and sobbed. "And his were not the only moist eyes that were present,"[13] wrote Niles in the *Weekly Register*.

Lafayette, nominally Catholic, had attended two Presbyterian services in Connecticut the same morning during his trek toward Boston. This earned a letter of reprobation from a Catholic priest, who admonished him "for having sacrificed to false gods and to remind him that outside the church of our good mother, there is no hope of salvation!"[14] The priest, however, offered absolution. This was the Nation's Guest, after all. But one stipulation was attached: He was to not again attend a Protestant service. Unmoved, the Frenchmen attended another Protestant service in Philadelphia.

But Lafayette ran afoul of Protestant ministers too because of his travel on Sundays. "What to do? My faith returns to the Catholic priests . . . our repentance would touch them perhaps," Levasseur cheekily wrote to Émilie Lafayette. Before leaving the city, Lafayette and his companions, joined by Charles Carroll of Carrollton, attended Mass in Baltimore, home of the first Catholic diocese in America. Maryland itself was founded by Lord Baltimore, as a haven for persecuted English Catholics. They sat through a lengthy service, received holy water, and filled the offering bag with money. "At the door we traverse an immense crowd that presses us from all sides, edified by our piety, and we enter the car with hearts filled with hope for the eternal life," wrote Levasseur. Minutes later, Georges discovered that his wallet, carrying 200 francs, was missing. Levasseur, realizing $10 had been pilfered from his pocket, declared, "That's what we get then for going to the Catholic church! As for me, I swear to go no more to the one nor the other."[15]

"Here I am on my too slow progress towards you," Lafayette wrote to James Monroe after arriving in Baltimore. "I much regret to have been so long in the U.S. before I have paid in person my respects to the president and embraced my friend."[16] So close, but yet so far from Monroe, Lafayette determined to move on to Washington. Accordingly, the visit to Baltimore was truncated.

On October 11, Lafayette left behind the cheering citizens of Baltimore and advanced, for the first time, by way of the Washington Turnpike, toward the national capital named for his adopted father. But if the French travelers envisioned a new Rome or Athens, they were sorely disappointed: Thirty minutes passed after they had entered the District of Columbia, on October 12, before a single dwelling came into sight.

"The History of the rise and Progress of the City is really delightful it is already a magnificent City—And in a few Years I think it must become one of the most beautiful Cities in the world," John Adams wrote in 1818, looking far off into the future.

During her visit in 1818, Fanny Wright described Washington as a "skeleton city." Six years later, the capital was still mostly the barren frame of a potential metropolis. There were broad avenues and diagonal roads, surrounded by sweeping vistas of the Potomac River, but little else of Pierre L'Enfant's original vision of the city was yet realized. There was a notable exception: The French architect, a veteran of the American Revolution, whose original plan for the federal city had drawn inspiration from Versailles, selected an incline, Jenkins Hill, to place the home of Congress. The hill, he wrote to Washington, was "a pedestal waiting for a monument."[17] On the morning of October 12, it was from the portico of that monument that a crowd spotted a line of cavalry accompanying several open carriages approaching from the east.

Before Lafayette made his way toward Washington, Sarah Gales Seaton was busy procuring uniforms—"appropriate wreaths, scarfs, and Lafayette gloves and flags."[18] Seaton's husband, William Winston Seaton, in partnership with her brother, Joseph Gales, published the *National Intelligencer*, the capital's oldest newspaper. The two, who reported the debates in Congress, were also the official printers of the U.S. government. In addition to these jobs, Seaton was also a Washington alderman and a member of the Committee of Arrangements organizing the capital's reception of Lafayette. While her husband rode ahead to greet and escort the Nation's Guest into its capital city, Sarah organized the twenty-five girls—each representing a state plus the District of Columbia—the committee had placed under her charge. She outfitted and escorted them to the Capitol, where they would welcome Lafayette. "You will see, dear mother, that Lafayette is expected on the first; and nothing is heard but drumming, nothing seen but regiments from one end of the District to the other," she wrote home shortly before the general's arrival.[19]

Shortly before 1:00 p.m. on October 12, as Lafayette's carriage moved along East Capitol Street, the monument came into view: a white marble building with two short wings and a three-story front on its eastern side, topped by a wooden dome coated in copper. A park, bounded by a wooden fence, was laid out in front of the Capitol, which was accessed through an iron gate.

The military procession accompanying Lafayette into Washington led him into an expansive plain that spread between the building and the Anacostia River. Arrayed before him were twelve hundred soldiers, plus thousands of spectators. Arriving along East Capitol Street, his carriage halted by a market house near the Capitol grounds, decorated by a replica of the Declaration of Independence and a live eagle with a scroll in its talons.

When Lafayette reached the perimeter of the park, he passed under the requisite civic arch—placed there the night before—and was greeted by Sarah Gales Seaton's little troop. "The little girls were in uniform, long blue scarfs, hair curling down, and wreathes of eglantine on their pretty young heads."[20] Each held a small American flag in their hand. Sarah M. Watterston, daughter of George Watterston, the Librarian of Congress, halted Lafayette's progress toward the Capitol with a welcome recitation: "A new generation, as well as new cities and new states, have arisen to welcome thy to the land your valor assisted to make free," she began.[21] Once she concluded her welcome, two additional columns of girls strewed flowers in Lafayette's path as he walked into the north wing of the building and ascended the staircase leading to the rotunda at its heart.

William Thornton, the original architect of the Capitol, had envisioned a large central space connecting two wings. However, inadequate funding, as well as the near destruction of the building by the British army, had postponed this project. In 1817, Benjamin Latrobe, the architect of the Capitol, was in the midst of restoring the building and constructing its center when friction with the committee appointed by Monroe to oversee the project led to his resignation. Charles Bulfinch then applied for and won the vacant position. After relocating to Washington from Baltimore, he oversaw the construction of the massive rotunda, its sandstone walls rising forty-eight feet tall, inspired by the Pantheon. By the time Lafayette stood beneath it, the dome was mostly complete, save for a few coats of paint and unfinished columns, with light streaming through its oculus. One of the Committee of Arrangements' unrealized ambitions was to construct an arch made up of colored lights to mimic a rainbow—a project that would have required nearly six thousands lamps.

Lafayette moved from the rotunda onto the eastern portico, where he passed through Washington's tent, hauled back from Baltimore. After tributes and odes, Lafayette offered his own toast to the home of the American Congress, intended not only for the audience at its Capitol, but for the capitals of Europe as well: "A great political school, where attentive observers from other parts of the world, may be taught the practical science of true social order."[22]

A parade of cavalry marched by as Lafayette exited the building's eastern door. Outside, he resumed his place in a carriage and moved slowly—the crush of well-wishers made any other speed impossible—down the other realized segment of L'Enfant's plan: Pennsylvania Avenue, the mile-long thoroughfare, lined with poplar trees and the concentration of the city's homes and buildings in various states of finish.

The crowd came to a halt at the gate in front of "a plain building of white marble, situated in a small garden" (as one European visitor described it), where the president of the United States resided, which, to their surprise, was "defended by neither guards, ushers, nor insolent valets."[23] A servant greeted the party at the door and led them up a staircase and into an elliptically shaped room, "decorated and carpeted with a remarkable taste of richness and austerity."[24] At its far end, in a chair no larger than any other in the room, sat James Monroe, surrounded by members of his cabinet, including Adams and Crawford, generals, and members of Congress.

"Happy I am, my dear sir, to be arrived under your presidency. Happy I will be to tell you 'Viva voce' how respectfully, affectionally and grateful I am your old brother soldier and friend," Lafayette wrote to his friend upon reaching New York in August.[25] Now, at last, the moment was at hand. As he entered the room, everyone present rose, and Monroe rushed toward Lafayette and embraced him "with the tenderness of a brother."[26]

The president offered his home to the travelers during their stay but knew already that it was impossible for them to accept. "The people have claimed you, they say you are the guest of the nation, and that no one else but they themselves have the right to host you," Monroe told

Lafayette. The president's residence was "your own," he promised.[27] As for the house, the Frenchmen were struck by its simplicity and lack of pretense. It was "without the childish ornaments for which so many fools cool their heels in the antechambers of the palaces of Europe." Its doors were wide open; and indeed, after Monroe had finished speaking, for nearly two hours, a line of citizens entered to shake Lafayette's hand. Laborers with sooty hands, politicians in their overcoats, farmers and soldiers, and children too, "a picture of the most perfect equality."[28]

The president himself was simple and kind, wearing a braidless blue coat—and, much to his credit, a figure who would have been an object of ridicule among the high nobility in the neighborhood of Saint-Germain. "They would not leave his house without proclaiming: 'Dear God, how this "sovereign" house feels bourgeois!'" Levasseur imagined.[29]

But it was another "sovereign" who loomed over Lafayette in the capital and across the Potomac. "The spirit of Washington, this day looking down upon his own city," John Quincy Adams toasted at one of the state dinners held in honor of the Nation's Guest.[30] "Our sires behold our Washington and thee, breasting the fight and daring to be free," a student declared during Lafayette's visit to the seminary at Georgetown. At a dinner following his tour of the Navy Yard, Commodore David Porter presented him with a cane, carved from a tree near the crypt at Mount Vernon.[31]

On the 15th, Lafayette crossed the wooden bridge leading over the Potomac River, away from the capital and into Virginia. His carriage climbed the wooded hill to George Washington Parke Custis's home, Arlington. Shortly before his arrival, the Custis family had illuminated the mansion. "The effect was at once beautiful and grand," a guest recalled. The home's giant Grecian columns were bathed in light when Lafayette arrived and stepped into the house; inside he was introduced to Custis's wife and daughter. The former handed Lafayette a fresh rose, pulled from Mount Vernon's garden just that morning. Touched, he placed it on his breast, "with expressions alluding to the spot where it grew and altho' distinctly uttered were accompanied by emotions indescribable."[32]

The receptions and ceremonies in the capital only delayed the inevitable pilgrimage. "At this hollowed and revered spot a scene is to occur, which, if not in splendor, will, in feeling, vie, with any that has happened among our northern and eastern countrymen," a Virginia editorialist predicted.[33]

On October 16, rain poured as Lafayette crossed over the Potomac River and into the town of Alexandria, whose people paid little notice to the weather. "The gathering of troops, the sound of martial music, the delighted children, all gave the appearance of preparations highly pleasing, for it was that of joy and gratitude," a correspondent reported.[34]

Two of the town's residents, Benjamin Hallowell and Margaret Farquhar, had wed only the day before and rented a house on Oronoco Street, on the edge of Alexandria, with plans to open a boarding school. Observing the mania spreading about the area in anticipation of Lafayette's arrival, the day of his wedding, Hallowell wrote an appropriate poem:

> *Each Lover of Liberty surely must get*
> *Something in honor of Lafayette*
> *There's a Lafayette Watch Chain, a La Fayette hat*
> *A La Fayette this, and a La Fayette that*
> *But I wanted something as lasting as life*
> *And took to myself a La Fayette wife.*

Now, Benjamin and Margaret stood on their doorstep as the Nation's Guest rolled by their home on his way through Alexandria. Lafayette noticed the newlyweds, doffed his hat, and bowed, "not knowing it was to a lady who had been married the day before, and whom her husband had named, after the wedding, his La Fayette wife." The barouche stopped at the house next to the Hallowells'. He had come to pay respects to Anne Hill Carter Lee, the widow of Lafayette's old compatriot Henry Lee III, Light-Horse Harry, the man who eulogized Washington as "first in war, first in peace, and first in the hearts of his countrymen."[35] Though now, in their joy over his return, it appeared that Lafayette was, perhaps, vying for that last spot in the breasts of his adopted countrymen. Lee's son Robert, who would be one of Hallowell's pupils and depart for West Point the following year, was possibly among the cavalry marching with Lafayette into Alexandria. That evening, as he sat down to dinner, Lafayette was informed by John Quincy Adams that King Louis XVIII had died in September.

At last, on the following morning, October 17, a scene worthy of a playwright unfolded along the Potomac's west bank. Lafayette boarded the steamboat *Petersburg* in Alexandria and descended the river. Two hours later, cannon fire from Fort Washington indicated that Mount Vernon was ahead. A band on board began to play a dirge as the ship dropped anchor. A barge brought Lafayette, his son, his secretary, and John C. Calhoun—traveling with the party to Yorktown—to shore, where they were greeted by Washington's nephews, Lawrence Lewis and John Augustine Washington, and George Washington Parke Custis as well. A carriage took Lafayette up the hill to the home, while the others went on foot.

After his death in 1799, Washington's body, following family members who had gone before him and according to his will, was placed in a small redbrick enclosure built on a hillock on Mount Vernon's grounds overlooking the Potomac. His wife, Martha, joined him there in 1802. Although he had stipulated in his will for the construction of a new vault for the family, his heirs had failed to act on the request. Congress authorized the construction of a monument for Washington in the Capitol with the intention of placing his remains under it. In 1800, legislation funding a pyramid-shaped mausoleum passed in the House but stalled in the Senate. The prospects of a public grave for Washington was victim, in part, to changing political currents, as Jefferson's partisans, weary of ostentatious honors for Washington, gained power and seats in Congress. Virginia applied, unsuccessfully, to Bushrod Washington for permission to relocate his uncle's bones to a spot near its capitol in Richmond. But he remained at Mount Vernon.

The path to the crypt was shaded by tall oaks, some of their limbs absent, clipped as souvenirs by visitors. Trees grew from the hillock above the vault. Entry was through an old wooden door. No sign or marker indicated the significance of the man who lay within. Inside, a tattered silk drape covered the sarcophagus. "It is very humble; and it seems scarcely possible so mean a place can contain the remains of so great a man," wrote one visitor.[36]

The grave's modesty and dilapidated state was a source of some national embarrassment. Major John Reid, an aide to Andrew Jackson, was appalled after visiting the grave in 1818. "In a small vault on the riverside of the hill ill constructed and overgrown with shrubbery, repose the bones of the father of his country. Why is this so? Must the charge of ingratitude forever rest upon Republics?"[37]

"A low, obscure, ice-house looking vault testifies how well a Nation's Gratitude repays the soldier's toils," a British traveler disapprovingly observed the same year. "He gave them liberty—He made them a nation. What has he received in return? Neglect!" No such oversight would be found in a monarchy, he claimed. "The selfish genius of republicanism turns enviously away from the glory of the departed hero."[38]

But as the children of Mount Vernon stood before the crypt, its size or ornamentation mattered little. Near its door, Custis drew attention to a ring suspended by a ribbon of the Cincinnati around his neck. He had commissioned Greenbury Gaither, a Washington silversmith, to craft a plain golden ring, inside of which were placed clippings of the hair of both George and Martha Washington, which "slightly shows the frost of time."[39]

"When your descendants of a distant day shall behold this valued relic," he told Lafayette as he presented the ring, "it will remind them of the heroic virtues of their illustrious sire, who received it, not in the palaces of princes, or amid the pomp and vanities of life, but at the laureled grave of Washington." That grave, Custis now declared, was entirely appropriate. Speaking to the small gathering, he pointed to the spare nature of the crypt, which would never suggest to a European that a leader of men rested inside it. Would it have suited a Marcus Aurelius? It need not. "The father of his country lies buried in the hearts of his countrymen, and in those of the brave, the good, the free, of all ages and nations."[40]

When he had finished, Custis handed the ring to Lafayette, who pressed it to his chest. "The feelings, which at this awful moment, oppress my heart, do not leave me the power of utterance," he explained. "I can only thank you my dear Custis, for your precious gift, and pay a silent homage to the tomb of the greatest and best of men, my paternal friend!"[41]

The door to the crypt was opened; nearby were wreaths, some fresh, others weathered. The leaves on the mighty oaks wore their autumn colors; the Potomac River swept by down the hill. Lafayette disappeared into the small structure, striking his head against part of the crypt, resulting in a slight contusion.[42] A few minutes later, he reappeared at its entrance, tears rushing down his face. He summoned Georges and Levasseur. They entered the crypt, where he pointed to the graves of the Washingtons; now all three men wept.

The homage complete, they lingered at Mount Vernon, lost in memories, revisiting the house and its grounds. Lafayette had last been here forty years before, during his visit in 1784, a time of great happiness, when he reminisced about the war and discussed the new nation's future with Washington. His son had departed here almost thirty years earlier, leaving behind an adopted father who had welcomed him into his family when his own were prisoners. To Georges's eyes, so little had changed since then. There, affixed to a wall, was the key to the Bastille, which Lafayette had sent to Washington in 1790, complete with the original shipping ticket.[43]

After an hour passed, the men descended the path leading back to the Potomac, carrying clippings from the trees that shaded the grave. "We resembled a grieving family who was come from putting a cherished father who had recently died in the ground," Levasseur wrote.[44] When its horses grew restive, several men on the grounds attempted to carry Lafayette's carriage themselves. He refused and instead walked to the barge that transported him back to the *Petersburg*; on its deck the Marine band resumed its solemn song. As the boat moved downriver, away from Mount Vernon, the silence was interrupted only when Lafayette shared stories of Washington late into the evening.

No stranger to the dramatic, Lafayette characterized the visit in muted terms. "We made a stop at Mount Vernon. All the people who accompanied us stayed in the house, and let us visit with the family the simple and sacred grave where the General and his wife are buried," he wrote to his friend the Princess d'Hénin. "You can judge the feelings shared between George and I."[45]

The visit provided fodder for all manner of romantic depictions among writers. According to contemporary newspapers, for example, an eagle followed the boat from Alexandria downriver, hovered above Mount Vernon during Lafayette's visit, and then vanished upon his departure.[46]

"'Tis done! The greatest, the most affecting scene of the grand drama has closed!" waxed the Federalist newspaper the *Statesmen*. "And the pilgrim who repairs to the tomb of the Father of his Country will find its laurels moistened by the tear of La Fayette."[47]

The poet Robert Stevenson Coffin wrote an ode, "La Fayette at the Tomb of Washington":

> *Ah, who may tell the converse sweet*
> *Unheard by mortal ear.*
> *When two such godlike spirits meet,*
> *Each in a different sphere.*
> *Time, tho' shall ne'er again behold*
> *A scene so fraught with bliss . . .*[48]

Perhaps more powerful was the recollection of an American who, while making a pilgrimage to the grave at Mount Vernon years later, encountered an elderly man—formerly one of its owner's slaves, now freed. Their conservation, tellingly, was about two things: Washington, and the Nation's Guest's visit to his grave. "He cried like an infant," the old man said of Lafayette.[49]

Before the American Revolution, Yorktown was a bustling town, home to three hundred people. War scattered its population and demolished many of its buildings. A fire in the spring of 1814 destroyed much of what remained, and by 1824, the port was largely deserted.

When Lafayette arrived to its shores four decades after his departure—the steamboat *Virginia* met the *Petersburg* twelve miles upriver to retrieve him—Virginia's governor James Pleasants, Chief Justice John Marshall, thousands of volunteer troops, and interested spectators, some from several states away, were there to welcome him back, spread along the beach and across the hills above.

Planning for the siege's anniversary celebration began that summer. Laborers built a forty-five-foot triumphal arch near Redoubt 10, captured by Lafayette's Americans under Alexander Hamilton. Two obelisks marked key sites: where General Charles O'Hara surrendered on Cornwallis's behalf, and where the French, led by Baron de Vioménil, took Redoubt 9. An amphitheater accommodated the ladies in attendance, and artist James Warrell was commissioned to create transparencies.

Cooks and butlers were hired, and vast amounts of food and drink—fifty pounds of bacon, one hundred pounds of almonds, and brandy, rum, and champagne—were procured. Matching bedsheets and curtains were purchased for the former home of General Thomas Nelson, Lafayette's lodgings for the celebration. The tab for the event, redeemed by Virginia's General Assembly, exceeded $10,000.[50]

Tents were spread out near the field of battle, some occupied by the men who had fought there. When Lafayette walked ashore, veterans of the Revolution surrounded him. "I was with you at Yorktown; I entered yonder redoubt at your side," said one. They had all returned to relive that climactic scene of the contest, among the "half-decayed ramparts." During the evening, Lafayette and other veterans toured the redoubts. One of their number, Allan McLane, a member of "Light-Horse Harry Lee's Legion" and veteran of the Yorktown Campaign who had traveled from Delaware for the celebration (he welcomed Lafayette to that state the previous month), snuck off, "shouldered a corn stock and mounted guard." When his old compatriots approached, he demanded to know who goes there. "Friends," they responded. They were not allowed to pass, though, until providing the correct countersigns from 1781. The reenactment greatly amused Lafayette.[51]

At noon on the 19th, the day of celebration, Lafayette, supported by Virginia's governor, walked up the hill leading to Rock Redoubt and to the triumphal arch decorated with thirteen stars and an eagle with its wings spread. He was met there by Robert B. Taylor, major general of the Virginia militia, who had helped fortify Norfolk during the War of 1812 and repulse the British landing at Craney Island in 1813.

During his tribute, delivered—as Taylor reminded the crowd—among "these half-decayed ramparts, this ruined village, in which the bomb's havoc is still everywhere visible," the Virginian explained that for the head of a republican like Lafayette, only one crown was suitable: "the only crown it would not disdain to wear."[52] He then began to place a wreath around the old man's head. But Lafayette stopped him, taking the wreath in his right hand instead.

The celebration, he said, was not for him but for the other veterans of Yorktown. "Let me pay special tribute to the gallant name of Hamilton, who commanded the attack," Lafayette declared. He also honored the field officers who had followed him into the redoubts: Jean-Joseph Sourbader de Gimat, John Laurens, Nicholas Fish. Of the group, only the last remained—and was present. Lafayette drew him from the crowd.

"Here, half this wreath belongs to you," he said.

"No, sir. It is all your own," Fish retorted.

"Then take it and preserve it as our common property," Lafayette insisted.[53]

"Many wept; all were moved," a Virginian correspondent wrote of the exchange.[54]

Taylor then led the military maneuvers, as cavalry, infantry, volumeters, and regulars marched, flags held high, before fifteen thousand spectators. Lafayette was drawn in a barouche past the amphitheater, where two thousand women waved their handkerchiefs. "The whole scene defies description," claimed the reporter.[55] An attendee, summarizing the celebration, wrote, "I have seldom seen so much beauty congregated together. All the wealth of the state shewn in brilliant array."[56]

During the preparations for the festivities, a box of blackened candles was discovered in a cellar of a Yorktown home, a stamp on their box indicating they were part of Cornwallis's stores, captured after the American victory. On this night, they burned, casting their glow across the large marquee where the veterans celebrated. After dinner, the first toast was to the memory of General Washington. The second, to "our beloved guest," General Lafayette.[57]

10

They Who Sin Against the Liberty of Their Country

Fanny and Camilla Wright hoped to travel from Philadelphia to Washington and then arrive at Yorktown in time for the anniversary on October 19.[1] Yet the sisters were nowhere to be seen during the celebrations. "My young friends went straight from Philadelphia to Washington where they have acquaintances. I only saw them at public festivities or in large reunions, besides the time at the house of our friend in common from New York. The life I am leading is not very suitable for private company," Lafayette informed his daughters at La Grange, probably much to their relief.[2] Indeed, there was a growing distance between Lafayette and Fanny. One source was Nelly Custis Lewis.

Conflict was inevitable. Other than a reverence for Lafayette, the women had little in common and hailed from different worlds. Wright was a radical with little use for societal strictures—a woman who met publicly with Black men, declared her thoughts on all manner of subjects to any audience, and expressed opinions no matter how controversial. Lewis had grown up under George Washington's roof; she was raised among America's political elite and valued the decorum and codes Wright so eagerly scorned. That they would clash was natural, but the animosity was intensified on Lewis's part—not only because of what she regarded as Wright's crude manners, but also because she was irritated by Wright's pretensions to Lafayette's attention and time, and aghast at her determination to travel by his side and soil sacred places. "I pray devoutly that you may be released from those plagues of Egypt—which are far more to be dreaded than locusts," Lewis wrote to Georges Washington de Lafayette in reference to his father's "young friends."[3]

During the brief time they spent together, Fanny grated intensely on Lewis. "The eldest [sister] said to several ladies, 'we are going to join the gen'l, never to be separated whilst he remains in the United States,'" Lewis told Georges. "How will that be—I hope he will not permit them to go to Mount Vernon when he goes. It is impossible that you or he should visit that spot without thinking of the departed friends who rest there & I confess it would wound my feelings that their foreign characters should witness & partake of those feelings. "She was not insensitive, however, to the fact that her honesty about the Wrights would upset Lafayette. "I do not, I cannot like them, particularly the eldest, & that I fear will make me most unadmirable to one whom I will always love & and venerate."[4]

Lewis claimed credit for successfully obstructing Fanny from accompanying Lafayette on his visit to Washington's grave. "The Fair W[right]s did not go to Mount Vernon with the Gen'l, or to York with him, or Alexandria . . ." Lewis wrote to her confidante, Elizabeth Bordley Gibson.[5] "Entre nous, dearest Bet, do I not deserve well of my country for this good deed, cost what it may to myself, I shall always rejoice that I have served him, so far," she boasted. "I know that but for me, they would have now been tarnishing his glory by their presence. They were resolved to go, & and he could not say no, until I taught him how to set his mouth & pen to a negative position."[6]

Lafayette might be persuaded to visit Mount Vernon without the Wrights, but he was determined they join him on a pilgrimage to another venerated place. One where the elder Wright was held in higher regard.

"How Happy I will be to embrace you, my dear friend, I need not tell, and I know the pleasure will be reciprocated," Lafayette wrote to

Thomas Jefferson at the end of August from Boston.[7] The much-hoped-for reunion was slow in coming. In October, when he'd progressed as far as Philadelphia, Lafayette wrote again to Jefferson explaining that his schedule had been so "deranged" by the constant receptions in his honor that they would not meet until after the celebration at Yorktown.[8] Then he would rush to Monticello. Jefferson's own wishes to participate in the anniversary in the latter location were unfulfillable: "My spirit will be there; my body cannot," he informed Lafayette. "I am too much enfeebled by age for such a journey. I cannot walk further than my garden."[9] When he at least reached Jefferson's home, Lafayette hoped that the Wright sisters would be there as well.

In 1820, after reading her *Altorf*, Jefferson sent its author a short note of approval. "The approbation of such a mind as Mr Jefferson's does indeed make the heart of the poet proud;—and very proud does mine feel at this moment," Fanny replied.[10] In 1823, Lafayette shipped copies of her *Views of Society and Manners in America* and *A Few Days in Athens* to Monticello, championing his young protégé to his old friend.[11] Now, he hoped to introduce her in person to Jefferson and his daughter Martha Jefferson Randolph. "You and I are the two men in the World the Esteem of Whom She values the most. I Wish Much, My dear friend, to present these two adopted daughters of Mine," Lafayette wrote to Jefferson from Philadelphia.[12] Happily obliging the request, Jefferson promised that the sisters would not "find a welcome more hearty than with Mrs Randolph, and all the inhabitants of Monticello."[13]

Fanny and Camilla made their way south from Washington, while Lafayette's plans to reach Monticello were again frustrated. Leaving Yorktown, he traveled to Williamsburg. Levasseur described the former Virginia capital as a "second rate town," but its citizens prepared a dinner of venison, sirloin, and mutton at the Raleigh Tavern, recorded as "the richest and most delightful ever enjoyed in Williamsburg."[14] From there they embarked on the *Petersburg* for Norfolk across the James River. "Of all the towns which we have visited up to now, Norfolk, is the one that offers the least agreeable appearance," Levasseur wrote after seeing its shabby homes and narrow streets and breathing its foul air.[15] On the 25th, Lafayette and his companions traveled up the Elizabeth River to Richmond, where they docked at Rocketts Landing the following afternoon in a driving rain. The soggy weather precluded a planned procession by the city but did not discourage citizens from turning out on foot or horseback to escort him themselves. The scene was one of "deep-toned sentiments of gratitude and joy, which he has everywhere inspired. His presence seems to operate as a spell. All regular business is suspended—crowds rush from all parts to see him, and the most rapturous *welcomes* burst from every lip."[16]

At the Eagle Tavern, the city's preeminent hotel, where rooms were set aside for Lafayette and his party, forty Revolutionary veterans waited to take him by the hand or salute him in silence. Richmond's Committee of Arrangements had invited numerous Virginian veterans to attend the city's celebration shortly after Lafayette reached New York in August. Among those who accepted the invitation was William Broadus of the Virginia Line, who made the 160-mile trip to Richmond from his home in Harpers Ferry. Broadus could still remember splashing through four feet of the Schuylkill River, as Lafayette led his troops to safety at Barren Hill. But soon after he arrived in Richmond, Broadus, now sixty-three, took ill. He lay in bed, near death, as his fellow veterans gathered around and two of the city's preeminent physicians rushed to treat him. And then, by his bed, Lafayette appeared. Broadus was soon on the mend and back to his family.[17]

Lafayette's stay in Richmond coincided with the running of its fall horse races, a four-day affair. It was the third day, October 28, that attracted the largest crowd. Shortly before a climactic race between Flirtilla and Janette, a bay mare owned by William Ransom Johnson, whose Sir Henry had lost the great contest against Eclipse in New York the year before, Lafayette took his seat at the judge's table. On this day Johnson fared better, as Janette won a closely contested race and the $1,000 purse. In tribute to the honored guest, Johnson renamed the horse Virginia Lafayette. "May all nations enter the course of freedom. We Americans have won the first race, but there is a noble prize for every one of the competitors," Lafayette toasted at the dinner afterward.[18]

Additionally, there was an invitation from the people of Petersburg and a planned celebration at Richmond's Masonic temple, drawing in lodges from around the city. By the end of October, Lafayette informed Jefferson that he was "once more disappointed in my Eagerness to Reach Monticello." Another roadblock to travel, "the great business of the election," on the first of November, rendered it impossible to schedule any receptions or events.[19]

"You will have seen by our papers the delirium into which our citizens are thrown by a visit from Genl. La Fayette. He is making a triumphal progress thro' the states, from town to town with acclamations of welcome, such as no crowned head ever received," Jefferson wrote to Richard Rush about Lafayette's return weeks before Americans selected their next president, predicting "its effect here too will be salutary, as to ourselves, by rallying us together, and strengthening the habit of considering our country as one and indivisible."[20]

On the verge of leaving for America in the summer of 1824, Lafayette had affirmed to George W. Erving, anxious his visit would further exacerbate political tensions (and disadvantage William H. Crawford), that he would strive to unify the country and remind its people of the importance of union. Here, as voting began, Lafayette saw some evidence of success.

"Our trip to the United States has recalled in every heart, has transmitted to every generation, times and feelings that are good to remember," Lafayette wrote his family. "The care we witness in finding along our journey all of the population who can stand on two feet, and to take those who cannot into my arms from their mothers, next to the white horses of the soldiers of the Revolution, has for this people of great sense a more serious object than to merely throw flowers or give out compliments."

Then he continued: "This voyage has also contributed to strengthening the union between the states and to soften the parties by occupying their simultaneous and common benevolence for the returnee of the old world. This benevolence is great, no doubt, and beyond anything I could have permitted myself to hope for."[21]

A romantic notion, that the return of the remaining ranks of the Revolutionary army and the spirit of departed founders had helped, for a moment, reconcile the nation. Lafayette, though, was also clear-eyed about another cause in the lessening of the most partisan passions. One of the principal means of provoking them had found another fixation: His travels were simply more interesting to journalists and their readers than partisan editorials. "Our journey, in occupying the columns of the newspapers, has saved the candidates from columns of critique," he acknowledged.[22]

On November 2, Lafayette, "pleased with all, *pleasing all*" in Richmond, was finally on the road north to Jefferson.[23] Along the way, the small populations of Goochland County, Columbia, and Wilmington welcomed the Nation's Guest as he passed through. Levasseur was temporarily detained in the last of these villages, sick with a fever, and Georges, who attended the secretary during his illness, with him.[24]

Two days after leaving Richmond, Lafayette paused for a lunch at Boyd's Tavern in Fluvanna County, across the county line from Albemarle, whose Committee of Arrangements arrived to accompany him the remainder of the way to Monticello. Jefferson's landau was sent down the mountain to retrieve Lafayette, as well as two other carriages for the rest of the party and their baggage. After noon, the team of gray mares began their incline up Brown's Mountain. It was preceded by a small cavalry troop and trailed by the local volunteers, mostly schoolboys, the Lafayette Guards. They were followed by hundreds of citizens trekking toward Monticello to witness the mountaintop reunion.

Along the portico on the northwest side of the home, a welcoming line was formed, made up of Jefferson's relatives. The former president stood at its center. The sound of a bugle echoed across the mountain, announcing Lafayette's approach. At a distance from the portico, a procession came into view down the mountain. It wound upward and then vanished. Then it came into sight once more, the scarves of the cavalry blowing in the wind, the steel of their pikes glistening in the sun. It was a particularly warm and golden autumn day. The landau carrying Lafayette completed its upward crawl and came to a halt in front of the home.

The large crowd across from Monticello positioned itself in a semicircle on the northern edge of the home's yard. The Blue Ridge Mountains were visible in the distance. Silence reigned over the scene. As Lafayette descended from the landau, Jefferson stepped off his porch. The former limped toward the house, the latter stepped shakily in the opposite direction, but his gait grew quicker until they were in reach of each other. The two old men opened their arms and gently collided in an emotional embrace. "My Dear Jefferson! "My dear Lafayette!" they repeated, kissing one another on the cheek.[25] The silence that had hung over the mountain was now interrupted by muffled sobs. Jefferson led his old friend to the home, where his daughter, who Lafayette had last seen as a young girl in Paris, greeted him. The crowds disappeared down the mountain. "The whole was a scene for an artist—a grand historic picture should have commemorated this meeting—on this mountain-top," Jane Blair Cary Smith, then fifteen years old, a member of the Jefferson family who watched the drama from Monticello's portico, remembered later in life.[26]

Georges and Levasseur arrived at Monticello shortly after Lafayette. The secretary, still reeling, sat quietly in a corner, quickly excused himself, and went to bed. During a dinner in the home that evening, Lafayette and Jefferson were seated on one side of the table, separated by Jefferson's daughter and granddaughter. "The French hero ate fish, not only with his fingers, but with his whole hand dipped into the mess Arab style," to Smith's astonishment.[27] Opposite them were nearly twenty young women, whose beauty astonished the Frenchmen as much as the sun setting on the mountains visible outside Monticello's large windows.

James Madison, traveling from his home, Montpelier, in nearby Orange County, arrived before nightfall, in time for desert. "My old friend embraced me with great warmth," Madison wrote to his wife, Dolley, the following morning. "He is in fine health & spirits but so much increased in bulk & changed in aspect that I should not have known him."[28] Madison was not the only one struck by time's toll. "I was welcomed with strong emotion by Mr. Jefferson," Lafayette wrote to his daughters, "who I found definitely to have aged after thirty-five years of separation, but who wears wonderfully his eighty-one years of age, and who still enjoys all of the vigor of his soul and of his spirit."[29]

The following day, Jefferson, Lafayette, and Madison traveled down the mountain to Charlottesville, where a reception awaited them at the institution that now occupied what remained of Jefferson's energies, "his last public care."[30] The landau deposited them at the edge of the University of Virginia's lawn; they went the remaining distance to its rotunda, still unfinished, on foot. Atop its white dome waved three flags, the largest of which read, *Welcome Our Country's Guest*.

The three old men walked together up the steps and into the building, "arm in arm, hero of the Revolution, with two of its sages."[31] Inside, tables were arranged in concentric circles around the structure's supporting columns. A grand meal, eaten by four hundred diners, was followed by orations and toasts by Lafayette and his hosts. The echo of cheers repeatedly bounced across the room. None of the speeches were more moving than the one Jefferson composed but did not deliver. "I am old, long in the disuse of making speeches, and without voice to utter them," he explained in its text, which he handed to his friend Valentine Wood Southall, who read it aloud in a clear voice. The address was as much a tribute to Lafayette as it was a reflection on their shared history. Jefferson praised not only Lafayette's valor in the Revolution but also his efforts, on behalf of America in France after the war: "I only held the nail, he drove it. Honor him then, as your benefactor in peace, as well as in war." Yet Jefferson's words also sounded like a farewell. "In this feeble state, the exhausted powers of life leave little within my competence for your service." As Southhall read the address, Lafayette reached for and grasped Jefferson's hand, weeping audibly.[32]

A pause at Monticello was the first relief for the Frenchmen after traveling—according to Levasseur's calculation—forty miles a day over three months. But the unrelenting schedule and unceasing acclamation revived Lafayette. "We are running from kindness to kindness, from tenderness to tenderness, and, no matter how nice it is to travel in this way, we are happily taking advantage of our rest [break] in Monticello.

I don't know what has become of my gouty disposition," he wrote to his daughters.[33] These were happy days spent with Jefferson reminiscing on their shared history, discussing the prospect of American material support for Greek rebels, the fate of emerging republics in the hemisphere, and the search of a possible means of eventually eradicating slavery. An additional voice joined the discussions, on November 7, when the Wrights reached Monticello.

The journey there was an unhappy revelation for Fanny. During the voyage south, near Norfolk, their steamboat brushed against another vessel. On its deck, she spotted Black men and women in manacles, bound for the slave market in New Orleans. Instantly, all the joy and celebration surrounding Lafayette felt hollow. How could a people celebrate a champion of the rights of man while showing so little regard for those rights? She had once seen slavery as a blot on the character of a nation in which she invested so much hope—a nation that, through the goodness of its people and institutions, would surely erase this evil in time. But the sight of the slaves in Virginia had cured her of such optimism and lent an air of ridiculousness to the pomp and pageantry surrounding Lafayette's visit.

"The enthusiasms triumphs & rejoices exhibited here before the countenance of the great & good Lafayette have no longer charms for me," she confessed to her friends the Garretts. "They who sin against the liberty of their country—against those great principles for which their honored guest poured on their soil his treasure & and his blood are not worthy to rejoice in his presence—My soul sickens in the midst of gaiety & and turns almost with disgust from the fairest faces of the most amiable discourse."[34]

In *Views of Society and Manners in America*, Fanny wrote that no state could "point to a longer line of public services than Virginia." After all, "she issued the Declaration of Independence from the pen of her Jefferson; she bound the republic link of the federal Union by the hand of her Madison."[35] Now, she estimated, correctly, that Virginia was the "nursery" of slavery. If she looked to its two "purest patriots and wisest statemen," for a means of urgently abolishing it, Fanny was surely disappointed.

Israel Gillette Jefferson, one of the enslaved population at Monticello, recalled from the distance of the 1870s that he had taken his master and Lafayette for drives around the mountain a number of times during that October. Though he admitted that it was often difficult to understand Lafayette in the carriage, on one particular ride he understood exactly what the Frenchman was saying. "Lafayette remarked that he thought the slaves ought to be free; that no man can rightly hold ownership in his brother man," Israel remembered. Lafayette had fought in a war to secure the freedom of all men, not so that a portion of them would be kept in bondage. Human liberty was a noble idea indeed, and it should extend to the Black people. In Israel's memory, his master agreed but offered no solution, only that the slaves would be freed one day. When that day would come, though, Jefferson did not know.[36]

For all their genius, their deep faith and commitment to the natural rights of men, to which they had dedicated their lives, in twilight, the matter of slavery confounded both Jefferson and Madison. During their public lives, both men had, with their customary eloquence, decried the institution. In his *Notes on the State of Virginia*, begun in 1781, Jefferson asked, "Can the liberties of a nation be thought secure when we have removed their only firm basis, a conviction in the minds of the people that these liberties are of the gift of God? That they are not to be violated but with his wrath?"[37]

His proposed steps toward eventual abolition—legislation ending the importation of slaves into Virginia, the prohibition of slavery from the Northwest Territories, the promotion of less labor-intensive crops, such as wheat, and improving the treatment of slaves themselves—collided with the rapidly growing number of slaves in the Southern states, hastened by the advent of the cotton gin and the increased profitability of the crop.

Madison, like Jefferson, was born to a planter family whose subsistence was made possible through slave labor, but he wrestled with the conflict between his inherited class and the experiment in human freedom to which he lent his intellect and energies. His antipathy toward slavery peaked in 1783 when Madison sold a twenty-four-year-old slave who attended him in Philadelphia into an apprenticeship from which he was eventually freed. "Where slavery exists the republican Theory becomes still more fallacious," Madison wrote in a preparatory memorandum in advance of the Constitutional Convention in 1787.[38] He contemplated means of making a living without the use of slave labor. But the inheritance of one hundred slaves after his father's death in 1801 rendered his desire to see slavery ended more abstract ambition than personal responsibility.

In 1816, a Presbyterian minister named Robert Finley founded the American Colonization Society with the aim of encouraging the emigration of free Blacks to the West African coast. The resettlement would, in theory, achieve three ends at once: remove the free Black population that unnerved Southerners, fretting it would foment an uprising among their slaves; incentivize manumission; and, by establishing a colony on land purchased by the U.S. Navy, the future colony of Liberia, Christianize Africa. Madison, who in 1821 described slavery to Lafayette as "a sad blot on our free Country," invested his hopes for eventual abolition in Finley's society; Jefferson, though he did not join, roughly approved of the plan: "The idea of emancipating the whole at once, the old as well as the young, and retaining them here, is of those only who have not the guide of either knowledge or experience of the subject," he wrote in 1814.[39] Slaves, because of their degraded circumstances and limitations of their race, could not be instantly freed, he thought. And the possibility of their amalgamation with whites—a possibility that "no lover of excellence in the human character can innocently consent"—necessitated immigration away from America. Jefferson had likely fathered at least six children with one of his own slaves, Sally Hemings.

"The hour of emancipation is advancing in the march of time. It will come," he wrote a decade before Lafayette's visit.[40] But neither he nor Madison would live to see the day; and the great object of reaching it was now too much for even their powers. The task would fall on the shoulders of another generation. Fanny Wright arrived at Monticello burning to begin that work. After the experience in Norfolk, the subject of slavery, she wrote, "preys so continually on my mind that I find it difficult to write on any other."[41]

During their time together, Jefferson explained to Fanny that he was indeed eager to see "preparatory" steps toward gradual abolition, as outlined in his *Notes on Virginia*, implemented in the commonwealth's legislature. "God grant that it be acted upon & that shortly," she subsequently wrote. Her experiences in America thus far had left Fanny convinced—like Jefferson, though for different reasons—that the cohabitation of the races was an impossibility in America. "The prejudice whether absurd or the contrary against a mixture of the two colors is so deeply rooted in the American mind that emancipation without expatriation (if indeed the word be applicable) seems impossible."[42] She now believed the most realistic solution was the gradual emancipation of slaves and their expatriation abroad.

Madison was unable to provide additional inspiration. After spending ten days at Monticello, Lafayette bid Jefferson farewell and departed for Montpelier, Madison's home, without the Wrights. Camilla had caught a cold, forcing the sisters to remain with Jefferson. When Madison learned of Lafayette's arrival in New York during the summer, he immediately wrote, wishing to add his voice to the chorus of freemen hailing his return. "That of no one, as you will believe, springs more from the heart than mine. May I not hope that the course of your movements will give me an opportunity of proving it, by the warmth of my embrace on my own threshold."[43] Lafayette reached Madison's door on the evening of November 15; Virginia's senator James Barbour and Madison's nephew Conway Macon arranged carriages to transport him from Albemarle to Orange County; the hours before his arrival were, in the words of Ailsey Payne, one of the Madison's slaves, "stirrin times at Montpilier." The ice houses were filled with mutton, ducks, and chicken; slaves hurriedly shined up the home's silver and arranged its china, the entire estate "gone over to make it look as fine as possible." Madison's wife, Dolley, even dressed up her servants, lest she "disqualified herself in her own house."[44]

During their four days at Montpelier, Levasseur found Madison, now seventy-four, little touched by time and full of cheer. He was also enthralled by the conversation with Dolley and her charm. The days were occupied with walks around Montpelier's grounds, at the foot of the Blue Ridge Mountains. The evenings were occupied with conversations on the affairs of the republic. These inevitably turned to slavery. Lafayette's tone remained understanding of his planter friends and fully aware of the impossibility of immediate emancipation. Still, as Levasseur recorded, in the home where the blueprint for America's constitution was composed, "he never missed an opportunity to defend the rights that *all* men without exception have to liberty, and to raise in the midst of Mr. Madison's the question of Slavery."[45]

On November 19, Madison accompanied Lafayette to Orange Courthouse, where the population turned out in welcome. After a banquet, Madison mounted his horse and disappeared into the woods on his way back to Montpelier. The party continued north, reaching Fredericksburg on the 20th where it remained until the 22nd before boarding a steamboat and traveling back up the Potomac to Washington, where Congress was assembling to receive him. Georges Washington departed in advance of his father from Fredericksburg to visit Nelly Custis Lewis at Woodlawn.[46]

When he arrived in Fredericksburg, a welcoming committee was sent to greet Lafayette at the Spotsylvania County line; then a parade would carry him into town. A public notice from the Committee of Arrangements demanded not only total silence from spectators in the path but a request that would have grieved Lafayette had he seen it: "Owners of slaves are respectfully solicited to keep their slaves within their lots. All colored people are warned that they are not to appear on any of the streets through which the procession will pass."[47]

When he was escorted into the town hall, decorated with evergreens and flowers, a choir of the young girls rose from their seats and sang an ode composed for the occasion. One of its verses celebrated his role as a beacon of hope:

In our darkness and peril, the light of his brand
Blaz'd a beacon to point thro' the tempest to land
And Lafayette was the first when the deluge was o'er,
To bear us the palm branch from the shore,
When the ark of young freedom found rest from the wave
And our land was no longer the land of the salve

This "melodious effusion of infant love," the *Virginia Herald* reported, touched the entire room.[48] Had she been present, Fanny Wright would have been unmoved.

11

Republics Are Not Ungrateful

L ooking on snootily from across the Atlantic, British commentators laughed off Lafayette's visit. "One conclusion from the old General's voyage is irresistible: it is that the cause of liberalism in Paris is utterly defunct, and annihilated," one columnist observed. "Nothing but desperation could have made General Lafayette sacrifice the pleasures *la belle* France to dwell among the Dubbikinses of New England."[1]

Americans, in New England, and elsewhere, could take pride in such an insult, as happy as they were to have him among them for a spell. But the sleight in another English journal had teeth. "In some of the papers it is delicately stated that Lafayette pays nothing for his board—we have not yet seen that the Nation's Guest has been furnished with pocket money."[2]

The historian David Ramsay's two-volume *The History of the American Revolution* was among the earliest chronicles of the new nation's struggle for independence. Published in 1787, its value was aided by its proximity to the epoch and the perspective of its author: Ramsay was a player in the struggle, both on the battlefield and in politics, as a surgeon in the South Carolina militia and as a delegate to the Continental

Congress. Through his writing, Ramsay promoted republican virtue and national union through history. In the closing pages of his popular work on the Revolution, he enclosed some civic instruction to his fellow Americans: "Cherish and reward the philosophers, the statesmen and the patriots, who devote their talents and time at the expense of their private interests, to the toils of enlightening and directing their fellow citizens, and thereby rescue citizens and rulers of republics, from the common and too often merited charge of ingratitude."[3]

The axiom that polities governed by crude and selfish popular sentiment were loath to honor debts owed to their forbearers, their soldiers, and their statesmen was frequently and self-consciously expressed by Americans in the early years of the republic. "Ingratitude has been experienced in all Ages & Republics in particular have ever been famed for the exercise of that unnatural & sordid Vice," George Washington wrote at the end of the Revolution, lamenting the Continental Congress's treatment of its soldiers, who had become estranged from their civilian counterparts.[4] Nearly a half century later, visitors gazed at his dilapidated grave at Mount Vernon and found confirmation of this ingratitude.

Perhaps James Brown was familiar with Ramsay's work; he certainly well understood his warning. When Lafayette stepped aboard the *Cadmus* in July 1824, he carried a letter from the American minister to France for President James Monroe. Brown, who had aided Lafayette in his efforts to obtain the financial assistance necessary in order to leave France, was aware of his sacrifices nearly half a century earlier and knew better than most Americans of their National Guest's pecuniary troubles in the present.

"I cannot repress a hope that, as he has delicately declined the offer of a National ship, and thus avoided subjecting the Country to a considerable expense the pledges he has been forced to give," Brown wrote, "will be redeemed and some equivalent allowed worthy the character of a people who, as it relates to the officers of our revolution, have but few remaining opportunities of proving that Republics are not ungrateful."[5]

When Lafayette returned to Washington at the end of November— he spent several days in Baltimore—after his visits with Jefferson and Madison, nearly five months had passed since Brown had written the letter. From the moment the man carrying it stepped onto America's shore, its citizens had not failed to show their gratitude. Yes, their civic leaders had organized elaborate parades and carefully choreographed fêtes to honor Lafayette. But the people along his path, no matter their station or color, had rushed to thank him at every point of his voyage, even if all they could offer was their presence in the vast crowds cheering at his arrival or weeping at his departure. Carved across the triumphant arches, inserted in all the speeches and toasts, was the word *gratitude*. And indeed, this was of incalculable value to Lafayette, whose spirits, so low at the moment of his departure, were now lifted; even his faltering health had somehow been revived. Admiring Americans had offered gifts and mementos, destined for places of honor in the collection at La Grange. But these would not repay Lafayette's debts, nor would they provide comfort or an inheritance for his grandchildren.

Monroe understood the source of his countryman's emotional reactions to Lafayette's return. "It has proceeded from a sacred regard to the principles of our revolution, and the service which he rendered in it," he wrote.[6] It was natural, then, that the instrument of their collective will would act to affirm its gratitude.

As Monroe composed his eighth and final annual message to Congress, he included a happy report on Lafayette's return near its conclusion. The president recounted to convulsions of joy elicited by the old hero's return. He painted the touching scenes of the old soldiers of the Revolution, "many of them in a decrepit state," rallying around the general. "A more interesting spectacle, it is believed, was never witnessed." And no American, young or old, had come away from these scenes oblivious to blessings won by the great sacrifices made by these men.

The republic had particular responsibility to Lafayette, Monroe insisted. "It is natural that we should all take a deep interest in his future welfare, as we do," the president wrote. "His high claims on our union are felt, and the sentiment universal that they should be met in a generous spirit." The president was speaking of more than the dinners and mementos: "I invite your attention to the subject, with a view that, regarding his very important services, losses, and sacrifices, a provision may be made and tendered to him which shall correspond with the sentiments and be worthy the character of the American people."[7]

As the year drew to a close, Lafayette returned to a transformed Washington. Legislators and diplomats drifted back into the capital expanding its population, enlivening its society as the presidential election neared its conclusion. "The long agony is over," Hezekiah Niles wrote, prematurely, at the beginning of December.[8]

Because of the number of contenders, the election was likely to end without a candidate winning the requisite 131 electoral votes, throwing, as the Constitution decreed in its Twelfth Amendment, the decision to the House of Representatives. There, delegations from each state would cast one vote. But only the three candidates who earned the most electoral votes could participate in the contingent election. So, in December, as results from the states were reported, the suspense surrounded which of the four would-be presidents would be culled from the field. By the middle of the month, when results from Louisiana arrived, the suspense ended: Jackson, with ninety-nine, Adams with eighty-four, and Crawford with forty-one, would stand in the contingent election to take place on February 9 of the new year, and Clay would not be president. In the meantime, jockeying and maneuvering began among the candidates, their supporters, and members of the House.

Lafayette and Jackson, who had returned to the capital from Nashville, both lodged at Gadsby's on Pennsylvania Avenue. The two men had not previously met and, upon learning they were in the same hotel, determined to seek each other out, as fate would have it, at the same time and ran into one another at the foot of the hotel's stairs. "It was truly interesting," Jackson's wife, Rachel, wrote. "The emotion of Revolutionary feeling was aroused in them both." She was immediately fond of Lafayette and impressed by his ability to recall names and faces and his stamina for the Washington social scene, of which he was the undisputed star. "He is very healthy, eats hearty, goes to every party, and that is every night."[9] William Winston Seaton noted his admiration for American cuisine: In Baltimore during one sitting, Lafayette ate six bay perch, a whole canvasback duck and hominy, and followed it with a bottle of Bordeaux. The publisher assumed all the constant movement and riding uncovered in carriages had stimulated his appetite.[10]

Seaton was the first to entertain Lafayette privately, crowding 360 people in his home for an introduction to the old hero. "He is very lame and we contrived to keep him seated as much as his extreme politeness would allow," wrote the evening's host. Besides the many parties, Lafayette frequented Washington's theaters, enjoyed the company of Washington's family at Woodlawn and Arlington, was received by Maryland's government at Annapolis, and returned to Baltimore, as well.

Congressmen whose constituents had yet to be blessed with his presence presented Lafayette with invitations. The governors of North and South Carolina had communicated their desire that Lafayette visit their states. In November, North Carolina's legislature had approved of a formal invitation; South Carolina followed days later. Other states were preparing their own resolution of invitation.

What had originally been a trip through the major metropolises of the East and a visit to the American capital, with a planned return to La Grange in the spring, was now transforming into a truly national tour lasting into the following summer. On his way to Yorktown, Lafayette had written to Henry Clay of his plans to visit the Southern and Western states before the year ended. As late as December, Lafayette still hoped to visit the Carolinas in that month and return to Washington by late January, then depart for a visit to New Orleans in March.

With the onset of winter, traveling into the South and across the American frontier was impractical. Nelly Lewis lamented to Elizabeth Bordley Gibson that "the roads and weather are so bad for his excellent father—exposure to cold will apt to make him liable to the gout. They ought to have mercy on him."[11] Members of Congress, Lafayette wrote Jefferson, "Have not only Assented to, but Advised My postponing the Southern Visit to the Opening of the Spring, When I may Go from Georgia to New Orleans and Up the River to the Western States." Lafayette would wait out the cold in Washington and be received by Congress, "whose unanimous invitation, has called to me the most honorable and gratifying enjoyments in which the human hearty can enjoy."[12] On this score there was more yet to come.

Congress gaveled into session on the 6th. The following day, while Lafayette was at Arlington with the family of George Washington Parke Custis, Charles Everett, Monroe's physician who doubled as his private secretary, read the president's annual message aloud. Two days later, on the 9th, at 1:00 p.m., the doors opened to the semicircular room just north of the rotunda in the U.S. Capitol. "We introduce General Lafayette to the Senate of the United States!" shouted Virginian senator James Barbour.[13] The words reverberated against the hall's domed ceiling as, for the first time in its history, the body received a citizen of another nation in its midst. Lafayette entered and walked slowly down the passageway between the rows of mahogany desks to the chair reserved for him, positioned to the right of the Senate president's own. On this day the vice president, Daniel Tompkins, was absent; in his stead, Barbour adjourned the Senate. Each member in turn advanced toward and welcomed Lafayette. "It was a scene of simple but imposing dignity," the *Daily National Intelligencer* reported. The House of Representatives had also invited Lafayette to be present at its session on the 10th. That occasion, the paper speculated, "will, perhaps, make this scene even more attractive than yesterday's."[14]

This was a prophetic observation. In the morning, clerks hauled seats and sofas into the House chambers, placing them wherever there was free space, so large was the crowd pouring into the Capitol to witness the first-ever instance of a foreign citizen addressing the U.S. Congress. "The galleries thronged with both sexes & the floor behind the seats of the Members filled with ladies for that day only the audience being admitted below," wrote Fanny Wright, who took her place among the crowd after arriving in Washington. Her sister, Camilla, described the reception as the "most grand and impressive scene that has passed since his arrival in this country."[15]

The venue no doubt enhanced the day. As the Wrights looked up from their seats in the semicircular amphitheater, they could see the dome with its square panels, the paint giving the appearance of a small recessed square, each with a flower painted inside. Across the room, above the Speaker's chair, a gold eagle kept watch, its wings spread wide. Twenty-eight-foot columns made of breccia were spaced throughout the chamber. As a matter of procedure, the House extended a formal invitation by sending a messenger to the Senate to join the reception. As a matter of procedure, the House dispatched a messenger with a formal invitation for the Senate to join the reception, though it was unnecessary, as the upper chamber had purposely not met that day. Soon, a line of senators entered the room and took their appointed seats. With their arrival, much of official Washington—members of the president's cabinet, the diplomatic corps, and others—was present.

While the spectators were still filing into the Capitol, twelve carriages had assembled at Gadsby's in order to retrieve Lafayette. Washington's military authorities had offered an escort, but the congressmen who had planned to attend the reception declined. Stripping away the pomp and pageantry that had followed Lafayette for six months, instead he was drawn to the Capitol in a simple civic procession. The way up Pennsylvania Avenue was lined with spectators who, rather than cheering, doffed their hats and stood quietly. When the carriages reached the Capitol, Georges and Levasseur entered the House chambers first, taking their seats on a sofa next to John Quincy Adams. At 1:00 p.m., when Lafayette entered the room, accompanied by the twenty-four members of the committee of reception, members of Congress rose from their seats and stood silently. Not a sound was heard from the galleries above. Lafayette made his way to the center of the room.

Though Lafayette was on the receiving end of so many speeches during his travel, with the exception of Edward Everett in Cambridge, he had not yet been given tribute by an orator the likes of the Speaker of the House. Henry Clay's powers of oration were so great that members of the House or reporters were often spellbound by his speeches, which were complemented by physical theatrics. Clay would contort his face, shrug his shoulders, and lift his words with sweeping gestures. During her prior visit to the states, Wright was awed by Clay's "fervid oratory" and his "animation, energy, high moral feeling." The Speaker, she wrote, was "without exception the most masterly voice that I ever remember to have heard."[16]

Clay began his remarks with a valedictory biography of Lafayette, recounting not only his disinterested contributions to a distant, foreign nation, but his efforts on behalf of liberty on another continent, where Lafayette's principles had held through the storms of another revolution. Another portion of Clay's remarks mingled gratitude with self-affirmation. "The vain wish has been sometimes indulged, that Providence would allow the patriot, after death, to return to his country, and to contemplate the intermediate changes which had taken place," the Speaker explained to a rapt audience, "to view to forest felled, the cities built, the mountains leveled, the canals cut, the highways constructed, the progress of the arts, the advancement of learning, and the increase of population."

Clay had traced Lafayette's long career. Now, he summarized the past six months.

"General, your present visit to the United States, is the realization of the consoling object of that wish. You are in the midst of prosperity!" Americans understood, Clay said, the surprise Lafayette must feel returning to a country so dramatically altered.

"Everywhere you must have been struck by the changes, physical and moral, which have occurred since you left us." What had not changed in his absence, Clay assured Lafayette, was America's devotion to liberty and gratitude toward the Revolutionary generation—a sentiment, he promised, that would be transmitted "down the tide of time."[17]

When Clay's speech concluded, the audience in the House remained silent, while Lafayette stood and walked toward the Speaker. He turned and paused to look over the crowded floor and gallery. Then, for the first time in American history, the citizen of a foreign nation addressed the U.S. Congress.

Instantly striking a note of humility, Lafayette assured Clay that his "obligations to the United States, Sir, surpass greatly the services that I have been able to render to them." The honors now bestowed, Lafayette said, did not belong solely to him, but rather to his fellow soldiers. He thanked Congress for their invitation, because of which "I find myself welcomed by a series of emotional receptions of which a single hour do more than compensation for the works and the sufferings of an entire life." The recognition here, this day, and the assurances of the American people's admiration for his less successful efforts on behalf of the rights of man in his native country, Lafayette, his head held high, said, was the "greatest thing that I could receive."

By contrast to that experiment in liberty, Lafayette confirmed Clay's narration of his triumphant return. "I am called to witness the immense improvements, the admirable communications, the prodigious creations of which we find an example in this City, whose name itself is a venerated palladium; in a word, to see all the grandeur, all the prosperity of these happy Unites States."

He had returned to "the light of a far superior civilization" spread through "resistance to oppression" and institutions founded on and designed to preserve the rights of men, "government of the people themselves." As his address neared its end, Lafayette recalled visiting the Congress of thirteen states in Trenton, forty years before, when he expressed "the ardent wishes of an American heart" for the nation's future. As he looked out on the representatives of twenty-four states, Lafayette concluded the wish was realized beyond his wildest dreams; "its nearly infinite prospect that we can certainly foresee." After he had returned to his seat, beginning with Clay, the Members of the House saluted Lafayette one by one.[18]

Lafayette wrote to his daughters of the reception in "this superb capitol, this admirable hall, much prettier than the Chamber of Deputies in Paris." When he rose to deliver his remarks, Lafayette explained, "it was thought that I would, as in other times when General Washington had in the public audience of Congress renounced his powers, that I would take out from my pocket a paper and my glasses."[19]

To Levasseur it was a scene "so simple and yet so majestic."[20] The *National Intelligencer* claimed it was a spectacle to which "no resemblance in history can be traced. And which will hereafter occupy one of its most delightful pages." The paper noted that the pomp that had followed Lafayette was dispensed with. "Here was no glorious parade, no gorgeous pageantry, no piercing clarion or mellifluous horn, to dazzle the eye, or astonish the senses . . . It was purely a civil ceremony."

"For this time, at least, the Congress and the people are of one mind," the paper concluded.[21] To Fanny Wright it was an event that, temporarily at least, transcended her growing disenchantment with America's hollow honors for her "father." She struggled to find adequate words to describe the occasion. "But how shall I convey to you the deep silence the breathless attention of the crowded hall," she wrote to the Garnetts. Clay's powerful tribute; Lafayette's emotional response. "No, my dear friend, no pen or pencil could portray that moment."[22] In his diary entry for December 10, 1824, John Quincy Adams wrote, "G.W. La Fayette's observation to me—what a glorious day for his father!"[23]

In fortuitous timing, at the end of the year, Francis Allyn, captain of the *Cadmus*, arrived in Washington with the full-length portrait of Lafayette—his preferred likeness, clad in informal black suit, brown overcoat, and top hat, and cane in his right hand—painted by and sent as a gift by the subject's friend Ary Scheffer, a frequent guest at La Grange. In a letter, read by Clay in front of the House of Representatives, the artist asked Congress to accept the work as a gift from a fellow admirer of Lafayette and as an expression of "my grateful feeling for the national honors which the free people of the United States are bestowing . . . on the man who has been so gloriously received by you as the 'Nation's Guest.'"[24] Congress accepted. The portrait was hung behind and to the left of the Speaker of the House's chair.

The American government's tributes to Lafayette were not yet concluded though: After the reading of Monroe's message to Congress with its suggestion of an act of federal generosity, both houses had created select committees to draft bills creating a "provision" for Lafayette—Congress was preparing a national gift to ensure that America did not simply have him over for dinner, as Jefferson had worried.

The chairman of the Senate's committee was Robert Y. Hayne, a thirty-three-year-old South Carolinian. He was only a year into his first term in the Senate, but in time he would become one of its most eloquent speakers in defense of Southern interests. In his role of arranging a national gift for Lafayette, he was, as fellow senator Thomas Hart

Benton wrote, the "organ of the expositions, as delicate as they were responsible, which reconciled such grants to the words and spirit of our Constitution and adjusted them to the merit and modesty of the receiver, a high function."[25]

Support for the allocation of federal money to steady Lafayette's finances was unanimous in principle, but not, however, in practice. Members of Congress disagreed on the means of the provision: Some members advocated for money. Others believed stock would provide lasting income in Lafayette's last year and that land would induce his family to relocate to America. Two days after Lafayette spoke in the House of Representatives, Clay visited Adams to discuss the matter. The Speaker's minimum was $100,000. His limit was $150,000, supplemented by a township of land. But even the lesser of these two figures was too much for some members of Congress: Clay's colleague from Kentucky, Robert P. Letcher, was unlikely to vote for a gift, no matter the sum.[26] But as the committees worked on their bills, Monroe quietly lobbied Congress for $200,000, accompanied by a township of land. Any smaller sum, the president insisted to South Carolina representative John Roberts Poinsett, "will not put him at ease, nor as I presume, acquit us, to the expectations of a beholding world."[27]

On December 21, Hayne's committee reported its bill to the Senate: Following Monroe's wishes, it granted Lafayette stock worth $200,000 with 6 percent interest, as well as any unsold township of public land. The bill was read twice and referred to a third reading the following day. When the Senate prepared to read the bill a third time, Nathaniel Macon interrupted before it could proceed. In the history of the republic, public expenditures never knew—a more steadfast foe than Macon. A critic of the Constitution, he had built a lengthy career in the House and Senate on parsimony and fear of debt.

He had opposed a national government, refusing to represent his native North Carolina at the Constitutional Convention and later advocating against the government it produced during his state's ratifying convention. After this effort failed, he spent the rest of a lengthy career in office demanding the strictest interpretation of the powers granted the government by the Constitution. His name and *nay* were synonymous. He opposed a standing army or navy, the Bank of the United States, and the U.S. Mint. In 1801, he blocked a proposed monument to George Washington. When Henry Lee III, then a congressman from Virginia, urged the House to approve a design for the project with a $200,000 price tag, Macon said absolutely not. The cost, he predicted, would surely exceed the estimate. But his objection was not about money alone. Macon argued, though unsuccessfully, that the federal government paying for and building such a monument would squander "millions in acts of useless and pernicious ostentation."[28] Such idolatry, he believed, was incompatible with the spirit of the republic.

True to form, as the Senate prepared its "Lafayette bill," Macon rose once again, this time with "painful reluctance," to say "nay." The objection was not to the sum of the gift, but the principle behind it. He made no attempt to dispute the value of Lafayette's services to America. True, he was "a son, adopted into the family, taken into the household," Macon explained. But should he not be "placed in every respect, with the other sons of the same family"?

When it came to Lafayette, Macon willingly conceded, "I have no doubt that every faculty of his mind and body were exerted in the Revolutionary war, in defense of this country; but this was equally the case with all the sons of the family."[29] Ethan Allen Brown of Ohio then requested documentation verifying the sum actually proposed was not a magical number but could be connected to Lafayette's own expenditures on behalf of the nation.

Upon these objections to the bill, Hayne, who would later participate in a storied oratory duel with Senator Daniel Webster over the national tariff, rose to give it an impassioned defense—the fact he was forced to do so, the senator confessed, was painful. But Macon's arguments he naturally understood: The senator from North Carolina would oppose any expenditure of money for any purpose. But regarding Brown's questioning of the justification of the compensation he could not let go unanswered.

He would demonstrate to the Senate that the measure to compensate Lafayette was "not only an act of justice to him, but a duty which we owe ourselves." Here in his hands, Hayne said, were documents that would establish the first part of that formulation. He had shared their contents in private with other members, but Brown's comments had forced him to now make them public and enter them into the Senate record. The documents laid out Lafayette's early expenses from his participation in America's Revolution: He had left France with an income of 146,000 francs, the equivalent of $27,800. From the time of his arrival until the end of the war in 1783, he had spent 700,000 francs, roughly $140,000. There was a unique nature to this sacrifice that Lafayette had made. If an American soldier had lost his fortune during the war, he would have surrendered it in pursuit of his freedom and suffered the common fate of his countrymen "whose lives and fortunes were necessarily exposed during the vicissitudes of a contest for the right of self-government." Lafayette was not one of these men, though. He had no stake in the fight; he could have remained in France where he was "cheered by the smiles of a sovereign, and rich in the treasures of domestic joy."

"And yet he tore himself away from his country and his home, to fight the battles of freedom in a foreign land, and to make common cause with a people to whom he owed no duty—a people then engaged in a contest considered almost hopeless," Hayne reminded the Senate.[30] From his own estate, he had equipped and armed American soldiers, put shoes on their bare feet, and had never submitted a bill for the services.

"He spent his fortune for you; he shed his blood for you; and without acquiring anything but a claim on your gratitude, he impoverished himself," Hayne admonished his colleagues. The American government had not been uncharitable to Lafayette, Hayne admitted. But nor had its charity been particularly prompt. It was not until 1794 that the government gave him any financial support. Numbers were meaningless though. There was no figure that could correspond to Lafayette's service. So, no, Hayne now argued, the bill would not be tabled or reconsidered to haggle over a sum. There were "higher and more generous considerations," he said. "It is not that an account is to be settled, but a debt of gratitude is to be acknowledged—a debt which can never be discharged."[31]

There was more in the document before Hayne. Surely, the members were aware that, in 1803, Congress had granted Lafayette 11,520 acres of Louisiana land. But did they also recall that after Lafayette's agent had claimed land near New Orleans—land the city government had also claimed and been granted by Congress—Lafayette had the legal standing to challenge New Orleans? He would do no such thing; entering into litigation with the American government was unthinkable. Instead, he willingly ceded the land—the title of which, at the time, was worth $50,000—for far less valuable acreage. Now, in 1824, the value of the land Lafayette had relinquished had increased to $500,000.

If members of the House were worried about establishing a precedent, Hayne argued, such concerns were misguided. Congress had already provided for other veterans. In 1790, Congress had granted Baron von Steuben, the German-born major general who had drilled the Continental Army into a fighting force at Valley Forge, an annual pension for life. In 1816, it had awarded Alexander Hamilton's widow, Eliza, a five-year pension worth $10,000.

But precedent be dammed. "Can such a case as Lafayette's ever again occur?" Hayne asked. Here he argued the singularity of Lafayette's story and relationship with America: Something his countrymen and women in their current delirium over the returned hero certainly understood. Then came the dénouement: The bill before the Senate was not simply about Lafayette. It was about America. "It is, that the provision to be made, should not only be worthy of the distinguished person for whom it is intended, but that it should be worthy of the character of the nation. National character is national wealth."[32]

Hayne claimed not to care about what European monarchs thought of the American republic. But he couldn't deny that Americans, by their invitation and now celebration of Lafayette, had caught the eye of the watching and cynical continent. "Now what will be thought of us in Europe, and, what is much more important, how will we deserve to be thought of, if we send back our venerable guest without any more substantial proof of our gratitude, than vague expressions of regard?" he asked. Americans had embedded Lafayette into their history; now every single citizen of this country who set foot in France would be duty-bound to visit La Grange. "At least let him not, after this, want the means of giving welcome to the American who, whenever they visit the shores of France, will repair, in crowds, to his hospitable mansion, to testify their veneration to the illustrious compatriot of their fathers," Hayne concluded, regretting he even had to argue the case for the bill.[33] When the vote was taken, the bill had passed, 40 to 8. Macon and Brown were among the nays.

Corresponding legislation, though with the stipulation that the $200,000 be awarded in money rather than stock, met with its own opposition in the lower chamber of Congress. When the House of Representatives took up the matter on the same day, James Gazlay, a high-toned populist from Ohio, serving his lone term in Congress, attempted to thwart it. Among the few members who objected to the provision for Lafayette, the common refrain was the speed at which the leaders in the House and Senate had pushed the bill, limiting time to debate its merits. But Gazlay's opposition went deeper. There was a sense of injustice in the act now before Congress. "No member of the House could be ignorant of the multitude of claims for these ten years past, have continually presented to it notice for pensions for revolutionary services," Gazlay reminded his colleagues.[34] Congress was prepared to hand over a national gift to Lafayette when so many of his fellow veterans had been turned away from or abandoned their pursuit of relief.

During the war, Congress had created pensions—half pay to injured or disabled soldiers, though these were "recommended" to the states. The near mutiny of the army in 1782 had forced the government, with Washington's encouragement, "to never leave unpaid the debt of gratitude" to its warriors, to expand the scope and availability of pensions, allowing officers to swap out half-pay for life in exchange for five years of full pay.[35] But it was not until 1818, just six years before Lafayette's return, that the American government provided a pension with a much wider accessibility. A law passed that year made both officers and enlisted soldiers eligible for lifetime support, if they could prove a dire financial need. Once evidence of the applicant's income was presented to a judge, the secretary of war then had final discretion on acceptance or denial. But in 1820, Congress amended the process, demanding that applicants provide "certified" evidence of their income, a cumbersome hurdle that discouraged many veterans from pursuing assistance, and reduced the number of them on the pension rolls.

"The soldier of the American Revolution, and the American soldier, have been again and again at their door, asking compensation for services and sacrifices in the cause of this country," Gazlay said. "Was it sufficient that he should merely mention his claim? No—he must state and explain the grounds on which it was founded. Was it enough that he should do this once? No—he had to do it again and again—he must do it twenty times over—there was no eye to pity him, no hand to relieve him. After waiting on this House for years, he often had to go away at last without reward, because he could not explain and prove the precise extent and amount of his services."[36]

The argument here was that it was only fair that the House scrutinize Lafayette's record in the manner it would for any applicant. At the very least, the House should reflect on the bill before passing it. Another representative, Ansel Sterling of Connecticut, proposed a compromise, stripping the township of land. This was rejected. Joseph Vance, also from Ohio, proposed reducing the amount of the bill to $150,000. When this failed, Gazlay went even further, suggesting the sum be reduced to $100,000. At an impasse, the discussion ended.

Debate resumed in the House the following day with several members pushing for additional time to consider the bill and whether the sum—or any sum—was owed to Lafayette. One member, Ebenezer Herrick of Maine, even suggested postponing the debate indefinitely. At this point, one of Lafayette's own friends intervened. Edward Livingston, who represented New Orleans, had advocated for a national invitation to Lafayette in February and helped write the bill before the House. He believed no defense of the gift was necessary; it was the "echo of the voice which is heard from one end of the country to the other." The facts of Lafayette's service to America were widely known. The House, when it unanimously invited Lafayette and offered him the use of a national ship, made this clear. The cost of that ship, which Lafayette declined, Livingston pointed out, would have nearly equaled $200,000.

"I consider the proposed appropriation not as an affair of account—not as a payment of a debt to Lafayette, but as the expression of a national sentiment, which would do honor, not only to this House, but to this people—as an act which would, as far as it goes, serve to take away from us the reproach that Republics are ungrateful," Livingston stated.[37] He echoed much of Hayne's address from the previous day, eliding Lafayette's financial contributions to the Revolutionary cause and selflessness regarding the matter of the Louisiana lands. Other members of the House decried the speed with which the bill was processed, "like a comet through the atmosphere," said John Wilson Campbell of Ohio, who proposed reducing the sum to $50,000.[38]

Toward the end of the debate, Charles Fenton Mercer, a Virginian and founding member of the American Colonization Society rose. He revealed himself as the source of the document detailing Lafayette's estate during the war; he verified its authenticity and antiquity: It was prepared by Lafayette's accountant, Jacques-Philippe Grattepain-Morizot. But there were details Hayne had not disclosed: The accountant had omitted 333,000 francs related to Lafayette's two voyages to America during the war. If it was all calculated with interest, the sum would far surpass $200,000. Mercer followed this with an impassioned exposition, claiming the value of Lafayette's services were "immeasurable." Placing his hand on his heart, he said, "It is here. It belongs to the soul and no gauge can graduate it."[39]

A last attempt to reduce the sum of the bill to $100,000 was made by Gazlay. When this was voted down, the bill was read once more and then voted upon. The yeas were 166; the nays, 26. When the voting ended, Clay, in the Speaker's chair, who refrained from participating in the debate, asked that his vote be recorded among the affirmative.

The following day, when the Senate prepared to take up the House's bill, Lafayette, following the debates, wrote to Monroe with his willingness to accept a lesser sum than the original figure, "to reconcile the minority to the measure, would be, for me, and perhaps for them, highly desirable, and the increasing of the minority on this day would be very unpleasant."[40] When the Senate received the bill, it passed, giving Lafayette $200,000 and a township of land containing twenty-four thousand acres. Of the former, at the encouragement of Nicholas Biddle, he invested $120,000 in U.S. stock and kept the remainder to redeem his debts. For the latter, Monroe appointed John McKee, an Alabama congressman, to select the site within three months. The following year, he suggested, and Lafayette approved of, land near Tallahassee, the capital of the Florida territory, recently ceded by Spain. By 1856, sales of the land, which McKee described as the "best in Florida," had netted Lafayette's family $103,000.[41]

"In a word, my dear friends, here is your father escaped from all pecuniary burdens, and in a state to promise for his grandchildren a sum very clearly greater than what we had already," Lafayette wrote to La Grange after Congress had concluded its deliberations. "All that I owe to the excellent Americans, whose Congress, in offering me fifteen hundred thousand francs, is more unanimously agreed than it has been since Independence on the use of money."[42]

Soon enough, he was writing home with instructions to send money to revolutionaries in Spain and Italy—"The unfortunate patriots needs to feel our better fortunes." And there was the matter of melodies in his home's drawing room. "Now that we have money, my dear friends, we must get La Grange the most perfect piano one can have. It is a great pleasure for me to offer (from a distance) our musical youth the best there is in this category, waiting for when I have the pleasure of hearing them."[43]

Newspapers heaped approbation on the national gift and scorn on those who had second-guessed it. The *Washington Gazette* assailed Gazlay's "limited intellect" and false motive. The congressman responded in a lengthy rebuttal published in the *Daily Intelligencer*. "I was opposed to this course," he wrote, "not because I was ignorant of the historical services of Gen. Lafayette—not because my patriotism was cold—not because I felt no gratitude—but because I regarded my country and its character as much above Genl. Lafayette."

Gazlay further explained that he took umbrage with the assertion that there was any difference between Lafayette and the most impoverished Revolutionary soldier; the latter beseeched Congress for a crust of bread; the former was now granted a fortune, on the justification of supposed debts and a large family to provide for. This, similar to providing for the offspring of a king, was the behavior of monarchies, not republics. It was a form of idolatry, not a sincere expression of thankfulness. "It is national vanity in appearance, and national gratitude by name only," Gazlay contended.[44]

"I am very anxious not to be a burden to Washington and Columbia now that I am become a rich man," Lafayette, overjoyed by but self-conscious of the gift, told Monroe after the vote; after all, it was granted by members of Congress "whose compensation is far from being equal to the provision made for me by their munificence."[45] As it turned out, Lafayette did not entirely disagree with the dissenters. "I was very well received when I said that they were right, and that I would have voted with them," he wrote to his daughters.[46]

This put him in the decided minority. To many Americans, Congress had now defied history with the world watching on. Prosper Rudd, a New York jurist, was appalled when members of Congress sought to thwart or reduce the size of the national gift; he was aghast there was an attempt to audit Lafayette's expenditures. The moment required "a good generous ample sum, that a grateful and magnanimous people could have no reason to blush at hereafter; nor our noble visitor feel dishonored in receiving," he wrote to an acquaintance in Connecticut. "Then let the crowned heads of Europe, the Legitimates! The Holy alliance! Sneer, and faint at the ingratitude of Republics, if they please—who cares."[47]

12

The Approaching Crisis

"S tate of the weather in Washington since January 1st: The earth covered by hardened snow—the sky pure, air calm—the sun, from 9 in the morning until 3 in the afternoon, ardent as in the month of May in France," Auguste Levasseur wrote as 1825 began. "State of our health—bodies robust and ready—soul mildly taken by homesickness—hearts entirely given to our friends, our families, and our country."[1]

On New Year's Day, a line of congressmen, cabinet secretaries, high-ranking military officials, and, eventually, Lafayette all made their way into Williamson's Hotel on Pennsylvania Avenue. The spacious room they gathered in was decorated with flags loaned from the Army and Navy Departments; the meal they ate there was the "most memorable feast that has ever taken place in this country." There had been many such occasions so far on his trip and many more on the next leg of his tour, which, he wrote to his granddaughter Clementine, "will really fatten us up if we keep putting on weight at the same rate as on our previous routes. Of all of us, Levasseur is the one who has profited most in this way."[2]

After the historic dinner on New Year's was consumed and the tablecloths removed, the Marine band played while Lafayette stood and toasted to "perpetual union among the states; it has served us in our times of danger; it will save the world."[3]

John Quincy Adams and Andrew Jackson were seated next to each other, with a vacant chair between them. Noticing this, Henry Clay approached his former rivals for the presidency and slid into the empty seat. "Well, gentlemen, since you are both so near the chair but neither can occupy it, I will slip in between you and take it myself!" he said, sparking uproarious laughter. Adams and Jackson, however, were not smiling.[4] Though Clay could not claim the presidential chair, his support now became essential to the candidates who still could. That evening at Williamson's Hotel, the Speaker whispered in Adams's ear: Could the two men have a confidential conversation? he asked. "It is not possible to mistake Clay's object in this interview," William Plumer Jr., Adams's ally, wrote to his father after learning of the proposal from the secretary of state.[5] On the evening of January 9, the requested meeting took place: a three-hour discussion after which Adams wrote in his diary that Clay's "preference would be for me." He also noted that the Speaker had dismissed "any personal considerations for himself" in forming a potential alliance that would lead to Adams's victory in the House of Representatives.

Despite past animosities, support for Adams was the most likely path for Clay. He believed Crawford incapable of administering the presidency because of his diminished health. Jackson, on the other hand, "was ignorant of the laws and the country" and possessed none of the requisite skills of a statesman.[6] Regarding "personal considerations," of course there were many. An Eastern-Western alliance would nationalize Clay's American System. An appointment as secretary of state would position him for the presidency. And, hypothetically, eight years of an Eastern presidency would make a Western president more palatable nationally.

On January 13, a Philadelphia newspaper decried the "intrigue" in Washington—"not for General Jackson, God forbid! no, but Mr. Adams, which is by no means marvelous. The very Mr. Adams whom this same Mr. Clay not long ago denounced!"[7] But pledging Kentucky's vote for Adams was not quite so simple: In late January, the commonwealth's legislature passed a resolution instructing its congressional delegation to vote for Jackson. After all, the Hero of New Orleans had won a majority of Kentucky's votes; he was the choice of its people. Ignoring this message, Clay pushed forward in support of Adams, seeking to incentivize a union of Western states by introducing legislation appropriating $150,000 in order to extend the National Road, funding new construction in Ohio and surveys that would presage passing through additional Western states.

By January 24, Clay and the majority of his Kentucky colleagues had agreed to pledge their support for Adams. Ohio's delegation would do the same. The commitments of the two Western states to Adams, and Clay's refutation of the popular will of Kentuckians, caused an uproar in the House. "I was advised by a friend if I do succeed it will be in opposition to all the aristocratical influences here—meaning as I understand him, a coalition of all the influential interests of the Cabinet," wrote Jackson. "I envy not the man who may climb into the presidential chair in any other way, but by the free suffrage of the people."[8] A near-fall—he had misjudged a step—had aggravated the musket ball lodged in his breast, confining Jackson to bed for a week, while, as Adams observed, "the excitement of electioneering is kindling into a fury."[9] Crawford's partisans, led by New York senator Martin Van Buren, hung their hopes on a deadlocked ballot that would open the door to their man as a compromise option.

When Lafayette arrived in August, the nation was embroiled in a bitter presidential contest. His presence, a reminder of common history, had eased the enmity and driven much of the bitter rhetoric from the newspaper columns. But as the contingent election, on February 9, neared, party passions flared once more. The House's coming decision, Levasseur observed, had "reawakened all the desires, all the fears, all the hopes, and returned to journalism, all its violence and all its exaggerations."[10]

Waiting for the weather to turn before departing for the Southern states, Lafayette visited Arlington, where George Washington Parke

Custis recorded and would latter publish their conversations reflecting on his life and the Revolution as "Conversations with Lafayette." Lafayette, "ever true to the cause of freedom, in all its forms," was made a perpetual vice president of the Colonization Society, which had established a colony for the resettlement of free Blacks, from where a member had recently returned.[11]

Lafayette traveled, at the invitation of their governors and legislatures, to the capitals of Virginia and Pennsylvania. During the trip to the latter, in Harrisburg, he paused at the town of York, on January 28. There, at the conclusion of a banquet held in Lafayette's honor, members of the town's militia had let loose their party spirits. "If trickery and corruption make the pretentious of Adams prevail, well then, our bayonets will do justice!" came the protests. "We will go to the Capitol! We will proclaim there, we will cause to triumph there, Jackson's rights by the force of arms . . ." as the room erupted in applause. Depressed, Levasseur wondered now if this republic, constructed on the rights of man, was destined to endure after all.[12] Anonymous letters from Philadelphia arrived for Adams threatening civil war should he, not Jackson, prevail.[13]

And it was not only Jackson men: New Hampshire representative William Plummer Jr. reported to Adams that Louis McLane, a representative from Delaware, had sworn to him that he "would overthrow the Capitol sooner than he would vote for Jackson."

True to character, Lafayette remained sanguine. He had purposely avoided any appearance of favoritism toward the candidates and not involved himself publicly with American politics. "I know little of the presidential election. Was I a member of the House, I would support my choice as long as possible, and endeavor to bind the next one, before I gave Him a vote, to examine political conditions," he told Jefferson, which was as close as he came to offering an opinion on the contest.[14] The outcome of the election in the House, he was confident, would demonstrate the durability of America's institutions. "The ministers of the Holy Alliance, including and even especially also the English government, flatter themselves in thinking that the Constitutional Republic will be ripped apart by the violence of the candidates' three parties, during this moment of passage from the veterans of the Revolution to new men," he wrote to La Grange from Washington. "On the contrary, they will see that everything will occur in the most reassuring way."[15]

The atmosphere in the capital, however, was not entirely reassuring. "A great number of strangers have been attracted to city by interest of the approaching crisis, and many more are expected," reported the *Daily National Intelligencer.* "Lodgings have already become scarce, and, by to-morrow's eve, there will not be a bed to be had in the city, for love or money."[16] On the 7th, Lafayette joined Monroe, Jackson, Adams, Crawford, and at the Washington theater. "The house was more crowded than I ever witnessed it," Adams wrote in his diary.[17] Fear grew among some Washingtonians about how the lower classes would react to the likely victory of the secretary of state. In some of Washington's wards, rumor had it, residents had constructed effigies of Adams and were prepared to light them should he win; fear grew of violence among the crowds gathered in the city.[18]

A large snowstorm on the morning of the 9th discouraged the congregating of "idle people," but not the one thousand spectators who cramped into the House gallery—diplomatic crops, members of British parliament, and Lafayette, to watch the brilliantly lit civic ceremony unfold on the floor below.[19] At noon, members of the Senate paraded into the hall and took their seats to join with the House to open and count the electoral votes of the states, beginning with New Hampshire and concluding with Missouri, from the first state to enter into the Union to the last. When it was confirmed that John C. Calhoun had won the vice presidency and no candidate had won the requisite 131 electoral votes in order to win the presidency, the Senate departed and the balloting began. Each state delegation was provided, by the Sergeant at Arms, a box in which to place their votes; they then assigned a single member to read and tally the votes, which were then submitted to the two groups of "tellers," led by Daniel Webster and John Randolph, who were assigned the responsibility of reading the cumulative results.

Earlier in the day, a member of the New York delegation, Stephen Van Rensselaer, had been invited into Clay's office upon his arrival at the Capitol. Inside, the Speaker aggressively lobbied him to vote for Adams, arguing that by not doing so he was endangering the Union and, more particularly, his considerable estate in New York. But the old patroon had pledged to Van Buren he would not vote for Adams on the first ballot: Disagreement among New York's delegation would preclude an Adams victory on the first ballot and open the door to a possible Crawford movement in the negotiations during subsequent votes. In the moment of decision, Van Rensselaer broke his pledge to Van Buren and voted for Adams. According to Van Buren, in the moment of decision, Van Rensselaer, finishing a prayer, supposedly spotted an Adams ballot on the floor, interpreted it as a divine sign.[20] True or not, this was likely determinative: The results of the first ballot were read: John Quincy Adams had thirteen votes; Andrew Jackson, seven; and William Crawford, four. When Webster announced the results, hissing erupted from the gallery, which Clay then ordered cleared. Randolph reiterated the fact that Adams had won, and a committee was then ordered to bring the news to both President Monroe and President-Elect Adams.[21] When the news was delivered to Adams, "sweat rolled down his face—he shook from head to foot and was so agitated that he could scarcely stand or speak," according to the Washington socialite and author Margaret Bayard Smith. "If success, thus discomposed him, how would he have supported defeat?" the diarist and Crawford supporter playfully asked.[22]

After the election, both Lafayette and his son consoled a distraught Crawford at his home outside of Washington. During their three-hour conversation, Lafayette observed that, had Jackson won, George Erving, the former minister to Spain who had worried that his voyage to America would disadvantage Crawford, would have held him directly responsible and never forgiven it. It was one of the reasons, Lafayette explained why he never wore a uniform and reviewed troops in civilian clothes, lest his actions be seen as favoring the one soldier among the candidates.[23]

The suspense settled; crowds in and around the Capitol peacefully scattered. Despite the threats from partisans to claim the presidency by force should their man not win it by votes, "one did not hear any recrimination, any complaint," Levasseur recorded.[24] That evening, Monroe held a party in the drawing room of the Executive Mansion. The crowd was so great that it was difficult to move freely; an attempt by a marshal to limit entrance failed; a few pickpockets even snuck in. Inside, a congratulatory circle formed around Adams. Then a commotion came from one of the house's doors. Jackson had arrived. After absorbing the many conciliatory greetings, the defeated candidate strode toward the victorious and extended his arm. In front of the assemblage, the two men graciously shook hands while Jackson heartily congratulated Adams. "He was altogether placid and courteous," the president-elect wrote in his diary.[25] Soon after, a jubilant Clay sauntered in with a lady on each arm.

Levasseur was engrossed by the scene, relieved to see Jackson's magnanimity after hearing the violent threats of his supporters, a few of whom he recognized in the room. These men had vowed to storm the Capitol if Jackson had lost. "What are you going to do? Will you soon begin the siege of the Capitol?" he claimed to have asked them. The men laughed off his questions. They were "busy shouting," they explained, and their opponents rightly paid little attention. But now that the matter had been settled in the manner prescribed by the Constitution, they had only one course of action. "Now that the law has spoken, we have only to obey it," they declared. They would support Adams as if they had voted for him; at the same time, however, they promised to "hold a candle near his administration, and according to whether it will be good or bad, we will defend or attack it." As the conversation ended, they reminded the Frenchman of the singularity of America's system of government in a world ruled by so many monarchs. "Four years are passed very soon," they explained. "And the consequences of a bad election are very easy to repair."[26]

Among those who congratulated Adams that evening was a thirty-three-year-old painter who had arrived in Washington two days before carrying a coveted commission. Tall, elegant, black-eyed Samuel Finely Breese Morse was the first son of Jedidiah Morse, a Calvinist preacher, educator, and distinguished geographer who wrote one of the first widely used textbooks on the subject as well as an early biography of

George Washington. Samuel enrolled at Yale at fourteen. An unserious student, his interest was stirred during lectures on electricity; his talents were demonstrated, not in classes, but on the wall of his dormitory where his drawings and caricatures amused his fellow students. By his third year in New Haven, Morse had taken up painting as a means of earning extra income. Before graduation, Morse met and was enthralled with Washington Allston, the "American Titian," so called for his mastery of color evoking the Venetian master of the High Renaissance. Morse conceived of studying under Allston in London but instead, following his parents' wishes, returned home with considerable disappointment to Charlestown to clerk for a bookseller.

"I still think I was made for a painter," Morse wrote to his parents before leaving Yale.[27] Refusing to abandon his dreams, he continued to paint, now focusing on landscapes. At last, bowing to their son's ambitions, the Morses agreed that he should study in England under Allston. He departed in the summer of 1811. In London, he was introduced to Benjamin West, the American master who was, at the time, the president of the Royal Academy. Quickly Morse was reporting "rapid improvement" in his technique under the eye of Allston and West. His *Dying Hercules*, modeled off the Farnese Hercules, was entered in the Royal Academy; the plaster model for the painting earned the gold medal in the Adelphi Society of Arts competition. In London, Morse did not simply study great works from antiquity and the Renaissance; he sought to surpass them. "My ambition is to be among those who shall rival the splendor of the fifteenth century; to rival the genius of Raphael, a Michel Angelo, or a Titian."[28]

Morse returned to Charlestown in 1815, planning to earn enough money from portrait commissions for a return trip to Europe the next year. Travels in New England in search of clients were unprofitable, but in Concord, New Hampshire, he met and fell in love with Lucretia Pickering Walker, the beautiful dark-haired granddaughter of one of the town's influential judges. They wed in 1818. "Never, never was a human so blessed as I am," Morse reflected on the union.[29] His fortunes and ambitions as an artist waxed and waned. Spending winters in Charleston, South Carolina, he acquired more work and income and matured his style, exchanging the romanticism of Allston for realism, capturing his figures in full, including their flaws. When James Monroe passed through Charleston in 1820, its city council paid Morse $75 to paint his portrait. The result, which made no attempt to obscure its subject's rosy complexion or cleft chin, was among the few portraits the president believed accurately captured his likeness. The economic panic in 1819, though, leveled the market in South Carolina for portraiture.

In 1821, the entire Morse family moved from Charlestown to New Haven, where Lucretia, along with the couple's daughter, Susan, stayed with her in-laws while Morse lived the life of an itinerant artist. Inspired by the success of John Trumbull's *Declaration of Independence*, which won great acclaim as a lucrative traveling exhibit, Morse conceived of an equivalent historical scene. Traveling to Washington in 1822, he began work on an elaborate painting of the House of Representatives. The painting, which incorporated studies of dozens of congressmen, captured the beauty of the hall illuminated by the enormous brass chandelier in the center of the room. Exhibitions of the painting in Boston were unsuccessful. Frustrated, Morse planned to escape to Mexico as part of the delegation accompanying the newly appointed American minister, Ninian Edwards. This too collapsed when Edwards resigned from the appointment caught up in the A.B. affair. Morse roamed on in search of work, once again separated from Lucretia, frustrated and lonely, sleeping on the floor of a rented studio on Broadway in New York in 1824.

The arrival of Lafayette in August proffered one more chance at the success and stability that so eluded Morse. On August 18, before he departed the city on his way to Boston, the Common Council had opened its competition for a full-length portrait of the Nation's Guest to be hung in city hall. Numerous painters had petitioned the council for the job. Morse leveraged his existing contacts in the city to ingratiate himself with members of the council, particularly Philip Hone, a member of the planning committee for Lafayette's reception.

He quickly won work painting Hone's niece and the wife of another member of the council and planning committee, Elisha King. The networking paid off: On January 4, Morse wrote to Lucretia that a member of the committee had informed him, in confidence, that the commission was his. The official announcement of the award came two days later, with the promise of a prize between $700 and $1,000. It was a great reversal of fortune and, perhaps, the opportunity that would establish his reputation and reunite Morse with his family once and for all after years of painful separation. "The only thing I fear is, that it is going to deprive me of my dear Lucretia," Morse wrote to his wife with the happy news. "When I consider how wonderfully things are working for the promotion of the great and long desired event—that of being constantly with my dear family all unpleasant feelings are absorbed in this joyful anticipation, and I look forward to the spring of the year with delightful prospects of seeing my dear family permanently settled with me in our own hired house here."[30]

Morse reached the capital on February 7 and presented his letter of introduction to Lafayette the following morning, planning to begin the portrait at once: Time was limited, as his subject planned to depart for the South at the end of February. As Lafayette read through the papers, Morse studied his subject's features. "He has a noble face," Morse wrote to his wife. "In this I am disappointed, for I had heard that his features were not good. On the contrary, if there is any truth in expression of character, there never was a more perfect example of accordance between the face and the character."[31] Then the painter was overcome with reverence. He slid into the same trance that had dazed so many of his countrymen. "While he was reading my letters I could not but call to mind the leading events of his truly eventful life," he confessed to Lucretia. Here, standing feet away from Morse was "the very man who spent his youth, and his fortune, and his time, to bring about (under Providence) our happy Revolution; the friend and companion of Washington, the terror of tyrants, the firm and consistent supporter of liberty, the man whose beloved name has rung from one end of this continent to the other, whom all flock to see, whom all delight to honor; this is the man, the very identical man!"[32] When Lafayette had finished looking at Morse's papers, satisfied, he reached for the painter's now trembling hand. "My feelings were almost too powerful for me as I shook him by the hand and received the greeting of —'Sir I am exceedingly happy in your acquaintance, and especially on such an occasion.'"[33]

Morse began work at once, drawing Lafayette's portrait; he found the old man most pleasant company during their sittings. "This is Mr. Morse, the painter, the son of the geographer; he has come to Washington to take the topography of my face," Lafayette jokingly introduced Morse to Georges.[34] Though he was making quick progress, the constraints on Lafayette's time due to the burden of social commitments in and around Washington presented a challenge. But Morse was optimistic about the final painting given additional time with Lafayette later in the year when he returned to New York.

While he was busy in Washington, a courier arrived at Morse's hotel with a letter from his father in New Haven. The Connecticut author Samuel Griswold Goodrich spotted the painter alone in the hall visibly distraught. When Goodrich approached, Morse was unable to speak. Reeling, he walked away, leaving the letter behind. Goodrich glanced at its contents: "My heart is in pain and deeply sorrowful while I announce to you the sudden and unexpected death of your dear and deservedly loved wife," it read. The cause, "an affection of the heart—incurable, had it been known."[35] The commission that promised to reunite Morse with his family lost all meaning; he was unable to continue work on the portrait. He would return at once to New Haven, and Goodrich agreed to accompany him and inform Lafayette of this sad development.

The general received the news with terrible shock. He then determined to go with Goodrich to see Morse in his quarters. When they arrived, Lafayette took the younger man in his arms and kissed his face and together they wept.[36] "I have feared to intrude upon you, my dear sir, but want to tell you how duly I sympathize in your grief, a grief of which nobody can better than me appreciate the cruel feelings," he consoled Morse.[37]

The same terrible feelings would visit Lafayette's own family days later. On February 15, President-Elect Adams received an apology from Georges: He was unable to accept an invitation to dine with the president-elect that evening. Levasseur had received a letter from France with news of the sudden death, at seventy, of Countess Émilie

Louise de Durfort Destutt de Tracy—the mother of Georges's wife, Émilie, and a much-loved member of the extended Lafayette family. "This fatal news seized me so strongly that I was unable to take the smallest caution in sharing it with my two poor friends, who in hearing it were as if defeated," he communicated to Georges's wife after sharing the terrible news with her husband and father-in-law.[38]

"La Grange is no more what you have seen it. I have lost my wife's respectable mother, and that young family which you have seen so gay and so happy, is now spending its whole days and nights in tears, and mourning," Georges disclosed to Francis Allyn, the captain of the *Cadmus*, who carried letters and cargo from the Lafayettes back to France. "She was the tie, the life, the animation of all around her, and the thought of her death will always rend my heart which was here so much exulting in joy and gratitude."[39]

Looking back decades later, Josiah Quincy remembered Georges Washington de Lafayette sympathetically. "His manners were not prepossessing, and he generally moved about as if depressed by the gigantic shadow cast by his father. His position was in some respect awkward," he recalled. "He was not popular; but the opinion of the time very likely did him injustice."[40] Quincy's cousin Charles Francis Adams thought Georges was homely—"his appearance is a little against him," and simple—"not a man of remarkable mind."[41]

One Revolutionary veteran, thrilled to meet Lafayette, wrote that "his son looked like a man who had seen much mental trouble; he seemed to be pleased at the reception given to his father, but was not a man to talk, was stiff and I thought not an intelligent man whatever, but a proud, weak man."[42] Jane Blair Cary Smith, writing decades after she had met him at Monticello, remembered Georges as a middle-aged man who said little. She noticed, though, a quiet air of gallantry in his fatherly kindness to a shy young girl at Monticello.

As Americans celebrated his father, and through him their past and present, Georges Washington de Lafayette had a mostly unrecognized role in this euphoria. He had separated himself from his wife and children in order to make the entire trip possible, to support and stand behind Lafayette. He endured the exhausting journey and was wearied too by the deeply emotional scenes surrounding his father transpiring at every single stop. Most Americans were too preoccupied with Lafayette to take much note of his quiet son, but he had sacrificed much to make them so happy.

There was one American for whom Georges's return meant as much as that of his father. And it was one of the most touching reunions of a tour filled with them. Nelly Lewis considered Georges her brother, a relationship that endured after their time living as siblings under the roof of Mount Vernon. She had feared, for years, they would never again meet. Now that Georges had returned, she doted over him like a concerned and protective older sister, though they were the same age. She worried over his health: "By the way, remember, that taking care of yourself is a sacred duty, & if you injure your health, or your enjoyments, you will not do as your sister requires."[43]

She chafed at how he was treated by other Americans. "I have watched with a jealous eye the movements of the Baltimoreans lest they should push you too far behind your father & I scold the Philadelphians at every good opportunity for the place they gave you in the procession," she wrote. "I charge you to tell me whenever my countrymen neglect what I think their duty in this respect . . . I will scold when I see cause."[44]

The postponement of Lafayette's trip to the South, which she had advised, was an opportunity for Lewis and Georges to visit often at Woodlawn during the winter in Washington. Her own brother, George Washington Parke Custis, had presented Lafayette with the gift of a ring containing the hair of his grandparents. Nelly believed that Georges too was deserving of a relic of the honored dead. "I will tell you a secret; you must keep it entirely to yourself until you receive the article," she wrote to him from Woodlawn. She had discovered a sleeve button with strands of both George and Martha Washington's hairs intertwined inside. This relic she had transformed into a breast pin for her "beloved brother" to wear on his trip to the South. On its back were engraved *GMW, George and Martha Washington*, and *GWLF, Georges Washington Lafayette*. Her children already had their own strands of the hair, but "no one will value it more than you will," she assured Georges, whom she hoped would pass it on to his own son.[45] Nelly worried over his other children, whom she had never met, as if they were her own nieces and nephews. Saddened to learn that Mathilde suffered from headaches, she suggested remedies, such as Seidlitz powders. She thought often of Émilie, so far away. "Your good wife counts every day, I have no doubt, until your return & yet I shall be selfish enough to wish you and your father to stay as long as possible," she confessed. "The difference, is, tho, when you meet again, it will be 'to part no more,' when we part, it will probably be to meet no more, in this world."[46]

And she rushed to comfort him after the death of Madame de Tracy. "My dearest friend, you know that you cannot suffer without my participation—tell me how I can give you any consolation & believe that it is my duty as well as my inclination to give up every thing to soothe & comfort my afflicted brother and truest friend."[47] In his grief, Georges visited Woodlawn seeking solace from his American sister. He had withdrawn from the Washington social scene in which his father was in so great demand, and Nelly was happy to join in his seclusion. "I much prefer exerting myself to console him as far as it is possible for friendship to accomplish, to any party that I could attend," she wrote to her friend Elizabeth Bordley Gibson.[48]

Georges was torn between staying by his father's side or rushing back to his wife's. And according to Lafayette, he had encouraged his son to return to France. But though Georges fretted over the health of Émilie, he was devoted as always to his father. The choice, though difficult, was obvious. "However great has been the temptation of going immediately to Europe to weep in the arms of the best of wives, I had to consider that two sacred duties enforced upon me the obligation of staying in this country," he explained to Allyn. "In leaving it, I would have transgressed my duty towards my father, and perhaps might have appeared ungrateful to your admirable countrymen. I determined to stay, but my father himself is so good for his children and grandchildren and was such a friend to my venerated mother in law, that he has taken the firm determination of going away on the fifteenth of August."[49] The tour would continue, regardless of the family's pain. "Poor George is most painfully situated as he cannot leave his Father, & is so far from his wife whom he adores. He has the best heart in the world," Nelly wrote.[50]

Since arriving in Washington, Lafayette had received additional invitations from across the Union. Joining the Carolinas and Kentucky were now Georgia, Tennessee, Louisiana, Alabama, Indiana, and Vermont. Lafayette was determined to revisit the earliest scenes of his time in America, in South Carolina, as well as states that were wilderness when last he had visited. There was a complication, however. He had promised to participate in the fiftieth-anniversary celebration at Bunker Hill, helping place the first stone in the foundation of a new monument to the Revolution's earliest heroes. That event would take place on June 17.

Keeping his promise to the Bunker Hill Monument Association and visiting the Western and Southern states would be difficult. He would cross over dodgy roads and through dense forests in carriages and travel mighty rivers by steamboat. The trip would send the aging Lafayette, his son, his secretary and valet into the wild American frontier and then back east to Boston in little more than four months. "I Contemplate to set out for the Carolinas, georgia, alabama, new orleans, and the Western states as far as pitsburg from where I must Hasten to Boston for the Corner Stone of the 17th June," Lafayette shared with Jefferson. "Upwards of 5000 miles to be performed in 99 days with only 13 days Rest to be distributed along the [. . .] places, and 300 miles through a sort of Wilderness. We Will do the Best we Can."[51]

Best efforts aside, this was an audacious proposal—a trip unlike any other in American history. While George Washington and James Monroe had traveled across regions of the country, this was something entirely different: the first celebrity tour in American history. If travels from New York to Washington constituted a trip, venturing into the Southern and Western states would be a grand voyage, full of adventure, peril, and considerable wonder to the Frenchmen who had seen nothing of the American frontier.

Naturally, Lafayette was eager to embark. Georges, shaking off his sadness as best he could, conferred with Simon Bernard, the French engineer, who had earned a commission in the U.S. Army Corps of

Engineers with Lafayette's recommendation and had traveled extensively along the American coast assessing existing military fortifications and suggesting sites for new construction and an inland communication network connecting each installation. These assignments gave Bernard an extensive knowledge of the country Lafayette would travel. Additional input came from Postmaster General John McLean, who expanded the nation's postal network and had overseen the management of the republic's public lands as commissioner of the U.S. General Land Office.

Members of Congress from the states along Lafayette's proposed path planned to visit. The result was an incredibly detailed and precise itinerary, taking him as far south as New Orleans, as far west as St. Louis, and then at its conclusion and most northerly point, Boston.

In order to reach Bunker Hill by the 17th, a departure was set for late February. Amid the planning, Lafayette received a letter from DeWitt Clinton, elected once again as New York's governor the previous year. On behalf of New York's legislature, Clinton invited Lafayette to visit Albany. On the verge of departing Washington, Lafayette informed the governor that, on his return east, he hoped to pass through New York, "and enjoy the navigation of the canal." For now, though, Lafayette told Clinton, he must make haste. "My progress must be rapid and shall be so."[52]

Eliza Custis, elder sister of Nelly Lewis and George Washington Parke Custis, offered a fine carriage. Lafayette acquired draft horses and invited a promising young French author, Francisque Alphonse de Syon, to join his entourage. There was another addition: a little dog, the gift of military engineer George Bomford and his wife, Clara Baldwin Bomford, named Quiz.

Along with her sister Camilla, Fanny Wright had remained in Washington during the winter as well. She read *Altorf* to small audiences, increasingly consumed with the matter of slavery, studied the laws and registers of the Southern states, and was frequently in the House of Representatives' galleries. "They very frequently attended the debates, and that the most distinguished members were always crowding around them," Frances Trollope wrote. "For this unworthy gallantry they apologized to their beautiful countrywomen by saying, that if they took equal interest in the debates, the galleries would be always thronged by the members."[53]

As the thaw approached, the Wrights prepared to embark on their own voyage: They would travel into the South and then meet Lafayette in New Orleans at the beginning of April. Along the way, Fanny planned to compose an essay on slavery for the radical English journal the *Westminster Review*. "Alas! Alas! The more I consider the subject the more I shudder the more I tremble!" she wrote to the Garrett sisters. "This plague spot so soils the beauty of the robe of American liberty that I often turn in disgust from the freest country in the world."[54] The Wright sisters' pending journey was as unprecedented as Lafayette's: two women traveling into the American frontier, and down its rivers, alone. Later in 1825, the German prince Carl Bernhard of Saxe-Weimar-Eisenach arrived in America and inquired about Fanny. "I was told that this *lady* with her sister, unattended by a male protector, had roved through the country, in steam-boats and stages," he wrote.[55]

Time was now of such essence in order to reach Boston by June 17, Lafayette elected to skip Adams's inauguration in March. There was one civic celebration he would not miss, however: On the 22nd, he was present at a Masonic celebration of George Washington's birthday in Alexandria. The following day he boarded the steamboat *Potomac* and descended its namesake river destined for Norfolk.

Niles's *Weekly Register* subsequently published the astonishing particulars of the adventure: Lafayette would travel 2,655 miles overland, 2,610 on water—a total of 5,265; the trip would take ninety-nine days and cross into fifteen states. As the publication editorialized, "What a journey."[56]

PART THREE

The Grand Voyage

13

———— ≈ ————

The Living and the Dead

I t took two days for Lafayette to descend the Potomac River, enter the Chesapeake Bay, and land at the port of Norfolk, in southeastern Virginia, and another to reach the North Carolina line at Murfreesboro. Along the way, his party stopped at a dilapidated inn near the town of Suffolk to water their horses. While Lafayette sat in his carriage, the proprietor appeared in the doorway, imploring him to come inside if only for a few minutes. Obliging, he and his companions entered the home, the insides of which were so humble they communicated the impoverished state of its owner. This did not prevent him from offering hospitality, however humble, to the Nation's Guest. On the white wall, *Welcome Lafayette* was scrawled with charcoal, circled with fir branches, freshly cut from a nearby forest. On a table was an offering of bread and brandy.

While the travelers enjoyed the refreshments, their host vanished and reappeared with his wife and young son. After the innkeeper introduced his family, he lifted the child and placed his little hand in Lafayette's. "General Lafayette, I thank you for the freedom that you won for my father, for my mother, and for myself," the boy recited at his papa's urging, while tears streaked down both his parents' cheeks.

Lafayette held the child for a moment and then, fighting back tears of his own, retreated to the carriage.[1]

"The volumes of history furnish no parallel—no one like La Fayette has ever *re-appeared* in any country," mused Hezekiah Niles. "To us he is like a venerated father, returned from the grave."[2] The remaining Revolutionary veterans, he could have added, had reemerged along with him, receiving a last tribute before descending to theirs. And what of the soldiers who had helped win the freedom which that child in Virginia tenderly thanked Lafayette for, who had not lived to receive their own laurels?

As the nation approached the fiftieth anniversary of the Declaration of Independence, patriot graves were left unmarked; dead heroes of the Revolution reposed inconspicuously, their stories in jeopardy of vanishing from memory with the passing generation. There were but a handful of shrines to the soldiers of the Continental Army. In St. Paul's Chapel in Lower Manhattan was America's first monument for one of its first martyrs: In January 1776, Congress commissioned the sculpture after the tragic and much-mourned death of Richard Montgomery during the Battle of Quebec. Benjamin Franklin contracted the royal sculptor Jean-Jacques Caffieri for the work in France, which once completed, spent years in purgatory between Le Havre and the port of Edenton, North Carolina, before installation in St. Paul's east window in 1788; Montgomery's body, originally buried in Quebec, was not placed under it until 1818. An obelisk in Lexington, Massachusetts, marked the spot where the minuteman fell and another in Malvern, Pennsylvania, commemorated the Americans killed during the Battle of Paoli. Jean-Antione Houdon's statue of Washington, commissioned by Virginia's government, stood in its state capital in Richmond, and Antonio Canova's sculpture of the same subject was displayed in North Carolina's seat, Raleigh. Another monument to Washington was begun during the previous decade in Baltimore but was unfinished.

Both the Continental Congress and the Congress of the Confederation had endorsed monuments for other fallen generals, but these were ultimately suggestions rather than orders. Even an equestrian statue of Washington, proposed by Congress in 1783 for a to-be-built national capitol, went unfunded, victim to politics and debate over the suitability of building ostentatious monuments to public men. With few civic organizations to plan them and little in the way of industrial capacity to build them, Revolutionary monuments and memorials were few and far between, even in the early decades of the nineteenth century.

Lafayette's return, coinciding with a growing interest and reverence for the founding era, presented an opportunity to make amends, to properly commemorate the Revolutionary dead, and to build enduring reminders of their sacrifices and valor, which the living could look to for instruction. Indeed, his tour catalyzed monumental campaigns at Bunker Hill, as well as in Philadelphia, where a subscription drive was underway to transform a park in the southwest part of the city, where Revolutionary soldiers were buried in trenches, into a monument to Washington. Now, as Lafayette began his great voyage, traveling into the American South, he served as an officiant, presiding over much-delayed memorial services for long-departed friends.

In December 1776, when Lafayette first dreamed of military glory across the Atlantic, it was Johann de Kalb who presented him to America's agent in Paris, Silas Deane, and wrote the contract between the two men that made him a major general. When Lafayette embarked on *La Victoire* bound for the new world, then trekked from Charleston to Philadelphia, it was with de Kalb. A Bavarian-born soldier of fortune, he fought with honor for France during the Seven Years' War and later visited the American colonies to ascertain the feasibility of fomenting a rebellion against Great Britain. Deane offered de Kalb, who was fifty-five at the time, a commission as a major general in the fall of 1776, an appointment that the Continental Congress later recognized only with Lafayette's intervention. Washington sent de Kalb, who had wintered with the army at Valley Forge and fought at Monmouth, south at the head of a division of volunteers from Maryland and Delaware to reinforce the beleaguered Americans as the British sieged Charleston. In August 1780, the rebel army, under the command of General Horatio Gates, was routed near a British supply post in Camden, South Carolina, by a smaller force, led by Lord Cornwallis.

During the battle, the Continental lines broke, but de Kalb refused to retreat. As he steadied the Maryland Division, the general's horse was shot out from under him; he crashed to the ground and was bayonetted repeatedly and shot three times. Three days later, he died in a small house near the battlefield. De Kalb's body was then buried by several American soldiers in a Masonic ceremony at the bottom of a sloping field not far from where he had died.

In 1780, Congress ordered a monument to be built for de Kalb in Maryland. Like so many other proposed tributes, it was never constructed. In the years after the war, the location of his body became a mystery, and the hero laid in an unmarked, obscure grave. In the first years of the nineteenth century, though, residents of Camden located one of the soldiers who had helped bury him and eventually discovered the whereabouts of de Kalb's remains. After visiting Camden, the author Parson Weems lamented the general's nondescript grave: "No sculpted warrior mourned his low-laid head; no cypress decked his heel."[3] Residents did, at last, place a simple tablet above it, with an inscription composed by David Ramsay, the early historian of the American Revolution. Still, de Kalb's bones remained in a lonely field, where children played on his grave, likely paying little attention to the inscription carved upon it:

A CITIZEN OF THE WORLD

HIS LOVE OF LIBERTY

INDUCED HIM

TO LEAVE THE OLD WORLD

TO AID THE CITIZENS OF THE NEW

IN THEIR STRUGGLE

FOR

INDEPENDENCE

In the early 1820s, a committee of businessmen, planters, and revolutionary veterans began a drive to relocate the body to a more central spot in Camden and build a more suitable monument to place over it. The urgency of the effort grew with Lafayette's announced intention to visit South Carolina. The Charleston-born Robert Mills, designer of the Washington Monument underway in Baltimore, was hired to create the tribute. A yard in front of the town's Greek Revival Bethesda Presbyterian church, completed in 1822, and also designed by Mills, provided a location. In the fall of 1824, the De Kalb Monument Committee formally invited Lafayette to lay the cornerstone of his old mentor's new tomb. Granite was quarried and brought back to Camden from a nearby plantation at White Oak. When the hero's body was then exhumed from its forlorn resting spot, the citizens who had volunteered for the task discovered that de Kalb was buried in the "custom of knighthood," with his helmet, sword, and spurs.[4] After the invitation of the area's Revolutionary veterans, all that remained was Lafayette's benediction.

He began the journey south to Camden burdened by grief. The loss of Madame de Tracy weighed on the entire party. "We are now on route for our big trip, my dear friends, bringing along with us all our pain and sadness. The circumstances of my situation have become a torment," Lafayette wrote to his daughters. "It is impossible to escape from these unanimous and ever-growing displays—without doubt they are a product of an unbelievable and very touching sentiment, but today they painfully strain my heart." His health, though, Lafayette reassured his loved ones, was fine. "It will pull itself through this most painful of moral situations, between my regrets, my thoughts, and the obligation to be always on display, just as it has pulled through the fatigue of our journey."[5]

The way through the Southern states was altered by politicking in Washington: Competing congressmen naturally wanted the Nation's Guest to pass through their districts or hometowns. North Carolina's senator Nathaniel Macon suggested he take the Warrenton Road, which would have taken Lafayette through his hometown; "some busybody," according to William Winston Seaton, publisher of the *National Intelligencer*, had convinced him that way was too dangerous and he should instead pass through Halifax. Seaton suspected this advice originated from North Carolina's other senator, John Branch, who resided in the area.[6]

Despite the precise itinerary made before departing from the national capital, a sense of anxiety over fulfilling the wishes of each state and making the ceremony at Bunker Hill bothered Lafayette and limited his availably. On this voyage, he wrote, "Contingences may be anticipated, and actual calculations show that unless I gain a few days it will become impossible to comply with the invitation of the assembly and executive of the state of New York to return along the Canal to Albany and through Vermont to Boston." Even an invitation to return to Georgetown, near where he had first set foot in America in 1777, was apologetically declined. This, in turn, brought a touch of regional antagonism from the *Charleston Daily Courier*: "Long before the attractions of the sacred spot, Bunker Hill, the Marathon of America existed, he was received by us, in a manner, only characteristic of such feelings, as we shall always be proud to boast."[7]

Traveling southwest from the North Carolina border, Lafayette rode in the rain, through forests and swampland, the wilderness occasionally interrupted by a crude plantation. Roads were really just ruts that jostled the carriages and exhausted their horses. The pageantry of the Northern cities gave way to humbler celebrations. The efforts to organize these festivities for Lafayette in Southern towns were not commensurate with the amount of time he remained in them. "The celerity of General Lafayette's movement through our state may not inaptly be compared to a meteor, which dazzles for a moment, and leaves no track behind," lamented the *Raleigh Register*.[8]

Near the North Carolina capital, Lafayette was met by a cavalry company that rode 150 miles from Charlotte to escort him into Raleigh in a gesture of Revolutionary symbolism: Their county, Mecklenburg, claimed to be the first in the nation to declare independence from Britain. In the statehouse, he wept with old veterans of the Revolution in the shadow of Canova's statue of Washington.

Lafayette had once told Horace Say, who presented him with a sketch of the North Carolina town named in his honor, that he so appreciated the gift providing him with an idea of its appearance, because he would likely never see the place himself. Fate proved him wrong. "Here we are, my dear friends, in the city of North Carolina that you have a view of at Lagrange," he wrote to his daughters from Fayetteville on March 5, 1825.[9]

Lafayette's party reached his namesake town on the Cape Fear River under a cloud—the rain had not ceased for days before his arrival. Six inches of mud and water accumulated in the streets. Paying no mind, more than one hundred of Fayetteville's citizens waited in the rain, their clothes drenched, to welcome their benefactor and tell him, "Here you are in your city, you are in your house, in the midst of your children."[10] When Lafayette left town the following day, the rain had subsided and the sun reemerged. "He was here and is gone, though his was too short for our wishes, his visit can never be forgotten," lamented the *Carolina Observer*, Fayetteville's local paper.[11]

In 1820, while he was studying in Europe, William C. Preston, making the compulsory pilgrimage, was graciously welcomed by Lafayette in Paris. Now, sent by Governor Richard I. Manning, Preston was able to reciprocate, leading an immense line of cavalry, infantry, and militia, as well as civilians, to welcome the general to South Carolina. He merged with their procession and pushed on through the night, bonfires illuminating both their path and the immense forest that surrounded it. When they reached Cheraw, the welcoming committee apologetically explained to Lafayette that there were no living veterans of the Revolution in town. "Alas," he said, "my brethren in arms are almost gone; but I am happy to see their children."

The passage from there to the town of Camden, sixty miles to the south, was especially arduous. Roads were rendered impassible because of the rain-swollen rivers. In the morass and under the darkness of night, the small procession was scattered. The carriage carrying Georges and Levasseur came to a violent halt and sunk into the marshy ground when the shaft linking the vehicle to one of its horses broke. Two riders who had accompanied them offered their horses to the Frenchmen, who then rendezvoused with the rest of their party in a house in the wilderness on Lynches Creek, where a feast was underway and warm beds waited.[12]

The next morning, March 7, when Lafayette set out for Camden, was clear. Trees were in flower, gardens in bloom; the air was scented by spring flora reminding the travelers of French summers. One of

Camden's finest homes, owned by John C. Carter, was not only designated Lafayette's temporary residence, but also renamed Lafayette Hall
in his honor; when he walked through its gate, leaning on Georges,
schoolgirls strewed flowers in his path and sang their ode: "Welcome,
mighty chief, once more, welcome to this grateful shore."[13] On the
portico, Henry G. Nixon, a lawyer, one of the town's most promising young men, only twenty-four, read Lafayette his soaring welcome,
which concluded with a tribute to de Kalb. "With you he first touched
American soil in Carolina, and doubly sanctified it by his first visit and
his last sigh," he declared, "and you are now, in your old age, to deposit a
stone over his ashes which will speak to coming years."[14] Nixon assured
Lafayette that delivering the oration was the happiest moment of his
life—a life that would end four years later, when he was shot through
the chest during a duel in Augusta.

At noon on March 8, as the procession prepared to march to
the Bethesda Presbyterian Church, two thousand people gathered
in Camden. As the sun reached its apex in the sky, a child pointed
upwards, drawing attention to a clearly visible star on the horizon, an
auspicious anomaly followed by the appearance of Lafayette, limping
slowly toward the churchyard; ahead of him a band played a mournful
dirge; behind him, six veterans of the Revolution carried the casket with
de Kalb's remains.[15] Boys climbed up trees to see the ceremony, women
congregated on the church's portico, and its reverend, Robert McLeod,
waited with a prayer. The Masonic rites were performed, and master of
the Grand Lodge of the Free Masons of South Carolina, John Geddes,
handed Lafayette a trowel made of Mexican silver. Taking hold of its
ivory handle, Lafayette then laid the cornerstone and handed the tool
to the architect Robert Mills. Both he and the town's superintendent
of public works, Abram Blanding, delivered speeches. Lafayette spoke
only briefly with an emotional reflection on de Kalb, "the tribute of an
admiring witness, of an intimate companion, of a mourning friend."[16]
Then, as the slab of granite was lowered, Lafayette guided its descent
with his hand until it had sealed off the vault containing de Kalb's
bones forever, forming a foundation for the memorial promising his
memory would endure for the ages. Indeed, etched on the granite

cornerstone that Lafayette had laid read, *Foedus: Esto Perpetuum—May It Be Eternal.*[17]

Days after Lafayette laid the cornerstone in Camden for the memorial over de Kalb's grave, citizens of Savannah, expecting his arrival, seized the moment to honor their own Revolutionary heroes. Nathanael Greene, who had preserved the American supply lines as quartermaster general and had driven Cornwallis into Virginia with his innovative, asymmetrical strategy as commander of the Southern Department, died in June 1786 at age forty-three. He passed away on his plantation, Mulberry Grove, built on land along the Savannah River, that Georgia had granted to the Rhode Islander. "It is a Great loss for the United states to which He Has Been an Useful servant, and I May add a Great Ornament," Lafayette wrote to Thomas Jefferson after learning of Greene's death. "I Have personally lost a friend, and Heartily Mourn for Him."[18] When he was interred in Savannah's Colonial Cemetery, silk gloves, a gift from Lafayette, were placed on his hands. The connection between the men continued after Greene's death: In the summer of 1788, his fatherless son, George Washington Greene, like Georges, godson to Washington, traveled to France, where Lafayette oversaw his education; after returning to Mulberry Grove, the younger Greene met an early demise too, drowning in the Savannah River in 1793.

Casimir Pulaski, like Lafayette, was a nobleman but born in Warsaw and had been a cavalryman seasoned in battles against Russian forces invading Poland. His desire to join the American cause was motivated not only by ideology and ambition but also by necessity: A foiled attempt to kidnap Poland's king forced Pulaski to wander Europe, eventually landing in France, where the government was wary of the Pole. But Benjamin Franklin recognized Pulaski's battlefield experience and recruited him to join the American war effort. Upon his arrival, it was Lafayette who introduced Pulaski to Washington. Without a formal command at Brandywine, Pulaski led an improvised countercharge that saved the American right flank and likely prevented Washington's capture. He was made a brigadier general, awarded for his efforts, and tasked with training and leading his own dangerous legion of cavalry and infantry. They were sent south in 1779, where Pulaski was shot in the saddle during the Siege of Savannah in October and died days later.

After their deaths, Congress ordered monuments for both Greene and Pulaski, neither of which were built. For the time being, the responsibility for creating tributes to both rested with the people of Savannah. Before Lafayette's arrival, a committee was quickly created, capitalizing on the excitement around his upcoming visit, to begin the process of posthumously honoring Pulaski and Greene. This was only a first step—money would have to be raised in the future to construct the monuments, but Lafayette presiding over the laying of cornerstones was a vital symbolic down payment. The memorials would be raised through a subscription paper distributed across Georgia; donations of $2 were requested. "The occasion of General Lafayette's visit has been selected as the most fit time for laying the corner stones of these monuments," it read. Contributions were part of a "work of duty, that the state of Georgia may give another example to the world that Republics are not unmindful of the obligations which they owe, both to the living and the dead."[19]

They had less than two weeks to prepare: Lafayette departed Camden on the 8th and reached Savannah on the 19th. The way there led through Columbia, sixty miles to the south. When he reached the capital on the afternoon of the 10th, its streets were illuminated and decorated with arches. Francis Huger, who had participated in an unsuccessful attempt to free Lafayette from Olmütz—it was Prospect Hill, the plantation of his father, Benjamin, where Lafayette was received on his arrival to America in 1777—traveled north from Charleston to meet again with Lafayette. He walked by his side as he passed by the ranks of soldiers, who extended their hands, which he grasped and said, over and over, "Very happy, very happy."[20]

On the way to Charleston, the rains resumed. The narrow pathways through the dense pine forests were nearly imperceptible. Between Columbia and Charleston, Levasseur's carriage broke again. Because of the dark, Lafayette's carriage rode on ahead, unaware the party had split. The horses pulling Georges's carriage, which was behind Levasseur's, startled by the obstacle ahead, bolted off into the forest until it, too, was stuck. Georges and William C. Preston hopped out and wrestled the carriage free. They then offered Levasseur a seat in the freed vehicle and attempted to move on but quickly abandoned the idea, unable to see the road ahead. A rider was eventually sent to fetch a resin torch. For an hour they waited until the horseman returned, enabling them to journey on to their lodgings for the night, a plantation twelve miles from Charleston. There the weary, wet, mud-covered men found Lafayette at the dinner table surrounded by beautiful women and the dignitaries of the state.

The next morning, on the way into Charleston, the travelers were welcomed by the stately magnolias; the scents of orange, pear, and almond trees mingled to create an agreeable bouquet. "The entrance to the City appeared to us like a delightful garden," Levasseur recorded.[21] The locus of Charleston's celebrations was a ball staged in the city's theater on the 16th. Planners had converted a two-hundred-foot-wide room into an amphitheater, placing rows of boxes upon a series of platforms increasing in height, all under a giant eagle painted on the ceiling.

When Lafayette entered the room at a little past eight in the evening, preceded by the sound of a bugle, pandemonium followed. "The ladies became frantic—with curiosity, I suppose—one hollered, another clapped her hands, a third jumped and skipped," H. W. Conner, who attended the gala, wrote to his family. A manager of the event rose to quiet the commotion, waving his hands wildly, but this was futile. "He might as well have said to the sea 'cease to rage,'" according to Conner. The pleas for quiet ignored, Lafayette then appeared to deafening applause, supported by a small platoon of Revolutionary veterans, walked around the room, bowing to the ladies, who grabbed him by the hand. When he saw Lafayette's face, and the grace with which he received the adoration of his American friends, Conner became enraptured himself. "Here forty years afterwards when the heroes of that day sleep with their fathers this same Hero after experiencing all the vicissitudes of fortune, but still retaining all the purity of virtue suddenly appears amongst us. He rises as it were from the dead."[22]

Lafayette had planned to arrive in Savannah by March 19; hours were lost, though, in the route south. At the insistence of Charleston's planning committee, the terrible roads were abandoned for the comfort of a well-outfitted steamship, the *Henry Schultz*. The boat's course southeast was through the channel between the mainland and the isles off South Carolina's coast; a stop on the way at Edisto Island was a favor: Congressman James Hamilton Jr. likely requested Lafayette visit his constituents there. One of them, William Seabrook, hosted the Nation's Guest in his home and provided a unique honor: During his American travels, parents held their children up to Lafayette as if seeking some sort of civic benediction. At the home of Seabrook, he participated in the baptism of a baby girl, who was named, of course, Lafayette Seabrook.[23] Inland to Savannah, Lafayette's boat passed through Hilton Head, and Beaufort, the islands dotting the coast, moving down the inland channel, so narrow that the boat seemed to brush the earth on each side during the night; the next morning, crocodiles appeared on the banks and in the water around their boat. The captain shot one of the reptiles, measuring nearly nine feet. Lafayette had hoped to ship its skin back to La Grange, but the men on board performed this task too poorly, and the carcass was thrown back in the water.

The days preceding Lafayette's arrival in Savannah mirrored those in other cities, a time when "the bustle and anxiety appears to increase," the *Georgian* reported. Crowds gathered on the banks of the Savannah River, waiting anxiously for a sign he might appear. "During the morning, many an eye was strained in the hopeless task of transforming the fog banks and mists which hung over the low lands between Savannah and Tybee, into the steamboat bearing the Guest of the Nation."[24] The view downriver was obscured though thick clouds of mist. But then the vapors disappeared and a pleasant breeze ran up the river. A bell on the City Exchange, which housed Savannah's government, rang, as a puff of smoke appeared on the horizon. The militias formed along the riverbank, spectators secured their positions, as the boat approached and anchored. A barge was dispatched to bring Lafayette ashore where the city's mayor, William C. Daniell, and a line of local officials, judges, and members of civic societies waited to greet and help him up the bluff, away from the shore. At its summit was Georgia's governor, George M. Troup, receiving the guest on his state's behalf.

The aged veterans gathered around. Among them, John Shellman, whose Maryland cavalry troop had joined Lafayette's army in Virginia in 1780; he still remembered riding to the general's headquarters where Lafayette complimented the men that they "were well mounted, armed and accoutered," and promised them every opportunity of earning glory.[25] And Hugh Rees, who took Lafayette by the hand, said, "I remember you! I saw you in Philadelphia," and then recalled the encounter in detail. "Ah, I remember," replied Lafayette.[26]

After the reunions, he walked on, reviewing the troops. "As the general marched down the line with hat off bowing, I could almost imagine that Gen. Washington was also along, so closely had they both been associated in my mind," wrote John Stevens in his diary shortly after Lafayette's arrival. Stevens commanded the Chatham Artillery company, charged with firing a salute once Lafayette arrived, stationed in front of the City Hotel. By the time their gun had fired its third round, all the hotel's windows had shattered, as well as those of the drugstore in a building next to it, which brought its irate owner out to complain about the damage. "I told him not to fret, that the City Council would pay all the damages," wrote Stevens.[27]

Between his arrival in Savannah by a procession on the 19th and the monument dedication on the 21st, there were public dinners, illuminations, including a transparency depicting his landing at Georgetown in 1777, a reception with the city's French residents, the city's clergy, and Savannah's citizens at the Exchange, during which a number of women fainted. While Savannah celebrated the apostle of liberty, its leaders pointed out who was allowed to do the celebrating. "The City Marshalls and City Constables are required to take into custody all such negroes and persons of color as may be found at all trespassing upon or attending the procession, parades, etc., during the stay of General Lafayette in this city," read a letter from the mayor, published in the *Savannah Georgian*.[28]

Regardless of the restrictions, Lafayette still had an emotional and public reunion—the local paper reported the meeting—with an eighty-five-year-old Black man named Nelson, a slave belonging to the McQueen family, who had been Lafayette's servant during the

Revolution. Nelson's sight was gone, but his mind was sharp, and he and Lafayette traded memories of the war.[29]

According to Maurice Moore, whose militia company traveled to Columbia for Lafayette's reception in South Carolina's capital, in the midst of a welcoming reception, an elderly Black man appeared at the door, asking to enter in order to see Lafayette. When the guards crossed their bayonets in his path, he pushed them away. He had seen guns fired in war, and the guards' display did not threaten him. They parted and the man walked into the house and, in front of the crowd, asked to see the general. "An old acquaintance, don't tell me who it is," Lafayette said when he turned around. "Do you remember me?" the man asked. "Yes, stop; don't tell me your name," the general answered. Then it came to Lafayette. "Ah, I have it, Pompey." The man, once a slave of John Buchanan, was the first to attend him when he reached America in 1777. Reintroduced after so long, Lafayette then ordered a glass of champagne for Pompey.[30]

As Lafayette traveled across the Southern states as the representative of the Revolutionary Army and eulogizer of its lamented heroes, he did what his hosts would not: By meeting with Nelson and raising a glass with Pompey, he was acknowledging that there were other Americans, to whom there would be no monument, whose names would never be toasted at banquets by politicians, who had contributed to but were not afforded the same freedoms Americans were now celebrating. Thousands of Black men, both free and enslaved, whether for pay, freedom, or belief in the cause, fought in the American Revolution, both in state's militias and with the Continental Army.

On March 21, the city's Freemasons met at the City Exchange and marched to Lafayette's quarters, a boardinghouse run by a local named Mary Maxwell. They left the home trailed by Lafayette, accompanied by Troup in their carriage. They marched to the bay, formed a larger procession, and then moved through the city's streets before reaching Johnson Square, the site designated for Greene's memorial, where schoolchildren were assembled; the boys doffed their hats as Lafayette passed. A makeshift stage had been constructed at the center of the square. Lafayette climbed the short staircase onto the platform, and the ceremony commenced.

"To raise monuments of renown, to perpetuate the fame, and cherish the memory of distinguished men, has been customary in all ages and all nations," John Shellman, who chaired the committee leading the effort to build the memorials, said as the rites began. "They lead youth, to meditate on the honors they inscribe, and inspire active emulation, which is the source of Moral dignity and National glory."[31] After the oration, Shellman formally asked Lafayette and the grand master to participate in the dedication. Lafayette, in turn, accepted the request; it was his duty. He was not simply the Nation's Guest but now the surrogate for a vanishing army. "I stand before you, before these rising generations, as a representative of that army of General Greene's departed or absent friends," he said. A hymn was sung—"Author of Light! Author of Love! Look from thy mercy seat above, Let marble crumble into the earth, and aid us by thy power to raise a monument to deeds of praise, a monument to heroes gone"[32]—the grand chaplain offered his prayer; and mementos, continental money, and medallions of Greene, Washington, and Lafayette were deposited into the foundation. The stone was lowered into a designated spot. After receiving the spade, level, and square, the deputy grandmaster, William Schley, declared the stone "well-formed true and trusty." Gold and silver vessels were lifted to the stage and ceremoniously handed to Lafayette. He then proceeded to pour the contents of each—corn, wine, and oil—over the stone, symbolizing the Masons' ancient wages, offering their wealth in hopes the monument that would rise above the stone would be useful to man and looked on favorably by God.

Lafayette then walked to the stone, tapped it three times with a mallet; the high priest, holding a vase of incense, gave his benediction. The trowel was handed to the principal architect, who delivered his own address: "To you is entrusted the superintendence of the workmen to be engaged in the construction of this Cenotaph, to the memory of a departed soldier of the Revolution." The stone was then lowered into place, a volley was fired, and the students gave a cheer; the procession then moved onto the Johnson Square, where the monument to Pulaski was to be built and the ceremony repeated, with Lafayette recalling the fallen general as "one of the most brilliant sons of which Poland had to boast."[33]

The ceremonies concluded, then, after the presentation of a flag, sewn for the Chatham Regiment, featuring the arms of Georgia on one side, a bust of Lafayette on one side, and then a Masonic dinner, he was gone. "We regret that the urgent haste of the general compels him to leave us at so early an hour," reported the *Savannah Georgian*, noting "pressing engagements" dictated his departure for Augusta on the steamboat *Altamaha*.[34]

"I consider it a very fortunate circumstance in my life to have had the opportunity after so long a lapse in time to take part in the honors paid to the memory of Kalb, Greene and Pulaski, which being added to the cases of the Washington monument at Philadelphia, and the monument at Bunker's Hill will form a very gratifying and remarkable event of my Happy visit to the U.S.," Lafayette wrote George Bomford after departing Savannah.[35]

The foundations were laid on future monuments to safeguard the memory of Revolutionary heroes for centuries. The inscriptions on both, reminders that they had been placed there by Lafayette, also guaranteed that, for as long as they stood, Americans would also recall Lafayette's visit. Shortly, the citizens of Utica, New York, met to establish a subscription of their own in order to build a monument for Baron von Steuben. "His remains lie undisguised; there is nothing to mark the place of his isolated grave," noted the *Onondaga Register*. This could be remedied, however, by the construction of a modest but more fitting tomb for the general. And, of course, there was only one man to preside over the dedication of this tribute.

"General Lafayette has already assisted in doing honor to the neglected remains of Generals Greene, de Kalb, and Pulaski," the correspondent reasoned, imagining "the public will experience delight, in embracing the opportunity, afforded by the visit of the nation's guest, to manifest, by this impressive ceremony, their feelings of respect, veneration and gratitude, both for the living and the dead."[36]

14

---~---

If Only You Knew
These Poor Indians!

The *Altamaha* sailed up the Savannah River on the 22nd, destined for Augusta. Its departure was slightly delayed because of the most recent addition to Lafayette's little troop. "Quiz has become very fond of me and on her account much trouble was occasioned last evening," he wrote to George Bomford, who had given him the dog in Washington. She had developed the habit of rushing toward large crowds of people or troops of soldiers in search of Lafayette when she was separated from him. As they were preparing to leave Savannah, Quiz escaped and ran off after her master. Bastien, Georges, and Levasseur all gave chase before she was finally wrangled and brought on board the steamboat.[1]

The trip upriver to Augusta, passing through low marshes and then by tall poplars, concluded in grand, dangerous fashion: As the *Altamaha* drew near its destination, two other steamboats intercepted it, packed with the townspeople shouting greetings and firing off salutes. Then the ships embarked together toward the harbor in a three-way race. "There was something frightening in this contest," Levasseur wrote.[2] Black smoke coughing from their stacks obscured the boats from one another, the roar from their engines sent a terrible sounds across the water, ceasing only when the *Altamaha* arrived in victory at the wharf ahead of its friendly rivals. The ship's captain, Lafayette's secretary observed, would rather his boat explode than lose with the Nation's Guest aboard.

Lafayette reached Augusta on March 23, a day behind schedule. The original intention to remain there one evening proved impossible when his hosts explained they had planned a ball the next evening. It was not until the morning of the 25th that he was on his way west for the next leg of the trip: 350 miles overland to Montgomery, Alabama. Before they departed, much to Levasseur's and Georges's alarm, Lafayette, for the first time on his trip, began to grow weary. That so many miles had passed before the sixty-seven-year-old's stamina began to buckle itself was astonishing. In the month since he had left Washington, Lafayette had traveled over 1,000 miles, through dozens of towns and cities, and had endured in most of them parades, processions, addresses to which he was required to respond, dinners, balls, and memorial ceremonies for long-dead friends.[3] When the party had reached Georgia's capital of Milledgeville by way of the Milledgeville Stage Road, after pausing overnight at Warrenton and Sparta, on the 27th, there was no rest—there was a banquet to attend, veterans of the Revolution to greet, and reception with the town's Masons. Even when the public ceremonies concluded, Lafayette found little rest at his quarters in the governor's house, where "the lodgings have been filled with people every time I am not at a public ceremony," he wrote his daughters. "These excellent people come from so far for a visit of just two to three minutes that it is impossible to refuse it to them."[4]

The party departed Georgia's capital on the 29th for the town of Macon. The roads leading there, like those he had traveled in the Carolinas, were little more than trenches cut through wilderness. The carriage given to Lafayette by Eliza Custis proved a warhorse. Its wheels were shaken violently, sickening Lafayette, but the vehicle held together. Georges and Levasseur, on the other hand, were forced to ride on horseback much of the way of their journey from Milledgeville, where they arrived on the evening of the 29th. "We dined the same day in Macon, a pretty little city that did not exist 18 months ago. Two years ago the place where the city now sits was still covered in forests and savage Indians," Levasseur wrote to Émilie de Lafayette. "In truth, I believe that on this happy land cultivated by liberty, men, women, and houses grow overnight like the mushrooms in the garden beds in the areas around Paris."[5]

The cultivation of this "happy land," though, came at a terrible cost to its original inhabitants. Lafayette arrived in Georgia during an unfolding tragedy that would lead, in a decade, to the devastation of the Creek nation, the same people who were already displaced in order to make the development, so remarkable to the Frenchmen in Macon, possible.

The term *Creek* referred to a multi-ethnic alliance of mostly Muscogee-speaking groups, primarily Indigenous to the land constituting the states of Georgia, Alabama, and in the north of the territory of Florida. A matrilineal culture, Creek society, political organization, and identity were centered around towns, or *talwas*. During the Revolution, the tribes remained largely neutral between the colonists and Great Britain. After American independence, the Creek faced Georgia's expanding population encroaching on their lands and the new federal government's efforts to alter their way of life, encouraging them to adopt farming, Christianity, and European-style political structures. A series of agreements with the U.S. government culminated in the 1805 Treaty of Washington, which ceded territory east of the Ocmulgee River—a waterway running through central Georgia—and permitted the construction of a federal road. This road, intended to connect Washington, DC, with the port of New Orleans, included a portion built by 1825 linking Fort Hawkins (later the site of Macon) to Fort Stoddert, thirty miles from Mobile.

Divergent responses to white settlement provoked a fissure among the nation. The Lower Creek, whose towns were near the Chattahoochee and Flint Rivers, included many leaders who were the children of Scottish settlers and Creek mothers. They were more amenable to assimilation. In contrast, the Upper Creek, living along the Tallapoosa and Coosa Rivers in Alabama, resisted such changes, attempting to preserve their identity. A faction of the upper Creek, the Red Sticks, allied with the British during the War of 1812, leading to a civil war between the two Creek divisions. This conflict drew in the American army on the side of the Lower Creek after the 1813 attack on Fort Mims, north of Mobile, where white settlers and multiracial Creek were massacred. Creek resistance ended when Andrew Jackson's forces defeated the Red Sticks at the Battle of Horseshoe Bend in 1814. The subsequent Treaty of Fort Jackson forced the Creek to cede another twenty-two million acres—much of what would become Alabama—to the U.S. government.

Lafayette traveled from Savannah to Milledgeville with Georgia's governor, George M. Troup. A protégé of William H. Crawford, Troup was allied with John Calhoun, Henry Clay, and the other war hawks in Congress during his three terms in the House of Representatives. Like Calhoun, Troup was nationalist in perspective, a slave-owning South-erner educated at the College of New Jersey, and a fervent believer in the inevitably of the white population's spread westward across the continent and with it the cultivation of cotton, regardless of who or what lay in its path. Localized to his domain, that meant removal of the Creek and Cherokee from the fertile and much-coveted soil of central and western Georgia.

Troup was locked in a bitter fight with John Clark, another Georgian politician and rival of Crawford's. In 1819 and 1821, they had battled for the state's governorship, which was decided by a vote of its legislature, with Clark victorious. The outcome was reversed in 1823. But in 1825, for the first time, Georgia's voters would directly pick their governor. There was additional incentive for Troup, who was disinclined to campaign, to usher the exodus of the Creek from Georgia.[6] In 1802, the U.S. government had purchased the land that became Alabama and Mississippi from Georgia, predicated on securing for it all remaining Indian land within its borders. Washington was too slow for Georgians' tastes in keeping their end of this bargain.

On February 12, 1825, acting as U.S. commissioners, two Georgians, Duncan G. Campbell and James Meriwether, wrote and signed the Treaty of Indian Springs. His co-signatories were fifty members of the Creek Nation, led by William McIntosh, a mixed-blood headman of the Coweta town—his father was Scottish, his mother Creek—and a first cousin of Troup's. An earlier treaty, signed in 1821, had surrendered the Creek land east of the Flint River, running through west-central Georgia. The second Treaty of Indian Springs surrendered their remaining land east of the Chattahoochee River, which travels along the southern stretch of the border between Georgia and Alabama. In return, the Creek were given as compensation land, "acre for acre," west of the Mississippi, where they were to depart for by September 1, 1826.[7]

McIntosh personally selected his co-signers, including his son Chillicothe, "Chilly." He had no authority from the Creek National Council, the tribe's governing body, to sign the agreement. Other members of the council were aghast. "My friend, you are about to sell our country; I now warn you of your danger," warned Opothle Yoholo, an emissary for the Upper Creek.[8] In agreeing to the Treaty of Indian Springs, McIntosh had not only endorsed his death warrant, but doomed his people as well. As this tragedy unfolded, Lafayette crossed into the Creek nation.

After their brief stay at Macon, he proceeded west on the Federal Road. As the party—Lafayette in his carriage; Georges, Levasseur, and their escort on horseback—struggled on the terrible roads, black clouds descended from the sky, coming to rest atop fir trees, lightning bolts lit the darkened forest, and thunder claps shook the travelers' carriages. A torrential rain, accompanied by powerful winds, beset the party. It was a storm "with a violence unknown in Europe, that cannot be expressed in words," Levasseur wrote.[9] Roads transformed into rivers, trunks crashed to the forest floor, and the travelers were pulled in different directions through the wilderness, some seeking shelter under trees, others stranded in the middle of the woods. Lafayette's carriage continued on, followed by Georges; Levasseur fell far behind, only catching up with the rest of the party at a cabin, Spain's Inn, two hours later, where the men dried their clothes. Here for the first time they met Creek Indians, who were also gathered around their fire and engaged in limited communication via pantomime and sign language with the Frenchmen.

By the evening, Lafayette and his party set out again and reached a farm known as Calfrey's Stand, a series of cabins constructed of tree trunks and bark that served as both a trading post and resting spot for travelers. At the front door, they encountered two Creek men, one old, the other young. They were dressed in coats made of fringed material, cinched around their waists with belts decorated with beads, with buckskin boots covering their legs and brilliantly colored shawls wrapped around their heads. The younger man, whose name was Hamley, greeted Lafayette in English—he had, they learned, attended an American college but had escaped and returned to his people in Georgia. Lafayette and the young man conversed pleasantly until the general broached the subject of the recently signed treaty.

Hamley's mood darkened, his head bowed. He gazed at the ground and stomped his boot into the dirt. "McIntosh sold our father's land," he cried. "Seduced by the whites he sacrificed his brethren to his own greed. Now we must adhere to a treaty that is impossible for us to break . . . But McIntosh!" Then his hand began to search for the knife hanging on his belt. Lafayette attempted to soothe the man, quickly turning to other subjects of conversation.[10]

After the exchange, Hamley invited Levasseur to visit his home, a cabin built on a nearby hill, just beyond an enclosed reserve filled with deer. Joined by two of Troup's aides, Levasseur entered the abode where a violin hung on the wall next to rifles and bows and arrows. The older Creek man pulled the instrument down and began to play. The guests were then invited to dance. The governor's aides refused, but Levasseur, "Young or less reserved than they," awkwardly attempted a few moves from France. "Hamley did not ask for more," he wrote afterward. Instead, he grabbed a cape, leapt onto the floor, and danced passionately, "improbably more daring and more expressive than our opera dancers," according to Levasseur, who pitied Hamley, writing that he had little else to be so proud of than this dance, and had only asked his white visitors to demonstrate their own in order to prove its superiority. "I was entirely pleased to procure him this little satisfaction," he wrote to Émilie de Lafayette.[11]

On the morning of March 31, Lafayette and his party traveled two hours to the banks of the Chattahoochee River, passing by the bark huts of the Muscogee nestled in the forest, a novel but depressing sight, for the travelers knew they would soon enough be torn down and replaced with the homes of white settlers. At the riverbank a ferry would take them to the opposite shore and the state of Alabama. As Lafayette and his companions loaded their belongings on the ferry waiting to carry them across, a few Creek women holding their babies, and boys carrying bows and arrows, appeared, gazing at the strangers through the woods. Then, across the bank, fifty Creek warriors made their way down the slope leading to the water, "stripped naked and finely painted."[12] Georges and members of the Georgia escort loaded the ferry with their equipment and crossed the Chattahoochee. When he reached the opposite shore, and the Creek there learned he was the son of Lafayette, a celebration began; they touched his clothes, cried in joy, danced around him. Once the merriment concluded, the warriors fell into ranks, forming a line across the shore, ready to welcome Lafayette himself. One Creek, clearly the chief, let out a high and sustained welcome call. His warriors followed with three short cries of their own; their leader howled again three times, and so did his warriors.

Beckoned across the water, Lafayette boarded the ferry and began his crossing. As the boat reached the shore, several of the Creek stepped on board and communicated that he would not be permitted to put his foot upon the muddy banks of the Chattahoochee. Instead, they insisted, he should sit in the party's sulky, the two-wheeled, one person carriage, while they grabbed drag ropes tied to the vehicle and carried it themselves away from the water up the bank and to a more appropriate and dry place for Lafayette to disembark, some eighty yards from the river. "That was the greatest show I ever saw at the crossing of any river," wrote Thomas S. Woodward, part of the Alabama delegation watching in silence while waiting for Lafayette above the river. "The Indians seemed to take as much interest in the matter as the whites," he recalled.[13]

When the Creek warriors, with great care, had removed Lafayette far enough from the shore, a young man, no older than thirty by appearance, with dark, sad eyes, and mournful air, approached the carriage. In fluent English, to the travelers' surprise, he expressed to Lafayette the joy of his people in welcoming a man who, as Levasseur recorded, "in his affection for the inhabitants of America, had never made distinctions by blood or color; that he was the father dear to all races of men who inhabited the continent."[14] Upon introductions, the travelers learned that this chief was Chillicothe "Chilly" McIntosh, who had signed the Treaty of Indian Springs only weeks before. Like his father, the younger McIntosh inhabited two worlds, Creek and white; he had been educated at the Green Academy in Milledgeville, Georgia's finest school. To Levasseur he resembled Apollo; his eyes alternatively sparkling, "mournful and constantly turned toward the earth, giving him a meditative air."[15] Weeks before, the younger McIntosh wrote Troup an urgent note: He had heard that a hostile part of the Creek had approached his friends; they "ran them off, threatened to kill them, cut their throats, sit up by the road for show." These men were now in council at Broken Arrow and were determined to kill him, his father and other signatories of the Treaty of Indian Springs.[16]

When McIntosh's band had carried Lafayette up the bluff overlooking the river, they approached Fort Mitchell, constructed during the Creek War, and now the headquarters of American Indian agent John Crowell. On the western bank of the Chattahoochee, they passed into a new world, where the sun glistened off the helmets and swords of two rows of Alabama militia arrayed on the road. Alabama governor Israel Pickens dispatched a delegation of the state's "most respectable citizens," led by former congressman Bolling Hall and John Dandridge Bibb, whose brothers were previous governors of Alabama. With them, they brought three fine carriages; the one designated for Lafayette was painted white, drawn by four gray horses; twenty riders were sent to accompany the party. General William Taylor, accompanied by troops of state militia, meticulously outfitted, and Woodward, a brigadier general in the Georgia militia, who, as a boy, lived among the Creek, were to guide Lafayette through Indian country, roiled by the treaty, to the town of Montgomery. "I have always been looked upon as rather dry faced; but gazing on the face of the most distinguished patriot that it had ever fallen to my lot to look upon . . . caused me, as it did most others that were present, to shed tears like so many children," Woodward wrote of Lafayette's arrival in Alabama.[17]

When he stepped out of the small carriage and to the ground and received their welcome, Lafayette stood, for the first time on his travels, on a state that was not one of the original colonies: Alabama had joined the Union in 1819. Even in the forests of the sparsely settled states, there were remembrances of the Revolution. Among the delegation waiting for Lafayette at Fort Mitchell was Isaac Smith, who had enlisted in an infantry regiment of the Virginia Line in 1776, fought with the American army at Brandywine and Monmouth, and after his discharge in 1779, joined a Virginia militia present at Yorktown. Smith, now sixty-four, had moved from South Carolina to Alabama and was now the minister at the Asbury School, a Methodist Mission, a few miles north of Fort Mitchell. "He appeared glad to see an old soldier," Smith wrote his son in South Carolina. Their conversation swiftly turned to the Revolution, and the two men were transported, fleetingly, back to their youth. "I could not refrain from tears at the sight of him. It brought fresh to my recollection, many scenes, that had nearly been forgotten in the lapse of almost half a century," wrote Smith.[18]

At the sight of the Alabama reception, the Creek were visibly upset. It was, Levasseur observed, "a challenge that does them an injustice." They dispersed quickly toward the fort to ready their own celebrations. "These," Levasseur predicted, "will be less brilliant but perhaps zestier than those of the whites."[19] The party climbed into the carriages and proceeded to a large field, surrounded by a few huts, where the elderly Lower Creek headman, Little Prince, addressed Lafayette, proclaiming that he was indeed "bound to be the very man the Americans were looking for."[20] Speaking to his warriors, their faces painted vivid colors, with feathers in their hair, Little Prince introduced him as a great warrior who had fought on both sides of the ocean, and had visited with the Iroquois Confederacy. Little Prince then announced that, in Lafayette's honor, they would begin a game of holliicosi, a Creek antecedent to lacrosse, a brutal sport played among towns and an outlet for the pent-up energy of warriors in the absence of battle.

The men picked up racquets and broke into two teams on opposite sides of the square field, and then McIntosh let out a howl. "The ear is struck with cries of rage, of despair, of pain, and of death," Levasseur explained. "It produces, it is said, on the savages in the moment of action the same effect that the Marseillaise would produce on republicans flying to the defense of their frontiers menaced by the Holy Alliance." Lafayette watched excitedly as the men formed into two lines and began to run in circles around the field, before the ball was thrown in the air and the game began. The object was to throw the ball into the opponent's goal seven times, which the men competed intensely to do, or prevent the other team from doing so, leaping into the air to hit or block the ball. The game concluded when McIntosh, the most skilled player on the field, scored the winning goal for his team.

While the Creek entertained Lafayette, Alabama's civic authorities grew impatient for his arrival. "I have sent two officers on to meet the General to inform him of the disappointment that will take place should he fail to arrive at Montgomery to day,"[21] J. B. Chambers, a general of the state's militia, informed Pickens from Line Creek, the boundary between Indian country and the white settlement. The march there was underway on April 1 and quite different than any of the previous processions that had carried Lafayette through city streets, by homes and buildings from which elegantly dressed women waved their handkerchiefs: Through the forest Lafayette marched, accompanied by the Alabama militia in their elegant uniforms and McIntosh's warriors, now wearing European clothing; pausing on the night of the 31st, at the home of Haynes Crabtree, an Indian agent, whose tavern was at the confluence of the Big and Little Uchee Creeks. The following day they reached and slept at Warrior Stand, the tavern of the Upper Creek Chief, Big Warrior, one of the principal opponents of the Treaty of Indian Springs, who had died weeks before during a trip to Washington. The daylong journey there was hampered by constant rain. When the convoy came to uncovered bridges flooded by overflowing streams, Creek warriors rushed into the water, positioning themselves along the length of the bridge, holding hands, allowing the carriage drivers to see its path and proceed forward. All they asked for in return was to grab the hand of "the great French warrior."[22]

After a storm passed in the night, and the travelers were setting their encampment at Big Warrior's home, the forest began to glow intermediately with brilliant flashing lights both rising from the ground and drifting down from the sky. "This phenomenon was entirely new to me," Levasseur, who walked toward the lights to discover their source, wrote. "Running into the woods, I quickly crossed a few grooves crudely dug by Indian hands and began running towards the mobile sparkles that evaded my activity by subtly fading out each time my hand was close to grabbing them." Unable to catch or determine the source of the mysterious light—"they led me through the forest, as illusions lead us through life"—he returned to Big Warrior's house to inquire about the phenomena. They were called, he was told by his hosts, fireflies.[23]

By the evening of April 2, the party reached Line Creek, the boundary between Indian country and the white settlement, where an escort of Creek warriors was waiting for Lafayette. Their chief delivered a lengthy oration, relayed to the Frenchmen by a translator. "The youngest among us will tell their grandchildren that they have touched your hand and seen your face," he said. "Perhaps they will see you yet again, because you are the favorite of the Great Spirit and you do not grow old." Lafayette replied, encouraging the Creek to embrace the Americans as their guardians. "That's good! You are right, my father!" the chief yelled as each line of the address was interpreted. "But it was easy to see, however, on the faces of all his brethren how much more agreeable the French name sounded to their ears than did the American name," wrote Levasseur.[24]

Indeed, the travelers were appalled by what they found when they crossed back into "civilization": a village peopled by avaricious impresarios who had settled in the frontier, hoping to acquire riches through dishonest deals with Indians for toxic spirits. The night of Lafayette's arrival at Line Creek, Georges and Levasseur visited a store in order to buy a few supplies. While the proprietor was attending to the Frenchmen, a Creek entered and asked for 12 cents' worth of whiskey. The store owner took the money and told the man that he would have to wait while he helped Georges and Levasseur. Fifteen minutes passed. The Creek inquired about his whiskey. Indignant, the owner lectured him that if he wanted liquor, he would have to pay for it first. "I gave you 12 cents just a bit ago," he replied. The owner leaped over the counter and grasped the man's ears, and with the help of a clerk, threw him out the door. The Frenchmen had witnessed the entire transaction; the Creek man had indeed given the store owner the 12 cents. "I was convinced of the good faith of the one and the deceit of the other. I felt my blood boil with indignation," Levasseur wrote to Émilie, recounting the episode.[25]

When he left the store, the Indian walked a few feet from the store. He crossed his arms over his chest as he strode toward Line Creek, splashed into the water, and crossed back into Creek territory. Then he turned toward the white village, looked up at the sky, raised his closed fists, and shouted aloud. Levasseur did not recognize the words but understood them nevertheless. "No doubt he called on the vengeance of heaven against his persecutors; this vengeance he well deserved, and yet his prayer was in vain!" he wrote. "In that moment, I wanted to be an Indian. I would have called my brethren to arms and the land of our fathers, this land usurped by the whites would be soaked in the blood of its usurpers . . . poor Indians! Plundered, beaten, poisoned by strong liquor, by dishonest treaties you are chased from your father's land, and are called savages!"[26]

When Levasseur had followed the young Creek, Hamley, into his home, he watched him dance with an amused, condescending air; the Indian had little else to boast or be proud of than his ability to dance with more energy than his white interlocutors. Now, though, his blood boiled at the treatment of the Creek by the whites. "If only you knew these poor Indians! I am sure you would love them," Levasseur told Émilie de Lafayette. "The whites, who at all times have abused the advantages conferred to them by the light of civilization over men of color, accuse the savages of being thieves, lazy, intemperate, vindictive, and cruel. If time allowed me, I could easily prove that the vices they are accused of having are the result of close proximity with civilization, and that in robbery and cruelty they are well behind their corrupters."[27]

Lafayette reached Montgomery on the 3rd. The procession concluded on Goat Hill, an incline offering a picturesque view of the village's homes and the surrounding farmland. Two tents were set up with an arch erected where Pickens waited for Lafayette. The governor, overwhelmed by the burden of addressing the Nation's Guest, apparently struggled initially to speak, before eventually regaining his composure. "Your present arduous tour is to us gratifying evidence that your generous concern has extended to these more recent members of the American Union," the governor told Lafayette, reminding him that "the beautiful country now passing under your review, was but a very few years ago only known as the hunting ground of the savage."[28] Lafayette, in turn, politely replied, praising the young state's "rapid improvements."[29] During the ceremony, an elderly veteran of the Revolution, Thomas Carr, straining to catch a glimpse of Lafayette in the large crowd of over three thousand—and perhaps drunk—slipped and fell into a well. The ceremonies were temporarily paused while he was safely fished out.

If Carr was indeed intoxicated, it could have been from the ample drinks provided for the occasion. Indeed, in planning for Lafayette's tour of their state, Pickens and Alabama's planning committee had taken the notion of disproving the ingratitude of republics to an entirely new, and not especially prudent, level. A lieutenant, John B. Hogan, was stationed to receive a rider with word of Lafayette's arrival at Fort Mitchell and to send a rider on to Montgomery with the news. When he heard of the welcome McIntosh and his tribe planned for the Nation's Guest, he reacted with jealousy. "I hope our citizens will not be outdone in patriotism by the Creek Indians," he confided to Pickens.[30] If measured by expenditures, that was impossible. In their excitement to stage a celebration for the Nation's Guest equal to their more established sister states, Alabama planned extravagantly.

The state spent wildly on food (ham, beef, lobsters, oysters, pickles, capers) and drink (champagne, raspberry brandy, Madeira, claret, Irish whiskey). It paid for refurbishments on the trapezoidal brick statehouse in the town of Cahawba; for a giant national flag, handbills, invitations, for the brass brand brought up from New Orleans to play on board one of the two steamships, the *Balize* and the *Henderson*, provided to Lafayette for his journey down the Alabama River. On the night of April 2, an argument erupted between one of the musicians in the band, Joseph Toussint, and a man named Reuben Green Bates in Montgomery, ending in the latter stabbing and killing the former. A local doctor attempted to save Toussint's life. Alabama picked up the tab for his services and a burial shroud for the victim. The state spent nearly $17,000 on Lafayette festivities; a sum that required an additional appropriation of $4,000 from the state legislature, a figure in total that surpassed funds designated for more enduring capital projects such as the construction of a new statehouse. On top of it all, when a crewman on one of the boats provided for Lafayette was injured while firing a canon salute, it was the first personal injury lawsuit in the history of Alabama.[31] "We gaze upon the object of our affections, with a mixture of love, gratitude and admiration," one Alabama newspaper explained unapologetically. "Our feelings are so blinded and confused that we find it impossible to analyze them, and rapt in the intensity of our sensations, we become lost and absorbed in a dreamy reverie of the mind."[32]

Following the schedule prepared by Pickens, the *Henderson* transported Lafayette and his companions to Mobile Gulf, stopping for balls, banquets, barbecues, and illuminations along the Alabama River from Montgomery, to Cahaba, then to Selma, Claiborne, and, finally, to Mobile, to the constant sound of a brass band and cannons booming and the sight of bonfires burning on their departures and arrivals.

On April 7, Lafayette boarded the *Natchez*, sent by the city of New Orleans; Alabama surrendered the Nation's Guest to Louisiana. "I consider this a very fortunate occurrence, which has given me occasion to be the fellow traveler & host of one of the finest men that ever graced and adorned the human family," wrote Pickens, who accompanied Lafayette from Montgomery to Mobile. "In private life & as a companion he is not less valuable and worthy than his exalted public character. He is gone & our prayers are with him."

Relinquishing Lafayette to Louisiana was moving for Pickens, though not likely the most emotional farewell in Alabama. "The goodbyes MacIntosh [sic] made to the General were very sad. He seemed

overwhelmed with funereal forebodings," Levasseur wrote. After parting with Lafayette, McIntosh encountered his secretary in a courtyard
in Montgomery. He asked the Frenchman to put his right forearm on
top of his own, a sign of friendship, and look upward toward the sky.
"Always accompany and watch over our father," he asked Levasseur
standing in the moonlight, his voice growing somber over the fate of
his father and his people. "It will be to the Great Spirit to watch over
him as well and to have him soon arrive, without misfortune, amid his
children in France. He children are our brothers, and he is our father. I
hope he will not forget us." Before Levasseur could respond, McIntosh
vanished from sight.[33]

Shortly after Lafayette had passed through Alabama, the Creek
National Council met at Broken Arrow, near Fort Mitchell. The Indian
Agent, Crowell, attended the gathering, having recently returned from
Washington with word that the Treaty of Indian Springs was now ratified. The Creek were in disbelief. "The countenances of the Chiefs
spoke their disappointment," wrote the Rev. Isaac Smith, who was also
present. Crowell encouraged the headmen to accept the agreement, and
to warn their young warriors to treat the white settlers who would pass
through their land peacefully. After this appeal, the Creek requested
that Crowell leave them. "The Council broke up different than any I
had seen in the nation," wrote Smith, who believed a decision was then
made regarding the fate of William McIntosh.[34]

On April 30, punished by a band of Creek for the illegal sale of
their land, the elder McIntosh was shot and stabbed, dragged across the
yard of his burning plantation.[35] In two years hundreds of Creek, many
aligned with McIntosh, departed Georgia for Fort Gibson in the future
state of Oklahoma. Over a thousand more made the grueling journey
west before the decade was over. Despite an additional treaty with the
American government, those who remained in Alabama were prey to
white land speculators and eventually rose up in a second war with the
US, which provided a pretext to their final, forced removal west.

15

---≈---

Vive la Liberte! Vive L'Ami de L'Amerique! Vive Lafayette!

On the evening of April 7, the steamboat *Natchez* departed the bay of Mobile, bound for the Gulf of Mexico. Returning to the water was a reprieve from the wretched roads Lafayette traveled across in the Southern states thus far. "Now we have gone through all the material difficulties of our journey, we will go for a great while by water and after that we will find good roads," Georges Washington de Lafayette wrote to Eliza Custis on the eve of their exit from Alabama.[1] Predictions of smooth sailing were premature.

In order to expedite its arrival at New Orleans, the boat's captain chose to swing into the Gulf and then steam across its confluence with the Mississippi River before anchoring off the Louisiana coast. Quickly, the entire voyage appeared doomed: As the *Natchez*'s paddle wheel turned, its passengers merrily gathering on the bridge to take a last look at Mobile, a fire erupted in the kitchen, which the crew quickly subdued.[2]

The journey south had just began when the winds rose and water convulsed, tossing the boat. Dizzied, vomiting passengers scurried to their cabins and attempted to sleep. Waves crashed high against the boat, splashing through its portals, soaking their beds, flooding the cabin floors. One of the passengers, who only the day prior had professed to the Frenchmen that he believed "in neither God nor the devil," sat alone in a corner praying. Lafayette, however, slept though the danger. At daybreak, the turbulence eased and the wide expanse of the Mississippi appeared. It was a river, Levasseur wrote, "whose terrible course and prodigious size suggests a conqueror of rather than a tributary to the ocean." Uprooted tree trunks lay in piles on muddy islands, and large alligators "with sideways glances and a heavy walk, placed on thrones of floating trees, menace the explorer and seem to want to block his passage," while tall magnolias stood on the banks, draped in Spanish moss.[3]

The boat's progress continued, dark returned, and near midnight, the muffled roar was perceptible in the distance, followed by repeated cannon blasts. The origin of the sound was New Orleans, readying to receive the Nation's Guest. At morning, the *Natchez* neared Chalmette Plantation, southeast of the city, where, in January 1815, Andrew Jackson's hastily organized army, an amalgamation of militia, backwoodsmen, pirates, and free Black soldiers, reduced the British army advancing on their earthworks in an attempt to take the vital port of New Orleans to a sea of dead bodies in red coats. Lafayette was still below deck, when shouts rang from the shore: "Vive la liberté! Vive l'ami de l'Amerique! Vive Lafayette!" He climbed to the deck and discovered, on the bank, a troop of militia wore the uniforms of the National Guard. "For a moment," Levasseur wrote, "we believed ourselves transported into our freed fatherland, and our hearts beat with joy."

After stepping on the shore, he was ushered to the home of William Montgomery, Jackson's headquarters, then, after the usual welcome oratory, took his place in the lengthy procession into the city, halting at the Place d'Armes, where, despite the miserable wet weather, an enormous crowd—and a sixty-eight-foot-tall arch—awaited at the square in the city's heart. The Cabildo, where the mayor and city council met, was refashioned "Lafayette House," for his stay and their offices transformed into a luxurious suite, furnished with new sofas, tables, chairs, beds and bedding, stocked with napkins, washboards, knives, and forks.

All of which, "lately used by 'the Nation's Guest,'" were sold off upon his departure from the city like precious relics.[4] He entered "Lafayette House" to a sustained ovation, and to church bells chiming, walked onto a balcony looking out on the square and watched the militias march by. Toward the end of the parade, an interesting sight: one hundred Choctaw warriors marching in a single line.

"I behold this city, so interesting to me," Lafayette exclaimed upon reaching New Orleans.[5] Over the previous seven months he was reunited with old soldiers and statesmen, had seen familiar scenes and shrines that touched memories from five decades prior, visited cities and trekked through the wilderness. He had seen nothing in America, though, quite like New Orleans.

In 1825, *half* of New Orleans's population was of French origin; some were assimilated, some could not even translate *bonjour* into English; the city was separated into Anglo and French districts, each with its own newspapers and theater. But New Orleans was far more than a melding of two cultures; it was an amalgamation of many. It was home to Spanish exiles, taking refuge from the Holy Alliance; free Blacks, whose movements in the city were limited without passes; Choctaw Indians, who sold their palmetto baskets; a legendary Catholic friar; and old heroes of the American Revolution. Its culture, relative to the Northern cities, was one of slightly loosened morals: The theaters, hosting balls, and masquerades were open on Sunday, while musicians wandered the streets strumming guitars.

New Orleans languished as an afterthought of the French and Spanish empires, who had possessed the city until the Louisiana Purchase in 1803. Louisiana entered the Union seven years later. By the time of Lafayette's visit, New Orleans had become a prospering city, one of America's most economically vibrant ports. "Under the European regimes, this city had five or six ships at its port—now it has three to four hundred," Lafayette wrote.[6] Indeed, New Orleans, Lafayette remarked, "offers one of the most incontestable arguments in favor of the doctrines for which my companions and myself have fought, by the comparison of that which it was for a long time under the former successive governments of France and Spain, and that which it has rapidly become since it has governed itself under the influence of American principles."[7] New Orleans lagged behind its Northern peers, but advancements were evident; only two streets were paved, but many of the city's sidewalks were covered in brick, imported from the North.

Though his published itinerary placed him there one day before his arrival on April 9, and the necessity to move quickly in order to reach Boston by June 17 necessitated his visits remain brief in the towns along his route, Lafayette remained in New Orleans for five days—the longest stop during his tour of the American South and West. Here he was addressed by fellow Frenchmen, held high as the hero of the Revolution of '76 and '89. He was able, in a fascinating hypothetical, to observe them living under the American system of government. Its mayor, Joseph de Roffignac (Count Louis Philippe Joseph Roffignac), was a colorful French nobleman.

Spaniards praised him for opposing the French invasion of their nation in the Chamber of Deputies, and with the death of Rafael del Riego, "unfortunate and without a home, come to you General," they cried. Lafayette, in return, offered encouragement: "Let us all enjoy the thought that the cause of liberty will end up by triumphing everywhere over hostile alliances and fallacious intrigue."[8] And an elderly Capuchin friar, Père Antoine, the much beloved former pastor of the Church of St. Louis, known for his generosity and "indifference to niceties of ecclesiastical form"—it was said "Sin seemed to concern Pere Antoine hardly at all"—threw himself into Lafayette's arms. "Oh my son!" he cried. "I have found grace before the Lord since he has allowed me to see and hear the most worthy apostle of liberty before my death."[9]

In one instance, the admiration of Lafayette in New Orleans nearly led to bloodshed. Members of both the Louisiana Legion as well as the state's militia were to march to Lafayette's lodgings; the first group, however, departed early, a breach of decorum offensive to the men in the second, leading to a near brawl between the two groups after they were received by the Nation's Guest. When he learned of the dispute, Lafayette spent nearly half an hour conciliating the men, telling them that had he known such a fight would break out, he would have sent a polite letter of regret from Mobile and bypassed New Orleans. He said also that if the soldiers had acted on their antagonisms, and news of it reached Europe, "I will have to suffer the pain of having sown the seeds of discord where I had found at first only peace and harmony." The council concluded with Lafayette successfully encouraging the estranged parties to embrace.[10]

In New Orleans, Lafayette was fêted by his fellow Masons and reunited with fellow soldiers of the Revolution. In one case, Lafayette's dinner was interrupted by the introduction of an old veteran who claimed to have come all the way from Delaware to see the general. He was ninety-six years of age—"They call you old, but you are quite a boy to me." Examining Lafayette's face, he said, "You are much altered since I first saw you at Brandywine."[11] Evenings ended with the city's buildings and homes illuminated, "the iron railing which surrounds the square, appeared like a wall of fire."[12]

"I am throwing myself into the kindnesses and honors that, here, due to the mix of different populations, take on a very unique character," Lafayette wrote to his daughters from New Orleans. "You will take notice of the Spanish address that touched me deeply. This almost entirely French republic has something pointed about it, and I am especially sensitive to everything I am experiencing here."[13]

There was also the matter of settling, at last, the matter of the location of his remaining Louisiana lands that Congress originally granted to him in 1804. Working with James Harper, his current agent, Lafayette found a plot of land six hundred yards outside the city's defensive perimeter. As it turned out, however, much of this was previously claimed, dragging the matter on further.[14] Lafayette was also reunited with Vincent Nolte, the cotton merchant who had helped him get his finances in order before leaving France the previous summer. Nolte, at Lafayette's request, had also handled the finances of Fanny and Camilla Wright; the sisters, as planned, arrived in Louisiana shortly after their "father." But where Lafayette was fascinated by New Orleans, Fanny was revolted.

"Slavery I expected to find here in all its horrors, and truly in all its horrors it is found," Fanny unhappily observed after arriving in the city.[15] She and her sister Camilla departed Washington in early March when a carriage was dispatched from Montpelier, where the Wrights spent a day with James and Dolley Madison.[16] They then traveled over the Allegheny Mountains, and then by boat on the Ohio River, to the port of Mount Vernon, in the southwest corner of Indiana, and then overland to a would-be earthly paradise on the Wabash River.

At the beginning of 1825, while the Wrights were in Washington, Robert Owen visited the capital and delivered two widely attended and much-discussed addresses in the House of Representatives. The subject was the ambitious experiment soon to begin in the town of Harmonie in southwest Indiana. Owen was born into poverty in Wales, had no formal education, still succeeded in business, and purchased a share of the largest Scottish cotton mill, New Lanark, in 1800. Laborers there worked long hours in terrible conditions, living in cramped, squalid homes. Alcoholism was rampant, and any formal education, for workers or their children, was nearly nonexistent. Compensation came in tokens redeemable only at factory stores that sold goods at inflated prices. Owen sought not just to cure these ills, but to redeem society and perfect the human condition. At New Lanark, he oversaw successful reforms, instituting an eight-hour workweek for employees, schoolhouses for their children, and factory stores offering quality goods at fair prices. Disputes with the co-owners of New Lanark, and failed reform projects elsewhere, led Owen to leave England for America in the autumn of 1824, lured by the possibility of conducting an even grander experiment in human improvement.

After arriving in America, Owen set out for southern Indiana in search of Harmonie, the utopian community founded on the Wabash River by George Rapp and his followers. Outcast from the Lutheran Church in Germany, Rapp and his flock, which practiced a form of radical pietism, emigrated from Württemberg to America in 1803 in search of religious freedom. Convinced that the Second Coming would occur in the New World, Rapp and his adopted son, Frederick Reichert, established their first commune in Butler County, Pennsylvania, where they prospered both in farming and manufacturing. The Harmonists held their property and earnings in common; marriages were rare, and most members were celibate. Under Father Rapp, members of the community worked diligently, lived piously, listened to their Father's sermons, and awaited Christ's return—the earnings of their labors were intended to support his coming reign. With increasing migration into western Pennsylvania, and in search of a more hospitable climate for their vineyards, Rapp and his followers relocated to the Indiana Territory in 1814 and established Harmonie, where they happily planted and tended to orchards and vineyards, built and operated their saw and grist mills, a distillery, store, and churches. There was even a band at Harmonie merrily making music. But, believing his work exhausted in Indiana and fearing the development of bad habits among his flock, Rapp purchased another tract of land northwest of Pittsburg and offered the entire settlement on the Wabash for sale.

In December 1824, Owen reached Indiana where he agreed to purchase Harmonie, which he would rechristen "New Harmony." There he would create a utopia: a community shielded from the toxins that so distorted human character—private property, marriage, and religion—on the American frontier. "He is doubtless a very honest and benevolent man, but a mistaken visionary," a Washington editorialist wrote after Owen unveiled the plan during his visit to the capital.[17]

Whether Fanny attended Owen's lectures in Washington is unknown, but she was interested enough in his ideas to visit Harmonie, where she and Camilla arrived March 19. Robert Owen was not present during the visit, but his son, William, served as a host. "Miss Wright is a very learned and a fine woman, and though her manners are free and unusual in a female, yet they are pleasing and graceful and she improves upon acquaintance," he wrote in his diary after their meeting.[18]

This was during an interlude between the Harmonists' departure and the beginning of Owen's community. Five hundred of Rapp's followers remained, working away in the fields. Watching these industrious and by all appearances contented people laboring for a common good, with no apparent self-interest, fascinated Wright, who wondered if, in this utopian arrangement, there might be the germ of a possible answer to the question of slavery.

What she failed to recognize, though, was that the Harmonists were motivated less by altruistic idealism than by fear of their leader.

Another traveler, Owen Gwathmey, a slave owner from Louisville, visited Harmonie in early 1825 as well, and though he believed it was one of the most delightful places he had ever visited, assessed the dynamic among its residents and their leader more perceptively. "They appear to be the most happy people and at the ringing of a bell they spring to their work and I believe they are more afraid to offend him than one of our negros are us," Gwathmey wrote. "Wrap [sic] himself is a very sensible man but I presume the generality of them are ignorant. He preaches to them himself and tells them if they do not mind and do what he tells them to do, Hell and Damnation will be their portion."[19]

After their stay at Harmonie, the Wrights rode across the Illinois border to another commune, Albion, in the company of a new acquaintance, George Flower. He and Morris Birkbeck, a fellow idealist, had immigrated to and founded the utopian English Prairie in Southern Illinois. A rift between the two pioneers led Flower to found his own community, Albion. After the Wrights had departed for New Orleans, Flower reported to William Owen that, visiting the commune, Fanny was "very much interested in the system."[20] And indeed, she resolved to revisit Harmonie after reconnoitering with Lafayette in Louisiana. On March 25, the sisters, accompanied by Emily Ronalds, an Englishwoman whose brother was married to one of Flower's sisters, sailed on the Ohio River from Shawneetown, Illinois, caught the Mississippi at Cairo, and headed downriver. "Surely this is the Babylon of revelations, where reigneth the great western slavery mud and mosquitos," she wrote after arriving in New Orleans in early April. "These are the first objects to greet your senses."[21]

Bernhard, Duke of Saxe-Weimar-Eisenach, who also visited New Orleans, though later in 1825, roomed at the same hotel, owned by a Mrs. Herries, in which the Wrights stayed. There he observed a ghastly, though not uncommon, scene in the city. One morning a French guest requested water from a slave who served as the hotel's chambermaid. When it was not brought immediately, he stalked from his room, found and punched the girl in the face, causing blood to gush down her forehead. When she grabbed his neck, the attacker fled back to his rooms. For the temerity of defending herself, to placate the irate Frenchman,

Mrs. Herries ordered another slave, the girl's best friend, to administer twenty-six lashes to her back. Unsatisfied, the Frenchman reported the incident to local police, who arrested the girl and gave her another round of lashings.[22]

Even on the lower level of Cabildo, home of the city government offices that were transformed into a luxurious suite for Lafayette and his companions, there was a prison holding runaway slaves; nearby, a cannon was fired to announce hours when no Black resident could travel New Orleans's streets without a pass.[23] It was a city, Fanny observed, where the clank of chains was constantly audible in the streets. A place where the first white soul a slave, running for freedom, encountered would apprehend or arrest them. "In proportion as you travel south, the features of slavery grow harsher, until they find their ne plus ultra in New Orleans," she wrote.[24] Another source of anger for Fanny was the treatment of the Free Men of Color.

At the end of 1814, with the British army advancing on New Orleans, Louisiana's governor, William C. C. Claiborne, suggested to Andrew Jackson the possibility of battalions formed of the state's free Black men to assist in the defense of New Orleans. Jackson eagerly accepted the idea; the nation was under attack and "She wants soldiers to fight her battles," he reasoned. Jackson issued messages encouraging the state's six hundred "free men of color" to enlist, promising the same compensation as white soldiers: 160 acres of land and $124. Jackson believed the free Black citizens of Louisiana would be "excellent soldiers," who would not remain neutral. "They will not remain quiet spectators of the interesting contest. They must be for or against us."[25]

Two battalions were formed, the First Battalion of Free Men and D'aquin's Second Battalion, consisting largely of immigrants from Saint-Dominque and led in the field by Second Major Joseph Savary, a former colonel in a mixed-race French legion. The second unit, during a nighttime raid on the British position, delayed the enemy's advance. Both battalions fought bravely during the Battle of New Orleans and earned Jackson's approbation. Anxiety in Louisiana over armed groups of Black men forced him to send the battalions out of the state. They eventually disbanded, and the soldiers never received their promised pay.[26] "They were afterwards deprived of the arms with which they had cooperated in defense of the country!" Fanny seethed after learning of the soldiers' service and fate. "This indignity has cut more deeply than any other."[27] In her heartache over the matter, she was not alone.

Lafayette's loathing of slavery was nearly as old and great as his love for America. In his heart, the two emotions were not incompatible. What was irreconcilable were the virtues of his adopted homeland and its institutions and the sin of human bondage. The first was destined to eradicate the second. In fact, he readily defended the country from accusations of a double standard from abroad during his visit. "This also I wish to be often repeated that Slavery was entailed upon the U.S. in spite of the Bills, entreaties, and Representatives of the Colonies who are now Bitterly attacked by England for what England has forced them to adopt," he wrote at the opening of the trip into the American South.[28]

Nor did the sight of slavery diminish Lafayette's joyful reaction to the advancements he withheld across America that had materialized since his last visit. In a sense, they were interconnected; the rights won in the Revolution, which had fueled such growth, could lead the nation toward a better realization of the values expressed in the Declaration of Independence. Visiting New York's Free School, drinking champagne with Pompey in Columbia, or visiting with Nelson in Savannah, he could subtly indicate his views on the inequality of the races and the hypocrisy of involuntary servitude in a nation dedicated to the rights of man—life, liberty, the pursuit of happiness—and whose freedom he had helped win. Lafayette could take incredible pride in the progress he saw across America but also politely signal to its citizens and leaders where great work remained.

In New Orleans, Lafayette had specifically requested a meeting with the "free men of color," who had helped defend the city. A new commander was appointed, John Mercier, and a battalion re-formed in order to address Lafayette. "I have often, during the War of Independence, seen African blood shed with honor in our ranks for the cause of the United States," Lafayette said after Mercier presented his men, before shaking each by the hand.[29]

"There is only one issue for which I am less resigned than ever, and that is slavery and anti-black prejudice. I think that my trip will have been worthwhile regarding this issue as well," Lafayette wrote to his daughters from New Orleans after the meeting with free men of color. "The way in which I asked to see and welcomed the colored men who fought in defense of the city on January 8th will make for another proof of the feelings that I am always going around preaching. This is not an empty gesture, but rather a way to gradually bring about a remedy."[30]

For Fanny Wright, though, a gradual remediation of slavery was now impracticable. Conversations in New Orleans with planters revealed the fear among some that they would eventually be outnumbered by their slaves—the Black population in Southern states was growing at a faster rate than the white—who would in time revolt and seize power. Gradual emancipation would come "too late." But, Wright asked these men, why then did they continue to purchase slaves from Virginia? It was cheaper, she was told, to import them and clear and work new plantations than to care for the slaves already in the state. The Southerners were "too ignorant & brutal" and fixated on quick profit to see the danger they courted.[31]

She and her sister were with Lafayette on April 15 as he departed New Orleans. A forlorn affair—much of the city's population gathered at the Place D'Armes to see him off. "An air of sadness appeared on every countenance, the more remarkable, from the contrast with the rapturous joy displayed on the morning of his arrival," the *Courier* observed. Sullen crowds followed him, passing under balconies from which women waved their handkerchiefs, toward the waiting steamboat *Natchez*, which Louisiana's government had dispatched to Mobile to bring Lafayette to their state, now ready to carry him up the Mississippi River. But when the ship came in sight, the crowds turned away—"all had wished to see him come to New Orleans, none seemed willing to see him depart."[32]

The *Natchez* began its ascent of the Mississippi ultimately destined for St Louis, but more immediately, Baton Rouge, where, on the day after leaving New Orleans, citizens of the town intercepted the boat and successfully summoned Lafayette to visit; from there he steamed on to the port of Natchez. During the journey upriver, the clustered homes of New Orleans slowly disappeared and in their place appeared sugar and cotton plantations adjoined by starkly white homes with gorgeously manicured gardens; groves of orange trees and palmettos delighted the *Natchez*'s passengers.

But as the boat traveled north, Fanny Wright was preoccupied with the horrors of New Orleans and the promise of Harmonie; the first increased an urgency to conceive of a solution to this stain on the experiment in self-government she so admired; the second, though Wright had yet to fully grasp its form, suggested a solution. In Indiana, she wrote, "a vague idea crossed me that there was something in the system as there in operation which might be rendered subservient to the emancipation of the south."

The terrible blot that now so consumed Fanny only made the beauty that surrounded her—"such woods such lawns such gently swelling hills such glorious trees, such exquisite flowers & and the giant river wafting the rich produce of this unrivaled land to the ocean"—painful. "I could have wept as I thought such a garden was wrought by the hands of slaves."[33]

16

Majestic River, Republican Shores

Since his return to America, Lafayette had endured countless speeches, odes, and lectures delivered by ambitious local magistrates and nationally known politicians, nervous schoolchildren, and erudite academics. Some were sublime. Others, less so. "Of course, in most instances, the speaker was more occupied in exhibiting his cleverness and oratorical talent, than with the object of his mission, or a desire to give pleasure to the hearer," the entrepreneur Vincent Nolte, who traveled with Lafayette from New Orleans to Natchez, wrote. "And the good general had no remedy for this evil, but was compelled to listen attentively to the longest, stupidest, wordiest discourses possible."[1]

And yet Lafayette's expression during these speeches never revealed any boredom or impatience. As the speakers ran out of wind, he was always ready with a thoughtful reply. How, exactly, did he do this, Nolte asked. Lafayette explained that he listened until the speaker mentioned something of interest. He seized on this in order to fashion his reply while they droned on. From that point, he told Nolte, "I do not hear a syllable—it all blows over me."[2]

Sure enough, as soon as his boat docked at Bacon's Landing below Natchez on April 17, Lafayette was carried away in a barouche to Tichenor's Field for a review of the gathered militia. He was then whisked to the entrance of the city, where the president of its selectmen, William Burns, delivered a lengthy address—though not without some predictive merit. Toward its conclusion, Burns prophesied that Lafayette, on leaving Natchez for St. Louis, would explore a region once inhabited by Indians during the Revolution but now home to white communities and see "the rich produce of their fields," the result of "regulated liberty." When Burns finished, Lafayette, serene as ever, offered a brief reply: "Well may your Majestic River be proud now to wash none but republican shores."[3] Soon after, he stepped back on board the *Natchez* ascending the river in search of these republican shores.

The purchase of the Louisiana Territory in 1803 settled the navigation rights of the Mississippi River in favor of the U.S. government, while acquiring 827,000 square miles west of it. The Corps of Discovery, co-captained by Meriweather Lewis and William Clark, explored this land, discovered an overland passage to the Pacific Ocean, and documented the topography of the territory, providing a template for future migration west. This hastened an incredible migration away from the Eastern Seaboard and into the American interior, as pioneers, adventurers, discontents, debtors, speculators, and squatters—all manner of citizen with great aspirations and various degrees of scruples—departed the exhausted, overcrowded lands of the East, clawed their way across the continent, over mountain ranges, over swamps, along trails cut with their hands, arriving in the wide-open spaces of the Mississippi and Ohio Valleys. They brought little with them, other than their ambition and an idealistic faith in liberty and equality, bequeathed by the founders.

Now, traveling to St. Louis on the Mississippi River, Lafayette began a new leg of the great adventure: Five Frenchmen, Lafayette—as well as his dog, Quiz—Georges, Levasseur, Bastien, and de Syon, attended by delegations from Louisiana and Mississippi, would steam north on an oft-mysterious waterway. On its shores, explorers, dreamers, and children of the Revolution waited to greet them.

But when the Nation's Guest exited New Orleans two days before reaching Natchez, the city's newspaper claimed it was akin to an old father leaving his children in order to undertake a "perilous journey." And they were justified to feel this way. "Just for this section, this will be a trip of two thousand leagues, thanks to the steamboat without which we would be on the road for more than a year," Lafayette, estimating the amount of time he would spend on the water, wrote to his family from aboard the *Natchez.*[4]

Steamboats, first appearing on the Mississippi River at New Orleans in 1811, contributed to the westward population rush by economizing and accelerating the flow of goods and people. But with this revolution came danger. Like Lafayette, Americans marveled at how the steam engine reduced heretofore vast distances between remote places. Commenting on the journey from St. Louis to St. Peter's—a trip that by any other boat would take fifty days, but by steamboat took *three*—one observer marveled that "such is the progress of an invention, which has produced a new era in the history of navigation."[5] Francis Trollope described the steamboats as the "stage coaches and fly wagons of this land of lakes and rivers."[6]

But the progress was unattended by little in the way of precaution. Regulation was nearly nonexistent. Boats, particularly above the main deck, were poorly constructed: Brittle wood, covered in paint, carrying cotton, made the ships highly flammable, fast-moving fire hazards. Improperly vented steam caused spectacular boiler explosions, showering and sometimes skinning alive crew and passengers with scalding water, or maiming or killing them with shrapnel. The Western rivers they traveled were full of dangers: snags and sawyers—felled trees planted in riverbeds whose limbs punctured hulls, or spinning with the current, ripped through them. There was risk of stranding on sandbars or colliding with traffic or even into the ghostly remains of partially submerged steamships, monuments to the dangerous Western waters. Just days before Lafayette began his journey upriver, fifteen miles below Natchez, the boiler of the steamboat *Teche* burst. The explosion sent the boiler's aft cap ripping through the cabin floor, ignited oakum on board, and set fire to the cotton it carried. Crew members were scalded to death or suffocated, while a lifeboat to the nearby *George Washington* met disaster when the latter's wheel was somehow put in motion as they approached, drowning all on board.[7]

"The navigation of the Mississippi is even more hazardous than I had apprehended, particularly the ascent," Fanny Wright observed. "But as is usually the case in this country, the more numerous the perils, the less the caution."[8] She and Lafayette would not face those dangers together: Parting company once more at Natchez, she and her sister Camilla traveled from Mississippi to the mouth of the Ohio River and then to Louisville. From there, they planned a return to Harmonie in southern Indiana, where Robert Owen had established his commune, New Harmony.

Meanwhile, Lafayette had the entire cabin of the *Natchez* at his disposal, with a saloon above his quarters stocked with food, drink, sofas, card tables, and books. Fanny, however, was stuck on a cramped steamer carrying five hundred passengers. "I could have arranged for them to come on the same steamboat [as us]," Lafayette explained to his daughter, Virginie, "but as we are traveling with [as] men, and official men, and as we are stopping for receptions, I found it most convenient for them and for their comfort to not press the matter, neither to the government of Louisiana who put the Natchez at my disposal, nor to my friends themselves."[9]

Before departing for St. Louis, however, an elderly man hollered for Lafayette's attention, baring his pockmarked chest. "These wounds, they are my pride!" he screamed, according to Levasseur. The old soldier had received them, he said, at Brandywine. "It was indeed a rough day," Lafayette reflected. "But have we not since been amply indemnified?" he asked. "Oh that is very true!" answered the old man.[10] With that, Lafayette sailed off, into the fruitful garden, toward the living evidence of that indemnification.

"On withdrawing from Natchez, we parted from the civilized world, so to speak," wrote Levasseur.[11] They began their ascent of the Mississippi early on the morning of April 19. It was not long before the beautiful plantations lining the shores upriver from New Orleans grew scarce and then vanished. There were no cities, few settlements to speak of, and only dilapidated plantations remained. The gentle hills north of New Orleans gave way to flat, flooded banks bordering the broad, muddy river. Trees were liberated from Spanish moss, and low-lying wooded islands—each identified by number rather than names—appeared below the mouth of the Ohio. At Petit Gulf, 340 miles from New Orleans, the river twisted sharply, as travelers, in turn, observed the Red, Yazoo, and Arkansas Rivers, flowing into the Mississippi.

On board the *Natchez*, bouts of monotony alternated with battles against swarms of mosquitoes that feasted on the passengers. "Monuments of recent disasters"—evidence of storms and tornadoes—lined the shore: uprooted trees, snags, and sawyers in the water, which Captain Robert Davis pointed out, were additional, though worrisome, distractions.[12] When Lafayette had traveled the Hudson the previous September, citizens rushed from their homes to cheer or fire salutes. Now, the only form of tribute was the ragged pioneer who emerged from the forest with cords of wood for the *Natchez*'s furnace. At some stops, when no woodsman appeared, the crew would step ashore, gather wood, and leave a note nailed to a tree with the captain and ship's names, the amount taken, and the date.[13]

The original schedule of the Western leg of Lafayette's trip placed him in Nashville before St. Louis. From the latter city he would travel overland through Illinois, Indiana, and Ohio on his path east toward Boston. The itinerary was altered before leaving New Orleans, perhaps for the sake of time: After visiting St. Louis, the *Natchez* would descend the Mississippi and then by way of the Ohio and Cumberland Rivers travel to Nashville. By the 24th, as they neared the mouth of the Ohio, he reported to Joel Poinsett, who had helped plan the route, "we don't find ourselves far from the mark." They were on track to accomplish the arduous goal of passing through all the Southern and Western states and returning east by June 17.[14]

Sure enough, on the 25th, when the *Natchez* reached the confluence of the Ohio and Mississippi, and Captain Davis, unacquainted with the upper stretches of the latter, diverted the boat a few miles into the Ohio in search of a second pilot, they encountered another boat, the *Mechanic*. On board was a delegation from Tennessee unaware Lafayette was headed to St. Louis, demanding he transfer to their boat and travel to their state. A compromise was reached: Part of the delegation would come aboard the *Natchez* and travel to St. Louis. The *Mechanic*, meanwhile, would wait for Lafayette when he came back to the Ohio and then would take him to Nashville.[15]

Back on the Mississippi, steaming north, the ghosts of earlier French settlers appeared on the shores: Cape Girardeau to their left in Missouri and Fort de Chartres on their right in Illinois. The fate of Lafayette's visit to the latter state, however, was uncertain. Its legislature in Vandalia extended an invitation at the end of 1824, which Edward Coles, its governor, forwarded to Lafayette while he was in New Orleans. "I don't doubt that by rapid movements, we can gratify my ardent desire to see every one of the western states, and yet fulfill a sacred duty as the representative of the Revolutionary army, on the half secular jubilee of Bunker Hill," Lafayette replied.[16] To accommodate Illinois's wishes, he proposed a plan: A representative from the state could meet him along the Mississippi River and accompany him to one of the Illinois towns along its banks or the Ohio River's path—Kaskaskia or Shawneetown. Coles knew exactly which young man to send to St. Louis.

"This will be handed to you by my friend and Aid de camp Colonel William Schuyler Hamilton who I take a particular pleasure in introducing to you, as the son of your old and particular friend, General Alexander Hamilton," wrote Coles.[17] Perhaps of his five brothers, in appearance and character William S. Hamilton most resembled his father.[18] The sixth child of Alexander Hamilton, he was just six when his father died in 1804, leaving his mother, Elizabeth, to care for their fatherless children and shoulder his debts, limiting opportunities early in life for the youngest among them. His elder brothers, like their father, studied at Columbia; William enrolled at sixteen at West Point in 1814 but stayed little more than a year, embarking on his own adventure in search of opportunity along the Mississippi River, where he arrived in 1816. Other than a single visit to his mother in New York, he never returned East again. Hamilton lived for a time in St. Louis, joining the staff of William Rector, newly appointed land surveyor general for the Illinois, Missouri, and Arkansas Territory. He drifted to Illinois, where he was made U.S. surveyor of public lands, and settled in Sangamon County, where he was elected to the Illinois House of Representatives in 1824.

The son of a founder by blood, Hamilton was an example of the second generation of Americans who helped form the nation's future: A hearty risk-taker with the appearance of a backwoodsman, he possessed, in his brother John's words, "a roving spirit" but an intellect much like his father's, whose library he inherited, carrying a copy of Voltaire's works into the wilderness.[19] Shortly after Lafayette's visit, Hamilton drove a herd of cattle north to Fort Howard on the Fox River; later he was lured away to the future state of Wisconsin during the lead rush along the upper Mississippi Valley and wandered farther west after the discovery of gold in California, where his life ended, a world away from where it began.

Hamilton set out for St. Louis while the *Natchez* neared. On the evening of April 28 it anchored at Carondelet, seven miles south of the city, an impoverished community of French Canadians who surrounded the boat, first welcoming Lafayette to their homes and then explaining that American settlers were regularly arriving to lay claim to the land they lived on. Two members of the Louisiana delegation accompanying Lafayette hurriedly dashed off a note to Missouri's governor, Frederick Bates, inquiring in what manner he would prefer to receive the Nation's Guest.[20]

Lafayette need not worry about remaining composed in the face of grandiloquent oratory from this politician. Bates had begun his political career at the opening of the nineteenth century as a Federalist before conveniently aligning with Democrat-Republicans during their ascendancy. A rival of Meriwether Lewis during their respective tenures as secretary and governor of the Missouri Territory, Bates had not extended a formal invitation to the Nation's Guest. Nor had Missouri's legislature. No funds were appropriated for his visit, and if St. Louis's leaders wanted to host him, they were on their own.

During his travels, some citizens had privately, and sometimes publicly, though politely, as was the case with Hezekiah Niles, expressed unease with the extravagant and sometimes undignified way Americans had celebrated Lafayette's return. Bates, in a memo concerning Missouri's own part in the national celebration, unleashed the sharpest articulation of this divergence from popular opinion—one that resembled an act of defiance of popular sentiment.

He recounted the splendid scenes of Lafayette's visit so far, which, he suggested, "one would think be sufficient to exhaust the patience of the General." Missouri's government needn't burden him any further and belabor the point. "There is no personal sacrifice we would not make on this occasion—but enough of pageantry—something is due principle—and I am afraid that amidst this ostentation and waste," he wrote, "the wounds of our revolutionists which yet survive, many of them in poverty or but lately relieved might cause these veterans to make comparisons very little to the credit of the nation. As an individual it would be altogether immaterial whether I kissed the hem of his garment or not."[21]

Bates said he had heard rumor that Lafayette might like to meet with him. If this was the case, and he was to travel to the capital of St. Charles or to his home in the settlement at Bon Homme, Lafayette would be disappointed: "He would find me at neither place for I have long since promised my family a visit to some friends about that time."[22]

The responsibility of welcoming Lafayette fell to other men. The following morning, they appeared: William Clark, the former governor of the Missouri Territory and its long-serving superintendent of Indian Affairs, accompanied by Senator Thomas Hart Benton. They were joined by Illinois governor Edward Coles, who had arrived in time to meet Lafayette in person. Boarding the *Natchez*, the party made its way to St. Louis. Another steamboat, packed with cheering men and women, pulled to its side, and, Levasseur wrote, "the forests of Missouri echo with *Welcome Lafayette*."[23]

Shortly, St. Louis appeared on the river's right bank. Established in 1764 as a fur trading post on elevated ground south of the Mississippi's junction with the Illinois and Missouri Rivers, the site not only made the city a hub for fur trading but also protected it from flooding. Another advantage, with the arrival of steam-powered travel, was the Mississippi's deeper channel at St. Louis, which allowed larger boats to anchor and transfer their cargo to smaller vessels better suited to navigate the treacherous Des Moines Rapids farther north. This fueled the city's growth: In 1810, St. Louis's population was fourteen hundred. A decade later, it was nearly nine thousand—many of whom now stood along the Mississippi, cheering to the sound of artillery fire.

After the ritual oration by the city's mayor, Will Carr Lane—"Few of us have seen your face before; but, your heroic deeds are engraved upon our memories and our hearts . . ."—and Lafayette's improvised reply—"I highly enjoy the pleasure to find myself on the soil of Missouri"—a carriage waited to take him into the city.[24] They traveled along Main Street, lined with two-story brick homes fronted by beautifully cultivated gardens. Auguste Chouteau, the son of one of St. Louis's founders, lent his own home as a reception hall where the city's residents came to meet Lafayette. There, William Hamilton introduced himself and was received with great joy by Lafayette; the meeting "excited particular feeling," reported a St. Louis newspaper.[25]

When Bernhard, Duke of Saxe-Weimar-Eisenach, visited the city not long after Lafayette, he thought he saw, because of its location on the map, a future capital of the United States.[26] Levasseur called it "the great warehouse for all the commerce of the regions to the west of the Mississippi."[27] St. Louis already had one singular distinction in the young nation, as Lafayette learned after arriving: It was home to the only museum west of the Mississippi River, Governor Clark's Indian Collection. In 1818, he built a two-story home on Main Street and the corner of Vine; shortly after, Clark added a brick annex to this home, intended as a chamber for meetings with Indian leaders; he adorned the space with artifacts, specimens, and objects from his travels and interactions with tribes. "We believe this is the only collection of specimens of art and nature west of Cincinnati, which partakes of the character of a museum, or cabinet of natural history," a visitor, Henry R. Schoolcraft, wrote in 1821.[28]

It was, according to an early St Louis directory, "probably the largest collection of Indian curiosities to be found in the Republic, and the Governor is so polite as to permit its being visited by any person of respectability at any time."[29] And many did. The museum was a destination within the destination of St. Louis for those traveling west. Technically, all doing so were required to confer with its owner: In order to go west into Indian Territory, travelers obtained a pass from Clark. Lafayette and his companions could not come to St. Louis without visiting the museum. "This collection is the most complete and the most varied that it may be possible to find," wrote Levasseur.[30]

Inside the low brick building, Lafayette and his companions examined displays of buffalo robes, tomahawks, and war clubs. There were bows made from elk horn, quivers full of arrows, saddles and canoes, shot pouches and powder horns. And, amazingly to the Frenchmen, several necklaces made from grizzly bear claws. By contrast, the London Cabinet of Natural History had only one grizzly bear claw, Levasseur wrote. There were natural wonders, as well: an eight-foot-long alligator, bear skins, porcupine quills, and the horns of an elk, shot by Clark in the Rocky Mountains. There were geodes pulled from the Des Moines River and gypsum from the Kansas River. During the visit, Lafayette presented Clark with the gift of a travel chest. Clark later sent a stuffed grizzly bear to La Grange, which Lafayette claimed was the first such creature, "living or dead," to appear on the other side of the Atlantic.[31]

Items in the collection were brought back from Clark's voyage with Lewis, though many of those were displayed in Peale's Museum in the old State House in Philadelphia; others were acquired through Clark's congress with Indian leaders in his decades-long role as the superintendent of Indian affairs: a difficult role that required fulfilling his mission to remove the native population farther west to allow for increased white settlement while also maintaining the trust of their leaders and acting as their primary representative. Clark was sympathetic to the plight of the Indians, advocating, for example, for smallpox inoculations to halt the disease's spread. At the same time, he presided over numerous treaties that led to the loss of ancestral lands and the destruction of their ways of life. The museum reflected a growing sense of self-identity, once mocked by European naturalists, that America's ecology was evidence of its ascendency. But Clark's museum, which was supplemented by portraits of Indian chiefs, was a means of preserving what was soon to be lost because of it.

In the evening, a crowded ball was held at Massie's Hotel—"the company was more numerous than had ever been seen on such occasion west of the Mississippi"—and then Lafayette was back on board the *Natchez*, much to the displeasure of the numerous men who had traveled through the night from distant counties to see him.[32] "In the rapid visit to our city, we have but one subject of regret, the shortness of it," lamented a local editorialist. The following morning, the boat traveled eight miles south on the Mississippi to Kaskaskia, fulfilling Lafayette's wish to visit Illinois; on board was its governor, Coles.

On the fringes of the American frontier, Lafayette met the son of one of America's fathers in William Hamilton. Now he was reunited with one of their ideological descendants. Hamilton sought adventure and fortune in the West; Edward Coles had come to reconcile the principles of the Revolution with the inaction of the founders.

Coles grew up in the shadow of—and idolized—America's architects. Enniscorthy, the Cole family plantation, sat on Green Mountain in the Virginia Piedmont, along the same range as Jefferson's Monticello, and James Monroe's Ash Lawn–Highland. Dolley Madison, by marriage, was Coles's cousin, and her husband, James Madison, became his mentor. The Madisons were associates of Coles's father, John Coles II, and frequent guests at their home. At the College of William & Mary, where he studied but left without a degree in 1805, Coles fell under the influence of the college's president, the Rev. James Madison, first bishop of Virginia, a second cousin of the Constitution's author. Grappling with the Enlightenment ideals and natural law that informed that document—principles Coles absorbed under the bishop—and their incompatibility with human bondage provoked a crisis of conscience. "As soon as I was capable of reading and reflecting on the nature of man, his duties to himself, to his fellow man, and to his creator I became strongly impressed with the belief that it was wrong to hold a fellow being in slavery," Coles wrote in 1827. "And at an early period of my life determined not to do so, whatever might be the sacrifice."[33]

The path there was full of twists and delays. After his father's death in 1808, Coles inherited a 782-acre plantation on the Rockfish River, fifteen miles from Enniscorthy, along with twelve slaves. He had kept his intentions secret from his father, fearing he might be bequeathed some other form of property. Liberating them, however, in Virginia was unfeasible: In 1806, the state had passed a law requiring freed slaves to leave the state within twelve months, this in addition to laws that restricted the rights of free Blacks. Accordingly, as Coles wrote, "I turned my face to the North West."[34]

In 1809, Coles traveled west to Kentucky, briefly crossing the Ohio River into free territory. Returning to Virginia, he put the Rockfish Plantation up for sale and began planning a relocation west. However, his plans were delayed when his older brother Isaac, who had served as private secretary to both Jefferson and Madison, assaulted a Maryland congressman. After dismissing Isaac from the post, President Madison offered the position to Coles, who, encouraged by Monroe, eventually accepted the role. From 1810 to 1815, Coles drafted Madison's correspondence, carried his messages to Congress, served as the president's political aide, and undertook special assignments on his behalf.

During this period, in the summer of 1814, Coles nervously struck up his own correspondence with Jefferson, seeking the old sage's advice and help in his efforts to end slavery. "This difficult task could be less exceptionably, and more successfully performed by the revered Fathers of all our political and social blessings, than by any succeeding statesmen," Coles, wrongly, asserted. He hoped that his hero, in his retirement, might "put into complete practice those hallowed principles contained in that renowned Declaration, of which you were the immortal author, and on which we founded our right to resist oppression, and establish our freedom and independence."[35]

As Fanny Wright discovered a decade later, any hopes that Jefferson could supply the magic answer to a riddle so terrible were sure to be disappointed. "I have overlived the generation with which mutual labors and perils begat mutual confidence and influence," he explained while discouraging Coles from freeing his slaves. "This enterprise is for the young; for those who can follow it up, and bear it through to it's [*sic*] consummation. It shall have all my prayers, and these are the only weapons of an old man." Coles disappointedly contended that Jefferson's order was reversed: "To effect so great and difficult an object great and extensive powers both of mind and influence are required, which can never be possessed in so great a degree by the young as by the old."[36] Yet, in a way, Coles ultimately proved Jefferson correct.

In the summer of 1815, Coles ventured west again, into Kentucky, across the Northwest Territory, across Ohio and the future states of Indiana and Illinois, then to Missouri, and, by keelboat, down the Mississippi River to New Orleans and then to his sister's home in South Carolina. Upon his return to Virginia, Coles quelled, on Madison's behalf, a diplomatic flap in Russia, during which he traveled across Paris, where he met Lafayette in 1817. The following year, Coles once more traveled west, exploring Illinois, where he attended the soon-to-be state's constitutional convention in Kaskaskia, acquired land in several spots—including the town of Edwardsville—and, with the assistance of President Monroe, was appointed its register of lands. Coles then returned to Rockfish, which he had sold to his brother, ready to relocate and emancipate his slaves in Illinois, "to take a stand, and set an example, promotive of an object so dear to my heart, as restoring the blacks to their liberty, and the whites to the consistency of their republican and Christian professions."[37] His family and friends, who vehemently opposed the plan, secured a promise from Coles that he would not inform his slaves—now numbering close to twenty—of their fate until they were gone from Virginia, lest they demand their own freedom.

In March 1819, guided by Coles's servant Ralph Crawford, they traveled to Brownsville in western Pennsylvania. Coles followed later, and together they set out with horses and wagons on two large flat-bottom boats down the Ohio River to its falls across from Louisville. From there, they would travel overland through Indiana to their new home in Edwardsville. It was on the water that Coles informed his slaves of their new condition. "The Negroes were in this state of hope and fear, when on one fine April day, while floating down the gentle current of the Beautiful

Ohio, I called on deck the whole party, old and young, and proclaimed to them their freedom," he recalled. "I never shall, I never can forget the expression of their countenances." The men and women were stunned. "At first they seemed to doubt the reality of what they heard. Then with a wild and hysterical laugh they gazed alternatively at me and each other."[38]

Coles retained some of his former slaves as employees and assisted others in finding employment. In 1822, he was narrowly elected governor of Illinois and quickly took up the fight against slavery. Despite its prohibition, slavery had arrived in Illinois a century earlier with French settlers and persisted as American settlers—many from Southern states—subverted the law.

When pro-slavery legislators attempted to call a convention to amend the state constitution and legalize slavery, they used the subterfuge of eventually emancipating and relocating slaves or their children once they reached a certain age. However, this effort was undermined by the fact that the state's original convention had never been properly ratified by its population, which had grown significantly since its writing.

After a year of political warfare between conventionists and their opponents, Coles successfully rallied anti-slavery sentiment with the help of idealists and preachers. Among them were Morris Birkbeck, whom Coles had met in England and persuaded to immigrate to Illinois, and George Flower, whom Fanny Wright had visited in New Albion. In 1824, voters rejected the call for a constitutional convention, preserving the Northwest Ordinance. Lafayette's arrival in America roughly coincided with this victory, news of which the general happily shared with his daughters-in-law.

Due to Coles's efforts, when the *Natchez* arrived at Kaskaskia on the afternoon of April 30, Lafayette stepped onto free soil for the first time during his tour of the American South and West. Although the visit came with little notice, the citizens of the Kaskaskia, along with those of Coles's home of Edwardsville, had already held meetings to prepare for the possibility of Lafayette's arrival. A messenger went from the shore to the town, from which a carriage was sent to bring him, and a large crowd gathered to accompany him into Kaskaskia.

Kaskaskia was a river town with a storied past and an inglorious future. Settled in the eighteenth century by Jesuit missionaries and members of its namesake tribe, the town thrived thanks to its fertile soil and access to the Mississippi River, becoming a hub of economic activity in Upper Louisiana. When American settlers arrived, it was the most established city in Illinois, serving as both the territorial capital and briefly the state capital before the government moved to Vandalia in 1819. This was the first knell. The final was when the flooding Mississippi mostly erased the town later in the nineteenth century.

In Kaskaskia, Lafayette was escorted to the home of John Edgar, an Irishman who had commanded a British vessel on the Great Lakes before the Revolution. Edgar had switched allegiances during the war, only to land in a Montreal prison on suspicion of corresponding with the colonials. While imprisoned, he uncovered a plot to surrender Vermont to the British, which he shared with New York's governor George Clinton. For his efforts, Edgar was awarded 2,200 acres of land, made a captain in the American navy, and immigrated to Kaskaskia in 1784, where he thrived as a merchant.[39]

Edgar's home—the largest in town, a one-story, French-style building surrounded by porches—was filled with Revolutionary veterans, rough-hewn frontiersman, and French Canadians eager for news of France. When Levasseur recounted the history of the past thirty years, culminating in the restoration of the Bourbons, they were in disbelief. "And you have suffered all that?" they asked. "How, in beautiful France, in great France, is one not free like in the state of Illinois!"[40]

On the town's square, joyous pioneers mingled with Kickapoo and Miami tribespeople. In the encampments outside of town, where Indians had gathered to sell their furs, de Syon, the young Frenchman traveling with Lafayette, encountered a woman who presented a letter of thanks. Written by Lafayette in 1778, it was "a little darkened by time but rather well preserved."[41] The letter was addressed to her father, Panisciowa, chief of the Six Nations in New York who had fought alongside the Americans during the Revolution. Her father had given it to her on his deathbed, telling her it was a powerful charm, received from "a great French warrior, whom the English dreaded as much as the

Americans loved." When Levasseur learned of the letter, he escorted the woman, named Mary, into Kaskaskia, where she presented it to Lafayette, who remembered the correspondence well.[42]

Despite the short notice, the people of Kaskaskia quickly staged a dinner and ball. During the dinner, Lafayette sat under an arch of flowers, constructed by the townswomen to resemble a rainbow. Spontaneous toasts were offered—to Illinois, the memory of Washington, and to La Grange. But it was Coles, naturally, who spoke most meaningfully that day.

During a reception for Lafayette at John Edgar's home, the governor delivered his address. Growing emotional, he paused to collect his thoughts, reflecting on battles recently won. He made a special point of welcoming the Nation's Guest, the "father of our political institutions," to "a state the offspring of those institutions, and which has not only inherited the precious boon of self-government but been reared in the principals and in the practice of liberty—and had her soil in an especial manner protected from oppression of every description."

Then, the governor looked back further—toward a generation to which Lafayette belonged, and to which Coles was the ideological heir. He also looked far into the future, to an America unbound by the Mississippi River. "And judging from the past," Coles said, "do I hazard too much in saying, the time is not far distant when the descendants of the Revolutionary worthies, inheriting the spirit of their fathers, and animated with the same attachment to liberty, the same enthusiastic devotion to country, and imbued with the same pure and divine principles people the country from the Atlantic to the Pacific."[43]

This prediction proved true, though it was a complicated proposition: The spread of liberty would not always keep pace with the spread of population. Yet, as Coles himself imperfectly exemplified, the next generation of trailblazers spreading across the continent and soon to arrive in Illinois—the family of Thomas Lincoln crossed the Wabash in 1830—would continue the founders' project. In Coles's words, they would strive to restore the consistency of their forbears' "republican professions."

17

———— ≋ ————

General Lafayette and General Jackson
Marched Arm in Arm

While Lafayette began his tour of the Southern and Western states, Andrew Jackson commenced a victorious march of his own, even if it was in the aftermath of defeat. Leaving Washington at the end of February with his wife, Rachel, Jackson was celebrated along his route back home to Tennessee. At banquets and military reviews, cavalcades of adoring citizens turned out to bid him welcome and wave goodbye.[1] At a dinner during his stop in Cincinnati, a toast was raised to "Washington, Lafayette, and Jackson." When he reached Nashville, a procession, including the Lafayette Guard, escorted him into town.[2]

By the time he reached his plantation, the Hermitage, east of Nashville, on the Cumberland River, Jackson was ailing. The exhaustion of travel and time in the saddle caused an infection that spread to his bladder. He was confined to bed for days after reaching home.[3]

While Jackson lay in agony, on May 2, the steamboat *Mechanic*—to which Lafayette and his companions had transferred from the *Natchez* on the Cumberland River—began its hairpin ascent, sailing in the dark of the night. In the morning, the rising sun shone on numerous boats carrying cargo along the river and its level, forested banks. There was little sign of any settlement. On the morning of the 4th, after anchoring three miles from Nashville the previous evening, the quiet of the wilderness was interrupted by the faint sound of bells off to the east. Soon, little by little, a series of spires revealed themselves on the vista and a mass of humanity perched on a plateau by the Cumberland came into view. Another traveler, after passing through the wilderness, described the city ahead as "quite what an oasis in the desert would be."[4] Now cheers of "Welcome, Lafayette" rang out across the Cumberland. It was Levasseur wrote, "the greeting of the inhabitants of Nashville for the Nation's Guest.[5]

Unlike St. Louis, or Kaskaskia, which had so little time to arrange receptions, Nashville was prepared for the Nation's Guest. "The near approach of the nation's guest is the theme of almost every tongue," the *Republican Banner* reported over a week before his arrival.[6] Tennessee's legislature passed a resolution of invitation and requested its governor, William Carroll, extended an invitation to Lafayette as early as September, which Jackson had conveyed when they met in Washington three months later. In advance of Lafayette's arrival, a committee gathered in Nashville in March to plan an appropriate welcome.[7]

The ringing of bells, the ones heard by the *Mechanic*'s passengers as they neared Nashville, would summon citizens to the town center. There they were to break into two platoons and line Lafayette's path into town; organizers suggested those who participated should wear Lafayette badges; no breaking ranks during the procession was permitted. All horses and carts were to be removed from the streets along the procession route.[8]

His arrival was declared a holiday: "That citizens suspend their ordinary labors on the arrival of Lafayette, to close their stores, shops and offices, and to afford to all in their employ a full opportunity to engage in festivity, and pay their respects to the venerated patriot."

The *Mechanic* slid past the roaring crowds and stopped at Fairfield, the home of William B. Lewis. And there on the shore, waiting to welcome Lafayette, was Old Hickory, Andrew Jackson himself. "The arrival of General Lafayette aroused me from my bed to hail him welcome," Jackson wrote later.[9] Lafayette was arguably the most popular man in America in the spring of 1825. But Jackson could lay his own claim on the title as well. In Nashville it was a draw. Lafayette embarked for America intent on conciliating its divided citizens. During the presidential contest, he had expressed friendship and fondness for all four of its participants and had gently avoided the discussion of politics in public. He was satisfied that his presence had united estranged parties.

But even the memory of the Revolution could not long suppress the unruly character of American democracy. In Charleston and Savannah, toasts at receptions held in Lafayette's honor turned political, courtesy of Jackson partisans. In Natchez, a speaker reflected on how the "expressed will of the majority is surrendered without tumult," a reference to Jackson's and Adam's respective vote totals in the general election.[10] Lafayette noticed, writing, "The fact is for the first time since my landing party sentiments have been toasted." He felt compelled to declare himself a friend of the new president and explain that he had missed his inauguration only because of the necessity of commencing his tour of the Southern and Western states.[11]

If Lafayette's presence had helped cool party tensions upon his arrival in New York the previous August, by the time he reached Nashville, and the gaunt Jackson took him by the hand, they had not simply woken once more, but a new era of democracy was begun; another election was already underway, and a new party was forming with Jackson as its star. The election of 1824 was only a prelude to the beginning of a new party system and a new era that would bear Jackson's mark.

Early on the day of the contingent presidential election, Hezekiah Niles sat with Jackson for an interview. The candidate, Niles claimed, had been reticent to discuss the election. But on that morning, he was sanguine about his chances. Should Adams win, and he may well, he would accept the result, striking a conciliatory note. "It was well he said, that persons should differ in opinion," wrote Niles, revealing that Jackson cautioned him that "we should always recollect that, in maintaining our own opinions, we naturally grant the right to others of supporting theirs, or lose every pretention to republicanism." It mattered not much, Jackson said, who won the presidency, as long as they performed its duties faithfully.[12] And the day of his defeat, Jackson had cheerily congratulated a rather stiff Adams at the president's house.

Days later, Adams nominated Henry Clay as secretary of state. The appointment was made on merit, and Adams had discussed the Speaker's suitability for the office as far back as 1821. Clay deliberated for a week before accepting. But the line between Clay's rousing the support of Kentucky and Ohio for Adams and the appointment intimated a deal between the two men at Jackson's expense, a "corrupt bargain," in the eyes of the losing candidate and his partisans.

"So you see, the Judas of the West, has closed the contract and will receive thirty pieces of silver," Jackson wrote upon news of Clay's nomination. "His end will be the same. Was there ever witnessed such a barefaced corruption in any country before?"[13]

It was, he fumed, "the most open daring corruption that has ever shown itself under our government, and if not checked by the people will lead to open direct bribery in less than twenty years."[14] Jackson, a reticent candidate in 1824, would take upon himself to do the checking in 1828—by the end of 1825, he was nominated for president by Tennessee's legislature. His supporters and allies would break into a new party, and American politics would be reordered because of it.

Lafayette and Jackson sat, side by side, in a carriage drawn into Nashville by four gray horses, mounted soldiers leading their way, followed by admiring citizens, down College Hill, up Market Street, to the civic arch at the center of town, decorated with evergreens. Hanging from this construction, next the American flag, a pennant with seven stars, representing each state whose representative in the House had voted for Jackson.[15]

Lafayette joined Tennessee's governor on the platform near the arch. "At the period of our eventful struggle, the fertile and delightful country which surrounds you, was a savage wilderness," Carroll said. "It is now filled with a population of hardy and enterprising yeomanry, in the enjoyment of the blessings of social life, of civil and religious liberty." In his reply, Lafayette made mention of Jackson, "an illustrious Tennessean hand," and delighted in "witnessing the blessed results of our old republican struggle."[16]

The backdrop for this ceremony was the impressive town hall, situated in the public square surrounded by taverns and a post office,

Georgian brick buildings, and fine homes. "It contains more elegant mansions and pleasant seats, in and around it, than any other town, of equal size, in the United States," one visitor wrote.[17]

The governor requested that all veterans of the Revolution in the vicinity of Nashville be present for Lafayette's arrival and ordered the state to help pay for their travel costs. After the governor's welcome address, thirty-five of them, "most worn out by age, some mutilated by war," appeared from opposite sides of the civic arch in Nashville's town square.[18]

One of these survivors, an ancient man, was helped up to the platform. "Why, John, is this you?" Lafayette was heard to ask. Indeed, it was John Hagey. The two men embraced and wept. Then Lafayette turned to the dignitaries gathered on the stand and explained that it was one of his old soldiers. Hagey claimed to have walked all the way from Huntsville, Alabama, to see his old general, telling him, "Now that I have seen you again, I have nothing more to wish for, I have lived enough." The crowd, stunned, fell silent for several moments.[19]

"General Lafayette and General Jackson marched arm and arm with their aides through long files of open ranks," remembered James N. Smith, a pioneer educator whose pupils included future president James K. Polk, and whose father, James Turner Smith, was a veteran of the Revolution.

Standing nervously across from his brother Charles as Lafayette moved along the lines while Jackson introduced him to individuals in the crowd, Smith, who had traveled to Nashville from his home in Maury County, waited to relate their own history to the general. "It was a great pleasure to me to shake hands with this great general and I had heard my father tell many things about him," wrote Smith. "My brother told him that our father had fought with him through the War of 1776."[20]

During the recent presidential election, partisans sought— sometimes through tortured logic—to connect their candidates to the Revolution. They channeled the soothing nostalgia for an earlier epoch during an uncertain time. Jackson, by virtue of his brief involvement in the Battle of Waxhaws in 1780, was portrayed by his supporters as a link to the spirit of '76, proof of his republican virtues. Some of his supporters even argued that voting for any other candidate betrayed the spirit of gratitude toward the old revolutionaries, a sentiment rekindled by Lafayette's return to America.[21]

To further solidify this revolutionary connection, partisans referenced Jackson's triumph in New Orleans and labeled him a "Second Washington." These were powerful political stratagems for a presidential candidate. Across his travels, Lafayette's name was often uttered alongside Washington's. Now, in Tennessee, Jackson's name joined theirs, forming a symbolic bridge from the Revolution of 1776 to the election of 1828.

At a dinner on the evening of Lafayette's arrival at the Nashville Inn, Jackson presided, offering the first toast to the illustrious guest of honor: "The Nation's Guest, tyrants have oppressed him, but free men delight to do him honor."[22] Lafayette remarked that he was doubly honored, by the toast and because of who had articulated it. Afterward, when a procession of Nashville's Masons brought him to the Grand Lodge of Tennessee, where three hundred of their brethren gathered, there was a portrait representing wisdom on one wall and another of Jackson, signifying strength, opposite. Likenesses of Lafayette were present too. Old Hickory, a former grandmaster, was in attendance, of course.[23]

Early the next day, May 5, Lafayette visited the militia encamped on a field south of town. Four thousand soldiers had come to the city from surrounding counties for his visit. He then saw firsthand an example of the impressive progress among the young western states, as well as Nashville's own growing affluence. At the Female Academy, one hundred students arranged in two columns serenaded him, welcoming him to their "retreat of science and the muses."[24] Lafayette was joined by Jackson at Cumberland College, where the institution's president, Philip Lindsley—who had declined an offer to become Princeton's president in 1824 to remain in Nashville[25]—conflated the two men's Revolutionary service in his address of welcome: "You, gentlemen were fighting the battles of liberty and independence, while the banks of the Cumberland were yet a part of the 'great unknown western wildness.'" Jackson, he continued, was like Washington, and Lafayette, when "crowned with the laurels of victory, and encompassed with all the 'pomp and circumstance of war,' gladly exchanged the sword for the plough." And of course, like those two men, he answered when pulled "by the voice of a free people from his beloved retreat."[26] The visit concluded with the school's board endowing two new faculty positions—the Lafayette professorship and the Jackson professorship of Cumberland College.[27]

The Nation's Guest and the Hero of New Orleans, with a large party on board, then sailed up the Cumberland to the Hermitage. At the sight of the rather plain Federal-style home, Levasseur was puzzled. "The first thing that struck me upon arriving at General Jackson's home was the simplicity of his residence," he wrote. "Still a little influenced by my European customs, I asked myself if this could really be the home of the most popular man in the United States."[28]

Over lunch, Lafayette and Jackson discussed revolutions, both American and French, as well as Napoleon. The Battle of New Orleans was similar to Waterloo, Lafayette said, with only "conditions reversed." The comparison pleased Jackson. "The subject of the election was not mentioned," according to one guest.[29]

On Jackson's gardens and farm, Levasseur found them so well organized that he observed, "We would have been able to believe ourselves at the home of one of the wealthiest and most capable farmers in Germany if, at each step, our eyes had not been afflicted by the sad spectacle of Slavery."[30]

Responding to requests from his guests, when the party returned to his house, Jackson showed off some of his trophies: a sword, gifted to him by Congress, and a saber from the men he commanded in Louisiana. Then, Jackson brought out the pride of the collection: a pair of saddle pistols, forged of Damascus steel, decorated with gold and silver inlay, attached to walnut stocks. Jackson asked Lafayette if he recognized the arms. He scrutinized them for a moment. They were the pistols he had given to Washington, made by a French gunsmith named Jacob Walster, likely around the beginning of the American Revolution. The pistols had passed from Washington's nephew, William Augustine

Washington, to his son-in-law, William Robinson. In 1824, congress-men Charles F. Mercer and Stephan Van Rensselaer, had presented them to Jackson on Robinson's behalf, another symbolic connection between Old Hickory and Washington.[31]

One of those present at the Hermitage shared the story with the pro-Jackson *Knoxville Register*. The paper's summary of the exchange portrayed a moment of blessing—Lafayette, the paper claimed, pressed the pistols into Jackson's hands, tears streaming from his eyes.[32] Lafayette, according to Levasseur, expressed his approval that they now belonged to a man worthy of Washington's legacy. At this compliment, Jackson blushed. Then he raised his voice. "Yes, I believe that I am wor-thy of them," he yelled, taking Lafayette's hand and pressing it and the pistols to his chest, "if not for what I have done but at least for what I desire to do for my country." The room erupted in applause.[33]

18

I Exclaim We Are Sinking!

Near midnight on May 6, Lafayette boarded the waiting steamboat *Mechanic*. Six hours later, at daybreak, with fresh stores, the vessel departed Nashville and descended the Cumberland River, caught the Ohio, and steamed toward the next point on Lafayette's rushed itinerary across the frontier, Louisville.

Early on May 8, the *Mechanic* stopped to take on firewood near the small community of Shawneetown, Illinois. There, Lafayette was greeted by a twenty-four-gun salute and the town's citizens standing silently in two long columns by the riverbank. Persuaded to disembark the *Mechanic*, he shuffled to the hotel built and owned by local merchant Moses Rawlings. On its steps he was greeted by a James Hall, a circuit judge, who offered the usual impassioned tribute—wistfully remarking on the passage of time and how it had claimed most of the founders. "But heaven," he rejoiced, "has spared Lafayette to the prayers of a grateful people." His statement would be tested in just a few short hours.

Lafayette and his companions—Illinois governor Edward Coles, who had traveled with Lafayette from Nashville, remained in Shawneetown—returned to the *Mechanic* and sped on. The day was brilliant, though Lafayette had little time to contemplate the weather. He spent the afternoon with Levasseur dictating responses to the many letters mailed to him from all over the country and notes of instruction for the caretaker of La Grange.

The Ohio, Thomas Jefferson, who never set his eyes upon it, wrote, was "the most beautiful river on earth."[1] For 980 miles it arched from western Pennsylvania, at the confluence of the Allegheny and Monongahela Rivers, before flowing into the Mississippi River at the southern Illinois town of Cairo. But as Washington, who had seen it, noted during an expedition up the river in 1770, travelers on the Ohio were likely to encounter "some ugly rifts and shoals" that were "somewhat difficult to pass."[2] In 1825, long before irrigation and canals transformed it into a broad and smooth waterway in the early twentieth century, the Ohio River was full of dangers.

Many of its passages were narrow and shallow. Its navigability was limited: Frozen and impassible in the winter, in spring its waters rose, providing a temporary pathway for the crops and livestock that were driven down to its banks and sent south. Under the water that transported them there were jagged rocks and hidden sandbanks for boats to run up on and snags to tear into their hulls. Vessels were regularly stranded on its shoals, sunk after running over its sawyers or pulled down its swift rapids.

By all appearances, the *Mechanic* was fit for the challenge: Built on the Little Muskingum River, near Marietta, Ohio, the boat was one hundred feet long, eighteen feet wide, capable of carrying tons of cargo and moving swiftly across shallow water, powered by an engine built by Phillips and Wise of Steubenville. Its captain, Wyllys Hall, boasted that the *Mechanic* was "equal to any boat on the western waters."[3] Like so many along Lafayette's path, Hall had revolutionary roots: His father, William Hall, rode express for George Washington. The captain shared his father's story with Lafayette, who searched his memory unsuccessfully for any trace of the older Hall.

On this evening, the *Mechanic*'s cabin was crowded: Nearly fifty passengers were on board, among them Western businessmen and lawyers, the Clarksville Blues (a Tennessee militia), and, perhaps most notably, Tennessee governor William Carroll, who had chartered the boat. Statuesque with a shock of white hair and an inconspicuously absent upper left thumb—it was blown off in a duel with Jesse Benton, younger brother of Senator Thomas Hart Benton—he was an ideal of the type of rowdy populist figure roaming the American political landscape at the time Lafayette arrived on the frontier.

As the night progressed, Lafayette retired to his cabin below deck while storm clouds arrived in the previously clear sky. The weather grew "boisterous," as Hall recalled, though the boat continued its swift pace. Georges stood on deck and stared worriedly across the darkened river. When he stepped into their cabin below, the younger Lafayette wondered with bewilderment to Levasseur why the captain of the boat continued to speed up such a perilous river on a moonless night. Agreeing on the danger, the men purposely turned the conversation to other subjects. "Accustomed as we are now to traveling at any hour and in any weather, these reflections were soon abandoned," wrote Levasseur.[4]

They were quartered for the trip in the women's cabin, the lowest on the boat, near the *Mechanic's* stern, accessed by a flight of ten stairs; lit by two windows, "almost pieced by the river's water."[5] At ten, Lafayette and Georges slept while Levasseur and de Syon composed letters nearby. As midnight neared, all the passengers aboard the *Mechanic* slumbered. Only Hall and his crew remained awake. On deck, the second watch prepared to take their positions, while the captain relayed instructions to one of his engineers. The *Mechanic* now was 125 miles from Louisville, nearing Deer Creek, a tributary fifty yards from the Kentucky shore. She steamed through a passage known as Troy Reach, roughly between the modern towns of Cannelton, Indiana, and Hawesville, Kentucky, having just maneuvered around a formation called Rock Island, when Hall's orders were interrupted by a loud crash.

The boat began to shake violently, then came to an abrupt stop. A tree had ripped through the bottom of the *Mechanic*, punched through the main deck, tossing a slumbering deckhand from his seat on the forecastle. The sailor was unscathed, but when Hall slipped below deck, he knew quickly that the *Mechanic* had no such luck. "A snag! A snag!" he screamed.[6]

The shock threw Levasseur and de Syon from their chairs, and Lafayette bolted from his bed. Bastien, Georges, and Levasseur ran to the bridge, where two passengers, unworried, claimed the boat had only touched a sandbar. Georges returned to the cabin to share the news with his father.

Levasseur grabbed a light and entered the main cabin, where he found the passengers, many still in their beds, in a state of confusion. Had the boat run aground? several wondered aloud. Pressing on toward the bow, he found Hall, who had ordered mattresses and blankets thrown below the deck in a futile effort to staunch the boat's wound. When the captain opened the *Mechanic*'s cargo hatch, he found it already half-full of water. The boat was certain to sink.

Hall's next thought was to get his most precious cargo to safety. "Hasten, Lafayette to my boat!"[7] he yelled, grabbing a deckhand and heading towards the cabin. Along the way he told the engineer he may as well let his engines continue to run—the boat was doomed. By the time he reached the cabin, the passengers, in various states of dress, were surmising that the boat had not run aground but had hit a snag. Hall confirmed this, admonished them to take care of themselves, and headed to the stern to prepare the yawl for Lafayette.

Levasseur returned below deck to find Lafayette putting on his clothing with Bastien's help: Before his arrival, a voice had shouted down to the cabin, "Dress yourselves!" Upon reaching the cabin, Levasseur laid out the dire circumstances. "We are sinking," he told Lafayette. "Hurry, we have no time to lose." At this point, the secretary began gathering the letters and documents scattered across the table and stuffed them into his portfolio. Lafayette finished dressing but lingered, questioning how the rest of his companions would escape. "Get out, dear papa, don't worry about us," pleaded Georges.[8]

He and Levasseur each grabbed one of Lafayette's hands and escorted him up the stairs. The old man, practiced at death-defying escapes, smiled at the two younger ones, tolerating their panic and concern. On his way to the deck, though, Lafayette did have a pang of worry. On a table in his cabin was left a treasured snuffbox, a portrait of George Washington on its lid, which Levasseur dutifully retrieved. Lost in the commotion, however, was the little dog Quiz.

When Lafayette reached the *Mechanic*'s main deck, the scene was one of total disorder. Passengers were attempting to salvage their belongings, while the boat—leaning leeward and taking on more water—was at such a pitch that standing was now difficult. There was one common concern across the entire boat: the safety of the Nation's Guest. Where was Lafayette? passengers cried. Though he was now on deck and among them, under the cover of night, he was unidentifiable. Screams of "General Lafayette! Save General Lafayette!" burst out from the listing *Mechanic*. But the passengers would not clear a space to let him pass; by now, in the panic, he was separated from Georges. "The boat leaned even more," wrote Levasseur. "The danger became pressing."[9]

At the boat's stern, Hall and two sailors had loosened the rope tying the *Mechanic*'s yawl to its taffrail and began to lower it into the water, yelling again for Lafayette through the chaos. Hearing the captain's call of "Lafayette, Lafayette!" Levasseur responded that he was present.[10] Now the chaos gave way to silence. The crowd parted as the general and his secretary pushed through toward the back of the ship.

Upon reaching the small lifeboat, Lafayette paused. There was limited space; he refused to take a spot when so many others would be left behind. Seconds before, the boats' passengers were caught in a commotion, saving their belongings and fearing for their lives. Now they temporarily discarded those worries and convinced Lafayette to flee to safety while he still could. He reluctantly stepped toward the yawl, which sat on the water four feet below the *Mechanic*'s deck. That distance, along with the boat's pitch and rocking and Lafayette's unsteady gait, made the short journey fraught.

Two passengers grabbed Lafayette by the elbows and lowered him into the boat, where Levasseur received him but lost his footing in the process. They might have toppled into the water if not for the steadying hand of Henry S. Thibodaux, an Anglo-French politician and adopted son of Philip Schuyler, a Revolutionary general and father-in-law of Alexander Hamilton. Lafayette was seated safely in one of the boat's wooden seats, near Allan Ditchfield Campbell, a Presbyterian minister from Nashville and his eight-year-old daughter, Anne. Hall ordered his sailors to row gently away from the *Mechanic*, and they reached the shore and safety within minutes.

Back on land, Lafayette had barely disembarked the yawl when he discovered that his son had not been on board the flight from the *Mechanic*. Lafayette's "habitual calm in the presence of danger abandoned him," Levasseur recalled. "Anxiety taking possession of him, he surrendered to the most animated excitement."[11] Limping along the shore he called for the absent son, only to be met with silence. His cries were futile: "His voice was drowned out by the shouts that arose from the ship, and by the horrible sound which the steam made in escaping from the engine, and he received no response," wrote Levasseur.[12]

After helping all of its passengers off, Hall redirected the yawl back toward the rapidly sinking *Mechanic* in order to rescue those remaining on board. Levasseur joined him, in search of his companion, Georges. When they arrived back at the *Mechanic*, the boat was still above water though nearly on its beam ends. Hall managed to temporarily step back on board and help passengers into the yawl. He ordered the boat's secretary, John F. Hall, to secure its records and the $1,000 on board before reboarding the lifeboat and heading back to the shore. The secretary promptly went to the desk containing the items, but as the boat leaned further to its side, he slipped. The desk, and with it the records and money, slid into the Ohio.

Levasseur sat in the rescue boat worried: There was no sign of Georges or Bastien. He purposely did not report this to Lafayette, now frantically asking the arriving rescues if they had seen his son. Instead, he returned again the *Mechanic* with Hall for another trek to secure more passengers. Before departing, though, a terrible cracking was heard across the water, accompanied by cries of terror in the dark as the *Mechanic* sunk, its boilers submerged in the water. There was a thrashing sound too, as passengers who had leapt for their lives swam to safety. One exhausted soul began to drown just feet from the shore in shallow water before Thibodaux once again saved the day, leading him to land. Conspicuously not among those paddling and thrashing or floating on timbers was Georges. There was a slim hope, however: The new arrivals reported that the *Mechanic* had not fully sunk: A small part of its roof and one wheelhouse remained above water and several passengers remained there, clinging to the boat.

Yet another rescue attempt was undertaken in the yawl. Arriving at the wreck, Levasseur called out for Georges. Instead of silence, though, a voice called out in French. "Is that you, Mr. Levasseur?" It was Bastien, awkwardly perched on the roof of the cabin. "Bring the rowboat, quick, because if I slip here, I drown," he yelled.[13] Levasseur helped him into the boat and then directed it toward the *Mechanic*'s stern. Levasseur called out for Georges. Finally there was a response: It was the younger Lafayette. He had purposely remained on the boat, refusing to leave until all those on board other than its sailors had been evacuated, and with the help of another passenger, Robert Walsh, he had endeavored to save as many of his father's belongings as time allowed. Shortly before their cabin filled with water, only minutes after the initial snag, he was able to secure some sixty of the two hundred letters Lafayette had composed that day, a coat rack, and his night bag. Levasseur returned with the salvaged items and the happy news to an overjoyed Lafayette, while Georges, accompanying the boat's remaining passengers, including de Syon, swam to safety shortly afterward.

Georges, Levasseur learned, once assured of his father's safety, had gone back to their cabin, as water poured in, to force de Syon and Bastien, who were attempting to secure the party's belongings, out. "His calm and presence of mind greatly contributed to reassuring the people who, without him, would have lost their heads and perhaps even their lives," wrote Levasseur. "He only left the boat when he was certain that those who remained were professionals and could do without him."[14]

No more than twenty minutes had passed from the instant the snag had burst through the *Mechanic* to the moment it capsized in the pitch of night. Now, suddenly, all on board sat on a strange shore buffeted by dense forest with no provisions, many soaked and half-dressed. The woods did provide kindling, which was set ablaze with candles preserved from the boat, creating large bonfires that warmed the drenched castaways. A mattress from the boat washed ashore. So too did an umbrella. Exhausted, Lafayette rested on the former. When a sudden rain arrived, he was shielded by the latter.

Soon the extent of the damage was visible. "The day shed light on a disastrous picture," wrote Levasseur. "The shore was covered in debris of every sort. Each searched desperately to find a few fragments of his property."[15] Carroll led an expedition from the shore, strewn with residue from the boat, back to the wreckage, in search of any salvageable items, securing a few pieces of luggage, a box of ground coffee, a leg of smoked venison, biscuits, and bottles of Bordeaux and Madeira. Levasseur watched with awe the egalitarian and particularly American spectacle of the governor of a state commandeering a salvage operation in a rowboat sans shoes or stockings.

The food and drink consumed around the bonfires lifted the spirits of the shipwrecked travelers. After the discovery of a home across the shore, at 9 a.m., Lafayette, along with Bastien and Thibodaux, was ferried to the other side of the river to shelter from an approaching storm. Neither Levasseur in his correspondence or published journals, or Hall, in a later letter detailing the wreck, made mention of which shore the passengers were stranded on or which one Lafayette was transported to in the morning. It is likely Kentucky in the case of the former, and Indiana in the latter: Lafayette is reputed to have briefly stayed at the cabin of a Hoosier pioneer named James Cavender in Perry County.[16] If this is the case, at the time, a sixteen-year-old Abraham Lincoln was likely rising for the day at his family's cabin at the Little Pigeon Creek community in neighboring Spencer County, whose residents included Thomas Turnham, veteran of Brandywine and Yorktown.[17]

Across the Ohio, there was still the riddle of how these fifty people would find their way to Louisville or even off their beach. Despite the momentary cheer from warmth, food, and drink, the travelers were still stranded.

Fatefully—decades later, Hall ascribed it to "a kind Providence"— soon after Lafayette departed and the crowd milled about its makeshift camp, two ships, one after another, came into view down the river. A signal went up from the shore and both boats sailed toward it. They were the *Paragon*, a large steamer carrying whiskey and tobacco from Louisville to New Orleans, and the smaller *Highland Laddie*. The *Paragon* had room enough to take the stranded travelers up to Louisville, but the jaunt would delay the delivery of its cargo and void the insurance covering it. Rescuing Lafayette would be costly, $25,000 in fact. Only the boat's owner could make that decision. Here, fortune again shined: That man, William H. Nielson, was on board and immediately determined to take the party back to Louisville, regardless of the expense.

The *Mechanic*'s passengers came on board the *Paragon*, where they were fed and given blankets. Levasseur and Georges quickly rowed the yawl back across the river to fetch Lafayette. While they were returning to meet the *Paragon*, another steamboat, the *Patriot*, arrived on the scene and offered to transport Lafayette and his friends in the *Paragon*'s stead. When Nielson politely declined, the two ships traded salutes and steamed off in opposite directions. Illinois senator Jesse B. Thomas, a passenger on board the *Patriot*, reported to the *Illinois Gazette* that Lafayette "appeared to be in good spirits and health and was only uneasy lest an exaggerated report of this accident should unnecessarily alarm his friends."[18]

Hall, accompanied by his crew, remained with the wreck a few days longer, venturing out on the yawl to save anything of value from the mostly sunken boat. He was less mortified by the damage to the *Mechanic* and apparent loss of money than he was about the shame of having piloted the boat that wrecked with Lafayette on board. "Never will my compatriots forgive me for the dangers to which Lafayette was exposed on this night!" he lamented.[19]

The Nation's Guest and his companions did not hold Hall responsible for the accident. "It was nobody's fault," wrote Lafayette, praising the captain's conduct, maintaining that there was "Nobody to blame but the snag."[20] A number of the passengers even signed a letter, later printed in the Louisville newspapers, claiming that "neither prudence or foresight could have prevented" the *Mechanic* from hitting the snag near Deer

Creek. Lafayette, absolving the captain from any blame, expressed his desire to "acknowledge my personal obligations to him." By some small miracle, the desk containing the boat's money was eventually retrieved and Hall arranged to have the *Mechanic* towed to New Albany, Indiana, across the Ohio River from Louisville, where she was repaired.

For his sacrifice, Kentucky's government offered full compensation to Nielson, the *Paragon*'s owner, for his losses incurred in rescuing Lafayette. He would have none of it, though: "Whatever renumeration the committee might think me entitled to, I relinquish it most freely for the benefit of Captain Hall feeling myself amply compensated for what I have done, by the honor of having been a passenger with our distinguished guest, Lafayette."[21]

"I exclaim we are sinking! And the sorry state of the papers that I am sending you were enough, I believe, for you to presume a shipwreck," Levasseur wrote to Émilie de Lafayette excitedly, relating the adventure. Lafayette took the near disaster in stride, accustomed to greater dangers. His only moment of panic was over his son's temporary absence while he rescued the boat's other passengers. "While I, on the riverbank, was shouting myself hoarse after him," Lafayette wrote. "It is true that after having been very politely placed in the women's cabin, below that of the men, we did well to get out before the water rapids had knocked over the partition and flooded the room." He lost the carriage given to him by Eliza Custis and his Bolivar hat. The latter item was quickly replaced by a Louisville milliner, Norborne Earickson, at no charge.[22] Also underwater was a trunk with hundreds of letters from around the country. In typical fashion, he was most upset about losing a letter from a Spanish refugee arriving in America and hoping to meet Lafayette before his return to France.[23]

At nine in the morning of May 11, the *Paragon* docked in Portland, three miles south of Louisville. The Lafayette Light Guard and the Lafayette Cavalry fired their salutes. Kentucky's politicians delivered their speeches. "The world will be here then—Man, woman and child are pressing to see the 'Nation's Guest,'" predicted one of the city's residents.[24] A carriage was waiting nearby. Lafayette climbed in with Richard Clough Anderson, his former aide-de-camp. Then began the procession into Louisville, where nearly ten thousand people greeted him. Women watched from windows; schoolgirls were stationed on sidewalks. They bowed and tossed flowers as the carriage passed by, down Jefferson Street, to Fifth, and then to his lodgings at the Union Hall. In the evening, during a ball held at Washington Hall, the "maidens of Louisville" wore star-shaped pendants from their necks containing miniature portraits of their newly arrived guest.[25]

"Here we are in the state of Kentucky where new kindnesses await us," Lafayette wrote to his daughters from Louisville. All those on board had survived the sinking of the *Mechanic*. But besides his hat, carriage, and some of his papers and letters, Lafayette had indeed suffered loss that night on the Ohio River. "No one has perished, thank God, but at present everything is under water," he wrote shortly after the accident. "But how I regret less our effects, our papers, but my little dog from Washington, who drowned because she wanted to make sure I was no longer in the lower cabin at the moment it was filling up with water."[26] The dog had run up to the deck in pursuit of her human after the boat began to sink; unable to locate him, she returned to their cabin as water rushed through its window, sealing the door and Quiz's fate. She drowned as the boat sank. For the remainder of his trip Lafayette lamented the loss of, in his words, "a most sagacious, affectionate little animal, and particularly attached to me." The general, according to one newspaper, "appeared to regret this loss, as the greatest that had befallen him."[27]

When he learned of the dog's valiant demise, Samuel Morse, grieving still but resuming work on Lafayette's portrait for New York City, sent his subject a condoling tribute to Quiz. "Lost from they care, to know thy master free, can we thy self-devotion e'er forget? T'was kindred feeling in less degree to that which thrilled the soul of Lafayette. He [*sic*] freely braved our storms, our dangers met, Nor left the ship till we had escaped the sea," it read. "Thine was a spark of noble feeling bright."[28] A feeling that burned for Lafayette, as Morse interpreted it, in man and beast alike.

19

In 1776, a Wilderness—In 1825,
a Civilized Community!

"The felicity denied by a curious providence to the Father of his country, has, it is hoped, been reserved for his adopted son," read the preamble to Indiana's resolution of invitation to Lafayette. "What the immortal Washington was permitted only to see through the dark vista of futurity, will be realized in the fullness of vision by his associate in arms and glory."[1]

Washington first ventured west over the Allegheny Mountains in 1754 as a twenty-one-year-old emissary sent by Virginia's governor Robert Dinwiddie. His mission was to deliver a warning to the French at Fort LeBoeuf in northwestern Pennsylvania, demanding they decamp from the land, which Britain claimed. A year later, as an aide-de-camp to General William Braddock, he helped lay a path for future migration west by helping cut a road wide enough to carry wagons over the mountains. This effort was part of a disastrous attempt to capture Fort Duquesne at the strategically vital Forks of the Ohio. It was there, on the banks of the Monongahela River, that he won his early military fame. After most of their command—including General Braddock—were killed or injured by French and Indian forces, he coolly rallied and led a force of British regulars and Virginia volunteers to safety.

The voyages west launched Washington's career and commenced his martial education. His impressions of the country west of the Allegheny—the richness of its soil and the abundance of its natural resources—helped shape his view of America's destiny. He was convinced that it lay westward, over the Allegheny, into the Ohio Valley, and to points even farther west. Along the waterways and in its hills, he saw a great stage for the creative dynamism of a young nation of restless freemen.

Tellingly, when Lafayette returned to America in 1784, Washington took leave of his guest to trek west from Virginia for the purpose of assessing the condition of his unsettled Western lands and to determine the feasibility of a waterway connecting the Ohio River to the upper Potomac, opening a channel for commerce to flow from the nation's interior to its Atlantic seaboard.

The Treaty of Paris in 1783 formally ended the Revolution and ceded the Northwest Territory—the land bounded by the Mississippi and Ohio Rivers, the Great Lakes, and the Appalachian Mountains—to America, though Britain stubbornly still held its Western forts. Four years later, in the summer of 1787, the Congress of the Confederation passed the Northwest Ordinance, providing a framework for the settlement, establishment of governments, and eventual statehood for the land. The Ohio Valley was opened to American migration. What had once been a matter of concern for Washington—violent conflict with and the eventual displacement of the Native populations on Western lands—became an inevitability.

"If I was a young man, just preparing to begin the world, or advanced in life, and had a family to make a provision for, I know of no country where I should rather fix my habitation than in some part of that region," Washington wrote in 1788, referring to the first white American colony in the Northwest Territory, at the confluence of the Muskingum and Ohio Rivers, settled by the Ohio Company, formed by Revolutionary soldiers, holding land grants for their service, and led by Rufus Putnam.[2] It was not only Washington's fellow veterans who concurred. Destitute farmers, wild-eyed entrepreneurs, and newly arrived immigrants—from Germany, Ireland, France, and dissident religious sects—began their adventures, setting out on the arduous journey into the Ohio Valley.

In 1800, the year following Washington's death, nearly 5 percent of America's population dwelled west of the Allegheny Mountains. A year later, Ohio achieved statehood; Indiana followed in 1816; Pennsylvania's population spread into the western reaches of the state. By 1820, 25 percent of Americans lived beyond the Allegheny Mountains. The introduction of commercial steamboat travel, which arrived on the Ohio River in 1811, vastly expedited the delivery of commerce—crops, livestock, and manufactured goods. This hastened the economic development and growth of cities in the Ohio Valley, including Pittsburg, Cincinnati, Louisville (Kentucky had joined the Union in 1792), and Wheeling in western Virginia. These cities were strung across the fertile country where Washington envisioned America's future.

He was long in the dilapidated crypt at Mount Vernon as the West took form, but as Indiana's General Assembly hopefully prophesied, when Lafayette arrived in Louisville after the wreck of the *Mechanic*, he had survived to see Washington's vision realized. The sight was not only gratifying but affirming: He could trace the path from the Revolution, the rights it had won, and the incredible material progress spreading across the continent, blooming on the banks of the Ohio River and its tributaries.

"The creations, improvements, dignity, prosperity, strength, and domestic happiness of this admirable republican confederation surpasses everything that my imagination, which is said to be quite lively in such matters, could ever conceive," Lafayette wrote during his venture into the American frontier. "The deserts are rapidly changing into fertile lands and flourishing cities, and everyone says this is the fruit of popular institutions and *self-governance*."[3]

Lafayette was delighted to behold the transformed Ohio Valley. But by now the grand celebration at Bunker Hill was little more than a month—and nearly one thousand miles—away. To fulfill his wish in the West, and discharge his duty in the East, Lafayette would resume his original itinerary, speed east overland across Kentucky, and pass through Lexington in route to Cincinnati. Then he would travel across Ohio by land, visiting Chillicothe, Columbus, Lancaster, Zanesville, and on to Wheeling. From there he would travel to Pittsburg, Philadelphia, and at last Boston. All in a single month. Visits would be truncated, sometimes lasting only a few hours; blue laws, discouraging travel on the Sabbath, would be apologetically ignored. The excited hopes of many citizens in settlements and towns between Indiana and Massachusetts would be dashed.

Indiana issued its invitation in February; its governor, William Hendricks, had hoped that Lafayette might visit the new capital in Indianapolis, but time and terrible roads leading into central Indiana made this impractical. "Happy would I be to visit every part of it [Indiana] but I am pressed by time, by engagements, and by the necessity to be on the heights of Bunker Hill by the 17th," Lafayette explained. He presented an alternative: "On my way up the Ohio, a place might be assigned to meet my friends of the state of Indiana."[4]

With no set day of arrival, Hoosiers living in the communities along the Ohio River were on high alert. When a steamboat neared the town of Lawrenceburg, with a band of musicians on board playing their flutes and fifes, its townspeople rushed to the riverbank—"the merchants dropped their yardsticks and scissors, and with unusual agility o'er-leaped the counter; the lawyer stopped in the middle of his harangue, and the justice for a while suspended the operation of the law." They waited by the water "with longing eyes, with gaping mouths and beating hearts" for Lafayette. "But alas!," wrote Lawrenceburg's newspaper, "how we are subject to disappointment." The ship was carrying only Harmonists on their way east to their new home and not the Nation's Guest.[5]

Indiana's moment arrived—and it was little more than a moment—when, beckoned by a delegation from the state once he reached Louisville, Lafayette steamed across the Ohio River to Jeffersonville on May 11. The village was, for a time, Indiana's pseudo-capital before statehood; its territorial governor, Thomas Posey, built his house there, preferring to reside near his doctor in Louisville rather than live in the second territorial and first state capital at Corydon. Posey, a Virginian whose father was an associate of Washington's, and who was even, some whispers said, his illegitimate son, had died in 1818. His mansion overlooking the Ohio River remained, though, and served as the backdrop for Lafayette's visit to Indiana.

There, James B. Ray, the state's thirty-year-old interim governor, delivered the requisite speech. (Hendricks, governor when Indiana issued its formal initiation in February, had since been elected to the Senate.) Lafayette's popularity was such that officeholders' odes to him were fodder for their rivals. "Cold, vapid and inflated, labored and pedantic without one vigorous or soul animating expression, it stands at an immeasurable distance below every address of the kind to that illustrious and venerable patriot, in the progress of his triumphant tour through our country," a foe wrote of Ray's remarks.[6]

Dinner was served on a 220-foot table, its decorations and the protective awning above it all crafted from wood harvested from nearby forests. As rain clouds emptied themselves from above, the guests dined beneath the sheltering canopy. At its far end hung a painted transparency. It read, *Indiana, In 76, A Wilderness—In 1825, a Civilized Community! Thanks to Lafayette and the Soldiers of the Revolution!*[7]

Jeffersonville was among the "infant towns," such as New Albany and Shippingport, emerging on both the Indiana and Kentucky banks of the Ohio near Louisville, a concourse of shipyards, flour mills, distilleries, sugar refineries, and pork houses. Louisville's population upon Lafayette's arrival was close to five thousand, but along with its satellite communities, the area was home to ten thousand people, busily shipping their goods—whiskey, flour, pork—along the river.

Back in Louisville, a few hours after his Indiana visit, a grand barbecue was nixed due to inclement weather. The city had other attractions, markers of developing economic and creative might. Victor Pepin, born in Albany but raised in France after moving there with his Canadian parents, established a circus in Louisville in 1824. A former French cavalry officer and dashing horseman, Pepin returned to America and, with a partner, established a series of circuses in eastern cities. Branding themselves the "First Riding Masters of the Academies of Paris," they

were among America's earliest circus promoters, in an era when performances were mostly equestrian. However, the War of 1812 reduced
demand for his shows, prompting Pepin to drift south and then west
into the frontier. In Pittsburg, Pepin's alleged seduction of a pupil—"a
respectable young lady"—from his riding school provoked the riot by
an angry mob during one of his performances.[8] One member of the
mob was murdered by one of Pepin's troupe.[9] On his second and final
evening in Louisville, Lafayette "witnesse[d] the extraordinary performance of Pepin and company." His performers leapt their horses over
fences and under poles, leaping out and back into the saddle, or, standing with one leg on their backs, rode two horses at once.[10]

After the spectacle at Pepin's circus, Lafayette was the guest of
honor at Sam Drake's City Theatre. Kentucky was a lucrative venue
for early-nineteenth-century thespians, who performed at theaters in
Louisville, Frankfort, and Lexington. Since its entry into the Union
in 1792 to 1820, more than six hundred performances took place in the
state. Drake, an English actor, immigrated with his family of performers
and, like Pepin, migrated west, bringing his company down the Ohio
River on a barge. In 1818, he purchased a shabby theater built by a local
amateur acting group, refurbished the building, and established the
long-running City Theatre. The walls were frescoed, gold and crimson
curtains were hung, and wax candles burned in large chandeliers placed
on opposite wings of the stage during performances of *Wives as They
Were and Maids as They Are* and *Pocahontas Saving the Life of Captain
Smith*.[11] On the evening of Lafayette's attendance, a crowd packed into
the small brick building. "As he approached his seat, the whole audience, male and female, rose and received him standing," wrote a correspondent. Once he reached a box, decorated for the occasion, and made
a bow of acknowledgment, the audience erupted in cheers.[12] It was a
formidable act for Mr. Drake's company to follow.

Before Lafayette left Louisville, Fanny Wright arrived with news
she could not quite steel herself to share. Since her visit to New
Orleans, she wrote, "we have lived half a life and seen half a world."[13]
After parting with Lafayette in Natchez, Wright returned to Harmonie,
or rather, New Harmony. Robert Owen's utopian community was now

gathering while the remaining members of George Rapp's flock were waiting for a steamboat to transport them to their new home in western Pennsylvania. Among the latter population was Rapp's son. Observing both the order and productivity of the Harmonists and inspired by Owen's theories, Wright formulated a plan to lance the "horrible ulcer" of American slavery.[14]

The concern Wright had heard from liberal-minded Americans regarding emancipation was the inability of the slave to exist with no education and no capacity to care for themselves in freedom. This, then, was the great object, to create a system in order to prepare the slave for freedom. She would purchase land and establish a farm in a slave state, perhaps Tennessee. Then she would purchase and bring slaves there, where they would work for their freedom. Once their labor was commensurate with their value on the market—four or six years, she estimated—they would be freed. In the interim, between their purchase and emancipation, the slaves would be provided with education in preparation for resettlement in, perhaps, Texas or Haiti. It was, typical for Wright, a highly idealistic plan based on faulty assumptions: The communal labor of the Harmonists, which partially formed her inspiration, was more a consequence of Rapp's iron-fisted rule over his followers and less the result of their sense of selflessness.

Wright was not yet willing to actuate the plan though. "Although thus far my arrangements were made they were only conditionally so until I could obtain the consent of the beloved Genl. to our remaining in America," she wrote.[15] Unnerved by Lafayette's wreck on the Ohio, perhaps fearing she would upset him, Wright remained silent. "I found no favorable moment to break to him the subject which occupied me at Louisville."[16] They parted with the plan unknown to Lafayette. Wright and her sister, who had obtained three horses and a Black servant, continued east, soliciting support for her project, to Pittsburg, where she and Lafayette agreed to meet.

Lafayette left Louisville on May 13. One of the city's newspapers, praising its demonstrations of admiration for the Nation's Guest, noted the "unprecedented rapidity" of his movement away from it. He departed Louisville quickly, but constant rain and muddy roads ensured he did not get far. The next afternoon, the party reached Frankfort, Kentucky's capital, where a dinner, held in the public square, ultimately cost the state $2,000. "Taking into consideration the nature of the occasion, the music, the decoration of the spacious and splendid ball room, the number, dresses and beauty of the ladies, there has never been so brilliant and interesting a display of the kind in Frankfort, if indeed the western country."[17] In the capital, Lafayette paid his own debt of gratitude, visiting Margaretta Brown, sister-in-law of the American minister to France, James Brown. During their hour-long visit, Lafayette told her son that, if not for his uncle, "he would never had been permitted to leave France."[18]

"It has not been the practice of General Lafayette to travel on the Sabbath; but the necessity he is under to be at Bunker Hill on June 17 compels him to expedite his journey," explained the *Frankfort Argus* the following morning. As he rode away from their town, he did so without the usual military escort or salute—a gesture of apology for his violation of Kentucky's "blue law."[19]

Unceasing rain and muddy roads delayed his arrival in Lexington until the next morning. His approach coincided with a clearing of the dark clouds over the heads of ten thousand people who had marched toward Frankfort to meet him as he entered town. "The scene, almost magical, increased the enthusiasm of the multitude whose joyful cheering blended with the continuous rumbling of artillery that thundered around us," Levasseur wrote.[20]

Old veterans made their way to the general with proof of their service—a hand missing two fingers, blown off at Brandywine; a powder horn that lit artillery at Yorktown. "When Ge. LaFayette got into Lexington the rush of many of the old soldiers was truly exciting. Everywhere his carriage was stopped by the surviving veterans who served with him and Washington," wrote Benjamin Netherland, a veteran of the Revolution who was in Charleston when Lafayette arrived there in 1777.[21]

Lexington, the "sweet Athens of the West," as the poet Josiah Espy affectionately labeled the town, was known for its beautiful homes, buildings, and plantations, including Henry Clay's Ashland, which

Lafayette visited though its owner was absent at the time. Its affluence stemmed from its position on the Kentucky River, a tributary of the Ohio. As Kentucky's most sophisticated city, Lexington represented the promise of America's future rather than reminders of its past. It was even forward-looking in fashion: Timed for his visit, a Lexington tailor named Lawson McCullough introduced the innovative "Lafayette coat." Cut without seams on the back or sides, it eliminated the gathering of dust, provided a better fit, and lasted longer. "This I believe is the first time that this mode of cutting coats has been used in the Western country," its creator bragged.[22]

Fayette County, named in Lafayette's honor in 1780—"the county that bears my name is the most fertile country in the world; we can call it the American Limagne," he wrote to granddaughter Nathalie—was home of the first newspaper, library, and college established west of the Allegheny Mountains, chartered by Virginia in 1790.[23] The visit to Transylvania University was among the experiences Lafayette found most rewarding on his western tour, Levasseur wrote, "was the picture of the development and the rapid progress of education among all classes of the people."[24] The school's president, Horace Holley, delivered one of the most perceptive of the hundreds of orations Lafayette endured during his travels.

Holley, a Yale-educated Unitarian minister, whom the school's trustees had lured to Kentucky, gracefully acknowledged Lafayette's sacrifice for America, but his purpose was not to flatter. He acknowledged the incredible transformation of the West, where "a few years since, wolves howled and buffaloes congregated, you find a community of six hundred thousand civilized, cultivated, and generous Freeman," but he did not seek to brag.

Rather, Holley reproached those who mocked America's national celebration of Lafayette or dismissed it as idolatry. "They, who see in it nothing but a popular pageant for the gratification of publick curiosity, know not its real character and effects," he said. Critics might liken the spectacle to "the homage paid to a king or an emperor" and incompatible with republican values, Holley acknowledged. But, Americans were not in fact celebrating one man, though.

"But we identify you, as we do Washington, with the cause, the sentiments, the institutions, the blessings, which the recollection, and still more the sight of you, can never fail to embody and present with paramount interest and force, to our minds. We see perfect consistency in this, the triumph of free principles and self-government. Your presence is the Jubilee of Liberty."[25]

Once Holley concluded, three of Transylvania's students delivered orations, interspersed with music in Latin, French, and English. Later, after dinner—"furnished with the best provisions the country affords at $2.50" per ticket—he visited the Lexington Female Academy. "Sir, you are now, literally, in a new world," declared its principal, Josiah Dunham. Its pupils delivered their compositions and sang a song penned by Holley's wife: "Never nation, since creation, hailed a hero like to thee!"[26]

"Such a literary reception has not, as far as we remember, been given La Fayette in any of the colleges of our country," commented the *Reporter*. The town's institutions, it continued, "unquestionably gave to the old hero a higher idea of the real advancement of our state of society in the West."[27] The paper failed to mention the "castled cake," baked by a local confectioner for a supper in Lafayette's honor. Its towering height and design were so impressive that none of the partiers could bring themselves to eat it, lest they destroy the great Lafayette Cake.[28] Even more telling of the region's cultural and artistic progress was the selection of Matthew H. Jouett, a "man born and nurtured in Kentucky, grown in its forests and cane-breaks," to paint Lafayette's portrait. Chosen by Kentucky's government, Jouett's work was destined to hang in the House of Representatives in the statehouse.[29]

The party pressed eastward on May 17. "Hundreds of the people of Lexington in talking of Lafayette cried out loud," as Netherland described it.[30] Twenty miles later, when they reached Georgetown, the road was lined with people from across the state as Lafayette's carriage rolled past. The teenage Ebenezer Stedman, whose father owned and operated a paper plant in town, recalled Lafayette "Bowing to Each Side of the Road & from thare to Getowin was on Live Mass of men women & Children Negros & Horses & Such Shouts with the Roar of Cannon & Musketry, the Like no one will Ever witness again."[31] Not to be outdone by Lexington's "castled cake," the people of Georgetown displayed for Lafayette their own unique proof of advancement: a five-hundred-pound cheese. With Lafayette in town, a competition arose among the young women of Georgetown over who would eat from his plate. Stedman's future wife emerged victorious, securing the treasured item when Lafayette left the table. "It was Made Much Talk of & fun amoungst all the girls," he recalled, "as Several of them Had Determined to have the Honor of the plate."[32]

Early on the 19th, Lafayette and his companions were rowed across the Ohio River from Covington. They were greeted with a twenty-four-gun salute and cheers from the citizens of Cincinnati, hailed by Mrs. Trollope as the "'Wonder of the West,' this 'Prophet's Gourd of Magic Growth,'—this 'infant Hercules.'"[33]

Settled between the Ohio River and numerous forested hills, Cincinnati was home to ten thousand people. Apothecaries and booksellers, shipwrights and stonecutters, factories and slaughterhouses filled the city, while hogs roamed freely, their blood often draining in the streets. It was the most populous city in the West and its economic powerhouse.

In preparation for Lafayette's visit—Ohio had not issued a formal invitation, but Lafayette included Cincinnati on his published itinerary—the city's elite, led by senator William Henry Harrison, began their preparations. Harrison, a former governor of the Indiana territory, a national hero after the battle of Tippecanoe, and a future president, lived in nearby North Bend. Alongside the city's mechanics and Masons, they worked to welcome Lafayette.

Lafayette badges were made available. One of Cincinnati's newspapers, the *National Republican*, proposed they be worn in tandem with Jackson badges. Another paper, the *Liberty Hall*, wishing to maintain the national character of the celebration, suggested a Revolutionary cockade instead.[34]

There were the usual tributes: Harrison and Ohio's governor, Jeremiah Morrow, delivered speeches upon Lafayette's landing, and

Masonic ceremonies were held. During his visit, the "Lafayette Lodge" was founded. But there was also something quite different.

In 1818, Dr. Benjamin Drake, a would-be Benjamin Franklin of the West, founded the Western Museum, which opened two years later after he had acquired the requisite exhibits. Drake intended to use the institution to enlighten and stir the curiosity of Cincinnatians. In a discourse delivered on the museum's anniversary, he outlined an American vision: Cultivating knowledge of national history would further decouple the New World from the Old. "A dependence on Europe is equally disastrous and degrading," Drake wrote. He believed "the increase of useful knowledge is the true secret of our happiness."[35] To that end, he displayed birds, fish, reptiles, and elephant bones. He even hired John James Audubon, a young artist, to paint exhibits and prepare taxidermy animals.

Laudable though it was, the museum floundered financially. Drake was dismissed, and in 1823, the exhibits were handed over to the museum's curator, Joseph Dorfeuille, a German immigrant with a murky past and a predilection for the morbid. Less a man of science than a frontier impresario, Dorfeuille transformed the Western Museum into a collection of shocking oddities. For a time, he made it a viable financial proposition with displays that did not quite adhere to Drake's original vision—such as the preserved heart and head of a local murderer, dancing skeletons, and a mechanized version of Dante's *Inferno*. These exhibits eventually earned the museum infamy.

Dorfeuille decked out the Western Museum for Lafayette, who arrived in the evening after a spectacular fireworks display. Exhibits were illuminated by colored lights and spermaceti candles placed in silver candlesticks "gave delight to the eye." Dorfeuille guided his guest through the museum, explaining each specimen in French; Lafayette "expressed himself surprised, delighted, and gratified," reported the *Cincinnati Advertiser*. "Such an exhibition, in the western wilds, within thirty years the haunt of the bear, the panther, and the more ferocious aborigines, was calculated to draw forth the astonishment, as well as the admiration of the Hero."[36]

On his second day in Cincinnati, fifteen hundred of the city's Sunday school students marched through its streets to Broadway, where Lafayette shook many of their hands and sat patiently for a discourse from their teacher and an address from Joseph Benham. The latter man, a U.S. Attorney, spoke with a trembling voice of the tranquility enjoyed by the American people under their free government, where "every branch of business is encouraged . . . the arts and sciences flourish . . . These Lafayette are the fruits of Thy soils and sacrifices!" he continued. "These are the laurels that bloom for thee in America—won by thy gallantry in the vales of Brandywine, on the plains of Monmouth, and at Yorktown."[37]

After Benham concluded his speech, crowds dispersed, and Lafayette retired briefly to the home of Christian Carson Febiger on Vine Street; Febiger's uncle and adopted father, Christian Febiger, was an original member of the Society of the Cincinnati. In Febiger's drawing room, a group of about forty men appeared. Their leader, an old man missing his left arm, requested an audience with Lafayette in French. "We are citizens of Vevay," he said. Levasseur went to fetch the general, but Lafayette, feeling indisposed, sent his son, Georges, to meet with the men instead.[38]

They were originally from the Swiss canton of Vaud; most had fled after the French army had invaded Switzerland and created the Helvetic Republic, ending autonomous rule under the previous Swiss Confederation. At the age of fourteen, their leader, Jean-Jacques Dufour, had read in newspapers unhappy letters from French officers fighting in the American Revolution regarding the lack of wine in the new country so blessed with natural resources. After examining maps of America, Dufour concluded that the country could be the equal to France or Italy in the cultivation of grapes. "I then made the culture of the grape, of its natural history, and all that was connected with it, my most serious study, to be the better to succeed here," he wrote.[39] In 1796, Dufour sailed to America, became John James Dufour, and traveled the Eastern states studying soil and climate. Concluding a viticulturist's prospects were fair on the Atlantic Seaboard, he ventured west with better luck. At one point he inquired about buying some of Washington's land on the Ohio River to establish a colony of Swiss winemakers.[40] Dufour eventually acquired six hundred acres on the

Kentucky River near Lexington, planted his clippings, and established the first vineyard of Kentucky.

Disease and a lack of stable financing—the enterprise was supported by subscriptions—led Dufour and his family members, who had joined him in Kentucky, to successfully petition Congress for a grant of twenty-five hundred acres in the Indiana Territory. "It would be useless for me to tell you how much vineyards would be advantageous for the country in general, or that there is no doubt of success in making them as productive as anywhere in Europe," Dufour wrote to Thomas Jefferson, appealing to his love of wine and desire to establish viticulture in American, for reasons related to commerce and establishing national self-identity.[41] In addition to the land granted on credit by the government, Dufour acquired and sold additional acreage. He named the settlement New Switzerland and established America's first commercial vineyard. The Vevay men recounted their story, explaining how they had left Europe "to seek in this hospitable land the free exercise of their rights and their industry; our quests have not been in vain; we have become American citizens and we are happy."[42] As the winemakers related their story, Lafayette appeared. Then, Dufour spoke on behalf of the group. "General, you see in front of you men who, disgusted by the tyranny and the misery which reigned in the old Europe, left their native land to come to seek in this hospitable land the free exercise of their rights and their industry," the old man explained, "our quests have not been in vain; we have become American citizens and we are happy."[43] In turn, each man then embraced Lafayette, and they presented him with their wine. Together, they toasted to prospects of America as well as the freedom of Switzerland. "The wine of Vevay, one must confess, is not an exquisite wine," wrote Levasseur, "yet it is agreeable enough to drink, and it is, in my opinion, the best of the wines produced in the United States."[44]

Gratifying as Cincinnati was to Lafayette, he arrived there six days behind schedule; it was no longer possible to tour the interior of Ohio on his way east. To the citizens of Chillicothe, one of his intended stops and the former capital, he sent a note of apologetic explanation, professing a desire to see their own "wonderful improvements." "But on calculating the days, hours, and miles, of the distance which still separates me from my solemn duty to be performed, as a representative of the Revolutionary Army, on the heights of Bunker's Hill, I find it impossible for me to indulge my very great desire to take the land tour to Wheeling."[45] In order to reach Boston by the 21st, Lafayette and his companions boarded a steamboat, the *Herald*, chartered by Ohio's governor, in Cincinnati. They traveled upriver to Wheeling, from where they would journey overland to Pittsburg. From there, they would continue into western New York, travel along the Erie Canal to Albany, and then proceed overland to Boston.

At midnight, as the *Herald* departed up the Ohio River, both banks were illuminated, cannons boomed, and the landing was thronged with people. Traveling by water led to the cancellation of several planned visits on Lafayette's tour, but it also created new opportunities. The party made lightning-fast stops along the river on its way to Wheeling. In the Kentucky port of Maysville, Lafayette reunited with fellow veterans of the Revolution. In Gallipolis, settled by French loyalists who had fled to America after being misled by a shell company in Paris, he reminisced about his days as commander of the National Guard. He spoke openly of the evils of slavery, congratulating the people of Gallipolis for settling in a land where the institution "cannot breathe."[46] When asked if he would settle in America, Lafayette, perhaps reinvigorated by the progress all around him, reminded his old countrymen that he was still a player in the affairs of France. In Marietta, the surprised citizens marched him into town, assembled to shake his hand, and just as quickly marched him back to the *Herald*.

On May 24, with thirty minutes' notice delivered by express from Grave Creek, volunteer companies quickly gathered, bands began to play, and men and women ran to the water's edge as clouds of smoke and vapor rose above the trees downriver. The sound of a gun signaled Lafayette's arrival in Wheeling, and soon the *Herald* came into view. Upon reaching Beymer's Landing, he was greeted by two columns of citizens, "awaiting in breathless anxiety the approach of the hero," and welcomed by local lawyer Alexander Caldwell, to "Western Virginia." Paraded into town, Lafayette repaired to Simm's Hotel to quickly dash off correspondence to the Bunker Hill Committee with an update of his progress.

Leaving Wheeling the following day, still accompanied by Ohio Governor Jeremiah Morrow, Lafayette saw another realization of Washington's dreams. In 1818, the first leg of a national road connecting the Potomac River at Cumberland, Maryland, to the Ohio River was completed, opening a passage into the interior for settlers and back East for commerce. Part of the road roughly followed the path laid out by Washington and Braddock during their doomed expedition. Stagecoaches now ran from Washington and Baltimore to Wheeling in less than four days. In 1820, Congress authorized an extension to St. Louis. The roads took Lafayette through southwest Pennsylvania to Washington, the first town named for the first president. From there, he crossed the Monongahela River in a barge accompanied by twenty-four young women—one for each state. He visited Brownsville, with its bustling shipyards, and then rode on to Uniontown in Fayette County, named for him in 1783 and home to the state's famed iron furnaces.

"The contemplated visit of the 'Nation's Guest' to this county, had excited great interest amongst the people, and all were on the tiptoe of anxious expectation to behold, him," reported the *Genius of Liberty*, Uniontown's newspaper, after his arrival. Local carpenters constructed four arches and a pavilion in the town's center in four days. Albert Gallatin, an intimate of Lafayette during his time as America's minister to France and whose home, Friendship Hill, was nearby, spoke under it on behalf of his fellow citizens. The women of Uniontown were given preferential seating, "except so far as might be necessary to seat the revolutionary soldiers comfortably within view of their companion in arms."[47]

Gallatin delivered a lengthy discourse on Lafayette's career, redeeming his role in France's Revolution, before extolling the results of America's. "Her villages are now populous cities: her ships cover the ocean," he exclaimed. "New states have, as by magic, arisen out of the wilderness: her progress in manufactures, in arts, in internal improvements, lately in science and literature have kept a pace with that of her wealth and her trebled population."[48] The next morning, Gallatin welcomed Lafayette and the people of Unionville to Friendship Hill, near New Geneva. "His best liquors were spread in profusion, on the tables," the local newspaper reported.

The following afternoon, Lafayette and his party traveled north to Elizabethtown, bound for Pittsburg. In the afternoon, they were rowed down the Monongahela River on a barge and landed at Braddock's Field, the site of the British rout at the hands of French and Indian forces. In the seven decades since the disastrous expedition, its history had been reinterpreted as the scene of Washington's heroism rather than British defeat. The expedition had also played a part in the eventual opening of the West and the creation of the advancements Lafayette had witnessed from Louisville and Pittsburg—rising cities, industries, arts, and a population of impresarios, educators, entertainers, and immigrants.

It was too late in the evening to see it when he and his companions arrived, but artifacts—tomahawks, sabers, rifles, and even bones of slain soldiers—were still regularly found on the battlefield. They walked to the home of George Wallace, who had acquired a deed to the land in 1791 and built a stately home. There, members of Pittsburg's Committee of Arrangements waited, ready to guide him into their city the next day.

Toward the end of the nineteenth century, when the original parchment deed to the 328 acres acquired by Wallace was discovered, a Pittsburg paper reported on the document with great interest, recalling Washington's valor on the site. "But," the columnist continued, "could the immortal Washington come back and view the famous battle ground, he would probably be astonished, to see acres of machinery and furnaces where once the stalwart oak sheltered the savage."[49]

20

≈

Here We Are Approaching the Ocean

For fifteen days, Fanny and Camilla Wright rode east, stopping at Economy, where the Harmonists were reestablishing themselves. Continuing west, now accompanied by George Rapp, they arrived in Pittsburg twelve hours before Lafayette.[1] There the sisters witnessed its citizens swoon as a barouche pulled by four white horses brought him into town. "Every countenance beamed with please, and every eye sparkled with delight," wrote a local reporter.[2] But in a quiet moment, away from the ball in his honor at Colonel Ramsey's, Wright at last shared her plan to end American slavery with Lafayette. "I had a long interview with that good angel and recd his blessing and permission," Fanny wrote to her friends Julia and Harriett Garnett.[3] But he did not bestow either so easily. Her proposal, her desire to remain in America, meant that father and daughter were to separate. "You will feel all that the Genl. feels, who passed a sleepless night after our conversation," she shared with the Garnetts.[4]

To Lafayette's objection, Fanny argued that a parting was inevitable if they returned to Europe, given the constraints on his time from "friends and strangers" once he was back in France, as well as the Wrights' own desires to revisit acquaintances after such a long absence.

She hoped that the pain of her absence would be offset by the "prospect of such misery being alleviated as that which disgraces & ruins a large half of this glorious country."[5] Even so, there were great dangers she perceived: "The ignorant white population of the South who have so long prohibited the instruction & very generally the emancipation of the slaves may attack us thro' law or thro' violence."[6] She was reassured by friends, and believed that her gender would protect her, at least from the second threat. But she was convinced her relative fame would engender her support and sympathy. "I am very generally known & I think I may add looked upon, as a friend by the American people," Fanny wrote. "I am assured that I am perhaps the only individual (who might) (with the exception of the beloved Gnl.) who could enter on or carry thro such an undertaking."[7]

Her next step was to present the plan to Andrew Jackson and DeWitt Clinton, the most popular man and the greatest man in America, respectively. Old Hickory's sanction of her project "would ensure its success."[8] And Tennessee, a relatively more liberal-minded slave state, was increasingly attractive to Fanny as a venue. New York's governor was a foe of slavery and perhaps a future president. Fanny hoped to arrange an interview with Jackson and travel to Nashville, but this would have to wait until after the celebration at Bunker Hill, which she promised Lafayette she would attend. So they parted once more, knowing a final goodbye was now inevitable. The sisters' path to Boston would lead through Philadelphia, to meet with members of emancipation societies, and then New York; Lafayette's would be "eastward by way of the lakes."[9]

As the summer of 1825 began, construction of the Erie Canal neared completion. In June, the Masons of Lockport readied a marble capstone for placement in the wall of a set of five locks, built to lift boats over the steep Niagara Escarpment, represented the most challenging and expensive portion of the project.

It read:

Let posterity be excited to perpetuate our free institutions, and to make still greater efforts than their ancestors, to promote public prosperity, by the recollection that these works of internal improvement by the spirit and perseverance of Republican Freeman.[10]

The canal connecting Lake Erie to the Hudson River, linking the Great Lakes to the Atlantic Ocean, was more than just a waterway, it symbolized a connection between America's past, the values of its founding, and its auspicious future of boomtowns, new industries, and expanded markets. Yet, it also brought incredible societal disruption: a reordering of how and where Americans worked, the structure of their families, the role of government in their lives, and the forced removal of the Iroquois Confederacy from their ancestral homeland.

Who better to bless this emblem of America's glorious destiny than the living embodiment of its sacred Revolution? In September 1824, during his trip up and back down the Hudson River, Lafayette traveled briefly along the eastern leg of the canal, running from Albany to Troy.

On the eve of his departure for the Southern states, New York's state legislature commissioned a portrait and extended a formal invitation to visit its seat in Albany, which DeWitt Clinton, reelected to New York's governorship, transmitted to Lafayette. He would enjoy returning to New York and traveling east to Vermont, whose government had also extended an invitation to the Nation's Guest, at the end of his Western voyage, Lafayette responded. The jaunt along the canal, however, was not reflected in the original itinerary, which planned an overland return from Pittsburg. This was abandoned; instead, Lafayette would travel up to western New York and then east along the canal, on a route apparently recommended by Clinton. It was proposed by the owners of the first steamer on the Great Lakes, the *Ontario*, that Lafayette travel to Rochester from Lewiston on their boat. "I would avail myself of their friendly proposal," Lafayette wrote in response to the offer, "but pressed as I am by time to reach Boston on the day appointed for the half-secular jubilee of Bunker Hill, it is necessary for me to take the shorter route, and I have reasons to believe I shall find it marked out by the Governor of New York."[11]

Speed was now paramount. Lafayette and his companions left Pittsburg in a stagecoach lent by Arthur M'Gill, who operated a mail route to Erie. They traveled seventy miles through western Pennsylvania's woods and valleys at a relentless pace toward the shores of Lake Erie, stopping briefly in villages that had, with little notice, improvised celebrations of welcome. Under hastily constructed arches, Lafayette shook hundreds of hands, shared stories of Brandywine with old veterans, and, turning to leave, said, "Farewell my friends; this is the last time you will see me."[12]

The party, now streamlined to just Lafayette, Georges, Levasseur, de Syon, and Bastien, accompanied initially by two representatives from Pittsburg to Erie, were exhausted after nearly four months of constant motion. They reached Mercer, Pennsylvania, after one in the morning on the first evening of June and were gone by dawn. "He appeared evidently fatigued," the county's newspaper reported after Lafayette's departure.[13] The southern shore of Lake Erie came into view on the following morning, the 3rd. From there Lafayette and his party crossed into New York, paralleling Lake Erie in new carriages provided by Nathaniel Bird, a veteran of the Revolution and owner of the Erie and Buffalo Mail Stages.[14] At Dunkirk, the steamboat *Superior* would take them across the lake to Buffalo. The men rode through the night, sleeping in their carriage. At the outskirts of Fredonia, fifty miles east of Erie, their slumber was interrupted by artillery fire. Outside the carriage was a completely illuminated village; light hung from each home and tree. Compelled to stop, Lafayette stepped down from the vehicle. Two columns came into view, one of Revolutionary veterans and young boys, and the other of young girls and grown women with babies in their arms. From a platform illuminated by resin torches, the village's leading citizens delivered an oration. It was two in the morning. "That ladies, too, should stay up all night to receive me, surely it is too much," Lafayette was heard to say.[15] There was little time to linger; he departed followed by a procession from Fredonia, which marched with him to the port of Dunkirk and then watched as he boarded the *Superior*, chartered by a committee of the county, and steamed on to Buffalo.

The Frenchmen were struck by the bustle in Buffalo's port. The same village that the British army had torched at the end of 1813, leaving only a handful of buildings standing, was resurrected. After much deliberation from its commissioners—and prolonged competition from Black Rock, three miles to the northwest—it was to be the terminus of the Erie Canal. Crowds, which began gathering two days in advance, formed a procession leading Lafayette to the Eagle Tavern, a hotel on Buffalo's main street. There, after speeches of welcome, an elderly Indian man was helped onto the stage prepared for Lafayette's welcome. From his neck hung a slender silver medal, depicting two men, one white, with his hand outstretched, and the other Indian, a peace pipe in his mouth. The old man, through an interpreter asked Lafayette if he remembered the negotiations at Fort Stanwix in 1784 between the American government and the Six Nations, which he had attended. Lafayette not only remembered, but specifically recalled a young Seneca who had eloquently opposed the agreement with the Americans, which robbed the tribe of their land in western New York. "And what became of the young Seneca who so forcefully opposed burying the hatchet?" he asked. "He is standing in front of you," the man answered through his interpreter.[16] It was Red Jacket, Seneca chief, diplomat, and storied orator. The medallion on his neck, which he wore constantly, was a gift from George Washington and depicted the first president and Red Jacket, optimistically projecting an era of peace between the American government and Iroquois nation. "He made, as usual, a somewhat ostentatious display of his medal," one present during his meeting with Lafayette wrote.[17] When he remarked how time had altered both men, Red Jacket ventured that it had been much kinder to the Frenchman than to himself, telling the be-wigged Lafayette, "It has left you with a fresh complexion, and a full head of hair." Then he removed a handkerchief, revealing the absence of it on his own. Levasseur observed that Red Jacket "seemed not to know the art of undoing the ravages of time."[18]

Lafayette's determination to press on toward Boston was momentarily softened by his desire to behold the great cataract. In 1816, Peter B. Porter, a politician who led the state's militia forces during the Niagara

Campaign in the War of 1812, and his older brother Augustus acquired the deed to Goat Island. Located at the foot of the Niagara River, the island divided its steep falls. Augustus, in particular, was convinced of the falls' commercial potential as an attraction—a prospect made even more lucrative by the construction of the Erie Canal. Travelers passing by on the waterway would pause to view the natural wonder and spend their money at nearby taverns or hotels. Peter Porter, who settled at Black Rock, was a member of the Erie Canal Commission. He had led the ultimately unsuccessful effort to locate the canal's terminus there rather than in Buffalo.

On the morning of the 5th, Lafayette arrived at Porter's House, twenty miles from the falls. During his travels to determine a route for the canal, DeWitt Clinton recorded in his journals how the home shook because of the force of the falls as he attempted to sleep. When the Frenchmen departed for Manchester, a mile above the falls, they heard a boom in the distance and could see large clouds of mist exploding in the sky. They impatiently endured a banquet at Manchester before Augustus Porter led them over his bridge to Goat Island. Astonished by the sight and frightened by the roar, they watched in silence as the Niagara River plummeted into the abyss before them. "Woe to the animals or men who would be rash enough to take on this irresistible current; no power could protect them from the insatiable voracity of the gulf!"[19] wrote Levasseur. Porter guided Lafayette around the island, whose natural landscape he had determined to preserve. As they crossed back over the bridge to the mainland, Porter shared that he was attempting to sell the property. Observing how reluctantly Lafayette pulled himself away from the falls, Levasseur was sure he would have purchased the island if not for its distance from France.

At Niagara Falls, Lafayette saw the terrifying face of nature. At Lockport, he witnessed humanity's efforts to conquer it. The day after the trip to Goat Island, the party left Lewiston, where they had spent the night, and stopped at Fort Niagara. As they approached the last remaining—and most complex—section of the Erie Canal, Lafayette's carriage entered Lockport, accompanied by eighty citizens on horseback. Laborers had chiseled holes into large rocks near the canal and stuffed them with gunpowder. Matches were lit as Lafayette arrived, blasting the rocks into thousands of particles that flew into the air in salute. In the summer of 1825, the final obstacle between Lake Erie and the Hudson River was the Niagara Escarpment, a tall formation of rock that intersected the canal's route as it turned southwest toward Buffalo.

This was an unavoidable obstacle: Another proposed, more direct, route to connect the lakes to sea ran too high above Lake Erie for its water to fill the canal. The canal's planners and engineers were forced to find a way to ascend the sixty-foot cliff. Nathan Roberts, a former math teacher and surveyor, proposed cutting two separate sets of locks—each with five steps—one to raise boats and the other to lower them. At the top of the locks, a channel was cut for boats to travel as the escarpment began its descent. When work began in 1821, the area was home to only a few families. Now, nearly three thousand people lived there, including twelve hundred workers—many of them Irish immigrants—who had arrived to dig and blast a channel to Lake Erie.[20] "What an astonishing change has a few years made at Lockport!" one visitor wrote. "It appears like the work of magic."[21]

Lafayette and his companions were stunned as well, observing the industry in the new town named for its locks. "In no other place have I seen the activity and industry of man grappling with nature as in this burgeoning place," Levasseur wrote. Houses were being built right before their eyes, and a fine hotel was open for business; there was a school and a printing press too, as well as luxurious carriages pulled by fine horses—ripples from "that work of giants, that great canal which, in tightening bonds of the American Union, is going to spread life and plenty in the wilderness that it traverses."[22]

The convergence of Lafayette's visit and the nearing completion of the locks brought Stephen Van Rensselaer, the current president of its commission, to Lockport. "To Lockport and to Niagara County: they contain the greatest wonders of Art and Nature, prodigies that can be surpassed only by those of liberty and equality of rights," Lafayette toasted at a banquet arranged after his arrival. After admiring the locks in person, Lafayette stepped aboard the packet boat *Rochester* as the day ended as the workers detonated rocks again, shooting fragments over Lafayette's head. The boat's team of horses moved forward on the towpath, pulling it toward Rochester, sixty miles to the east. Once the packet neared the village, playing and handsomely dressed passengers accompanied them back into town. Crowds lining both sides of the canal celebrated Lafayette and showed off the incredible highway that carried him into their village. When the Frenchmen stepped on deck to answer the cheers, their boat appeared to be floating in the air. Fifty yards below, the Genesee River rushed by. "We were some moments without comprehending our situation," Levasseur wrote. The *Rochester* was not floating by some form of magic, though. It was atop an eight-hundred-foot-long aqueduct, supported by eleven stone arches. The Frenchmen had never seen engineering of this sort. "This kind of construction," Levasseur wrote, "appeared to be familiar to the Americans."[23]

Since arriving the previous summer, Lafayette was treated to tributes in amphitheaters, city halls, hotels, pine forests, and river banks, to name only a few venues. Now, a first: From a stage placed over the Genesee River Aqueduct, he listened as William B. Rochester delivered his salutary speech. In his response, Lafayette could not fail to mention how the Americans had bent nature to their will in western New York. "I enjoy the sight of works and improvements equally rapid and wonderful—among which is this grand canal," he said, "an admirable work, which genius, science and patriotism, have united to construct, and which the grand objects of nature, which threatened to impede, have been made only to adorn, as we see in the striking spectacle which is at this moment presented to our enchanted eye."[24]

Travel along the canal was a reprieve from the bruising conditions of the roads in western New York. Lafayette briefly surrendered the comfort of the packet boat to pass through the towns on the north shores of the narrow Finger Lakes, which flowed to Lake Ontario. On June 7, he rode out of Rochester in local coaches, heading southeast onto the Seneca Turnpike. Most towns had little notice of his approach, as news came just hours before via an express rider. Some, however, had formed planning committees in the spring on the chance that he would pass through on his return from the West. Celebrations were improvised:

Military escorts formed, suppers prepared, and men and women rushed in from surrounding communities to shake his hand. Children scattered flowers in his path, Masons offered tributes, and Revolutionary veterans gathered to greet him. In villages like Mendon, Geneva, Waterloo, Lafayette appeared and was soon gone. Even these brief visits were hailed as unparalleled historic events. "Wednesday last was the proudest day that ever shone in this 'village of the plain,'" opined Auburn's newspaper after his pause there on June 8, "for it received to the enjoyment of its simple hospitalities, the only man now living, to deserve, as he has earned, the epithets, of truly *good* and truly *great*—the brightest day moreover, that can ever smile upon its spires, for another La Fayette will never live!"[25]

Aboard a new carriage and fresh horses, provided by a generous citizen of Geneva, Lafayette rode through the dark, under the summer stars, into the hamlets of Skaneateles and Marcellus. Their few streets, illuminated by bonfires, were clogged with citizens waiting to take him by the hand as his carriage slowed. In the village of Marcellus, the presence of an old man named Ebenezer Moore, who had stormed the redoubts at Yorktown, brought Lafayette's carriage to a halt. "I am very glad to see that man once more this side of the grave," Lafayette said.[26] There was no time to stop, and yet Moore and Lafayette, from his carriage, reminisced before the procession departed. Moore held his hands up to the sky, appealing to heaven to bless Lafayette, who, unable to respond, just offered his hand. The two men's grasp was only broken when the carriage moved away from Marcellus.

After nearly a day of continuous riding, on the morning of June 9, Lafayette arrived in Syracuse, seventy-five miles from Rochester. Periodically along the road, the party's exhausted horses were replaced by a fresh set, provided by citizens or local stage owners. The urgency to reach Boston was only growing: Lafayette received word that Massachusetts's legislature planned to meet and wished to receive him on the 16th, a day before the celebration at Bunker Hill. He still had three hundred miles to travel, and the last seventy-five, over land, were through stifling heat and clouds of dust. Happily, at Syracuse, the miserable road yielded to the Great Canal, the stagecoach to the packet boat. The race against time continued, however. In the towns that bloomed like flowers along the canal's path, citizens waited on both sides of the waterway. Processions of boats floated west to meet the Nation's Guest as he traveled east. On their right, Rome glowed with light in the night. Next came Oriskany, home of Gerrit Lansing, who had fought at Yorktown under Alexander Hamilton, and then Whitesboro, where a carriage waited to take Lafayette to Utica, collecting a procession of citizens as it sped along, entering the street named in his honor, which was lined on both sides by soldiers. It crossed a bridge spanning the canal, over which an arch had been erected. A flag hanging from it read, *La Fayette, the Apostle of Liberty, we hail thee welcome.*[27]

At Shepard's Hotel, Lafayette was besieged by Utica's politicians, ladies, schoolchildren, and Revolutionary veterans. Among them were members of the Oneida who had come to speak with Lafayette privately. The tribe, along with the Tuscarora, who inhabited land south of Lake Ontario, were unique among the Six Nations Iroquois in siding with the rebels, largely due to the influence of missionary Samuel Kirkland. The Oneida served as spies for the Continental Army and fought in several battles, including Barren Hill, where these men were with Lafayette.

Lafayette immediately recognized the men who came to speak to him at Shepard's Hotel—Henry Cornelius and Blatcop—though he was astonished they were still alive, given their advanced age during the Revolution. The meeting, however, was melancholy. In the same region where Lafayette had commanded the Northern Army in 1777, now transformed by the Erie Canal's defiance of nature, New York's government had displaced the Oneida and other members of the Iroquois Confederacy from their ancestral lands to make way for settlers and the canal.

"Our hunts are hardly productive any longer," the Oneida told Lafayette. "They cannot suffice for our needs, and we are forced to provide for our subsistence by agriculture, a state of affairs which makes us very unhappy."[28] Lafayette could only encourage them to regard the Americans as their brothers and insist they take a gift of money. When the Oneida later migrated westward to Wisconsin, many traveled there by way of the Erie Canal.

Before departing Utica and returning to the canal, Lafayette met with members of the committee planning the construction of a memorial over the grave of Baron von Steuben. Would he, they inquired, lay its cornerstone as he had done for the similar monuments of de Kalb, Pulaski, and Greene in South Carolina and Georgia? So rushed was Lafayette's pace toward Bunker Hill, his participation was not possible. As he explained to the committee, "It would not be the hardships of a long and speedy trip that would stop me, you should be persuaded; but a single day's delay would make me miss these sacred undertakings."[29]

Late in the afternoon of the 10th, Lafayette returned to the canal, on board the appropriately named *Governor Clinton*—packets were named for each of the canal's commissioners—and was pulled away from Utica by three white horses, to a twenty-four-gun salute and repeated cheers. Little boys standing on bridges at the edge of town dropped baskets of flowers into the boat as it passed under. As the boat moved on, a man sprinted down the pier, calling for the captain to stop. When the packet continued, the man ran to the nearest bridge and, just as the boat passed under, leapt onto the deck and said, "I want to see Kayewla." When Lafayette was introduced, the man claimed he was the son of Peter Otsiquette, the young Oneida who had lived for a time with Lafayette in Paris. In 1786, Lafayette had brought Otsiquette, a nineteen-year-old of French and Oneida heritage, to his household in Paris.[30] "My young Indiana," as Lafayette called him, stayed for nearly three years, captivating visitors with his manners and fluency in French and English. After returning to America, he was a figure of some public note among Americans and Oneida before dying in Philadelphia in 1792 while part of a Five Nations delegation. His funeral was attended by ten thousand people, among them Secretary of War Henry Knox.[31]

Briefly, the man related to Lafayette that his father had spoken of him often; then, as the boat continued its path, he leapt ten feet to the wall of the canal as the *Governor Clinton* pulled away. Lafayette then explained to his inquisitive companions Otsiquette's story, claiming that the boy, "disgusted by civilization, returned to his wild forests."[32]

From Utica, the canal began a southeasterly descent toward Albany. On the night of the 11th, Lafayette passed through the town of Little Falls, whose aqueduct was illuminated for the occasion, and by eight in the evening reached Schenectady, eighty miles from Utica, where people crowded on the canal's bridges and banks. There, he disembarked and, after traveling nearly three hundred miles, left the canal behind. "Here we are approaching the Ocean," Lafayette wrote to his daughters after quitting the canal. "I was planning on writing at my ease on the lovely canal that goes from Lake Erie to Albany, but this countryside that was until recently a desert is now so populated and cultivated that the banks were adorned with friends and we had to visit the cities. Great reunions awaited us on the riverbank."[33]

From Schenectady, a carriage carried Lafayette to Albany, where he arrived so late—at one in the morning—that a planned procession of six companies of militia and the reserved box at the city's theater, decorated with evergreens, went unused. The late hour did not prevent a crowd of bleary-eyed citizens from gathering to welcome him. The next day, he left the capital with an escort trailing him toward the Massachusetts state line. As Lafayette and his companions raced to Boston, they made brief stops in villages across eastern New York and western Massachusetts. After crossing the state line on the 13th, celebrations along the way were muted. At coffee houses, on bridges, and in taverns, the exhausted men received the last salutes of their great adventure.

They continued east across Massachusetts, through Worthington, Chesterfield, and then to Northampton for one final celebration, the last of the voyage. The escorts who had accompanied them thus far across the state departed. The Frenchman's party rode alone, late into the night, reaching Worcester at two in the morning on the 15th, forty miles from Boston. The following afternoon, the carriage passed into the city and, little noticed and with no fanfare, pulled up to a brick mansion on Somerset Street, the home of Senator James Lloyd.

Over five thousand miles, in carriages and steamboats, barges and packets, Lafayette had skirted the ocean, crossed a great river, wrecked on another, rode through forests and into the frontier, and sailed along the incredible canal, always caught in, as he called it, "a whirlwind of charity."[34] The sixty-seven-year-old had obliged almost every invitation, shook thousands of hands, memorialized his dead brother soldiers, and made history by simply pausing for an hour in communities that would remember the visit centuries later. No public man had ever successfully attempted such an endeavor. Duty-bound, hours after it had concluded, he paid his respects to the men of the Bunker Hill Monument Association.

PART FOUR

The Last Adieu

21

---≈---

The Lord Will Not
Permit It to Rain on That Day

W hen Boston's newspapers caught word the Nation's Guest had returned to their city, they quickly reassured readers that he had arrived unscathed. "In his capacity to endure fatigue General Lafayette is certainly a wonderful man," reported the *Boston Patriot*. "A journey for its length and rapidity alone, almost unparalleled, he had accomplished and really seems in better health than when he started."[1]

The Massachusetts General Court, the state's legislative assembly, had no reservations about intruding on a day when most men who had just concluded a five-thousand-mile journey would require rest. On June 16, he stood in the chamber of the state's House of Representatives, addressed by Governor Levi Lincoln Jr., who expressed his and his countrymen's joy at Lafayette's safely completed tour of the Union before yielding to their guest. William Eustis, the man who had welcomed Lafayette to Massachusetts the previous August and a fellow soldier of the Revolutionary army, had expired in office four months earlier—another reminder of that generation's disappearing ranks.

As Lafayette replied with his "pretty French" accent, it was difficult to believe, from a distance, that he was a brother-soldier of the veterans now flocking to Boston.[2] Only upon closer inspection of the lines on his face did it become clear, as he claimed, citing the year of his enlistment, that he was a fellow patriot of '76.[3] He had rushed eastward for the celebration of '75, though. "In the long and happy series of visits through the several parts of the Union to which you have been pleased to allude," said Lafayette, "Bunker Hill has ever been my polar star, and I now rejoice to be arrived in time to join, on the grand half-secular jubilee, with my companions in arms, as being together the representatives of the early and unshaken devotion of our Revolutionary army."[4]

Though not its conclusion, the event on June 17 was the culmination of Lafayette's return to and tour of America. It was a final unifying act, rallying citizens across regional and partisan lines in reverence for the old men who had won their freedoms—the fruits of which they so eagerly displayed for their guest.

Throughout his journey, Lafayette was often forced to pull himself away from—or miss entirely—the company of and celebrations staged by affectionate Americans. They generally accepted his departures and absences, however. "I must say that whenever the kindness of my friends, my own wishes, and even a sense of propriety, in other respects, should have detained me, in my progress through the Southern and Western states," he communicated to the Bunker Hill Monument Association, "it has supplied, on all parts, to expedite my journey, to have it remembered that I had the honor to be invited to Boston, as a representative of the Revolutionary Army, on that memorable occasion equally interesting to the whole Confederate Union."[5]

Accordingly, a Southern editor viewed the Northern memorial thusly: "A monument of the defense of Bunker Hill may justly be considered as a Monument of *American national existence*. It is to place a stone at the sepulcher of tyranny, whence it shall never rise more. It is to mark the birth-place of this great republic, whose path is in the Zodiac, among the stars."[6]

If the anniversary celebration of Bunker Hill drew Lafayette across the Union, he, in turn, helped bring the memorial's construction into reality. The battle had been a particular source of interest and debate in the years before his return. In April 1775, British regulars marched to Concord, twenty miles from Boston, to disarm Americans, prevent rebellion, and seize the Massachusetts militia's supplies. On the way, the Redcoats exchanged fire with Minutemen in Lexington, who were warned of their approach. After reaching and trading volleys with the rebels in Concord, the British retreated under fire along the way back to Boston. After the shot heard round the world, militia from New Hampshire, Rhode Island, and Connecticut joined their fellow colonists on the hills north and south of the city. When they fortified Bunker and Breed's Hills on the Charleston peninsula, the British army took notice. On June 17, 1775, General Thomas Gage ordered his men to seize the hills in an effort to crush the rebellion. That sweltering afternoon, the British were blown back twice before finally capturing the American redoubt on their third attempt, marching over the dead bodies of their fellow soldiers and engaging in brutal combat with the outnumbered, underarmed, untrained colonists. The British victory came at a bloody cost of over one thousand dead. While Americans had fought first at Lexington and Concord, and Congress had created the Continental Army days before Bunker Hill, it was this battle—erroneously named for the colonists' original objective to secure that hill—that truly signaled their preparedness for a prolonged fight.

In 1818, Henry Dearborn, former secretary of war, published "An Account of the Battle of Bunker Kill" in the *Port Folio* literary magazine, criticizing General Israel Putnam's leadership during the fight. Dearborn, who had formed and led a New Hampshire militia to Massachusetts after the opening salvo at Lexington and Concord, provoked a fierce response from Putnam's son, Congressman and famed attorney Daniel Webster. Webster's rebuttal essay inspired Massachusetts governor John Brooks, who had helped fortify the hill but was absent from the battle, to revisit the battlefield for the first time since 1775. Subsequently, one of Brooks's aides, Samuel Swift, published his own history of the conflict.

Dearborn's essay had inadvertently stirred interest in the Battle of Bunker Hill right as the battlefield land went up for auction, with Charlestown's development encroaching on the site. At the time, an eighteen-foot wooden pillar, erected in 1794 by Charlestown's King Solomon's Lodge of Free and Accepted Masons stood on land donated by James Russell. The monument was a tribute to Joseph Warren, Grand Master of the Grand Lodge of Massachusetts and the driving force behind the Massachusetts militias, whose quill, voice, and energy had inspired the colonists' rebellion. Warren, who had been appointed a general only the day prior, was killed as a volunteer at age thirty-four during the final British charge on Breed's Hill.[7]

As development threatened the battlefield, a group of prominent Bostonians—including Webster, Harvard professor of Greek literature Edward Everett (who addressed Lafayette in Cambridge the previous summer), and *North American Review* publisher William Tudor—persuaded John Collins Warren, nephew of the fallen hero, to purchase and preserve the land. Over dinners, the Brahmans coalesced around the idea of preserving the Bunker Hill site and building upon it a shrine to the American Revolution. In 1823, after obtaining incorporation from the General Court, the group branded itself the Bunker Hill Monument Association and began raising money for their project. This was a novel enterprise; monuments to early American heroes were rare. Aside from the purchase of the garrison at Fort Ticonderoga in 1820 by a private citizen, efforts to preserve the stages of their glory were nearly nonexistent.[8]

Initial solicitations—membership in the association cost $5—to public men, politicians, and literary figures drew donations and pledges of support not only from New England but from states such as South Carolina and Virginia as well. These appeals were largely to transplanted New Englanders. The regional focus disappointed Americans in other regions of the country, also eager to see the monument built. "The glory of Bunker Hill is a common glory. Its rays are not confined to Massachusetts alone but are indiscriminately reflected over every portion of our country," asserted one Southern paper.[9]

By 1824, of the nearly twenty-four hundred Americans who fought at the Battle of Bunker Hill, there were at least two hundred still living. "The survivors, like setting stars, linger on the horizon of departing life," the *Charleston Daily Courier* lamented. Given their advanced age, there was little time to waste in building a monument if they were to enjoy it.[10] "I hope there will be no reason for delaying the commencement of the work beyond the time contemplated, as the heroes of '75 are falling like the leaves of the season around us, and all of them will soon be gone," worried the author Samuel K. Knapp, while adding his name to the subscription list in the fall of 1824.[11]

The Monument Association's efforts were aided by the happy timing of Lafayette's American arrival. Its members were quick to capitalize on the excitement inspired by his tour. "Now, would it not be well, while he is here, to have a general subscription among all classes of our citizens, for the erection of a Monument upon Bunker Hill?" wrote one of the members, Abbott Lawrence. "Feelings in the community will be excited, which, perhaps, never will again be felt and it does appear to me that there will not again be so favorable a moment to collect money as when the Marquis is here."[12]

Energized by Lafayette's tour and the resurgent memories of the Revolution, subscription books were distributed across Massachusetts and a circular was read by selectmen during the November election. "There is no longer a doubt that a monument will rise on the spot where the battle of the seventeenth of June '75 was fought. As it will commemorate the GREATEST EVENT in the history of civil liberty, as it should be, *and shall be*, the GREATEST MONUMENT IN THE WORLD," it read.[13]

When Lafayette reached Boston in August 1824, members of the association presented only a vague sketch of their plans. He happily signed his name in the subscription book and promised, if he had not yet returned to France, he would be present for the celebration of the fiftieth anniversary of the battle the following June. Progress accelerated in early 1825 when the General Court passed legislation helping the association acquire fifteen acres and promised to provide rock for the monument that would be hammered at the state's penitentiary, with the stipulation that Massachusetts would have say over the design of the monument and the association would cede the land upon its completion.[14] The association launched a competition for a suitable 220-foot column design, offering a $100 prize to the winner.

Additionally, the Grand Lodge of Massachusetts surrendered both its existing wooden pillar on the site and the patch of land on which it stood for the purposes of building a sturdier replacement.

Other than Webster delivering the day's keynote, the details of the ceremony for the fiftieth anniversary remained uncertain. In March, Everett reported to Lafayette that sufficient funds were already raised to obtain a cornerstone and commence the building of the monument. There was one minor complication, however, which troubled members of the Monument Association. While newspapers reported that Lafayette himself would lay the cornerstone, King Solomon's Lodge current Grand Master, John Abbott, was a more meaningful choice, as the lodge had donated the existing monument and its land, and Warren had been its Grand Master himself.

This was also natural, given the Freemasons' participation in the dedication ceremonies and construction of public buildings. The monuments for de Kalb, Greene, and Pulaski were conducted with Masonic rites, as was the U.S. Capitol, whose cornerstone was laid by George Washington, a Master Mason—the organization's highest rank—in 1793. The smooth, perfectly square cornerstone symbolized the beginning of an endeavor and guided its design.

During an era where voluntary associations proliferated in America—with communities forming mutual aid societies, reform organizations, libraries, firehouses, and schools—few groups were as numerous as the Freemasons. By 1820, the country's lodges had eighty thousand members, representing 5 percent of the white male population.[15] A venue for social networking and establishing status both before and after the Revolution, the Masons were also philanthropic, building orphanages and schools. They promoted values like tolerance and individual liberty, which underpinned the rationale for the Revolution and helped inform the design of the government. Among the founding generation, Washington and Benjamin Franklin were Masons; in 1825, so were DeWitt Clinton and Andrew Jackson, among the most popular man in America (outside of Lafayette, for a spell).

Fittingly, Masonic celebrations were a regular feature wherever Lafayette went, from New York to Alabama. If the Bunker Hill ceremony marked the apogee of Lafayette's tour, it also represented the high-water mark of Masonry in early America—a peak from which the organization would fall precipitously only a year later. In 1826, William Morgan, a Mason who had written and contracted to publish a book revealing the society's oaths and rituals, was seized from his home in Batavia, New York, thrown in jail, subsequently kidnapped, and vanished. The presumption that he was murdered by fellow Masons, who were never prosecuted, fanned existing suspicions that the group operated as a separate sovereignty, outside American laws—many lodges had resisted state incorporation—and that its oaths and ceremonies were violent. Critics argued that the fraternal order, like the Society of the Cincinnati at its founding, was an un-republican society of powerful elites.

These resentments, combined with Morgan's disappearance, and the increasing democratization of American politics, caused public opinion to turn dramatically against Masonry. Membership declined, lodges closed, and the first third-party movement in American political history—the Anti-Masonic Party—formed in upstate New York in 1828.

But in the days leading up to June 17, 1825, members of Grand Masonic Lodges across New England made their way to Boston, where they would play a central role in the procession to Bunker Hill and the laying of the cornerstone there. By May, a month before the anniversary, the Monument Association had raised nearly $50,000. Anticipation crescendoed, citizens pledged their money, and veterans of the battle made plans to be present, come hell or high water. Newspapers reported that "farmers are preserving their pocket money, in order to spend it on the 17th of June," and a survivor of the battle vowed "that if he can put one leg before the other, he will again visit the spot where he spilt blood in defense on his country."[16] Crews began excavating *that spot*, the land reserved for the monument, tilling up the land and carefully reserving the bones of the old veterans' brother soldiers. In anticipation of their presence, the Monument Association warned that, "As there will be in this assembly many persons of far advanced age and who are consequently infirm, all the ceremonies will be as SHORT as can be, consistently with the dignity of the occasion."[17]

On the night of June 16, 1775, American militiamen hurriedly dug their redoubt atop Breed's Hill under moonlight, readying for the British siege. Fifty years later, on the evening of June 16, 1825, calm reigned where the American lines once formed. The bridges leading into Boston, decorated with lanterns, shone, and lights in the homes in the city and along the bay flickered in anticipation of the next day's celebration. The morning of June 17, 1775, British warships bombarded Charlestown, as the regulars landed and prepared to march. The morning of June 17, 1825, broke to the sound of cannon fire once again, a gesture of salute, not the opening of an attack. Anxiety over the weather—storms loomed the day before—proved unwarranted when the sun emerged. "The Lord will not permit it to rain on that day," a man in Andover was heard to predict.[18] A few showers had only settled dust on the roads, which carriages thundered across on their way to Bunker Hill, while soldiers paraded on the Common.

Meanwhile, a more solemn scene unfolded at the Subscription House, the grand manse that had temporarily housed Lafayette during his visit the previous August. Now, it was being used to raise funds for the monument. There, the surviving veterans of the battle assembled. The old men were met by young Josiah Quincy Jr., son of Boston's mayor, recently appointed aide to Massachusetts's adjunct general, William H. Sumner, following his orders to arrive at nine. One interloper caught a glimpse of the soldiers at the house: "Their countenances and frames seemed to have been made of iron. One man had a scar on his cheek, which told that bullet had done large execution there."[19] Many of the survivors had not seen each other in fifty years. "The occasion would have been far from insignificant, even if it had accomplished no other purpose than to bring these men together once more before they die," this observer reasoned.[20]

Quincy Jr, following his instructions, affixed a blue badge of honor to the breast of each old soldier, and then asked for their name, which he repeated to Lafayette, who pronounced it again with emotion as he clasped his fellow veteran's hand.[21] "I stood the one young man among these honored heroes. If there was a dry eye in the room, mine were not among them" remembered Quincy.[22]

At 10:00 a.m., the procession formed outside the State House. Half an hour later, it moved toward Charlestown, passing twenty thousand spectators who had converged on Boston from all parts of the Union. The crowds were so dense that the sidewalks and window frames were filled to capacity, and churches were opened to accommodate the overflow. Some even climbed onto and sat atop chimneys. Trees were rented for the reasonable sum of $500.[23] "It seemed as if no spot where a human foot could plant itself was left unoccupied," remembered Quincy.

At its front were the militia: sixteen artillery companies drawn from Boston, Salem, Charlestown, Concord, and a corps of cavalry. Behind them marched veterans of the battle. Those who were able marched on foot, while others, having surrendered to the ravages of time, were carried back to the site in eight carriages. Leading the way were the captains: Dearborn; James Clark, now ninety-five; Samuel Russell Trevett, seventy-four; and Benjamin Mann, eighty-five. One man held the drum he had beaten that day; another swung a leather pouch over his shoulder. From the crowds came inquiries of its origin; "Bunker Hill," he exclaimed. Another veteran, dressed in the hat and coat he had worn during the battle, with bullet holes still visible in both, carried the shot bag containing the bullets he had brought into battle that day, waving it from left to right for all to see. "General Lafayette, the Knights as glorious as they were, shrunk into nothing, beside this war-worn soldier," recalled the writer Anne Royall. "It transported us back fifty years and we were in imagination fighting the battle of Bunker Hill. Not a word was uttered for several minutes. Every cheek was wet."[24]

Two hundred additional Revolutionary veterans followed, ahead of the members of the Bunker Hill Monuments Associations, each wearing a badge reading *B.H.M.A.*, indicating their authorship of the day's event. Then came the concourse of Masons, representing lodges from Maine, Vermont, New Hampshire, Rhode Island, and New Jersey—some two thousand of varying degrees and order, wearing their dark blue, purple, or crimson sashes and black aprons with silver embroidery. Massachusetts's Grand Lodge displayed the instruments designed for the ceremony. Following was a carriage carrying Webster and other high-ranking members of the monument association, and then, pulled by six white horses, came Lafayette. Trailing behind in carriages were Georges, Levasseur, and numerous dignitaries, including the Massachusetts governor, members of the legislature, representatives from Congress and other departments of the federal government, and leaders from other states. From front to rear, the column stretched a mile and a half. By the time the militia at its front reached the bridge to Charlestown, the rear had just moved away from the Common. President John Quincy Adams was invited but not present. One participant, far back in the procession, could not see Lafayette but tracked his progress by the twirling white objects extending out of the windows where he passed. "A Boston lady does not study to wave her handkerchief gracefully and sweepingly at Lafayette; but she twirls it with a violence resembling the gyrations of a fire-wheel," they wrote.[25]

From the hilltop, a breathtaking sight came into view below: a column of banners waving, plumes bobbing, muskets and rifles, and Masonic regalia reflecting the sunlight. When the entire procession had reached the hill, it broke into segments and formed a square around the spot reserved for the monument. Lafayette, Webster, and Abbott—the Grand Master of Massachusetts's Grand Lodge—alighted around the excavated ground readied for the cornerstone. An iron box containing coins as well as a silver plate inscribed with the day's program was lowered into the void. The stone, declared true and proper, followed, after which the Grand Master poured corn, wine, and oil atop it. After a benediction, the ceremony concluded. As artillery salutes fired and the crowds cheered, the procession moved again, now to the amphitheater built on the northeast side of Breed's Hill. Seats, reserved for the women in attendance, were arranged in semicircles on each side. In front of the stage were the survivors of the battle and the Revolution. Ascending the hill were rows of wooden benches for members of the processions and thousands of spectators, while many more watched from around and on top of the hill. A covered pavilion was designated for the guests of honor, shielding them from the afternoon sun. Lafayette, however, refused to take his place under it, insisting that he belonged among his fellow soldiers and the people as their living representative of the old army. He took his seat under the hot sun, surrounded by a sea of heads with whitened or thinning hair, as silver trumpets, reflecting the sun, were pressed to ears to amplify the speakers' voices.

A reverential silence hung over the foot of the hill as an old man raised his bony finger in the air and spoke in a trembling voice. The Reverend Joseph Thaxter, the chaplain present during the Battle of Bunker Hill, now eighty-one, had long been in seclusion after a series of personal tragedies. Now he reappeared onstage, his long gray locks resting on his shoulders, to offer the opening prayer. "We thank thee that when our country was invaded by the armies of the mother country, thou didst raise up wise counsellors and unshaken patriots, who, at the risk of life and fortune, not only defended our country, but raised it to the rank of a nation among the nations of the earth," he said, his reedy voice gaining strength. "We thank thee that thou has blessed us with a constitution of government, which, if duly administered, secures to all, high and low, rich and poor, their invaluable rights and privileges."[26]

When Thaxter finished, a chorus, supported by a full band, sang an ode to the melody of the hymn "Old Hundred," its lyrics penned by the poet, educator, and theologian John Pierpont. It began:

> Oh, is not this a holy spot!
> Tis the high place of freedom's birth:
> God of our fathers?! is it not
> The holiest spot of all the earth?

> Alexandria Gazette, June 25, 1825.

As the song neared conclusion, the singers' voices lowered to a whisper during the fourth verse, only to rise again into a stunning finale—a fitting prelude to the day's keynote. Once the music died, Daniel Webster, clad in a loose-fitting black robe, walked to the end of the stage. As he began his address, the crowds standing beyond the barriers around the amphitheater began to holler, angered at being unable to hear, as they were too far from the ceremonies. The men and women near the stage grew worried that the rabble would storm through the barricades; indeed, some moved forward, climbed upon the reserved seats, and pulled at the awning above them. A clash between the crowd and the constables and guards arrayed around the amphitheater appeared imminent. Then Webster raised his voice. "We frustrate our own work," he said, a fierce look in his famous black eyes directed at the guards. "Be silent yourselves and the people will obey!" The crowd hushed. Webster resumed his address.[27]

"We see rolling before us a probable train of great events. The future is full of pleasing promises, and we cannot turn back without interest to the circumstances which, before we were born were to influence so fortunately our future destiny." He opened with an account of the "discovery," settlement, and liberation of the country. The last of these events, Webster said, was "the greatest in the history of the continent [and] the one that we are met here to commemorate today, that prodigy of modern times, at once a wonder and a blessing, the American Revolution!" Though unnecessary, he explained the purpose of the monument now begun was "to keep alive in the generations to come similar sentiments to those which inspire us, and to foster a living and constant regard for the principles of the Revolution." It would not be a monument to victory in battle, but to America's independence, a reassurance to its citizens, now and in the future, in inevitable moments of national depression, so that its people, "in turning its eyes to it, may be reassured and be reminded on what solid foundations our national strength reposes."

And in the fifty years since the battle? A wise government had been created, twenty-four states established, and industry, letters, and science flourished. Webster spoke directly to the veterans who had lived to see this transformation, calling them the "venerable men" of the "broken band." And then he addressed Lafayette. "Fortunate, fortunate man! What measure of devotion do you owe to Providence which has plotted out the circle of your extraordinary life! You belong to both hemispheres, to two generations. Heaven saw fit that the electric spark of liberty should be conducted by you from the New World to the Old."

The speech, which lasted over an hour, concluded with a challenge to preserve these achievements: "See if we cannot also merit living in the memory of men; let us cultivate a true spirit of union and harmony, and, in pursuing these great objects which our current condition so clearly points out to us, let us act always with the feeling and the conviction that the 24 States are united as one Nation."[28]

After a final hymn, the old warriors and the distinguished guests retreated to a giant marquee sitting atop Bunker Hill. Beneath it were thirteen long tables, room enough for thirty-five hundred diners. The old warriors among them swapped memories, revisited the past, and lamented the passage of time. "We have not another 50 years meeting to look forward to here," one lamented, putting his hand on a printed program of the day's ceremonies. Noting the badge on his coat, he added, "All these matters will be put up in my desk; whoever goes to my funeral will see them all."[29]

"I like writing to you, dear friends, upon leaving one of the most beautiful patriotic celebrations that could have been celebrated; we can only compare it with the Federation of 1790," Lafayette wrote to his daughters that evening. "Two hundred thousand Americans, it is said, came for the fifty-year anniversary of Bunker Hill and for the first stone of a superb monument. You will see the details in the newspapers. Nothing can capture the effect of the republican prayer given before the immense multitude by an old chaplain who fought at Bunker Hill. The survivors of that day uncovered their white hair while the president of the association, the day's speaker, addressed himself to them—and I also was raised up at the head of the other Revolutionary soldiers to receive our compliments, not counting the compliments I had on my own part."[30]

As the sun retreated, the day's heat died, and a cooling breeze swept up from the harbor. Georges and Levasseur, struck by the beauty of the evening, decided to walk back to Boston. Behind them lay the foundation of a column that would stretch toward the sky, a bridge, its planners hoped, linking Americans to their original benefactors. As they descended Bunker Hill alongside thousands of dispersing spectators, Levasseur overheard, to his surprise, deep discussions of the history of the American Revolution, with an impressive knowledge equal among participants. "I am well aware that the reception given to Lafayette in each town furnished the occasion to recall all these facts," he wrote, "but often I also had proof that the other facts of the Revolution were equally known by all classes of citizens, from the veterans who speak of them incessantly to the schoolchildren who are proud of what their ancestors had done and of the freedom that they have the good fortune to enjoy."[31]

22

———≈———

Never to Meet Again,
Unless Beyond the Grave

The first act of *Charles II*, a comedy penned by the playwright John Howard Payne, concluded by the time Lafayette reached the Boston Theatre on the evening of June 20. A shout from outside the building announced his arrival. While the theatre's managers led him to the box decorated with flags, flowers, and evergreens, the entire audience stood, clapped, stomped their feet, and rattled their canes as the orchestra broke out in "Lafayette's March." The ovation was escalating into near pandemonium when a manager screamed for silence and the performance resumed. When the play concluded, a curtain dropped bearing a painting of Mount Vernon's crypt. An actress costumed as the Goddess of Liberty recited an ode to the guest of honor, and when another drop-scene descended, this one representing La Grange, the audience erupted yet again as Lafayette stared admiringly at his home.[1]

"I feel growing at every moment the need to be with you all again," Lafayette wrote to his loved ones there months before. "This feeling of awakening, when one is upset and when one has slept, comes incessantly knocking at the heart, in the middle of brilliant and touching displays for which one needs to surrender with affection and recognition."[2] As July approached, Lafayette had been absent from France for nearly a year. The length of his stay had done nothing to diminish America's joy over their guest. But his visit was nearing its end. "Soon we shall hear the veteran's last adieu—soon he will gaze upon the retiring shores of America, and with tear filled eyes bestow his blessing upon that country, whose fabric of independence, in his youth he fought and bled to raise, and whose freedom and happiness will cause his grey hairs to descend peaceful and honored to the grave," lamented a Maryland newspaper during the summer.[3]

Fewer parades and celebrations remained than tender goodbyes: The day after the celebration at Bunker Hill, Lafayette returned to Quincy, Massachusetts, to bid farewell to John Adams. The infirmed ex-president was buoyed by the Frenchman's visit: "When the Marquis is gone I hope to have letters from your Brother, John, and yourself, which will help to keep up my old spirits a little longer," he wrote to his grandson Charles Francis Adams.[4]

Improbably, after so many celebrations and so many miles traveled, there were still invitations to fulfill and unfamiliar states to visit: On the morning of June 21, Lafayette sat at the home of James Lloyd preparing to depart for a tour of the northernmost states of New England; Josiah Quincy Jr. was present, appointed to ride with the Nation's Guest away from Boston and to the New Hampshire border. During breakfast, he reflected happily over his travels across the country, but sounded a lone sad note. "I have one thing to regret in all my travels," he said according to Quincy, "and that is the loss of my little dog, who loved me so much."[5] At nine, three carriages arrived and Lafayette departed. "Sir, you have made us love you too much," cried the elder Josiah Quincy, Boston's mayor. "Ah!" Lafayette replied, "but I cannot love you too much."[6]

For the next nine days, from the 21st to the 30th of June, Lafayette traveled north to New Hampshire, then east to Maine, before retracing his path and riding west to Vermont. When he arrived there on the 28th, Lafayette had set foot in all twenty-four states. He was received by the legislatures and governors of each state—in Concord, Portland, and Montpelier—with the customary orations. In the villages along the way—Barnard, Royalton, Biddeford—the entire population emerged to greet him. Men reached into the barouche for a handshake, babies were lifted for a kiss, and flowers were tossed into his lap. Old veterans of the Revolution waited to introduce themselves. In the Vermont hamlet of Royalton, twenty survivors shook his hand, then stepped back one by one to discharge their muskets. Where old compatriots no longer lived, their children appeared. In Concord, a state senator named John Brodhead asked if he recalled the name of a man of the same name from the war. Yes, Lafayette answered, he had fought along him at Brandywine. "I am the son of that man," replied Brodhead. "I am very glad to see you," said Lafayette, "how happy I am that children of my companions in arms still love me."[7]

Far less happy were the children of William Barton, the former colonel in the Continental Army imprisoned in Vermont. Prior to Lafayette's arrival, pleas for Barton's release had been printed in the newspapers. During the visit, Barton's friends and family were saddened that the affection Lafayette showed his fellow soldiers was insufficient to inspire Barton's freedom.

"While the people of the United States are so enthusiastic for La Fayette, and the whole Union, from Maine to the Sabine is vocal with every demonstration of gratitude for this distinguished man, justice demands that claims of other patriots should be heard," argued one editorialist. It was right that Lafayette should be welcomed so generously, but "what shall we say of the base ingratitude of those who are stigmatizing another war worn veteran of the Revolution with the blackest crimes?"[8] Lafayette did not disagree. Though a rumored visit to Barton in Danville did not occur, in Vermont he met and conferred with the prisoner's creditor, Isaac Fletcher, the adjunct general of the state's militia.[9]

If the states of northern New England were the last on Lafayette's itinerary, in terms of pageantry, progress, and presents, they would not be the least: In Maine's capital, a triumphant arch sat atop a ship from which an inscription read, I SHALL PURCHASE AND FIT A VESSEL FOR MYSELF, a reference to *La Victoire*, which had carried Lafayette to America in 1777. In New Hampshire's seat of government, a "sumptuous" dinner was staged, allegedly accommodating the greatest number of people ever at "one table and under one roof" in the state's history.[10] The competition between communities continued as well. The east half of the bridge crossing the Salmon Falls River, separating New Hampshire from Maine, was decorated with an arch, from which a giant sign hung, proudly baring the latter state's name. "Our reception of Lafayette was one notch above South Berwick—even the Dover [New Hampshire] folks who attended him aver we beat them in ornaments," wrote one Mainer. "You know such a compliment could not have been drawn from them had it not been richly merited."[11]

The people of Biddeford had but thirty minutes' notice he would attend Sunday services in their town in southern Maine. "What will you say, my dear friend, when I tell you the Illustrious Lafayette worshipped at our little church on Sabbath morning!" wrote Ann Tracey, wife of the town's pastor. Her husband was left dazed by the news. "For a few moments my husband said he felt paralyzed by the unexpectedness of the thing—and the certainty that nothing could then be done suitable to the occasion," she admitted to a friend. Then he regained his senses and revised an early sermon relating the murder of the Babylonian tyrant Belshazzar. "Suffice it to say, that after having cast into merited contempt & obscurity the splendors of impious Kings and Emperor—the base oppressors and tyrants of the earth—that by a happy transition he directed the attention of his hearers to the Illustrious Individual before them—the friend of America."[12] He visited the academy in Pembroke, heard an oratorio performed by the New Hampshire Musical Society in Concord. In Portland, Lafayette was presented with an honorary Doctor of Laws degree from the president of Bowdoin College; in Burlington, he helped lay the cornerstone for the south wing of the University of Vermont.

After the last of these endeavors, on the evening of the 29th, Lafayette boarded a steamboat, the *Phoenix*, ornamented with American and French flags, a carved eagle on its engine frame, steamed across Lake Champlain, and landed at Whitehall, in eastern New York, the following day. There, soldiers formed in lines and seventy little girls, dressed in white and with garlands on their heads, threw roses from the baskets under their arms, creating a carpet for Lafayette as he walked past. "The scene so overcame the old veteran that the tear started under the smile of pleasure that it gave his feelings, that an infant generation should, half a century after his achievements, come to welcome him with their grateful little hearts, and strew his path with roses and with blessings," observed a reporter.[13] From Whitehall, he visited the battlefield of Saratoga, overnighted in Waterford, passed through the village of Lansingburgh, then once more to Troy and Albany, before returning, by way of the Hudson River on the steamboat *Bolivar*, to West Point, where he transferred to the *James Kent*, embarked again for New York, where he landed on July 3, in time to celebrate the national day of independence.

The village of Brooklyn had the privilege of—and took great pride in—hosting Lafayette's official act on the Fourth of July.[14] Early that morning, he crossed the Fulton Ferry in a canary-colored barouche drawn by four white horses, stepping down into a crowd of children and their parents, recently emancipated freed Blacks, and soldiers of the Revolution. They all watched as Lafayette laid the cornerstone for the new home of the Apprentices Library in Brooklyn Heights, established to broaden access to books and learning for the area's youth and laborers. Before the ceremony, children were moved away from the rocky excavation site and placed at a safe distance to observe the ceremony; one, a six-year-old boy named Walt Whitman, recalled sixty years later Lafayette sweeping him up in his arms and kissing his cheek before he placed him back on the ground.[15]

Later in the day, Lafayette returned to city hall, where he was first received the previous August, now met by New York's Senate. The intervening eleven months, he confessed, "will fill every one of the remaining days, and the last instant of my life, with a most lively sense of gratitude and delight." As for the holiday, "The fourth of July has begun the era of a new social order, hitherto unexampled and founded on the sovereignty of the people, on the plain rights of man, on the practice of unalloyed self-government," he declared. During dinner, when New York's mayor, William Paulding Jr., sliced into a large pie, a carrier pigeon fluttered out holding a tribute to Lafayette written on a small scroll.[16] In the evening, soldiers and members of civic associations strode through New York's streets, while Lafayette watched from the steps of city hall. Strangers flocked to New York; its museums and gardens were full; boats raced from Governor's Island to Whitehall Slip, during what a reporter described as "the pleasantest days known to an American summer," where "the adopted son of Washington was the magnet that attracted all eyes, and interested all hearts."[17]

With few days remaining with him, New York presented its final wonders to Lafayette: visits to the Chatham Theatre and the "Lafayette Circus," an exhibit of transparent paintings, among them portraits of himself and Washington, at Castle Garden. On the 9th, he visited his old friend Richard Varick, at Prospect Hall, in Jersey City. The boat that took him there was the *American Star*, which, the previous December, had vanquished *Certain Death*, owned by a British captain, in a race from Long Island to Castle Garden, winning $1,000. Its crew—who had worn handkerchiefs with the likeness of George Washington during their victory—volunteered to row Lafayette across the Hudson to Varick's home, Prospect Hill, in Jersey, now Jersey City. New carpets were installed and silver oars were mounted. Polished for the occasion, the boat would be a symbol not just of national might, but gratitude too. At the conclusion of the evening, the crew presented the *American Star* to Lafayette, successfully imploring him to take it back to France and place it in some spot of honor at La Grange as a token of thanks and a source of pride in his second home.

That evening, he returned to Castle Garden, where over seven thousand people collected to watch the French showman and aeronaut, Étienne-Gaspard Robert, whose stage name was Robertson, ascend to the heavens in his hydrogen balloon. When Lafayette cut the cord connecting the balloon, *E. Pluribus unum* painted on its side, the wicker basket containing Robert drifted up over the fortress and across the city, eventually touching down in a cornfield in Long Island.

He submitted to uncomfortable plaster casting by the artist John H. J. Browere by request of the Common Council. The artist, in a printed notice, claimed this to be an "equally correct method of taking his likeness," insisting he would "challenge any artist in the United States or Europe, to produce an equally correct Bust with mine of

General Lafayette. One thousand dollars shall be no bar to competition."[18] Samuel Morse, whose work on Lafayette's portrait was tragically derailed by the death of his wife, Lucretia, had since left their children with his parents in New Haven and returned to New York. Tormented by sleepless nights, lost in heartache—"I fear I shall sink under it," he told his father—Morse threw himself into the new work he had earned as the result of his elevated reputation after winning the Lafayette commission.[19] He saw his subject only fleetingly while they were in the city at the same time.[20] A year later, he was still working to complete the portrait.

Fanny Wright saw more of Lafayette, but not by much; their paths crossed briefly and then diverged for good in New York. She and her sister Camilla were present in Boston for the ceremony at Bunker Hill, but the younger of the two, sickened by the heat and crowds, was bedridden for days after. On their way to Boston, Fanny met with DeWitt Clinton for an hour in Philadelphia, and shared the design of her plan to remove slavery from America. New York's governor, "having listened with great attention observed that I had given him a more correct view of the whole surface of Southern slavery than he had previously received."[21]

George Flower, the Englishman Fanny had befriended in Illinois, joined her in New York. There, she courted support from abolitionists and funds from potential donors for her experiment, composing a circular explaining its intentions. Despite its ambitious title, "A Plan for the Gradual Abolition of Slavery in the United States without danger of loss to the Citizens of the South," it was a rather pragmatic proposal. Wright hoped to acquire two plots of public cotton land in the West. There, eventually, fifty to one hundred slaves would labor for the requisite span of years to recoup their market value and earn their liberty. The enterprise would cost, at its beginning, $40,000 but, Fanny believed, generate $10,000 annually. Taking inspiration from Robert Owen's reforms at New Lanark, a school would be established on the farm to educate the children of slaves and prepare their parents for freedom. The plan had a number of reasoned concessions—to Southern planters, whose capital and fortunes were intractably linked to slavery,

and to those, like Jefferson, who feared the blending of the races following the abolition of the institution. Fanny presented the concept as
a moneymaking enterprise: The productivity of communal labor that
had so impressed her at Harmonie would be supercharged by laborers
incentivized to break the chains of bondage. This, in turn, would give
her farm a competitive edge against other plantations; the model would
crowd out slave labor and spread across the states and attract investors
from abroad. Once workers had earned their emancipation, they would
live free lives elsewhere, away from America.[22] As she had failed to see
that the Harmonists' productivity was, at least in part, a result of their
fear of Rapp, she wrongly believed that Southern planters wanted to
end slavery if only the financial knot it trapped them in could be untied.

Fanny had the pamphlet published in Baltimore and sent to
Jefferson, Madison, as well as Henry Clay. The first of these statesmen
offered some encouragement. "At the age of 82, with one foot in the
grave, and the other uplifted to follow it, I do not permit myself to
take part in any new enterprises, even for bettering the condition of
man, not even in the great one which is the subject of your letter, and
which has been thro' life that of my greatest anxieties," he cautioned
her. Ridding America of slavery, though, was not unimaginable. "The
abolition of the evil is not impossible: it ought never therefore to be
despaired of. Every plan should be adopted, every experiment tried,
which may do something towards the ultimate object," he assured her.
"That which you propose is well worthy of tryal [*sic*]. It has succeeded
with certain portions of our white brethren, under the care of a Rapp
and an Owen; and why may it not succeed with the man of colour?"[23]

Lafayette agreed to promote the project. He promised to introduce
Wright to Andrew Jackson, given her interest in establishing her commune in Tennessee, and even offered her $8,000 (she had loaned him
money before his departure from France). Wright refused the offer
of reimbursement. She had described her plan for abolition as "the
great object the only one which could ever have brought his generous
& tender nature to bear a separation."[24] This made for a noble parting between the apostle and his disciple, separated by the pursuit of a
great good they both passionately wished to see realized. In its idealism,

Wright's plan for achieving this resembled Lafayette's own experiment with emancipation in Cayenne between the American and French Revolutions.

Of course the reality of their goodbye was more complicated. The Wrights no longer felt welcome at La Grange and saw no future there or with their "adopted father." For this they knew whom to blame: his actual family. As Camilla wrote, "Those who could not in return make our home theirs—unless you had witnessed as we have done the many prods of the increasing influence of certain persons over the mind of him for whose dear sake we have resolved to make every sacrifice, you cannot understand the change that has taken place in Fanny's mind & feelings." The younger sister, in a backhanded absolution, did not blame Lafayette for their estrangement, writing, that, "bedimmed" by advancing years, "he is himself too guileless to suspect duplicity in others."[25] Fanny pulled fewer punches. "I have never written & should probably never have told you (as I never shall him) all that we have seen at work secretly in the mind of George," she wrote her friends Julia and Harriet Garnett. "We have long foreseen that they will ever be between us & our revered friend. To leave him on their account I never could & yet to stay would make us wretched & him with all our care not happy."[26]

A horrified Nelly Lewis, Fanny's great detractor, heard rumors that the separation had another source. "Would you believe that *Miss W*[right] asserted in N.Y. that *she* had the refusal of Gen'l La Fayette's hand," she fumed to her friend Elizabeth Bordley Gibson." It is *sacrilege*. He said to George 'People little know the many ties I have. The devotion I feel for your Mother's memory, or they would not circulate such reports.'"[27]

And then, before Lafayette departed New York on July 13, there were inevitable goodbyes to his old brother soldiers—Richard Varick, Marinus Willett—who, after decades of separation, he had been reunited with so briefly, and as, Niles's *Weekly Register* commented, "with whom he can never expect to meet again, unless beyond the grave." In touching symmetry, one of his final goodbyes was to Hannah Tompkins, the wife of Daniel Tompkins. The former vice president, the first American official to formally greet Lafayette on his arrival on

Staten Island almost a year before, died on June 11. As his first visit to New York began at Tompkins's estate, he wished his final one to conclude in the company of his widow.[28]

"A profound dejection was imprinted on every face," when Lafayette departed New York on July 14, wrote Levasseur.[29] Only the sound of one final artillery salute interrupted the silence as he departed from the wharf at the foot of Barclay Street—where thousands of people watched. A New York paper reported that an elderly man attempted to place his hat over a gutter in the path of Lafayette, who politely refused the assistance and requested to place the item back on his head. He bid another round of difficult goodbyes to brother soldiers—Nicholas Fish and Philip Van Cortlandt. "They severally and warmly embraced, and while tears rolled profusely down their furrowed cheeks, the spectators unconsciously wept from sympathy," reported Wilkes-Barre's newspaper, the *Wyoming Herald*. "When the old veteran left the dock the immense concourse of people were silent at death and the solemn stillness was only broken by the loud peals of artillery, as the last salute in New York was fired in honor of the beloved 'National Guest.'"[30] He sailed to Hoboken, passed through and overnighted in Morristown, then on to Princeton and Trenton. He said farewell to Joseph Bonaparte at Point Breeze and then was conveyed on the Delaware River, aboard a steamboat bearing its name, to Philadelphia, where he arrived at the Chestnut Street wharf in the early evening. The previous fall, Lafayette was brought into the city in the midst of a triumphant procession. His return to Philadelphia was a more sedate affair. "It was thought on the present occasion, when we were again favored with the presence of Gen. La Fayette, nothing remained but to give him an honest and affectionate welcome, to make him master of his own time, in fact to place him at *home*," explained one of the city's newspapers.[31]

Over the following eight days, Lafayette returned to the Hall of Independence, where he visited with the ladies of Philadelphia—no men were allowed in other than as escorts—and members of the Society of the Cincinnati. For a second time, he inspected the Water Works at Fairmount and was presented with a model of the operation, which he had requested the previous fall. At the Castle, their clubhouse at Rambo's

Rock on the Schuylkill River, he was given a certificate of honorary membership in the State in Schuylkill, the nation's oldest angling club. "It is the more grateful to me, as it completes my tour to all the states," Lafayette said after receiving the honor, with a sly nod to the club's organization as a pseudo-government. Then, fulfilling his duty as a new member, he donned the club's signature straw hat and white linen apron and was led into the kitchen to help prepare dinner.[32] In his waning time in Philadelphia, he was treated to a display of fireworks at Vauxhall Garden, the city's preeminent park, which occupied an entire block.[33]

There was an excursion too, on the 20th, northwest of Philadelphia, to Germantown and a breakfast at Cliveden, the country estate built by the patriot Benjamin Chew, now owned by his son, Benjamin Chew Jr. Its walls still bore the marks of the bullets and cannonballs fired during the Battle of Germantown. "There was so much noise that I could not hear a word the General said, every person seemed so anxious to see him *eat* that a sentinel had to keep guard at the door with a drawn sword," wrote a neighbor who was present at Cliveden, Ann Johnson. Later he visited Mount Airy College and Germantown Academy. From atop Chestnut Hill, two miles away, he looked down at the battlefield of Barren Hill—his schedule was too pressed to allow a closer visit.[34]

"It is more than probable that our eyes will not again be blest with a sight of our nation's beloved guest, Lafayette," lamented a Delaware columnist during Lafayette's last days in Philadelphia, assuming on the way back to Washington he would not pass through their state.[35] To the people of Wilmington's surprise, he reappeared ever so briefly: He left Philadelphia on the morning of the 25th, traveling down the Delaware River and disembarking at Marcus Hook on his way to lodge with Victor Marie du Pont at his mansion, Louviers, on the north bank of Brandywine Creek. Du Pont, a French immigrant, along with his brother Éleuthère Irénée du Pont, had transformed the valley into an industrial hub, anchored by the family's gunpowder works, Eleutherian Mills.[36] It was a transformation Lafayette happily noted in a scrapbook kept by du Pont's daughters: "After having seen, near half a century ago, the banks of the Brandywine a scene of bloody fighting, I am happy now to find it the seat of industry, beauty, and mutual friendship."[36]

During Lafayette's first visit to Philadelphia, representatives from Chester and Delaware Counties had requested he visit their parts of Pennsylvania, where the battlefield of Brandywine lay. Time did not allow it in the fall of 1824, but the summer of 1825, as Lafayette made his way toward Washington to conclude his tour, provided an opportunity. Planning had begun for a celebration on September 11, the anniversary of the conflict, as a last sendoff for Lafayette. However, it was almost certain he would have left the country by that date, and newspapers reported that he was disinclined to celebrate the anniversary of a defeat.[37] Instead, he settled for a brief visit, escorted from du Pont's home on the morning of the 26th to the banks of Brandywine Creek with the intent to cross the stream near Chadds Ford, as the army had done. On approach, however, Lafayette alone realized that the spot was incorrect—the action had actually occurred farther upstream.

When they reached the creek, he was met by the chairmen of the two counties' committees, both veterans of the Revolution: William Anderson and Joseph McLellan. The latter had commanded a company of riflemen and was injured during the Yorktown Campaign, prompting Lafayette to send him a note saying, "I have no finer troops under me; always willing and ready to do their full duty."[38] Nearly half a century on, McLellan's charge was now to escort his old general around the Brandywine battlefield, where militia had formed along the former American lines and spectators gathered.

Lafayette toured the field, attempting to match his memories with the altered landscape, contending with the passage of forty-five years. As he moved along the site, he would periodically stand in the barouche, recognizing and pointing out the positions of General Maxwell's and Wayne's brigades. Where, he asked, was the bridge, made of rails, that had once spanned the creek? This mystery went unanswered.

A mile from Chadds Ford, he stopped at the home of Gideon Gilpin, a Quaker farmer whose abode he had used prior to the battle and whose farm the British had ransacked during and after.[39] Confined to his bed, and with only weeks to live, Gilpin instantly recognized his guest, returned after so long. As the procession moved on, Lafayette asked if any of his companions could find the Birmingham Meeting

House. When the building was identified, Lafayette realized exactly where he was. "Oh, it is here," he said. Rising again in the barouche, speaking emotionally in French to Georges, he gestured toward the spot where he bled for America's freedom. Lafayette's fellow veterans now surrounded him, and the militia escort filed by shouting, "Long live Lafayette!"[40] When the party repaired to the estate of Samuel Jones, which was used for a time by British General William Howe as headquarters, they were presented with relics from the battle—bullets and cannonballs pulled from the battlefield. "It was here he first met danger and received a wound in defense of the cause he had espoused," wrote one columnist, "the hour of suffering was past and the hour of triumph had come; he was sensibly affected."[41]

They continued on, passing through West Chester, and arriving in Lancaster on the 27th. Friedrich List, the German economist whom Lafayette unsuccessfully encouraged to immigrate to America and invited to join him on the *Cadmus* on his journey, had later acted on the advice. List arrived in New York in June, settling his family in Northern Liberties, above Philadelphia, and then joined Lafayette's trip through Pennsylvania. Still a stranger to America, he was bewildered by the scene in Lancaster, where "every farm boy asks about Lafayette." "Strange sight," he wrote in his journal. "Germans mixed with the English, in a place where the Indians resided, where they celebrate a Frenchman as their liberator. A look of joy is on all their faces."[42]

The farther the procession moved west, the larger the crowds grew. "Riders come out of every bush, groups of elegant ladies come out and join in," List recorded. Young boys climbed tall oaks to wave handkerchiefs; grown women waved theirs from the rooftops. Soldiers from 1776 waited on balconies, while bands played "Yankee Doodle" and a ten-year-old boy read aloud an address on freedom. "The youth of Lancaster," List wrote, "praise the heroes of the Revolution."[43]

On the 29th, Lafayette and his companions sailed from Port Deposit, on the eastern bank of the Susquehanna River, paused in Havre de Grace, then entered the Patapsco and landed at Baltimore— at the moment a fire, which was eventually subdued, raged through the city. After two days of rest, they left for the national capital. "General

Lafayette desired that there be no pomp and circumstance to mark his departure," wrote Levasseur.[44] And still the farewell ceremony lasted several hours. Outside of Washington, the party was met by John Adams II, the president's middle son, bearing a message that the people of the capital had ceded to his father's request that Lafayette be his personal guest at the Executive Mansion for the remainder of his time in America. Lafayette, whose son and secretary followed riding in the stagecoach, accompanied the younger Adams to the president's house, where for the following months he enjoyed, in Levasseur's words, the "sweetness of family life," among the first family in their unpretentious home.[45]

President John Quincy Adams had other, more symbolic, arrangements for Lafayette as well. On the death of Georges's mother-in-law, before their departure for the South, Lafayette had determined to sail for France on a packet ship by the middle of August, in order to return to their grieving loved ones at La Grange. The president dashed these plans.

The previous year, after Congress had invited Lafayette to visit America and offered him a national ship, Monroe and his cabinet debated for some time whether to actually send one, while Lafayette eventually secured his own passage on the *Cadmus*. There would be no debate or refusals now. In June, while Lafayette was racing toward Boston, President Adams was informed by Thomas Tingey, commandant of the navy yard, that a forty-four-gun frigate, built by the naval architect William Doughty, which had been in construction since 1821, was nearing its launch. It was named the *Susquehanna*. In a later meeting with Samuel Southard, the secretary of the navy, Adams inquired about this ship: Could it be renamed and readied to sail by August 15? To equip the vessel for a voyage across the Atlantic in so little time was a formidable task. But the purpose of doing so—conveying Lafayette back to France—was incentive enough. Adams, irritated by a congressional resolution that limited the names of new ships to towns, states, or rivers, conceived of a means to name the ship in a way that both honored the government's decree and Lafayette. "It is customary," the president informed Lafayette, "to designate our frigates by the names of the rivers of the United States; to conform to this custom, and make it accord with the desire we have to perpetuate a name that recalls that glorious event of our revolutionary war, in which you sealed with your blood your devotion to our principles, we have given the name of Brandywine to the new frigate to which we confide the honorable mission of returning you to the wishes of your country and family."[46] Brandywine had endeared Lafayette to America; now it would take him away from its shores forever.

Quickly, under the guidance of Southard, the secretary of the navy, the frigate was equipped: Guns, sails, provisions, and rigging were installed. Archibald Henderson, commandant of the Marine Corps, stopped by the president's house to offer his officers, his band, even himself to help carry the Nation's Guest across the Atlantic Ocean. Parents pleaded with the president to appoint their son a midshipman on such a momentous voyage; the number of those appointed was expanded to over twenty in order to include young men from each state (and with Revolutionary ancestry). Many, though not all, of the twenty-four states were represented, with one sailor (William Radford) even hailing from as far west as Missouri, and another (Solomon D. Belton) as far south as Georgia.

On June 16, Michael Shiner, an enslaved worker at the Navy Yard, who concealed his literacy but kept a diary in which he recorded many of the capital's most historic events, wrote that he had seen "the united States frigate *Branday Wine* Wher launch" and the boat "Wher fited out expresly to carry genral layet."[47] Crowds gathered on Smallwood's wharf, as carpenters freed the boat from its stocks and Sailing Master Captain Marmaduke, standing on its bow with the president nearby, christened the ship *Brandywine* to a twenty-four-gun salute and the Marine band playing "Yankee Doodle Dandy." "At first dip the water seemed to embrace up to her galleries, as if welcoming her home on the deep, in a cloud of pearly spray," wrote a correspondent for the *National Intelligencer*.[48] In July, Charles Morris, the naval commissioner who had served during the Barbary Wars and the War of 1812 and had sailed since the age of fifteen, when he was made a midshipman on the *Baltimore*, was given command of the ship and a departure date of early September was estimated.[49]

"You will see, dear ones, that the moment of our departure has become less certain than when we had to take a packet boat on the fixed day of August 15th," Lafayette wrote to his daughters, with word of the president's offer. "It is impossible to refuse the beautiful, 44 cannon frigate, to which the government has given the name of a stream instead of a river, of a defeat instead of a victory, only to recall my first battle and my injury."[50]

One editorialist wrote the *Brandywine* "flew to sea as if on eagles wings." It was not simply a tribute to prepare a mighty ship in such short order to carry Lafayette back to Europe; it was also a flex of American naval strength, aimed at the potentates and monarchs who ruled there. "Of all the occurrences which transpired, and the steps that were taken, to do honor to the Nation's Guest, none speak in a language more empathic and striking than those connected with the preparation of a national ship for his accommodation," opined the *Baltimore American*. Indeed, what a sight on both sides of the Atlantic. A forty-four-gun frigate, featuring an elliptical stern—an innovation in shipbuilding—commanded by a storied commodore, with midshipmen from across the American Union standing on its yards, and the hero of two hemispheres aboard. "We have given to foreign powers a practice exemplification of our naval skill and resources," bragged the Baltimore editor, "that may save us the necessity of showing them in a manner much more expensive and sanguinary."[51]

Accepting passage on the *Brandywine* necessitated pushing Lafayette's departure back a month, but doing so afforded him more time in Washington. The summer heat in the capital was oppressive; Congress was out of session. Adams was harried by a conflict with George M. Troup. The governor of Georgia, in defiance of the federal government, and personally insulting the president, was preparing to survey the Creek lands ceded by William McIntosh and his allies at Indian Springs earlier in the year. The lull offered an opportunity for farewells. "I strongly desire, before leaving the American coast, to embrace one last time my friends Jefferson, Madison, and Monroe," Lafayette had written earlier in the tour.[52] On August 6, after visiting the *Brandywine,* a party consisting of the president, the Nation's Guest,

Georges, and Levasseur left Washington for Monroe's home, Oak Hill, in Loudon County, thirty-seven miles from the capital.

After the small group reached the bridge crossing the Potomac, Adams paid its toll. As they began to move, the collector chased after the carriages with his palm outstretched crying, "Mr. President! Mr. President! You have given me eleven cents too little!" Adams counted the coins in his hand and conceded he had unintentionally shorted the man. After he produced the remaining amount, the collector recognized Lafayette in the carriage and now refused the fee. Adams insisted he pay, explaining the Nation's Guest was not traveling in an official capacity but as *his* guest. The collector accepted this reasoning. As Levasseur noted, this was the lone occasion during his entire stay in America when Lafayette or his party paid a toll.[53]

They spent three days with Monroe, returned to Washington, and then on the 13th left again for Fredericksburg on the steamboat *Mount Vernon*, arriving the following morning. "How beautifully interesting is everything which appertains to this great man!" cried the *Fredericksburg Herald*, showing no fatigue after a year of Lafayette hysteria.[54] An escort—including the town's mayor and Hugh Mercer, son of General Hugh Mercer, slain in the Battle of Princeton—accompanied Lafayette to Montpelier, where he arrived on the 15th. He then left for Monticello on the 18th, joined by Madison and then Monroe, who had traveled to Albemarle. There, Lafayette found an enfeebled Jefferson. So fragile was the former president that when the University of Virginia hosted a state dinner for Lafayette, its founder was unable to attend. "I am this day, with Very Heavy Heart, to part from my friend Jefferson," he wrote to Andrew Jackson from Monticello before leaving on the 21st.[55]

After another short visit at Montpelier, the party returned to Washington overland, lodging at Monroe's home in Loudon County again before bidding him farewell again and returning to the capital on August 25. "We just made a trip around Virginia to take our leave of my close friends of fifty years, Jefferson, Madison, and Monroe," Lafayette wrote upon returning to the president's house. "These goodbyes and many others are very painful."[56] There, he was disappointed to find no correspondence from Wright, now on her way to Tennessee, a feeling he aired in a letter apprising her of his discussions with the former presidents regarding her plan. Jefferson was ailing, he informed her, and their parting difficult. "Our mutual adieus very, very melancholy, as you may believe." Monroe and Madison supported her outline, and in the case of the second man, Lafayette assured her, "you have no better friend in the U.S." The former presidents said the project was "the best they have seen so far," Lafayette told his daughters. "It will make them some enemies who will take revenge of their success, if it does succeed as I do believe it will, with gossip and ridicule. But plenty of serious and enlightened men encourage the attempt. May they not lose their fortune."[57]

For his part, as his stay in America concluded, Lafayette was optimistic about the eventual demise of slavery in the South and confident his own subtle gestures against it and inequality in every region were not worthless. "I think I have done well in this respect. I have said that popularity, the primary treasure, is however, like all treasures, best spent usefully," he wrote his daughter-in-law earlier in the year. "The difficulties are immense, I admit, but nothing is insurmountable with time, and first steps must be made. The treatment of blacks is greatly improved; we need only wait for emancipation, and, after several circumstances that are too long to describe, it should be favored over recolonisation [*sic*] in Africa, Haiti, or anywhere else."[58]

By the end of the month a departure date was confirmed: The *Brandywine* would be ready to sail on September 7, the day after Lafayette's birthday. In the remaining days, he and Georges made final visits to Mount Vernon for a large dinner with Commodore Morris, and to Woodlawn for a goodbye to the family of Nelly Lewis. "I cannot rest without bidding you adieu once more, dearest and treasured friend," she wrote to Georges on the eve of his departure, "you leave me and I know not when we can meet again, but the time you have passed with me will be ever fresh in my recollection—it will be a happy dream that will comfort many a weary hour of my future."[59]

The parting from friends was no less painful for the elder Lafayette. "You see, my dear, friend, that the moment comes very rapidly upon me when I must leave this blessed, happy, and beloved shore," he wrote

Richard Peters.[60] "We leave Here for the Brandywine on the 7th. My Heart is too full to write more," he sighed to Jefferson. Adams, though, observed that he was not likely sailing off into obsolescence. During a conversion before he took his leave, the president discouraged Lafayette from resuming his involvement in revolutionary projects once he returned to France but was unconvinced he would take the advice. "He says he will go quietly to La Grange; that he is 68 years old, and must leave revolutions to younger men; but there is fire beneath his cinders."[61]

On September 6, Lafayette marked his sixty-eighth birthday with a celebration at the president's home. A delegation from New York made a surprise appearance, bearing the gift of a book chronicling the events surrounding his visits. Despite the jubilation, the Frenchmen were preoccupied. "Although the dinner joined a large number of guests, and it was intended to celebrate the anniversary of Lafayette's birth, it was nonetheless very serious, I may say almost sad," Levasseur reflected. "Each of us was too strongly preoccupied with the day that was going to follow to be able to surrender himself to mirth. We already felt, by anticipation, the regret of separation."[62]

There was so much consolation to look back upon, however. Prior to the birthday, Lafayette paid a visit to the home of William Winston Seaton, the co-publisher of the *National Intelligencer*. "He dwelt on the magic changes which a few short years had made in our cities, our art our wealth, and above all in our population," Seaton's wife, Sarah, wrote to her mother, "and in the most touching strain spoke of the spring-time of his youth when visions of hope were strong, and which in age he had the singular felicity of seeing realized."[63]

23

Go Then, Our Beloved Friend

When the melancholy September morning at last arrived, a brilliant sun rose to meet it. It shone across Washington's shuttered banks and businesses and over its empty homes, sporadically standing along broad and muddy roads and emerging from overgrown fields. Attention was fixed away from the Capitol and up poplar-lined Pennsylvania Avenue, toward the president's home. Outside its northern entrance, Marines stood expectantly in their uniforms of navy wool and gold lace, joined by the assorted cavalry and militia from the District of Columbia, their battle colors on display.

Crowds gathered and waited in anticipation in the park just across the home's doors. At noon, they swung open. In walked the officials of the district and its three cities, Alexandria, Georgetown, and Washington, their mayors, aldermen, and councilmen stopping in the great hall of the executive mansion. There they completed a circle already half formed by members of the U.S. government—cabinet officials, congressmen, and the chief magistrate himself, John Quincy Adams.

Silent minutes passed. Then, from a small room in the grand hall, in walked the old hero. He moved slowly, supported on one side by the president's secretary and middle son, John Adams II. And on the other,

Tench Ringgold, the U.S. marshal of the District of Columbia. He passed through a space in the ring of dignitaries, stopping in its center. The only audible sounds were sad murmurs from the throngs outside, floating in through the mansion's still-open entrance.

Nearly fifty years had passed since Lafayette first set foot on American soil. He had left behind a beloved wife, an infant daughter, and a disapproving family. It was the summer of 1777; he was nineteen years old, full of optimism about the outcome of a contest that was very much in doubt and burning with idealism for a people he hardly knew. "The happiness of America is intimately connected with the happiness of mankind," he prophesized aboard the *La Victoire*, riding the Atlantic's waves, birds overhead indicating that he had almost reached this new country he so esteemed. "She will become the safe and respected asylum of virtue, integrity, toleration, equality and tranquil happiness."[1] On this day, half a century later, he stood in a capital city that was then little more than woods, hills, and waterways.

Adams was, by his own admission, publicly austere and unfeeling. It was a measurement then of the task before him that the president fought back evident emotion in addressing the Nation's Guest. The silence in the great hall broke. "You are now about to return to the country of your birth," he began, his voice clear but distressed. The recent national discord that had culminated in his election was, for the moment, forgotten. "At the painful moment of parting," as Adams described it, "the nation was one."

He evoked its revolution and lamented the fading ranks of the men who had participated in it. "In the lapse of 40 years," he said, speaking directly to Lafayette, "the generation of men with whom you cooperated with in the conflict of arms has nearly passed away. Of the general officers of the American army in that way, you alone survive." The Frenchman was a living link to the Revolution, that his reappearance, like the ghost of a long-lost relative, rallied Americans together in celebration of a memory and tribute to a set of ideals.

"The ship is now prepared for your reception, and equipped for sea. From the moment of her departure, the prayers of millions will ascend to heaven that her passage may be prosperous, and your return to the bosom of your family as propitious to your happiness as your visit to this scene of your youthful glory has been to that of the American people," he said. "Go, then, our beloved friend, to the land of brilliant genius, of generous sentiment, of heroic valor."

The president mentioned a much-hoped-for but unlikely future reunion. Then, "speaking in the name of the whole people of the United States," he concluded, "at a loss only for language to give utterance to that feeling of attachment with which the heart of the nation beats as the heart of one man, I bid you a reluctant and affectionate farewell."[2]

A chorus of approvals followed. Lafayette, shaken, paused to gather his composure before responding. He reminisced about the grand displays of public affection that had "marked, each step, each hour of a 12 months' progress through 24 states." With pride, he remarked on the "self-felt happiness of the people . . . their rapid prosperity and insured security," and, above all else, "The cherishing of that union between the states . . . the dying prayer of every American patriot."

Then he bid his goodbye, crying, "God bless you, sir, and you all who surround us! God bless the American people, each of their states and the federal government! Accept this patriotic farewell of an overflowing heart: such will be its last throb when it ceases to beat."[3]

Lafayette moved forward, embraced Adams, then stepped away. Pulled back as if by an irresistible force, he walked toward and took Adams in his arms once more, murmuring only "Farewell! Farewell!"[4] Those watching sighed and wept; the large ring they had formed collapsed around Lafayette. Now they competed to clasp his hand, to look in his eyes one last time. He lingered among them, hoping to delay the inevitable. When the blast of cannons from outside the mansion announced that this was no longer possible, Lafayette, at last, reluctantly shook the president's hand once more, took leave of his house a final time, and climbed into a large, open-topped carriage. "No spectacle could be more sublime than the whole of this scene," observed a newspaper correspondent from inside the mansion. "It is one which can be more easily fancied than described—comment would be useless."[5]

Accompanying Lafayette were members of Adams's cabinet: Secretary of State Henry Clay, Secretary of the Treasury Richard

Rush, and Secretary of the Navy Samuel Southard. Final waves were exchanged, and the flags of the assembled military regiments fell. A column formed and proceeded away from the president's house and toward the Potomac River. Marines, cavalry, and rifle corps were in succession at its head, their battle colors once more aloft. Civil dignitaries came next, followed, finally, by Lafayette and his companions. The music of military bands competed with the thunder of artillery. A mass of spectators followed the pageant on its way down Pennsylvania Avenue, across to Seventh Street, and finally to Cana's wharf on the Potomac. There the steamboat *Mount Vernon* waited on the water.

When the procession reached its terminus, the carriages, their passengers disembarking, peeled off and away. Only Lafayette's remained. Atop a nearby ridge he beheld the militias and representatives of the three towns of the District of Columbia standing in long columns. They descended toward the river, making one more pass. Lafayette took to his feet and extended a final salute. Crowds numbering in the thousands pressed upon the wharf, filling the horizon. Cannons boomed. He waved, bowed, turned, and stepped aboard the small steamer and off American soil.

The *Mount Vernon*'s paddle wheel turned, churning water underneath, exhaling smoke overhead. It slipped into the river and glided southward, past the armory at Greenleaf's Point, by the navy yard, its guns ringing in salute, to Alexandria, whose citizens stood waiting on the wharves and ships, bursting into cries of "Farewell, Lafayette!" So quick was the boat's passage and so emotional its goodbye—and, wishing to allow the trailing boats, the *Surprise* and the *Potomac*, to catch up—the *Mount Vernon* was forced to make a second passage by Alexandria. Once this was completed, half a mile past the town, a shout of "man overboard" was heard on deck. Indeed, a man was swimming near the *Mount Vernon* and was soon picked up by the *Surprise*. He had not fallen in the water, but rather leaped in wishing to see Lafayette off. Only wanting to go as far as Alexandria, he determined to swim back to shore.[6]

Soon a salute was fired from Fort Washington, on whose walls women waved their handkerchiefs one final time, and to whom

Lafayette waved his hat in return. After four in the afternoon, an elaborate dinner began on board. This was interrupted with the announcement that the boat was approaching Mount Vernon. The Marine band on board began to play a pretty hymn. "At that moment I caught La Fayette's eye—it was pensive," a fellow passenger later wrote. "His communicative powers appeared suddenly suspended, and his complexion grew wan!" He quit the dinner and pulled away from the table. Leaning on Southard's arm, he walked the boat's deck and stopped near its stern, standing still and silent with his head tilted contemplatively to the right and downward as the sun began to drop in the sky above. When, after fifteen minutes, Washington's home—where his bones rested, where many dear memories remained—vanished, Lafayette quietly returned to his cabin. "There was an awe and a sanctity about it which could not have been increased, had we actually witnessed a communion between the hero who reposes at Mount Vernon and his devoted and admiring La Fayette!" observed an onlooker.[7]

Rain fell during the night, and the *Mount Vernon* ran against an oyster bank, which neither delayed nor harmed the boat. At nine the next morning, they approached the mouth of the Potomac, where the rigging and masts of the *Brandywine* appeared on the horizon. Two hours later, the smaller boat anchored near the larger one's stern. Barges were dispatched to bring the passengers from the former to the latter, but Lafayette, now seasick, was delayed from arriving for an hour—when he did, it was on an ornamented chair, arranged by Captain Morris, which was hoisted on board to the sound of fifteen guns saluting.

Refreshments were made available on board, and Morris provided a tour of the ship for the new arrivals. "We passed through the ship, and had disclosed what, to many of us was a world of wonders," wrote one. "It was hardly possible to satisfy the visitors, that such a ship, in all respects so perfect, was launched but two months ago!"[8] After dinner, the passengers who had come aboard from the *Mount Vernon* made their leave, said farewell, and offered wishes of a speedy and safe return to Lafayette. "The General was too much affected to reply, except in broken sentences."[9]

The *Mount Vernon*'s passengers returned to the boat, which circled the *Brandywine*, with its band playing "Lafayette's March." Then he appeared, visible atop the gangway. He bowed one last time, turned, walked toward the deck, and was gone from view. As the steamboat departed, the sun reappeared. Thirteen months earlier, when Lafayette arrived in America, a magnificent rainbow appeared over Staten Island. Now, as he took his leave, another arched over the *Brandywine*.

Despite the fortuitous omen, the return voyage to France was rocky. On the 9th, the *Brandywine* left the Potomac, entered the Chesapeake Bay, sailing eleven knots an hour, with a breeze from the north, passed Cape Henry, and entered the Atlantic. After a few hours on the ocean, the *Brandywine*'s crew discovered a leak: Eight feet of water had accumulated in its hold. Manning the pumps, sailors returned the ocean's unwanted gift and added their own, tossing thousands of pounds of ammunition and ballast overboard. Initially, the source of the leak was a mystery and a cause naturally for worry over the safety of such a precious mission. Returning Lafayette to an American port, though, Morris deemed unseemly after such an elaborate sendoff, and besides, unless out of dire necessity, he was disinclined to turn back. In time, the crew deduced that the leak was a result of oakum oozing from the *Brandywine*'s sides, perhaps a result of its hasty preparation for sail. The size and power of the Atlantic's waves precluded any attempt to remedy this, but the inpour of water eventually subsided once the planks of the ship, after enough time at sea, began to swell. Another, though more minor, unpleasantry: A bottle of turpentine, used by a steward to clean an officer's uniform, was placed on top of a sugar barrel and knocked over, spilling into a crack, greatly diminishing the taste of the sailors' desserts.

"We had a rough but short passage," wrote David Glasgow Farragut, who had been appointed a lieutenant shortly before sailing on the *Brandywine*.[10]

Lafayette, seasick and suffering from a flare-up of his gout, was rarely seen on deck and seldom joined Morris for dinner. "This was much regretted, for, besides the discomforts, we were deprived of most of the pleasure which had been anticipated from the society of the general, and the hope of listening to his reminiscences of some of the interesting scenes, and persons connected with his eventful life," wrote the captain.[11] Mercifully, the passage was relatively brief, taking only twenty-four days. This was enough time, though, for Lafayette to bond with the midshipmen, regale them with stories of the Revolution, and inquire about their own familiar connections to that epoch. Later, the sailors, through the American consul in Paris, Barnett, sent Lafayette the gift of a silver urn with bas-reliefs of the U.S. Capitol, his visit to Washington's crypt, and the *Brandywine* arriving at Le Havre.

Fifteen days into the journey, the ship encountered a small boat traveling from Liverpool to Philadelphia; the Frenchmen pressed its sailors to pass along their warm greeting to their relations there. "The chance to send you new assurances of our sincere friendship was too lovely for us to let it slip by," wrote Levasseur to Peter Du Ponceau, the French-born veteran of the American Revolution living in Philadelphia, though the sentiment expressed could have been spread more widely across the land they had departed.[12]

The *Brandywine* reached Le Havre on October 3. "I will not speak of the feelings that agitated us at the sight of our Fatherland," wrote Levasseur.[13] Adams had worried that the French government would block Lafayette's landing, smarting from his adoring reception and triumphant tour of America, but no objections were made. In the evening, the ship tacked back and forth, while Farragut was sent ashore to summon a pilot boat to guide the *Brandywine* to port. The next morning, the ship appeared but was unable to lead the frigate in. During this attempt, a steamboat pulled aside. On board were Émilie de Lafayette, her children, and other members of their family, as well as Levasseur's father. The crew of the *Brandywine* bid their guest a prolonged and emotional goodbye, presenting him with the ship's flag. They stood on its yards as Lafayette boarded the steamboat and returned to French soil, where the crowds, discouraged from watching his departure thirteen months earlier, had gathered once again to welcome his return.

After a day at Le Havre, Lafayette, accompanied by Captain Morris, who relinquished command of the *Brandywine* to his first lieutenant, planning to tour French and British naval installations, and his family departed Le Havre. On the way out of the city, crowds tagged behind his carriage, forming a final procession. The party dined in the village of Rouen—desserts were decorated with scenes of the American Revolution—then overnighted in Saint Germain-en-Laye. On the 9th, La Grange's towers once more came into view.

"I found the General big, fat, fresh, happy—in a word, not at all feeling the effect of several months without sleep or nearly without it, chatting, writing, traveling, and drinking for a good eighteen hours out of twenty-four," observed the Duc de Brogli after visiting Lafayette. Days after his return, four thousand of the inhabitants of Rozay-en-Brie held a festival in his honor; in the meadow near the home, illuminations were lit, fireworks launched, men and women danced, and calls of "Long live the friend of the people" were heard into the morning.[14]

By November, ships from Europe carrying newspapers confirmed to relieved Americans Lafayette's safe arrival in France after thirteen months, during which he had brought them joy, gratitude, and affirmation, and added one more chapter to their history. One man who had helped stage the festival of liberty around the memory of the Revolution, though he had not seen or participated in it, was pleased to learn of Lafayette's successful journey and safe return. "Genl Lafayette has arrived in good health at La Grange," wrote James Brown, the American minister in Paris, to his brother-in-law Henry Clay, "and I sincerely hope he will wisely avoid any interference with public affairs, and content with the public honors he has received in the United States, will pass the remainder of his days in tranquility."[15]

In December 1825, a rider on a stagecoach from Boston encountered an old man traveling to his home in Rhode Island. He carried a sword, its silver hilt decorated with gold, a gift, he would learn in conversation, from Congress for service in the War of Independence. His name was William Barton, and he was on his way home after an absence of fourteen years. Along the way he remarked with wonder at the transformation of the country he saw along the road after so long an absence. As he related his ordeal, Barton spoke of a man who was affected by his plight and paid for his release from a Vermont prison—General Lafayette—and "his eyes filled with tears of gratitude." As the stagecoach approached his home, Providence, where his wife, children, and grandchildren waited, the old soldier happily sang a song of the American Revolution.[16]

EPILOGUE

When Lafayette Was Here . . .

Contrary to the assurances made to America's president and the wishes of its minister in Paris, General Lafayette did not quietly retire upon his return to France. Having reentered the Chamber of Deputies three years earlier, he found himself in July 1830 at the center of another revolution. Years of economic stagnation and resentment toward the increasingly absolutist rule of King Charles X—who had curtailed freedom of the press, dissolved the Chamber, and restricted the franchise—had escalated from riots into full-scale revolt. Lafayette, now seventy-three, once again assumed command of the National Guard. In this role, he helped bring an end to the Bourbon monarchy for good. Standing on the balcony of the Hôtel de Ville, he handed the tricolor flag to Louis-Philippe, Duc d'Orleans, symbolically conferring the throne to the deposed Charles X's cousin and proclaiming him king of the French. This act came with the promise of a constitutional monarchy—a promise that went largely unfulfilled as Louis-Philippe restricted freedoms and violently suppressed workers' revolts during his reign.

Lafayette died at his home in Paris on rue d'Anjou on May 20, 1834. Until his death, Americans continued to visit him there and at LaGrange. When he was laid to rest at Picpus Cemetery, beside his wife, Adrienne, Georges scattered soil shipped from Bunker Hill over the grave. A French newspaper noted that this earth, brought from America to serve as his sepulchre, symbolized how little he had expected to see France become a republican land."[1]

Just as his return a decade earlier had sent Americans into a delirium, news of his death now plunged them into grief. Andrew Jackson, who had assumed the presidency in 1829, ordered honors similar to those bestowed upon George Washington after his passing: twenty-one-gun salutes, the lowering of flags to half-mast at military installations across the nation, and the wearing of black crepe armbands by officers for six months. Funeral processions were organized, eulogies delivered, and toasts—once raised to his longevity at countless banquets—were now made to his memory.

Georges Washington de Lafayette carried on his father's labors and guarded his legacy. Achille Tenaille de Vaulabelle, the politician and historian, who sat next to the younger Lafayette during the National Constituent Assembly of 1848, wrote that "his eyes would become moist and his voice would tremble with profound emotion each time he pronounced the name of his father; each of his votes testified, furthermore, to an unshakable loyalty to the principles of the first years of his life."[2] After his death on November 29, 1849, American friends were among the pallbearers who carried his casket to Picpus, where it was buried in a torrential rainstorm. The following year, his son Edmond traveled to America, retracing some of the journey his father and grandfather had taken a quarter of a century earlier. At Mount Vernon, accompanied by an elderly George Washington Parke Custis, they paid their respects to George Washington. Washington's body, now in a new marble sarcophagus—designed by William Strickland, who had refurbished the Hall of Independence in 1824—had since been removed from the decaying crypt and relocated to a vestibule outside the new family tomb.

In 1829, Auguste Levasseur published *Lafayette en Amérique, en 1824 et 1825 ou Journal d'un voyage aux États-Unis.* This account of Lafayette's American tour, written by his secretary, was subsequently translated into English, Dutch, and German. The last of these editions was completed by his wife, Agnese, whom he wed in 1826. Wounded in the foot during the July Revolution in 1830, Levasseur later served as French consul to Haiti and minister to Mexico. He was also a commander in the Legion of Honor and knight of the Order of St. Gregory. Levasseur died on May 10, 1871, and is buried at the church of St. Pierre-St. Paul in Clamart.

With Jackson's assistance, Fanny Wright purchased 1,240 acres in western Tennessee on the Wolf River near Memphis, on land from which the Chickasaw were forced, and began her great experiment to redeem liberty in America. She named it Nashoba—Chickasaw for "wolf." After purchasing ten slaves, in 1826 she began the great experiment and the difficult labor of clearing the land and establishing her commune. Nashoba was beset with difficulties, disease, and financial distress. Fanny traveled to Europe in 1827 to find money to sustain the project and regain her health after a bout with malaria. There she was reunited with Lafayette, who became one of Nashoba's trustees. She returned to Tennessee only to find many of its white residents had deserted the farm, around which rumors of interracial relationships had risen, tarring Wright's reputation and scaring off additional investors and champions for the project. This was only inflamed by articles Wright wrote endorsing sexual freedom and the cohabitation of the races. Under these strains, Nashoba disintegrated. Wright relocated to New Harmony, sold the farm, and then, in 1830, sailed with her slaves to Haiti and freed them.

Eleanor "Nelly" Lewis outlived her husband and seven of their eight children. She died in 1852 at her son's Virginia estate, Audley. As she had predicted, she never saw her "brother" Georges Washington de Lafayette again after 1825.

Samuel Morse completed his portrait of Lafayette in 1826. The painting was a high-water mark of early American painting, full of Revolutionary symbolism and suggestions of future American greatness. The portrait sealed its creator's reputation; he became president of the National Academy of Design, a means to further his ambition to raise the arts in America, but the value of these laurels was diminished without his wife, Lucretia. Decades later, after the discovery of electronic telegraphy and the code that bears his name, he reflected on the portrait of Lafayette, writing "a picture painted under such circumstances can scarcely be expected to do the artist justice, and as a work of art I cannot praise it."[3] Today, the painting hangs in New York's city hall.

The completed Bunker Hill Monument was dedicated by Daniel Webster on June 17, 1843. The 221-foot obelisk, consecrating the memory of the Revolution, receives 330,000 visitors annually.

In 1826, as America celebrated the fiftieth anniversary of the Declaration of Independence, Thomas Jefferson and John Adams died within hours of each other. The last living signer of that document, Charles Carroll of Carrollton, died in 1832 at ninety-five.

Three decades later, in 1864, as Americans fought a Civil War over the great contradiction to the ideals articulated in their founding document, a woman in Missouri named Sara Bodley reflected on an earlier, more felicitous time in the nation's history. "When La Fayette was here he toured to impress upon our statesmen that all Europe was watching us. That our government was a great experiment. Is it not somewhat of a failure?" she justifiably questioned.[4]

Lafayette, ever optimistic about man's capability for self-government and the future of the nation he had helped found, likely would have argued otherwise.

In 2026, America turns 250 years old.

ACKNOWLEDGMENTS

First and foremost, I am indebted to my agent, David Vigliano, for his trust and support, which predate this work. Thanks are due as well to Thomas Flannery, whose wise counsel helped make it a reality.

I am grateful to Matt Baugher and Austin Ross and their team at Harper Horizon for taking a chance on this book and remaining patient with its author.

David Bordelon was a welcome collaborator who did not simply translate manuscripts from French to English, but was always able to find exactly the passages that most brilliantly brought Lafayette and his adventures to life. Anna Plotnick traveled many miles, good-naturedly received constant requests for research help, and unearthed countless treasures in numerous archives. Without their assistance and partnership, this book would have been impossible. I am also indebted to Hadley McSunas, whose early research helped lift the idea off the ground.

The Achelis & Bodman Foundation and Gilder Lehrman Institute of American History respectively gave and administered support during the research and writing of this book, which was critical to its completion. Dr. Leslie Lenkowsky was instrumental in my earning this grant, and Kate Rizzo Smith helped manage it.

I would also like to acknowledge the numerous archivists and librarians around the U.S. who assisted in locating much of the material in this book. A special thanks is due to Vincent Bouat-Ferlier, director of the Chambrun Foundation, who entertained many questions regarding the items in Lafayette's home, La Grange.

Though not involved in the writing of this book, I am appreciative of Vice President Mike Pence and Senator Todd Young for their encouragement and example.

As always, thanks to my family—Jamie, Moose, the Whittakers, Neil Cole, Zorro, Shrimp, Dummi, and the late but much missed Piccino—for enduring another book.

There are so many friends, colleagues, relatives—to list them all would take pages—who have shown kindness, offered grace, and engaged in enlightening and thoughtful conversations, all of which contributed in ways big and small to the realization of this project. I am thankful for each one of you.

NOTES

Prelude

1. John Reynolds, *My Own Times, Embracing, Also the History of My Life* (Illinois, 1855), 257.
2. Jay Read Pember, *A Day with Lafayette in Vermont* (Elm Tree Press, 1912), 12.
3. Walt Whitman, *Lafayette in Brooklyn* (George D. Smith, 1905).
4. John D. Cladwell, *The Cincinnati Pioneer 1–3* (Cincinnati Pioneer Association, 1873), 15.
5. Charles Sumner, *Lafayette the Faithful One* (Wright & Potter, 1870), 30.
6. Ebenezer Hiram Stedman, *Bluegrass Craftsman: Being the Reminiscences of Ebenezer Hiram Stedman, Papermaker 1808–1885*, Edited by Frances L. S. Dugan and Jacqueline P. Bull (University of Kentucky Press, 1959), 75.
7. Ebenezer Hiram Stedman, *Bluegrass Craftsman*, 74.
8. Charles Sumner, *Lafayette the Faithful One*, 31

Chapter 1

1. Frances A. Trollope, *Frances Trollope: Her Life and Literary Work from George III to Victoria*, vol. 1 (London: Richard Bentley and Son, 1895), 86.
2. James M. Glassell, excerpt of diary, 1825, giving an account of his visit with Lafayette in La Grange, Taylor-Cannon Family Papers, Box 14, Folder 134, Filson Historical Society, Louisville, KY.
3. Sydney, Lady Morgan, *France*, vol. 2 (London: Henry Colburn, 1817), 300.
4. Sydney, Lady Morgan, *France*, 300.
5. Jules Cloquet, *Recollections of the Private Life of General Lafayette* (London: Baldwin and Cradock, 1835), 177.
6. The Marquis de Lafayette, *Memoirs, Correspondence and Manuscripts of General Lafayette, Published by His Family*, vol. 1 (London: Saunders and Otley, 1837), 3.
7. *Correspondance Entre Le Comte de Mirabeau et le Comte De La Marck Pendant Les Annees 1789, 1790 et 1791* (Auguste Pagny, Libraire-Editeur, 1851), 47.
8. The Marquis de Lafayette, *Memoirs, Correspondence and Manuscripts of General Lafayette*, vol 1., 4.
9. The Marquis de Lafayette, *Memoirs, Correspondence and Manuscripts of General Lafayette*, vol 1., 15.
10. A. E. Zucker, "An Unguided Tour from Charleston to Philadelphia," in *General de Kalb, Lafayette's Mentor*, vol. 53 (Chapel Hill: University of North Carolina Press, 1966), 127.

11. The Marquis de Lafayette, *Memoirs, Correspondence and Manuscripts of General Lafayette*, vol 1., 17.

12. The Marquis de Lafayette, *Memoirs, Correspondence and Manuscripts of General Lafayette*, vol 1., 19.

13. Octavius Pickering and Charles Wentworth Upham, *The Life of Timothy Pickering*, vol. 1 (Little, Brown, and Company, 1867), 151.

14. The Marquis de Lafayette, *Memoirs, Correspondence and Manuscripts of General Lafayette*, vol. 1, 106.

15. *The Papers of George Washington*, Revolutionary War Series, vol. 16, *1 July–14 September 1778*, ed. David R. Hoth (Charlottesville: University of Virginia Press, 2006), 153–155.

16. *The Papers of Benjamin Franklin*, vol. 30, *July 1 Through October 31, 1779*, ed. Barbara B. Oberg (New Haven, CT and London: Yale University Press, 1993), 260–261.

17. *The Papers of Benjamin Franklin*, vol. 31, *November 1, 1779, Through February 29, 1780*, ed. Barbara B. Oberg (New Haven, CT and London: Yale University Press, 1995), 276.

18. *Our Revolutionary Forefathers, The Letters of Francois, Marquis de Barbe-Marbois, During His Residence in the United States as Secretary of the French Legation, 1779–1785*. Translated and Edited by Eugene Parker Chase (Duffield & Co., 1929), 116.

19. From John Adams to James Lovell, February 29, 1780, *Founders Online*, National Archives, https://founders.archives.gov/documents/Adams/06-08-02-0254. [Original source: *The Adams Papers*, Papers of John Adams, vol. 8, *March 1779–February 1780*, ed. Gregg L. Lint, Robert J. Taylor, Richard Alan Reyerson, Celeste Walker, and Joanna M. Revelas (Cambridge, MA: Harvard University Press, 1989), 380.]

20. "From George Washington to Samuel Huntington, April 3, 1780," *Founders Online*, National Archives, https://founders.archives.gov/documents/Washington/03-25-02-0196. [Original source: *The Papers of George Washington*, Revolutionary War Series, vol. 25, *10 March–12 May 1780*, ed. William M. Ferraro (Charlottesville: University of Virginia Press, 2017), 298–307.]

21. To George Washington from Marie-Joseph-Paul-Yves-Roch-Gilbert du Motier, marquis de Lafayette, October 14, 1782, *Founders Online*, National Archives, https://founders.archives.gov/documents/Washington/99-01-02-09717.

22. To George Washington from Marie-Joseph-Paul-Yves-Roch-Gilbert du Motier, marquis de Lafayette, June 25, 1782, *Founders Online*, National Archives, https://founders.archives.gov/documents/Washington/99-01-02-08791.

23. To George Washington from Marie-Joseph-Paul-Yves-Roch-Gilbert du Motier, marquis de Lafayette, September 8, 1783, *Founders Online*, National Archives, https://founders.archives.gov/documents/Washington/99-01-02-11801.

24. From George Washington to Lafayette, February 1, 1784, *Founders Online*, National Archives, https://founders.archives.gov/documents/Washington/04-01-02-0064. [Original source: *The Papers of George Washington*, Confederation Series, vol. 1, *1 January 1784–17 July 1784*, ed. W. W. Abbot (Charlottesville: University Press of Virginia, 1992), 87–90.]

25. From George Washington to Lafayette, February 1, 1784.

26. Stanley J. Idzerda et al., eds. *Lafayette in the Age of the American Revolution: Selected Letters and Papers, 1776–1790*. 5 vols. (Ithaca, NY, 1977-83), 237–238.

27. Ibid.

28. From James Madison to James Monroe, December 4, 1784, *Founders Online*, National Archives, https://founders.archives.gov/documents/Madison/01-08-02-0092. [Original

source: *The Papers of James Madison*, vol. 8, *10 March 1784–28 March 1786*, eds. Robert A. Rutland and William M. E. Rachal (Chicago: University of Chicago Press, 1973), 175–176.

29. From James Madison to Thomas Jefferson, 17 October 1784, *Founders Online*, National Archives, https://founders.archives.gov/documents/Madison/01-08-02-0064. [Original source: *The Papers of James Madison*, vol. 8, *10 March 1784–28 March 1786*, ed. Robert A. Rutland and William M. E. Rachal. Chicago: The University of Chicago Press, 1973, pp. 118–122.]

30. *Maryland Gazette*, December 2, 1783.

31. George Washington to the Marquis de Lafayette, December 8, 1784, *Founders Online*, National Archives, https://founders.archives.gov/documents/Washington /04-02-02-0140. [Original source: *The Papers of George Washington, Confederation Series*, vol. 2, *18 July 1784–18 May 1785*, ed. W. W. Abbot (Charlottesville: University Press of Virginia, 1992), 175–176.]

32. *Journals of the Continental Congress 1774 -1789*, vol. XXVII, May 11–December 24, 684.

33. The Marquis de Lafayette to George Washington, December 21, 1784, *Founders Online*, National Archives, https://founders.archives.gov/documents/Washington /04-02-02-0167. [Original source: *The Papers of George Washington, Confederation Series*, vol. 2, *18 July 1784–18 May 1785*, ed. W. W. Abbot (Charlottesville: University Press of Virginia, 1992), 226–228.]

34. Louis Gottschalk, *Lafayette in America*, First Bicentennial Edition (L'Espirit de Lafayette Society, 1975), 423.

35. Laura Auricchio, *The Marquis Lafayette Reconsidered* (Vintage Books, 2014), 130.

36. *Letters of Mrs. Adams, With an Introductory Memoir by Her Grandson, Charles Francis Adams* (Charles C. Little and James Brown, 1840), 257–258.

37. From Thomas Jefferson to James Madison, 30 January 1787, *Founders Online*, National Archives, https://founders.archives.gov/documents/Jefferson/01-11-02-0095. [Original source: *The Papers of Thomas Jefferson*, vol. 11, *1 January–6 August 1787*, ed. Julian P. Boyd. Princeton: Princeton University Press, 1955, pp. 92–97.]

38. To George Washington from Lafayette, 25 May 1788, *Founders Online*, National Archives, https://founders.archives.gov/documents/Washington/04-06-02-0260. [Original source: *The Papers of George Washington*, Confederation Series, vol. 6, *1 January 1788–23 September 1788*, ed. W. W. Abbot. Charlottesville: University Press of Virginia, 1997, pp. 292–295.]

39. Ibid.

40. The Marquis de Lafayette, *Memoirs, Correspondence and Manuscripts of General Lafayette*, vol 1., 237.

41. The Marquis de Lafayette to George Washington, March 17, 1790, *Founders Online,* National Archives, https://founders.archives.gov/documents/Washington /05-05-02-0159. [Original source: *The Papers of George Washington*, Presidential Series, vol. 5, *16 January 1790–30 June 1790*, eds. Dorothy Twohig, Mark A. Mastromarino, and Jack D. Warren (Charlottesville: University Press of Virginia, 1996), 241–243.]

42. The Marquis de Lafayette, *Memoirs, Correspondence and Manuscripts of General Lafayette*, vol. II, 328.

43. Auricchio, *The Marquis: Lafayette Reconsidered*, 220.

44. Auricchio, *The Marquis: Lafayette Reconsidered*, 244.

45. Lloyd Kramer, *Lafayette in Two Worlds, Public Cultures and Personal Identities in an Age of Revolutions* (University of North Carolina Press, 1996), 44.

46. To Thomas Jefferson from Gouverneur Morris, August 22, 1792, *Founders Online,* National Archives, https://founders.archives.gov/documents/Jefferson /01-24-02-0298. [Original source: *The Papers of Thomas Jefferson*, vol. 24, *1 June–31 December 1792*, ed. John Catanzariti (Princeton, NJ: Princeton University Press, 1990), 313–315.]

47. André Maurois, *Adrienne, The Life of the Marquise De La Lafayette* (McGraw-Hill, 1961), 287.

48. To George Washington from Lafayette, 9 May 1799, *Founders Online,* National Archives, https://founders.archives.gov/documents/Washington/06-04-02-0041. [Original source: *The Papers of George Washington*, Retirement Series, vol. 4, *20 April 1799–13 December 1799*, ed. W. W. Abbot. Charlottesville: University Press of Virginia, 1999, pp. 54–59.]

49. To George Washington from William Vans Murray, 17 August 1799, *Founders Online,* National Archives, https://founders.archives.gov/documents/Washington /06-04-02-0212. [Original source: *The Papers of George Washington*, Retirement Series, vol. 4, *20 April 1799–13 December 1799*, ed. W. W. Abbot. Charlottesville: University Press of Virginia, 1999, pp. 258–263.]

50. Ibid.

51. The Marquis de Lafayette to Martha Washington, February 28, 1800, Peters Family Papers.

52. To Thomas Jefferson from Marie-Joseph-Paul-Yves-Roch-Gilbert du Motier, marquis de Lafayette, April 8, 1808, *Founders Online,* National Archives, https://founders .archives.gov/documents/Jefferson/99-01-02-7814.

53. To James Madison from William Eustis, August 18, 1815, *Founders Online,* National Archives, https://founders.archives.gov/documents/Madison/03-09-02-0534. [Original source: *The Papers of James Madison*, Presidential Series, vol. 9, *19 February 1815–12 October 1815*, eds. Angela Kreider, J. C. A. Stagg, Mary Parke Johnson, and Anne Mandeville Colony (Charlottesville: University of Virginia Press, 2018), 539–542.]

54. *Evening Post*, August 7, 1824.

55. Cloquet, *Recollections of the Private Life of General Lafayette*, 179–180.

Chapter 2

1. James Schouler, *History of the United States Under the Constitution*, vol. 3, *1817–1831* (New York: Dodd, Mead & Company, 1885), 1–3.

2. Harold H. Burton and Thomas E. Waggaman, "The Story of the Place: Where First and A Streets Formerly Met at What Is Now the Site of the Supreme Court Building," *Records of the Columbia Historical Society, Washington, D.C.* vol. 51/52 (1951), 138–147.

3. Samuel Eliot Morison, *The Life and Letters of Henry Gray Otis, Federalist, 1765–1848*, vol. 2 (Boston: Houghton Mifflin, 1913), 205.

4. *A Compilation of Messages and Papers of the Presidents*, vol. 2 (New York: Bureau of National Literature, Inc., 1897), 574.

5. *A Compilation of Messages and Papers of the Presidents*, vol. 2, 579.

6. Morrison, *The Life and Letters of Henry Gray Otis*, 205.

7. *Portland Gazette*, March 18, 1817.

8. *Boston Centinel,* July 12, 1817.

9. Murray N. Rothbard, *The Panic of 1819: Reactions and Policies* (New York: Columbia University Press, 1962), 121.

10. Ibid, 11.

11. Thomas Jefferson to Charles Yancey, January 6, 1816, Founders Online, National Archives, https://founders.archives.gov/documents/Jefferson/03-09-02-0209. [Original source: *The Papers of Thomas Jefferson, Retirement Series,* vol. 9, *September 1815 to April 1816,* ed. J. Jefferson Looney (Princeton, NJ: Princeton University Press, 2012), 328–331.]

12. Hezekiah Niles, *Weekly Register,* February 21, 1818.

13. Charles Theodore Greve, *Centennial History of Cincinnati and Representative Citizens* (Chicago: Biographical Publishing Company, 1904), 571–573.

14. Gorham Worth to Thomas Sloo Jr., August 2, 1820, *Quarterly Publication of the Historical & Philosophical Society of Ohio* 4, no. 1 (January–March 1909), 32.

15. Ibid, 34.

16. Thomas Jefferson to John Adams, 10 December 1819, *Founders Online,* National Archives, https://founders.archives.gov/documents/Jefferson/03-15-02-0240. [Original source: *The Papers of Thomas Jefferson,* Retirement Series, vol. 15, *1 September 1819 to 31 May 1820,* ed. J. Jefferson Looney. Princeton: Princeton University Press, 2018, pp. 271–273.]

17. Glover Moore, *The Missouri Controversy, 1819–1821* (Lexington: University of Kentucky Press, 1953), 33.

18. *Acts Passed at the Twenty-Eighth Session of the General Assembly of the Commonwealth of Kentucky* (Frankfort, KY: Kendall and Russell, 1820), 989.

19. David Johnson, *John Randolph of Roanoke* (Louisiana State University Press, 2012), 185.

20. Thomas H. Benton, *Historical and Legal Examination of That Part of the Decision of the Supreme Court in the Dred Scott Case* (New York: D. Appleton and Company, 1857), 94.

21. Abner Lacock to James Monroe, January 30, 1820. Appendix to *The Congressional Globe, Sketches of the Debates and Proceedings of the Second Session of the Thirtieth Congress* (Blair and Rives, 1849), 64.

22. Henry Clay to Adam Beatty, January 22, 1820. Calvin Colton, *The Life, Correspondence and Speeches of Henry Clay,* vol. IV (A.S. Barnes, 1857), 61.

23. Thomas Jefferson to John Holmes, April 22, 1820, *Founders Online,* National Archives, https://founders.archives.gov/documents/Jefferson/03-15-02-0518. [Original source: *The Papers of Thomas Jefferson,* Retirement Series, vol. 15, *1 September 1819 to 31 May 1820,* ed. J. Jefferson Looney (Princeton, NJ: Princeton University Press, 2018), 550–551.]

24. Lynn W. Turner, "The Electoral Vote Against Monroe in 1820—An American Legend," *Mississippi Valley Historical Review* vol. 42, no. 2 (1955), 250–273, https://doi.org/10.2307/1897643.

25. Thomas Jefferson to Albert Gallatin, October 29, 1822, *Founders Online,* National Archives, https://founders.archives.gov/documents/Jefferson/03-19-02-0076. [Original source: *The Papers of Thomas Jefferson,* Retirement Series, vol. 19, *16 September 1822 to 30 June 1823,* ed. J. Jefferson Looney et al. (Princeton, NJ: Princeton University Press, 2022), 104–105.]

26. Donald Ratcliffe, *The One-Party Presidential Contest: Adams, Jackson, and 1824's Five-Horse Race* (Lawrence: University Press of Kansas, 2015).

27. Worthington Chauncy Ford, *Writings of John Quincy Adams,* vol. VII, *1820–1823* (The Macmillan Company, 1917), 316.

28. Allan Nevins, *The Diary of John Quincy Adams, 1794–1845* (Longmans, Green and Co. 1929), 217.

29. George Dangerfield, *The Era of Good Feelings* (Rowman & Littlefield, 1989).

30. Hezekiah Niles, *Weekly Register*, May 25, 1822.

31. Robert V. Remini, *The Life of Andrew Jackson* (New York: Harper & Row, 1988), 145.

32. *The Letters of Wyoming, to the People of the United States, On the Presidential Election, In Favour of Andrew Jackson* (S. Simpson and J. Conrad, 1824), 4.

33. Article from the *N.Y. Statesman*, republished in the *Black Rock Beacon*, October 30, 1823.

34. Hezekiah Niles, *Weekly Register*, May 25, 1822.

35. Hezekiah Niles, *Weekly Register*, March 20, 1824.

36. *Nashville Whig*, quoted in Paul C. Nagel, "The Election of 1824: A Reconsideration Based on Newspaper Opinion," *Journal of Southern History*, vol. 26, no. 3, 315–329 (1960).

37. *Vincennes Western Sun*, November 23, 1822, quoted in Thomas W. Howard, "Indiana Newspapers and the Presidential Election of 1824," *Indiana Magazine of History*, vol. 63, no. 3 (1967), 177–206.

38. Hezekiah Niles, *Weekly Register*, July 26, 1823.

39. Paul C. Nagel, "The Election of 1824: A Reconsideration Based on Newspaper Opinion."

40. *Eastern Argus*, quoted in *National Intelligencer*, in Paul C. Nagel, "The Election of 1824: A Reconsideration Based on Newspaper Opinion."

41. Josiah Quincy, *Figures of the Past from Leaves of Old Journals* (Roberts Brothers, 1883), 99.

42. *National Advocate*, May 28, 1823.

43. *Richmond Enquirer*, quoted in *Milledgeville Georgia Journal*, February 25, 1823.

44. For a comprehensive analysis of the tensions surrounding the growth in early-nineteenth-century America, see Fred Somkin, *The Unquiet Eagle* (Cornell University Press, 1967).

45. Hezekiah Niles, *Principles and Acts of the Revolution in America* (Baltimore: Printed by W. O. Niles, 1822).

46. *Edwardsville Spectator*, August 17, 1822.

47. *Franklin Repository*, October 16, 1821.

48. *Gettysburg Compiler*, November 7, 1821.

49. *United States Gazette*, March 2, 1824.

50. *Lancaster Intelligencer*, November 23, 1822.

51. Philo-Jackson, *Presidential Election*, 26–27, quoted in Robert P. Hay "The American Revolution Twice Recalled: Lafayette's Visit and the Election of 1824," *Indiana Magazine of History*, vol. 69, no. 1 (1973), 43–62.

52. *The Letters of Wyoming, to the People of the United States*, 4.

53. Ibid, 5.

54. Hezekiah Niles, *Weekly Register*, January 24, 1824.

55. *Washington Republic*, quoted in *North Carolina Star*, May 23, 1823.

56. James Monroe to Marquis de Lafayette, March 16, 1821, Morgan Library and Museum, New York; James Monroe, *The Autobiography of James Monroe* (Syracuse, NY: Syracuse University Press, 2017), 32.

Chapter 3

1. Stendhal, *Memoirs of an Egotist*, translated by David Ellis (New York: Horizon Press, 1975), 66.

2. Extract of letter, dated April 25, 1821, printed in the *Christian Spectator*, quoted in the *Maryland Gazette, Western Carolinian*, October 25, 1821.

3. Stendhal, *Memoirs of an Egotist*, 66.

4. Victor de Broglie, *Souvenirs 1785–1870* (Paris: Calmann-Lévy Éditeurs, 1886), 326–327.

5. Victor de Broglie, *Souvenirs 1785–1870*, 326–327.

6. The Marquis de Lafayette to Charles and Lady Morgan, March 8, 1823, Lilly Library, Indiana University, Bloomington, IN.

7. Ibid.

8. The Marquis de Lafayette to Thomas Jefferson, January 11, 1808, *Founders Online*, National Archives, https://founders.archives.gov/documents/Jefferson/99-01-02-7183.

9. Sylvia Neely, *Lafayette and the Liberal Ideal, 1814–1824* (Southern Illinois University Press, 1991), 81.

10. The Marquis de Lafayette to James Monroe, January 22, 1822, New York Public Library, copy in Lilly Library.

11. The Marquis de Lafayette to James Monroe, September 27, 1822, New York Public Library, copy in Lilly Library.

12. Achille de Vaulabelle, *Chute De L'Empire Histoire des deux Restorations Jusqu'a La Chute de Charles X*. 10 Vols. (Perrotin, 1850), 275–276.

13. To George Washington from George Washington Motier Lafayette, August 31, 1795, *Founders Online*, National Archives, https://founders.archives.gov/documents/Washington/05-18-02-0405. [Original source: *The Papers of George Washington*, Presidential Series, vol. 18, *1 April–30 September 1795*, ed. Carol S. Ebel (Charlottesville: University of Virginia Press, 2015) 616–617.]

14. George Washington, *The Papers of George Washington*, vol. 1, 24–25.

15. Benjamin Henry Latrobe, *The Journal of Latrobe. Being the Notes and Sketches of an Architect, Naturalist, and Traveler in the United States, from 1796 to 1820* (New York: Appleton and Company, 1905), 57–58.

16. Maurois, *Adrienne, The Life of the Marquise De La Lafayette*, 406.

17. Cloquet, *Recollections of the Private Life of General Lafayette*, 35.

18. Stendhal, *Memoirs of an Egotist*, 67.

19. Kramer, 137–184.

20. Jeremy Bentham, *The Works of Jeremy Bentham*, published under the superintendence of his executor, John Bowring, Part XX (Edinburgh: William Tait, 1842), 526.

21. Frances Trollope, *Domestic Manners of the Americans* (London: Whittaker, Treacher, & Co., 1832), 33.

22. Celia Morris Eckhardt, *Fanny Wright: Rebel in America* (Cambridge, MA: Harvard University Press, 1984), 15.

23. Bernhard, Duke of Saxe-Weimar Eisenach, *Travels Through North America During the Years 1825 and 1826*, vol. 1 (Philadelphia: Carey, Lea & Carey, 1828), 41–42.

24. Frances Wright to Harriet and Julia Garnett, October 1820, in Cecilia Payne-Gaposchkin, "The Nashoba Plan for Removing the Evil of Slavery: Letters of Frances and Camilla Wright, 1820–1829," *Harvard Library Bulletin*, vol. 23, no. 2 (July 1975), 223–225.

25. Frances Wright to the Marquis de Lafayette, July 16, 1821, Bonaventure Lafayette Collection, University of Chicago Libraries, ms. 304.

26. Jeremy Bentham, *The Works of Jeremy Bentham*, 526.

27. Frances Wright to the Marquis de Lafayette, December 27, 1821, Bonaventure Lafayette Collection, University of Chicago Libraries, ms. 304.
28. Frances Wright to unnamed correspondent, December 18, 1822, New York Public Library.
29. Frances Wright to the Marquis de Lafayette, no date, 1822. Bonaventure Lafayette Collection, University of Chicago Libraries, ms. 304.
30. Frances Wright to the Marquis de Lafayette, March 21, 1822, Bonaventure Lafayette Collection, University of Chicago Libraries, ms. 304.
31. Frances Wright D'Arusmont, *Biography, Notes and Political Letters* (J. Myles, 1844), 13.
32. Frances Wright to the Marquis de Lafayette, December 27, 1821, Bonaventure Lafayette Collection, University of Chicago Libraries, ms. 304.
33. Frances Wright to the Marquis de Lafayette, December 29, 1821, Bonaventure Lafayette Collection, University of Chicago Libraries, ms. 304.
34. Albert Gallatin to John Quincy Adams, October 18, 1826, in *The Writings of Albert Gallatin*, ed. Henry Adams (Philadelphia: J.B. Lippincott & Co., 1879), 332.
35. Jacques Laffitte, *Memoires of Laffitte (1767–1844) Publies Par Paul Duchon* (Libraire De Paris Firmin-Didot, 1932), 135–136.
36. Marquis de Lafayette to Miss Sueuvelle, July 29, Lilly Library.
37. Sylvia Neely, *Lafayette and the Liberal Ideal, 1814–1824*, 195–197.
38. Laffitte, *Memoires of Laffitte*, 134–135.
39. Georges Washington de Lafayette to Tailhand, January 20, 1821, Lilly, Gardner Collection, Box 3, Folder 25.
40. Duc de Broglie, in George Morgan, *The True Lafayette* (J.P. Lippincott, 1919), 457.
41. Pierre Samuel Du Pont de Nemours to Thomas Jefferson, April 3, 1802, *Founders Online*, National Archives, https://founders.archives.gov/documents/Jefferson/01-37-02-0144. [Original source: *The Papers of Thomas Jefferson*, vol. 37, *4 March–30 June 1802*, ed. Barbara B. Oberg (Princeton, NJ: Princeton University Press, 2010), 170–171.]
42. *Annals of the Congress of the United States, Seventh Congress, Second Session* (Gales and Seation, 1851), 583.
43. Kathryn T. Abbey, "The Land Ventures of General Lafayette in the Territory of Orleans and the State of Louisiana," *Louisiana Historical Quarterly*, vol. 16, 1933.
44. Lafayette household account book, prepared by T.M. Pontonnier, appendix, January 30, 1824, Lilly Library.
45. Marquis de Lafayette to Thomas Jefferson, December 20, 1823, Chinard, Gilbert, *The Letters of Lafayette and Jefferson* (Johns Hopkins Press, 1929), 417-420
46. The Marquis de Lafayette to James Monroe, January 11, 1824, New York Public Library, copy in Lilly Library.
47. James Monroe to the Marquis de Lafayette, March 16, 1821, The Morgan Library and Museum.
48. The Marquis de Lafayette to John Trumbull, January 24, 1824, in Hezekiah Niles, *Weekly Register*, March 6, 1824.
49. The Marquis de Lafayette to James Thatcher, January 12, 1824, in Hezekiah Niles, *Weekly Register*, April 10, 1824.
50. William Willett, *A Narrative of the Military Actions of Colonel Marinus Willett, Taken Chiefly from His Own Manuscript* (New York: G. & C. & H. Carvill, 1831), 66–67.
51. The Marquis de Lafayette to Marinus Willett, July 13, 1822, Lilly Library.
52. The Marquis de Lafayette to Clara Baldwin, May 19, 1823, copy in Lilly Library.

53. William Lee to the Marquis de Lafayette, April 20, 1823, Lilly Library.

54. The Marquis de Lafayette to James Thatcher, January 12, 1824, in Hezekiah Niles, *Weekly Register*, April 10, 1824.

55. *Pittsfield Sun*, August 21, 1823.

56. Published in the *Baton Rouge Gazette*, November 9, 1822.

57. The Marquis de Lafayette to William Lee, December 20, 1823, Lilly Library.

58. John Jaquelin Ambler, *Journal of John Jaquelin Ambler of "Glen Ambler," 1801–1854*, Papers of the Ambler and Barbour Families, Accession #38-77, Special Collections Department, University of Virginia Library, Charlottesville, VA, 142–144.

Chapter 4

1. Ambler, *Journal of John Jaquelin Ambler of "Glen Ambler,"* 180–182.

2. Ambler, *Journal of John Jaquelin Ambler of "Glen Ambler"*; *Le Constitutionnel*, February 24, 1824.

3. James Brown to James Monroe, January 23, 1824, *Papers of James Monroe*, Library of Congress, Reel 8.

4. Lawrence Keith Fox, "The Political Career of James Brown" (PhD diss., Louisiana State University, 1946), 7–10, Louisiana State University Historical Dissertations and Theses, 8258.

5. Lawrence Keith Fox, "The Political Career of James Brown," 12.

6. John Quincy Adams, *Memoirs of John Quincy Adams*, 122–123.

7. Albert Gallatin to James Monroe, October 26, 1823, John Quincy Adams, *Memoirs of John Quincy Adams*, 323.

8. John Quincy Adams, *Memoirs of John Quincy Adams*, 186–187.

9. John Quincy Adams, *Memoirs of John Quincy Adams*, 187.

10. John Quincy Adams to James Brown, December 23, 1823, printed in *The Writings of James Monroe*, vol. 6, *1817–1823*, ed. Stanislaus Murray Hamilton (G. P. Putnam's Sons, 1902).

11. James Brown to James Monroe, January 10, 1824, *Papers of James Monroe*, Library of Congress, Reel 8.

12. *Annals of the Congress of the United States, Eighteenth Congress, First Session* (Gales and Seaton, 1856), 988.

13. *Annals of the Congress of the United States, Eighteenth Congress, First Session*, 1004.

14. *Annals of the Congress of the United States, Eighteenth Congress, First Session*, 1103.

15. *Annals of the Congress of the United States, Eighteenth Congress, First Session*, 1103.

16. *Le Constitutionnel*, March 10, 1824.

17. *Le Constitutionnel*, March 10, 1824.

18. John Jaquelin Ambler, *Journal of John Jaquelin Ambler of "Glen Ambler,"* 189–190.

19. The Marquis de Lafayette to James Monroe, March 18, 1824, New York Public Library, copy in Lilly Library.

20. James Brown to James Monroe, April 15, 1824, *Papers of James Monroe*, Library of Congress, Reel 8.

21. Ibid.

22. Ibid.

23. The Marquis de Lafayette to Josiah Quincy, May 16, 1824, printed in the *Lexington Weekly Press*, August 9, 1824.

24. James Brown to James Monroe, April 14, 1824, *Papers of James Monroe*, Library of Congress, Reel 8.

25. Vincent Nolte, *Fifty Years in Both Hemispheres, or, Reminiscences of a Merchant's Life* (New York: Redfield, 1854).

26. Thomas Jefferson to James Monroe, February 5, 1824, *Founders Online,* National Archives, https://founders.archives.gov/documents/Jefferson/98-01-02-4027.

27. James Brown to James Monroe, May 30, 1824, *Papers of James Monroe*, Library of Congress, Reel 8.

28. The Marquis de Lafayette to James Monroe, May 10, 1824, Morgan Library, New York, NY; copy in Lilly Library.

29. Lafayette to M. de Marcilly, June 3, 1824, Dean Collection, Cornell University Library. Box 25, Folder 46.

30. James Brown to James Monroe, June 11, 1824, *Papers of James Monroe*, Library of Congress, Reel 8.

31. Vincent Nolte, *Fifty Years in Both Hemispheres,* 299

32. Ibid, 300.

33. The Marquis de Lafayette to Jean Francois Girod, June 18, 1824, Morgan Library, copy in Lilly Library.

34. The Marquis de Lafayette to James Monroe, May 10, 1824, New York Public Library, copy in Lilly Library.

35. Frances Allyn to William Whitlock Jr., June 30, 1824, in *Reports of Committees*, 16th Congress, 1st Session, Vol 1, Index to House Reports, Second Session, Thirtieth Congress, Rep. No 12 4.

36. Franics Allyn to William Whitlock, July 5, 1824, New York Public Library.

37. Jonathan Mason, Jr., "Recollections of a Septuagenarian," 1866-1881, The Joseph Downs Collection of Manuscripts and Printed Ephemera, Henry Francis du Point Winterthur Museum.

38. Levasseur was also known as Andre-Nicolas Levasseur.

39. George W. Erving to James Monroe, *Papers of James Monroe*, Library of Congress, Reel 8.

40. George W. Erving to William H. Crawford, April 20, 1824, William H. Crawford Papers, Library of Congress.

41. Ibid.

42. George W. Erving to William H. Crawford, June 26, 1824, Crawford Papers, Library of Congress.

43. Ibid.

44. Ibid.

45. Ibid.

46. Charles Morris, *Autobiography of Charles Morris* (Naval Institute Press 2002), 72.

47. A. J. G. Perkins and Theresa Wolfson, *Frances Wright, Free Enquirer: The Study of a Temperament* (Harper & Brothers, 1939), 92.

48. Ibid, 95.

49. Ibid.

50. Ibid.

51. Ibid.

52. Ibid.

53. Ibid.

54. Ibid.

55. Ibid.

56. Ibid.

57. *The Leeds Mercury*, July 17, 1824.

58. The Marquis de Lafayette to Lady Morgan, August 4, 1824, Lilly Library.

59. *Le Constitutionnel*, July 17, 1824.

60. Auguste Levasseur to Émile Lafayette, July 20, 1824, Dean Collection, Cornell University. Box 68, Folder 12.

61. Marquis de Lafayette to Friedrich List, July 13, 1824, Lilly Library.

62. The Marquis de Lafayette to Mes Chéres Amies, August 11, 1824, Dean Collection, Cornell University. Box 26, Folder 3.

Interlude

1. *Painesville Telegraph*, July 24, 1824.

2. *Washington Gazette*, July 21, 1824.

3. Hezekiah Niles, *Weekly Register*, July 26, 1823.

4. *New-York Statesman*, quoted in the *Evansville Gazette* (Evansville, IN), August 12, 1824, quoted in *Indiana Magazine of History*.

5. *Richmond Compiler*, July 15, 1824, quoted in *Washington Gazette*, July 22, 1824.

6. *Elizabeth-City Star*, July 16, 1824.

7. Hezekiah Niles, *Weekly Register*, July 24, 1824.

8. *Richmond Enquirer*, January 27, 1824.

9. *Alexandria Gazette*, May 4, 1824.

10. *Richmond Compiler*, July 15, 1824, quoted in *Washington Gazette*, July 22, 1824.

11. Hezekiah Niles, *Weekly Register*, June 26, 1824.

12. *Elizabeth-City Star*, July 16, 1824.

13. *Washington Gazette*, July 22, 1824.

14. The Marquis de Lafayette to Mes Chéres Amies, August 11–14, 1824, Dean Collection, Cornell University. Box 26, Folder 3.

15. Ibid.

16. Ibid.

17. Mason, Jr., "Recollections of a Septuagenarian."

18. Auguste Levasseur to Émilie de Lafayette, August 9, 1824, Dean Collection. Box 68, Folder 14.

19. Ibid.

20. Ibid.

21. Mason, Jr., "Recollections of a Septuagenarian."

22. Auguste Levasseur to Émilie de Lafayette, August 9, 1824, Dean Collection.

23. The Marquis de Lafayette to Mes Chéres Amies, August 11–14, 1824, Dean Collection.

24. The Marquis de Lafayette to Mes Chéres Amies, August 11–14, 1824, Dean Collection.

25. The Marquis de Lafayette to Julie Garnett, August 14, 1824, Dean Collection, Box 26, Folder 4.

26. The Marquis de Lafayette to Mes Chéres Amies, August 11–14, 1824, Dean Collection.

Chapter 5

1. *Oswego Palladium*, August 7, 1824.

2. *National Advocate*, quoted in *Washington Gazette*, August 18, 1824.

3. DeAlva Stanwood Alexander, *A Political History of the State of New York*, vol. I, *1774–1832* (Henry Holt and Company, 1906), 282.

4. John Quincy Adams, *Memoirs of John Quincy Adams*, 236.

5. Auguste Levasseur to Émilie de Lafayette, August 24, 1824, Dean Collection, Cornell University. Box 68, Folder 17.

6. Jonathan Mason Jr., *Diary of Jonathan Mason, Jr.*

7. Auguste Levasseur to Émilie de Lafayette, August 24, 1824, Dean Collection.

8. *Alexandria Gazette*, August 21, 1824.

9. *Constitutional Whig*, July 27, 1824.

10. *Daily National Journal*, August 21, 1824.

11. Van Cortlandt Papers, Volume One, *The Revolutionary War Memoir and Selected Correspondence of Philip Van Cortlandt, Compiled and Edited by Jacob Judd* (Sleepy Hollow Restoration, 1976), 60.

12. *Evening Post*, August 17, 1824.

13. *Evening Post*, August 17, 1824.

14. *New York Merchant Advertiser*, August 17, quoted in *Pennsylvania Weekly Telegraph*, August 28, 1824.

15. Auguste Levasseur to Émilie de Lafayette, August 24, 1824, Dean Collection.

16. *Washington Gazette*, August 20, 1824.

17. *Washington Gazette*, August 20, 1824.

18. Auguste Levasseur to Émilie de Lafayette, August 24, 1824, Dean Collection.

19. Auguste Levasseur to Émilie de Lafayette, August 24, 1824, Dean Collection.

20. Bayles, W. Harrison, *Old Taverns of New York*, Frank Allaban Genealogical Company, 1915, 450.

21. *Constitutional Whig*, August 24, 1824.

22. *New York Commercial Advertiser*, August 17, 1824, quoted in *Constitutional Whig*, August 24, 1824.

23. *New York Daily Advertiser*, August 17, 1824, quoted in *Alexandria Gazette*, August 21, 1824.

24. The Marquis de Lafayette to James Monroe, August 18, copy Lilly Library.

25. Hezekiah Niles, *Weekly Register*, August 28, 1824.

26. Auguste Levasseur to Émilie de Lafayette, August 24, 1824, Dean Collection.

27. *New York Mirror, and Ladies Literary Gazette*, August 21, 1824, 31.

28. *Raleigh Register*, August 27, 1824.

29. *Independent Patriot*, September 25, 1824.

30. *New York Commercial Advertiser*, August 23, 1824, quoted in *Lafayette, Guest of the Nation, A Contemporary Account of the Triumphal Tour of General Lafayette, Through the United States in 1824–1825 as Reported by the Local Newspapers*, vol. I, compiled and edited by Edgar Ewing Brandon (The Oxford Historical Press, 1950), 100–101.

31. Benjamin Rush, *A Memorial Containing Travels Through Life or Sundry Incidents in the Life of Dr. Benjamin Rush* (Louis Alexander Biddle, 1905), 118.

Chapter 6

1. Josiah Quincy to the Marquis de Lafayette, March 15, 1824, in Brandon, *Lafayette, Guest of the Nation*, vol. I, 103.

2. The Marquis de Lafayette to Josiah Quincy, May 26, 1824, in Brandon, *Lafayette, Guest of the Nation*, vol. I, 103.

3. The Marquis de Lafayette to Josiah Quincy, May 26, 1824, in Brandon, *Lafayette, Guest of the Nation*, vol. 1, 103.

4. J. T. Headly, *The Chaplains and Clergy of the Revolution* (G. and F. Bill, 1861), 71–72.

5. *New York American*, August 23, 1824, in Brandon, *Lafayette, Guest of the Nation*, vol. 1, 63.

6. "Extract of letter from a Lady, now in Greenwich, Conn dated last evening" (August 26, 1824) quoted in *Richmond Enquirer*, August 27, 1824.

7. *London Courier*, September 29, quoted in *Washington Gazette*, November 30, 1824.

8. *New York Daily Advertiser*, August 20, 1824, quoted in *United States Gazette*, August 27, 1824.

9. *London Courier*, September 29, quoted in *Washington Gazette*, November 30, 1824.

10. *New London Gazette*, August 25, in Brandon, *Lafayette, Guest of the Nation*, vol. 1, 80.

11. *New London Gazette*, August 25, in Brandon, *Lafayette, Guest of the Nation*, vol. 1, 80.

12. *Connecticut Journal*, August 31, in Brandon, *Lafayette, Guest of the Nation*, vol. 1, 73.

13. Ibid.

14. *Connecticut Journal*, August 31, in Brandon, *Lafayette, Guest of the Nation*, vol. 1, 74.

15. *Harpers-Ferry Free Press*, September 2, 1824.

16. *New York Daily Advertiser*, August 25, 1824.

17. *Providence Gazette*, August 25, in Brandon, *Lafayette, Guest of the Nation*, vol. 1, 88.

18. *Springfield Weekly Republican*, September 8, 1824.

19. Josiah Quincy, *Figures of the Past from Leaves of Old Journals*, 88.

20. *Diary of Charles Francis Adams*, vol. 1, January 1820–June 1825, edited by Aida DiPace, David Donald (Belknap Press, 1964), 299.

21. Mason, Jr., "Recollections of a Septuagenarian."

22. Josiah Quincy, *Figures of the Past from Leaves of Old Journals*, 88.

23. John Graham to Richard Graham, September 13, 1824, Richard Graham Papers, Missouri Historical Society.

24. Josiah Quincy, *Figures of the Past from Leaves of Old Journals*, 90.

25. *Daily National Intelligencer*, August 31, 1824.

26. *Daily National Intelligencer*, August 31, 1824.

27. Ellen Woodbury, *Dorothy Quincy, Wife of John Hancock* (Washington: The Neale Publishing Company, 1905), 237–238.

28. Crosby identifies the girl as the daughter of "Dr. J. Ware" of Boston, brother of Henry Ware. It is possible she was in fact the daughter of Henry Ware.

29. Elizabeth Crosby to Emily Abbott, August 27, 1824, The American Revolution Institute of the Society of Cincinnati, Washington, DC.

30. Auguste Levasseur to Émilie de Lafayette, September 28, 1824, Dean Collection, Cornell University. Box 68, Folder 19.

31. Ibid.

32. John Graham to Orchard Graham, September 12, 1824, Richard Graham Papers, Missouri Historical Society, St. Louis.

33. *Diary of Charles Francis Adams*, 300.

34. Josiah Quincy, *Figures of the Past from Leaves of Old Journals*, 49–50.

35. Auguste Levasseur to Émilie de Lafayette, September 28, 1824, Dean Collection.

36. Josiah Quincy, *Figures of the Past from Leaves of Old Journals*, 56.

37. Ibid.

38. *Diary of Charles Francis Adams*, 300.

39. Ibid, 301.

40. *John Ware, Memoir of the Life of Henry Ware Jr.* (James Munroe and Company, 1846), 160–161.

41. *Daily National Intelligencer*, September 20, 1824.

42. Ibid.

43. Josiah Quincy, *Figures of the Past from Leaves of Old Journals*, 107.

44. John Ware, *Memoir of the Life of Henry Ware, Jr.* (James Munroe and Company, 1846), 160–161.

45. *Diary of Charles Francis Adams*, 301.

46. *The Recorder*, September 7, 1824.

47. John Adams to James Warren, April 16, 1783, *Founders Online*, National Archives, https://founders.archives.gov/documents/Adams/06-14-02-0260. [Original source: *The Adams Papers*, Papers of John Adams, vol. 14, *October 1782–May 1783*, eds. Gregg L. Lint, C. James Taylor, Hobson Woodward, Margaret A. Hogan, Mary T. Claffey, Sara B. Sikes, and Judith S. Graham (Cambridge, MA: Harvard University Press, 2008), 417–419.]

48. John Adams to James Warren, April 16, 1783, *Founders Online*, National Archives, https://founders.archives.gov/documents/Adams/06-14-02-0260.

49. John Adams to the Marquis de Lafayette, April 6, 1801, *Founders Online*, National Archives, https://founders.archives.gov/documents/Adams/99-02-02-4904.

50. John Adams to Marie-Joseph-Paul-Yves-Roch-Gilbert du Motier, marquis de Lafayette, August 22, 1824," *Founders Online*, National Archives, https://founders.archives.gov/documents/Adams/99-02-02-7912.

51. *Diary of Charles Francis Adams*, 303.

52. Ibid, 304.

53. Ibid.

54. Auguste Levasseur to Émilie de Lafayette, October 21, 1824, Dean Collection, Cornell University. Box 68, 21–24.

55. *Diary of Charles Francis Adams*, 304.

56. *Diary of Charles Francis Adams*, 305

57. Auguste Levasseur to Émilie de Lafayette, October 21, 1824, Dean Collection.

58. *Diary of Charles Francis Adams*, 305.

59. Auguste Levasseur, *Lafayette in America in 1824 and 1825, Journal of a Voyage to the United States*, translated by Alan R. Hoffman (Lafayette Press, 2007), 70.

60. *Proceedings, and Papers Relating to the History of the Town*, Lexington Historical Society, vol. 1 (Lexington, MA: Published by the Historical Society, 1889), 32.

61. Robert Gross, *The Minutemen and Their World*, revised and expanded edition (Picador, Farrar, Straus and Giroux, 2022), 238–240.

62. Auguste Levasseur to Émilie de Lafayette, September 5, 1824, Dean Collection, Cornell University. Box 68, Folder 18.

63. Auguste Levasseur to Émilie de Lafayette, September 5, 1824, Dean Collection.

64. The Marquis de Lafayette to Mes Chéres Amies, September 5, 1824, in Marie Joseph, Paul Yves Roch, and Gilbert Du Motier, *Memoires, Correspondance et Manuscripts du General Lafayette*, vol. 6 (H. Fournier Aine, Editeur, A Leipzig, Brockhaus & Avenarius, 1838), 170.

65. *Ontario Repository*, September 1, 1824.

66. Ibid.

67. The Marquis de Lafayette to Mes Chéres Amies, September 5, 1824, *Memoires*, vol. 6, 171.

68. Auguste Levasseur to Émilie de Lafayette, November 7, 1824, Dean Collection, Cornell University. Box 68, Folder 23.

69. *Valentine's Manuel of Old New York*, No. 5, New Series Edited by Henry Collins Brown (Valentines Manuel Inc., 1921), 101.

70. *New York American*, September 9, 1824, in Brandon, *Lafayette, Guest of the Nation*, vol. 1, 185; Levasseur, *Lafayette in America*, 87–88.

71. Anna J. H. Fitch to Sarah Smith Weed, September 9, 1824, Lilly Library.

72. Ibid.

73. *United States Gazette*, September 14, 1824.

74. Auguste Levasseur to Émilie de Lafayette, Nov. 7, 1824, Dean Collection.

Chapter 7

1. *Minutes of the Common Council of the City of New York*, vol. 14, 44.

2. Hall, John Elihu, *The Port Folio*, XVIII, Oct. 1824, 323

3. *New-York Evening Post*, September 18, 1824.

4. *New-York Evening Post*, September 18, 1824; Wayne Franklin, *James Fenimore Cooper: The Early Years* (New Haven & London: Yale University Press, 2007), 444.

5. *Evening Post*, September 15, 1824.

6. *New-York Evening Post,* September 11, 1824.

7. *New-York Evening Post*, September 13, 1824.

8. *New-York Evening Post*, September 8, 1824.

9. *New-York Evening Post*, September 9, 1824.

10. *New-York Evening Post*, September 8, 1824.

11. *New-York Evening Post*, September 8, 1824.

12. *New-York Evening Post*, September 8, 1824; *New York Commercial Advertiser*, September 11, 1824, quoted in Brandon, *Lafayette, Guest of the Nation*, vol. 1, 204.

13. *Albany Microscope*, printed in the *Pensacola Gazette*, December 4, 1824.

14. Fred Somkin, *The Unquiet Eagle*, 135.

15. *New-York Evening Post*, September 6, 1824.

16. *Washington Gazette*, August 24, 1824.

17. *New-York Evening Post*, Sept. 8, 1824.

18. *Minutes of the Common Council of the City of New York*, 1784-1831, vol. 14, 1824-25, City of New York, 1917, 123.

19. The Marquis de Lafayette to Émilie de Lafayette, September 14, 1824, Dean Collection, Cornell University. Box 26, Folder 8.

20. Charles C. Andrews, *History of the New York African Free Schools, from Their Establishment in 1787 to the Present Time: Embracing a Period of 40 Years* (Mahlon Day, 1830), 50–53.

21. Thomas Morgan, "The Education and Medical Practice of Dr. James McCune Smith (1813–1865), First Black American to Hold a Medical Degree," *Journal of the National Medical Association*, vol. 95, no. 7 (July, 2003).

22. Auguste Levasseur, *Lafayette in America*, 101–102.

23. DeWitt Clinton to Nicholas Fish, September 20, 1824, The Morgan Library and Museum, New York.

24. Evan Cornog, *The Birth of Empire, DeWitt Clinton and the American Experience, 1769–1828* (Oxford University Press, 1998), 147.

25. Peter L. Bernstein, *Wedding of the Waters, the Erie Canal and the Making of a Great Nation* (W. W. Norton & Company, 2006), 23.

26. Evan Cornog, *The Birth of Empire*, 115.

27. Donald Jackson, "George Washington's Beautiful Nelly," *American Heritage*, vol. 28, issue 2, 1977.

28. Benjamin Henry Latrobe, *Journal of Latrobe*, 57–58.

29. *George Washington's Beautiful Nelly: The Letters of Eleanor Parke Custis Lewis to Elizabeth Bordley Gibson, 1794–1851*, expanded edition, ed. Patricia Brady (University of South Carolina Press, 1991), 39.

30. Eleanor Parke Custis Lewis to Georges Washington de Lafayette, February 3, 1821, Dean Collection, Cornell University. Box 69, Folder 7.

31. *George Washington's Beautiful Nelly*, 9.

32. *George Washington's Beautiful Nelly*, 73.

33. Eleanor Lewis to Elizabeth Bordley Gibson, August 10, 1824, in *George Washington's Beautiful Nelly*, 158.

34. William Randall Waterman, *Frances Wright* (Columbia University, 1924), 85.

35. The Marquis de Lafayette to Émilie de Lafayette, September 14, 1824, Dean Collection.

36. *New York Evening Post*, September 15, 1824.

37. Ibid.

38. *Evening Post*, September 15, 1824.

39. James Fenimore Cooper, *The Traveling Bachelor, or Notions of the Americans* (Stringer and Townsend, 1856), 182.

40. Rodman Gilder, *The Battery* (Houghton Mifflin Company, 1926), 150.

41. James Fenimore Cooper, *The Traveling Bachelor*, 184.

42. *New-York Evening Post*, September 15, 1824.

43. Auguste Levasseur to Émilie de Lafayette, November 7, 1824, Dean Collection.

44. Auguste Levasseur to Émilie de Lafayette, November 7, 1824, Dean Collection.

45. The Marquis de Lafayette to Anastasie Lafayette, September 13, 1824, Dean Collection, Cornell University. Box 26, Folder 7.

46. Auguste Levasseur to Émilie de Lafayette, November 7, 1824, Dean Collection.

47. Auguste Levasseur, *Lafayette in America*, 105.

48. *Hartford Courant*, September 21, 1824.

49. Ibid.

50. Auguste Levasseur to Émilie de Lafayette, November 7, 1824, Dean Collection.

51. Ibid.

52. Ibid.

53. Ibid.

54. Ibid.

55. *Commercial Advertiser*, September 16–17, in Brandon, *Lafayette, Guest of the Nation*, vol. 1, 220–222.

56. Auguste Levasseur, *Lafayette in America*, 124.

57. Auguste Levasseur, *Lafayette in America*, 120–121.

58. Emma Willard, *A Plan for Improving Female Education* (Middlebury, 1819), 15.

59. Auguste Levasseur, *Lafayette in America*, 122.

60. Auguste Levasseur to Émilie de Lafayette, December 10, 1824, Dean Collection, Cornell University. Box 68, Folder 24.

61. The Marquis de Lafayette to Mathieu Dumas, September 27, 1824, Lilly Library.

62. Auguste Levasseur, *Lafayette in America*, 139–140.

63. Auguste Levasseur to Émilie de Lafayette, September 28, 1824, Dean Collection, Cornell University. Box 68, Folder 19.

64. Auguste Levasseur to Émilie de Lafayette, September 28, 1824, Dean Collection.

65. Ibid.

66. John S. C. Abbott, *History of Joseph Bonaparte, King of Naples and of Italy* (New York: Harper & Brothers Publishers, 1869), 335–336; Patricia Tyson Stroud, *The Man Who Had Been King, The American Exile of Napoleon's Brother Joseph* (Philadelphia: University of Pennsylvania Press, 2005), 11–15.

Chapter 8

1. *Philadelphia Inquirer*, April 5, 1824.

2. Ibid.

3. Charlene Mires, *Independence Hall in American Memory* (Penn Press, 2002), 67.

4. Auguste Levasseur to Émilie de Lafayette, September 28, 1824, Dean Collection.

5. The Marquis de Lafayette to Joseph Watson, August 18, 1824, Historical Society of Pennsylvania, copy in Lilly Library.

6. *United States Gazette*, August 20, 1824.

7. "Account of the Federal Procession in Philadelphia, July 4, 1778," *American Museum*, vol. 4 (July 1788), 57–60.

8. Harold Edward Dickson, *John Wesley Jarvis, American Painter, 1780–1840* (New York Historical Society, 1949), 21–22.

9. Committee of Arrangements Minutes, August 19, 1824, Pennsylvania Historical Society.

10. *United States Gazette*, October 1, 1824, Rembrandt Peale to the Committee of Arrangements, August 29, 1824, Lafayette Committee of Arrangements Correspondence, PHS.

11. *Philadelphia Inquirer*, September 30, 1824, and Lafayette Committee of Arrangements Minutes, September 14, 1824, Pennsylvania Historical Society.

12. *Lancaster Intelligencer*, September 24, 1824.

13. B. August to the Committee of Arrangements, Committee of Arrangements Correspondence, September 7, 1824, Pennsylvania Historical Society.

14. "A Citizen" to Lafayette Committee of Arrangements, September 7, 1824, Lafayette Committee of Arrangements Correspondence, Pennsylvania Historical Society.

15. Franklin Peale to Lafayette Committee of Arrangements September 17, 1824, Lafayette Committee of Arrangements Correspondence, Pennsylvania Historical Society.

16. Geo. Parkinson to Lafayette Committee of Arrangements, September 9, 1824, Lafayette Committee of Arrangements Correspondence, Pennsylvania Historical Society.

17. John Tremble to Lafayette Committee of Arrangements, September 17, 1824, Lafayette Committee of Arrangements Correspondence, Pennsylvania Historical Society.

18. Anonymous to Lafayette Committee of Arrangements, September 17, 1824, Lafayette Committee of Arrangements Correspondence, Pennsylvania Historical Society.

19. "A Citizen" to Lafayette Committee of Arrangements, September 7, 1824, Lafayette Committee of Arrangements Correspondence, Pennsylvania Historical Society.

20. A. Perier to Wm. Humphreys, October 12, 1824, Lilly Library.

21. *Philadelphia Inquirer*, September 25, 1824.

22. *Philadelphia Inquirer*, September 20, 1824.
23. A. Perier to Wm. Humphreys, October 12, 1824, Lilly Library.
24. Auguste Levasseur to Émilie de Lafayette, September 28, 1824, Dean Collection.
25. Auguste Levasseur to Émilie de Lafayette, September 28, 1824, Dean Collection.
26. Auguste Levasseur, *Lafayette in America*, 145.
27. The Marquis de Lafayette to Mes Chéres Amies, September 28, 1824, Dean Collection, Cornell University. Box 26, Folder 10.
28. Moses W. Jordan to Ruth Smith, October 10, 1824, Gilder Lehrman Institute of American Studies.
29. A.J.G. Perkins and Theresa Wolfson, *Frances Wright, Free Enquirer, The Study of a Temperament* (Harper & Brothers, 1939), 110.
30. Bernhard, Duke of Saxe-Weimar Eisenach, *Travels Through North America During the Years 1825 and 1826*, 91.
31. Cecilia Payne-Gaposchkin, "The Nashoba Plan for Removing the Evil of Slavery."
32. John Quincy Adams, *The Diary of John Quincy Adams, 1794–1845; American Political, Social, and Intellectual Life from Washington to Polk*, ed. Allan Nevins (Longmans, Green and Co, 1929), 330.
33. Marquis de Lafayette to Émilie de Lafayette, September 14, 1824, Cornell University. Box 26, Folder 8.
34. *New York Commercial Advertiser*, August 23, 1824, in Brandon, *Lafayette, Guest of the Nation*, vol. 1, 100–101.
35. Henry Clay to J. S. Johnston, September 19, 1824. *The Private Correspondence of Henry Clay*, 101–102.
36. The Marquis de Lafayette to Émilie de Lafayette, September 14, 1824, Dean Collection.
37. *Daily National Intelligencer and Washington Express*, October 18, 1824.
38. Auguste Levasseur to Émilie de Lafayette, September 29, 1824, Dean Collection. Box 68, Folder 19.
39. Auguste Levasseur to Émilie de Lafayette, September 29, 1824, Dean Collection.
40. A. Perier to Wm. Humphreys, October 12, 1824, Lilly Library.
41. Hezekiah Niles, *Weekly Register*, August 28, 1824.
42. *Philadelphia Inquirer*, August 27, 1824.
43. Timothy Pickering to John Jay, September 23, 1824, Gilder Lehrman Institute of American History.
44. A. Perier to Wm. Humphreys, October 12, 1824, Lilly Library.

Chapter 9

1. *United States Gazette*, October 1, 1824, in Brandon, *Lafayette the Guest of the Nation*, vol. II, 79.
2. *Alexandria Gazette*, September 7, 1824.
3. *Daily National Intelligencer and Washington Express*, September 4, 1824.
4. Memoirs of John Quincy Adams, 424.
5. Auguste Levasseur, *Lafayette in America*, 167.
6. Hezekiah Niles, *Weekly Register*, October 16, 1824.
7. *Richmond Enquirer*, October 14, 1824.
8. Auguste Levasseur to Émilie de Lafayette, January 25, 1825, Dean Collection.
9. Mannie Williams to Jared Sparks, October 19, Lilly Library.
10. *The Diary of John Quincy Adams*, 331.

11. Hezekiah Niles, *Weekly Register*, October 16, 1824.

12. Mannie Williams to Jared Sparks, October 19, Lilly Library.

13. Hezekiah Niles, *Weekly Register*, October 16, 1824.

14. Auguste Levasseur to Émilie de Lafayette, October 21, 1824, Dean Collection. Box 68, Folder 22.

15. Auguste Levasseur to Émilie de Lafayette, October 21, 1824, Dean Collection.

16. The Marquis de Lafayette to James Monroe, Baltimore, October 8, 1824, New York Public Library, copy in Lilly Library.

17. To George Washington from Pierre-Charles L'Enfant, June 22, 1791, *The Papers of George Washington*, Presidential Series, vol. 8, *22 March 1791–22 September 1791*, ed. Mark A. Mastromarino (Charlottesville: University Press of Virginia, 1999), 287–293.

18. *William Winston Seaton of the "National Intelligencer," A Biographical Sketch with Passing Notices of His Associates and Friends* (James R. Osgood and Company, 1871), 167.

19. *William Winston Seaton of the "National Intelligencer,"* 163.

20. *William Winston Seaton of the "National Intelligencer,"* 167.

21. *Alexandria Gazette*, October 16, 1824.

22. *Daily National Intelligencer and Washington Express*, October 14, 1824.

23. Bernhard Duke of Saxe-Weimar-Eisenach, *Travels Through North America During the Years 1825 and 1826*, vol. I (Carey, Lea & Carey, 1828), 170; Auguste Levasseur, *Lafayette in America*, 189.

24. Auguste Levasseur to Émilie de Lafayette, January 10, 1825, Dean Collection. Box 68, Folder 28.

25. The Marquis de Lafayette to James Monroe, August 18, 1824, copy in Lilly Library.

26. Auguste Levasseur to Émilie de Lafayette, January 10, 1825, Dean Collection.

27. Auguste Levasseur to Émilie de Lafayette, January 10, 1825, Dean Collection.

28. Auguste Levasseur to Émilie de Lafayette, January 10, 1825, Dean Collection.

29. Auguste Levasseur to Émilie de Lafayette, January 25, 1825.

30. *Wilmingtonian and Delaware Register*, October 21, 1824, reprinted in *Delaware Advertiser and Farmer's Journal*, October 21, 1824.

31. *Washington Gazette*, October 16, 1824.

32. Anonymous letter describing Lafayette's visit to Arlington House, undated, Thomas and Martha Custis Papers, Tudor Place, Washington, DC.

33. *Richmond Enquirer*, September 10, 1824.

34. *Alexandria Gazette*, October 19, 1824.

35. Benjamin Hallowell, *Autobiography of Benjamin Hallowell, Caroline H. Miller, for His Children and Grandchildren, Written at the Request of His Daughter, in the Seventy-sixth Year of His Age* (Friends' Book Association,1883), 98–100.

36. *Harrisburg Chronicle*, September 6, 1824.

37. *Alexandria Gazette*, February 20, 1818.

38. *Lancaster Intelligencer*, September 23, 1818.

39. *Maryland Gazette*, August 26, 1824.

40. George Washington Parke Custis, *Recollections and Private Memoirs of Washington, by His Adopted Son, George Washington Parke Custis, with a Memoir of the Author, by his Daughter; And Illustrative and Explanatory Notes by Benson J. Lossing* (Derby and Jackson, 1860), 592–593.

41. *Washington Gazette*, October 27, 1824; Custis, *Recollections*, 593.

42. *Philadelphia Inquirer*, October 22, 1824.

43. Auguste Levasseur, *Lafayette in America*, 198–199.

44. Auguste Levasseur, *Lafayette in America*, 198–199.

45. The Marquis de Lafayette to Princess d'Hénin, October 26, 1824, Dean Collection. Box 26, Folder 12.

46. *Philadelphia Inquirer*, October 22, 1824.

47. *National Intelligencer*, quoted in *Lancaster Intelligencer*, November 9, 1824.

48. Robert Stevenson Coffin, *Oriental Harp, Poems of the Boston Bard* (Smith and Parmenter, 1826), 95–96.

49. *Tramp's Note Book, or, Some Things a "Tramp" Has Seen, Heard and Said*, compiled by A. F. Chaffee (Tramps Note Book Company, 1889), 16–17.

50. Celebration at Yorktown Records of the Virginia Auditor of Public Accounts, 1824–1825. Accession APA 692, State government records collection, The Library of Virginia, Richmond, Virginia.

51. John Foster, *A Sketch of the Tour of Lafayette, on His Late Visit to the United States* (A. W. Thayer, 1824), 209–210.

52. *Daily National Intelligencer*, October 28, 1824.

53. *Alexandria Gazette*, October 28, 1824.

54. *Alexandria Gazette*, October 28, 1824.

55. *Alexandria Gazette*, October 28, 1824.

56. William P. Taylor to Professor John Maclean, October 25, 1824, Lilly Library.

57. *Richmond Enquirer*, October 22, 1824.

Chapter 10

1. Celia Morris Eckhardt, *Fanny Wright Rebel in America*, 80–81.

2. The Marquis de Lafayette to Mes Chéres Amies, October 10, 1824, Dean Collection.

3. Eleanor Parke Custis Lewis to Georges Washington de Lafayette, October 7, 1824, Dean Collection. Box 69, Folder 13.

4. Ibid.

5. Eleanor Parke Custis to Elizabeth Bordley Gibson, October 22, 1824, in *George Washington's Beautiful Nelly*, 154.

6. Eleanor Parke Custis to Elizabeth Bordley Gibson, October 22, 1824, in *George Washington's Beautiful Nelly*, 154.

7. The Marquis de Lafayette to Thomas Jefferson, August 29, 1824, in *The Letters of Lafayette and Jefferson*, Gilbert Chinard (The John Hopkins Press, 1929), 420.

8. Lafayette to Thomas Jefferson, October 1, 1824, in Chinard, *The Letters of Lafayette and Jefferson*, 421.

9. Thomas Jefferson to the Marquis de Lafayette, September 3, 1824, in Chinard, *The Letters of Lafayette and Jefferson*, 420–421.

10. *The Papers of Thomas Jefferson*, Retirement Series, vol. 16, *1 June 1820 to 28 February 1821*, eds. J. Jefferson Looney et al. (Princeton, NJ: Princeton University Press, 2019), 144–145.

11. *The Papers of Thomas Jefferson*, Retirement Series, vol. 19, 609.

12. The Marquis de Lafayette to Thomas Jefferson, October 1, 1824, Chinard, *The Letters of Lafayette and Jefferson*, 421–423.

13. Thomas Jefferson to the Marquis de Lafayette, October 9, 1824, Chinard, *The Letters of Lafayette and Jefferson*, 423–424.

14. Auguste Levasseur, *Lafayette in America*, 215; Cynthia Beverley Ticker Coleman, *The Annals of Williamsburg*, an unpublished history of Williamsburg, 1875, The Tucker-Coleman Papers, College of William and Mary.

15. Levasseur, *Lafayette in America*, 216.

16. *Daily National Intelligencer*, November 1, 1824.

17. *Richmond Enquirer*, November 2, 1824

18. *Daily National Intelligencer and Washington Express*, November 5, 1824.

19. The Marquis de Lafayette to Thomas Jefferson, October 28, 1824, Chinard, *The Letters of Lafayette and Jefferson.*

20. From Thomas Jefferson to Richard Rush, October 13, 1824, *Founders Online*, National Archives, https://founders.archives.gov/documents/Jefferson/98-01-02-4620.

21. The Marquis de Lafayette to Mes Chéres Amies, November 1, 1824, Dean Collection, Cornell University. Box 26, Folder 16.

22. The Marquis de Lafayette to Mes Chéres Amies, November 8, 1824, Dean Collection, Cornell University. Box 26, Folder 17.

23. *Daily National Intelligencer and Washington Express*, November 8, 1824.

24. Auguste Levasseur, *Lafayette in America*, 234.

25. Jane Blair Cary Smith, *The Craysbrook Memoir, The Cary's of Virginia*, ca. 1684, Special Collections, University of Virginia Library, 69–78.

26. Jane Blair Cary Smith, *The Craysbrook Memoir*, 69–78.

27. Jane Blair Cary Smith, *The Craysbrook Memoir*, 69–78.

28. From James Madison to Dolley Madison, November 5, 1824, *Founders Online*, National Archives, https://founders.archives.gov/documents/Madison/04-03-02-0418. [Original source: *The Papers of James Madison*, Retirement Series, vol. 3, *1 March 1823–24 February 1826*, eds. David B. Mattern, J. C. A. Stagg, Mary Parke Johnson, and Katherine E. Harbury (Charlottesville: University of Virginia Press, 2016), 425–426.]

29. The Marquis de Lafayette to Mes Chéres Amies, November 8, 1824, Dean Collection.

30. From a letter published in the *Virginia Herald*, November 15, 1824.

31. *Richmond Enquirer*, November 16, 1824.

32. *Daily National Intelligencer and Washington Express*, November 13, 1824; *Virginia Herald*, November 15, 1824, in Brandon, *Lafayette, Guest of the Nation*, vol. III, 131.

33. The Marquis de Lafayette to Mes Chéres Amies, October 25, 1824, Dean Collection, Cornell University. Box 26, Folder 14.

34. Cecilia Payne-Gaposchkin, "The Nashoba Plan for Removing the Evil of Slavery."

35. Frances Wright, *Views of Society and Manners*, 197.

36. Israel Jefferson, "Life Among the Lowly No. III," *Pike County Republican*, December 25, 1873,

37. Thomas Jefferson, *Notes on Virginia* (M.L. & W. A. Davis for Furman & Loudon, 1801), 241.

38. Reply to the New Jersey Plan, June 19, 1787, *Founders Online*, National Archives, https://founders.archives.gov/documents/Madison/01-10-02-0036. [Original source: *The Papers of James Madison*, vol. 10, *27 May 1787–3 March 1788*, eds. Robert A. Rutland, Charles F. Hobson, William M. E. Rachal, and Frederika J. Teute (Chicago: University of Chicago Press, 1977), 55–63.]

39. From James Madison to Lafayette, ca. October 7, 1821, *Founders Online*, National Archives, https://founders.archives.gov/documents/Madison/04-02-02-0336. [Original source: *The Papers of James Madison*, Retirement Series, vol. 2, *1 February*

1820–26 February 1823, eds. David B. Mattern, J. C. A. Stagg, Mary Parke Johnson, and Anne Mandeville Colony (Charlottesville: University of Virginia Press, 2013), 405–407]; Thomas Jefferson to Edward Coles, August 25, 1814, *Founders Online*, National Archives, https://founders.archives.gov/documents/Jefferson/03-07-02-0439. [Original source: *The Papers of Thomas Jefferson*, Retirement Series, vol. 7, *28 November 1813 to 30 September 1814*, ed. J. Jefferson Looney (Princeton, NJ: Princeton University Press, 2010), 603–605.]

40. Thomas Jefferson to Edward Coles, August 25, 1814, *Founders Online*, National Archives, https://founders.archives.gov/documents/Jefferson/03-07-02-0439. [Original source: *The Papers of Thomas Jefferson*, Retirement Series, vol. 7, *28 November 1813 to 30 September 1814*, ed. J. Jefferson Looney. Princeton: Princeton University Press, 2010, 603–605.]

41. Cecilia Payne-Gaposchkin, "The Nashoba Plan for Removing the Evil of Slavery."

42. Cecilia Payne-Gaposchkin, "The Nashoba Plan for Removing the Evil of Slavery."

43. From James Madison to Lafayette, August 21, 1824," *Founders Online*, National Archives, https://founders.archives.gov/documents/Madison/04-03-02-0356. [Original source: *The Papers of James Madison*, Retirement Series, vol. 3, *1 March 1823–24 February 1826*, eds. David B. Mattern, J. C. A. Stagg, Mary Parke Johnson, and Katherine E. Harbury (Charlottesville: University of Virginia Press, 2016), 365.]

44. "Old Times at Montpelier," *Sioux City Journal*, November 23, 1902.

45. Levasseur, *Lafayette in America*, 242–243.

46. Eleanor Parke Custis Lewis to Elizabeth Bordley Gibson, November 22, 1824, in *Washington's Beautiful Nelly*, 155.

47. *Virginia Herald*, November 20, 1824, in Brandon, *Lafayette, Guest of the Nation*, vol. III, 142.

48. *Virginia Herald*, November 27, 1824, in Brandon, *Lafayette, Guest of the Nation*, vol. III, 143–146.

Chapter 11

1. *Southampton Herald and Ilse of Wight Gazette*, September 13, 1824.

2. *Middlesex Gazette*, November 24, 1824, in the (Greenfield, MA) *Recorder*, December 6, 1824.

3. David Ramsay, *The History of the American Revolution*, vol. II (John Stockdale, 1793), 355.

4. From George Washington to Israel Putnam, June 2, 1783, *Founders Online*, National Archives, https://founders.archives.gov/documents/Washington/99-01-02-11360.

5. James Brown to James Monroe, July 12, 1824, *Papers of James Monroe*, Library of Congress, Reel 8.

6. James Monore to Henry Richard Vassall Fox, 3rd Baron Holland, November 6, 1824, Gilder Lehrman Institute for American History.

7. *The Speeches, Addresses, and Messages of the Various Presidents* (Robert Desliver, 1825), 517–518.

8. Hezekiah Niles, *Weekly Register*, December. 4, 1824.

9. Rachel Jackson to Elizabeth Kingsley, December 23, 1824, *The Papers of Andrew Jackson*, vol. II *1821–1824*, Harold D. Moser, David R. Hoth, George Hoemann, editors (University of Tennessee Press, 1996), 456.

10. *William Winston Seaton of the "National Intelligencer,"* 166

11. Eleanor Parke Custis Lewis to Elizabeth Bordley Gibson, November 22, 1824, in *Washington's Beautiful Nelly*, 155–156.

12. Lafayette to Henry Clay, October 18, 1824, *Works of Henry Clay, Compromising His, Correspondence, and Speeches*, vol. IV, edited by Calvin Colton (Henry Clay Publishing Company, 1897), 155.

13. *North Carolina Star*, December 17, 1824.

14. *Daily National Intelligencer*, December 10, 1824.

15. "Letters of Frances and Camilla Wright, 1820–1829," *Harvard Library Bulletin*, vol. XXIII, no. 3 (July 1975), 221–251.

16. Frances Wright, *Views of Society and Manners*, 262–263.

17. *Washington Daily National Intelligencer and Washington Express*, December 11, 1824.

18. *Washington Daily National Intelligencer and Washington Express*, December 11, 1824.

19. The Marquis de Lafayette to Mes Chéres Amies, December 24, 1824, Dean Collection, Cornell University. Box 26, Folder 20.

20. Levasseur, *Lafayette in America*, 272.

21. *Washington Daily National Intelligencer and Washington Express*, December 11, 1824.

22. Cecilia Payne-Gaposchkin, "The Nashoba Plan for Removing the Evil of Slavery."

23. *The Diary of John Quincy Adams*, 332.

24. *Daily National Journal*, December 24, 1824.

25. Thomas Hart Benton, *Thirty Years' View, or the History of the Working of the American Government for Thirty Years, from 1820 to 1850*, vol. II (D. Appleton and Company, 1865), 187.

26. *The Diary of John Quincy Adams*, 332–333.

27. James Monroe to Joel Roberts Poinsett, December 13, 1824, Lilly Library.

28. *Abridgment of the Debates of Congress, from 1789 to 1856*, vol. II (D. Appleton and Company, 1857), 505.

29. *Register of Debates in Congress, Comprising the Leading Debates and Incidents of the Second Session of the Eighteenth Congress*, vol. I (Gales & Seaton, 1825), 28.

30. *Register of Debates, Second Session Eighteenth Congress*, 29.

31. *Register of Debates, Second Session Eighteenth Congress*, 29.

32. *Register of Debates, Second Session Eighteenth Congress*, 31.

33. *Register of Debates, Second Session Eighteenth Congress*, 31.

34. *Register of Debates, Second Session Eighteenth Congress*, 33.

35. George Washington to Elias Boudinot, March 18, 1783, in Thacher, James, *A Military Journal During the America Revolution* (Cottons & Barnard, 1827), 331.

36. *Register of Debates, Second Session Eighteenth Congress*, 35.

37. *Register of Debates, Second Session Eighteenth Congress*, 46.

38. *Register of Debates, Second Session Eighteenth Congress*, 51.

39. *Register of Debates, Second Session Eighteenth Congress*, 53.

40. The Marquis de Lafayette to James Monroe, December 23, 1824, New York Public Library, copy in Lilly Library.

41. Kathryn T. Abbey, "The Story of the Lafayette Lands in Florida," *Florida Historical Society Quarterly*, vol. 10, no. 3, 1932, 115–133.

42. The Marquis de Lafayette to Mes Chéres Amies, December 24, 1824, Dean Collection.

43. The Marquis de Lafayette to Mes Chéres Amies, January 31, 1825, Dean Collection, Cornell University. Box 26, Folder 25.

44. *Daily National Intelligencer*, January 5, 1825.

45. The Marquis de Lafayette to James Monroe, December 24, 1824, Lilly Library.

46. The Marquis de Lafayette to Mes Chéres Amies, December 24, 1824, Dean Collection.

47. Prosper Rudd to Don C. Brigham, February 1, 1825, Lilly Library.

Chapter 12

1. Auguste Levasseur to Émilie de Lafayette, January 10, 1825, Dean Collection, Box 68, Folder 28.
2. The Marquis de Lafayette to Clementine de Lafayette, December 25, 1824, Morgan Library and Museum.
3. *Washington Gazette,* January 3, 1825
4. Louis McLane to Catherine McLane, January 1825, McClane Papers LC.
5. William Plumer Jr. to William Plumer Sr., January 4, 1825; William Plumer Jr., to William Plumer Sr., January 11, 1825; William Plumer Jr. to William Plumer Sr., January 20, 1825, in *The Missouri Compromises and Presidential Politics, 1820–1825* (Missouri Historical Society, 1926), 127–133.
6. William Plumer Jr. to William Plummer Sr., January 20, 1825, in *The Missouri Compromises and Presidential Politics,* 132.
7. *Harrisburg Chronicle,* January 13, 1825.
8. Stanley F. Horn, "Some Jackson-Overton Correspondence," *Tennessee Historical Quarterly,* vol. 6, no. 2, 1947, 161–175.
9. *The Diary of John Quincy Adams,* 339.
10. Levasseur, *Lafayette in America,* 282.
11. *Daily National Intelligencer,* February 21, 1825.
12. Levasseur, *Lafayette in America,* 282–283.
13. Philip Shriver Klein, *Pennsylvania Politics, 1817–1832: A Game Without Rules* (The Historical Society of Pennsylvania, 1940), 183.
14. The Marquis de Lafayette to Thomas Jefferson, January 26, 1825, Chinard, *The Letters of Lafayette and Jefferson,* 430.
15. The Marquis de Lafayette to Mes Chéres Amies, January 20, 1825, *Memoires,* vol. 6, 193–194.
16. *Daily National Intelligencer and Washington Express,* February 8, 1825.
17. John Quincy Adams, *Memoirs of John Quincy Adams, Comprising Portions of His Diary from 1795 to 1848,* edited by Charles Francis Adams, vol. VI (J.B. Lippincott, 1875), 500.
18. Margaret Bayard Smith, *The First Forty Years of Washington Society, Portrayed by the Family Letters of Mrs. Samuel Harrison Smith, from the Collection of Her Grandson, J. Henley Smith,* ed. Gaillard Hunt (Charles Scribner's Sons, 1906), 186.
19. Margaret Bayard Smith, *The First Forty Years of Washington Society,* 186.
20. George Dangerfield, *The Era of Good Feelings* (Elephant Paperbacks Edition, 1980), 342.
21. *Washington Gazette,* February 9, 1825.
22. Margaret Bayard Smith, *The First Forty Years of Washington Society,* 186
23. Margaret Bayard Smith, *The First Forty Years of Washington Society,* 189.
24. Auguste Levasseur, *Lafayette in America,* 285.
25. *The Diary of John Quincy Adams,* 342.
26. Levasseur, *Lafayette in America,* 287–288.
27. Carleton Mabee, *The American Leonardo: A Life of Samuel F. B. Morse,* revised paperback edition (Purple Mountain Press, 2000), 21.
28. Carleton Mabee, *The American Leonardo,* 47.
29. Samuel Finely Breese Morse, *Samuel F. B. Morse, His Letters and Journals,* vol. I, ed. Edward Lind Morse (Houghton Mifflin Company, 1905), 205.

30. *Samuel F. B. Morse, His Letters and Journals*, 261.

31. *Samuel F. B. Morse, His Letters and Journals*, 261–262.

32. *Samuel F. B. Morse, His Letters and Journals*, 262.

33. *Samuel F. B. Morse, His Letters and Journals*, 262.

34. *Samuel F. B. Morse, His Letters and Journals*, 264.

35. *Samuel F. B. Morse, His Letters and Journals*, 265.

36. Samuel Griswold Goodrich, *Recollections of a Lifetime, or Men and Things I Have Seen, in a Series of Letters to a Friend*, vol. I (Miller Orton and Company, 1857), 410–411.

37. The Marquis de Lafayette to Samuel Morse, February 11, 1825, Lafayette manuscripts, Box 1, Folder 12, Hanna Gray Special Collections Research Center, University of Chicago Library.

38. Auguste Levasseur to Émilie de Lafayette, February 21, 1825, Dean Collection, Cornell University. Box 68, Folder 30.

39. Georges Washington de Lafayette Louis Gilbert Du Motier, Marquis de, 1779–1849, Washington, DC, to Francis Allyn, New York, February 17, 1825, Hanna Holborn Gray Special Collections Research Center, University of Chicago Library, Box 1, Folder 31.

40. Josiah Quincy, *Figures of the Past from Leaves of Old Journals*, 95.

41. *Diary of Charles Francis Adams*, 304.

42. E. E. Hume, "LA FAYETTE IN KENTUCKY (Continued)," *Register of Kentucky State Historical Society*, vol. 33, no. 104 (1935), 234–251.

43. Eleanor Parke Custis Lewis to Georges Washington de Lafayette, October 7, 1824, in Dean Collection, Cornell University. Box 69, Folder 13.

44. Ibid.

45. Eleanor Parke Custis Lewis to Georges Washington de Lafayette, November 29, 1824, Dean Collection, Box 69, Folder 14.

46. Eleanor Parke Custis Lewis to Georges Washington de Lafayette, November 29, 1824.

47. Eleanor Parke Custis to Georges Washington de Lafayette, n.d. 1825, Dean Collection, Box 69, Folder 10.

48. *George Washington's Beautiful Nelly*, 163.

49. Georges Washington de Lafayette to Francis Allyn Louis Gilbert Du Motier, Marquis de, 1779–1849, Washington, DC, to Captain Allyn, New York, February 17, 1825, Hanna Holborn Gray Special Collections Research Center, University of Chicago Library, Box 1, Folder 31.

50. *George Washington's Beautiful Nelly*, 163.

51. The Marquis de Lafayette to Thomas Jefferson, January 26, 1825, in Chinard, *The Letters of Lafayette and Jefferson*, 428–429.

52. *Fredonia Censor*, March 16, 1825.

53. Frances Trollope, *Domestic Manners of the Americans*, 183.

54. Cecilia Payne-Gaposchkin, "The Nashoba Plan for Removing the Evil of Slavery."

55. Bernhard, Duke of Saxe-Weimar Eisenach, *Travels Through North America*, 41.

56. Hezekiah Niles, *Weekly Register*, April 9, 1825.

Chapter 13

1. Auguste Levasseur to Émilie de Lafayette, undated, Dean Collection, Box 68, Folder 26.

2. Hezekiah Niles, *Weekly Register*, November 6, 1824.

3. Peter Horry and Mason Locke Weems, *The Life of Gen. Francis Marion* (Joseph Allen, 1852), 107.

4. Thomas J. Kirkland and Robert M. Kennedy, *Historic Camden, Part II: Nineteenth Century* (The State Company, 1926), 74–82.

5. The Marquis de Lafayette to Mes Chéres Amies, February 26, 1825, *Memoires*, vol. 6, 195–196.

6. *William Winston Seaton of the "National Intelligencer,"* 74.

7. *Charleston Daily Courier*, March 18, 1825.

8. *Weekly Raleigh Register*, March 11, 1825.

9. The Marquis de Lafayette to Mes Chéres Amies, March 5, 1825, *Memoires*, vol. 6, 196.

10. Auguste Levasseur, *Lafayette in America*, 306.

11. *Carolina Observer*, March 10, 1825, in *A Pilgrimage of Liberty; a Contemporary Account of the Triumphal Tour of General Lafayette Through the Southern and Western States in 1825, as Reported by the Local Newspapers*, compiled and edited by Edgar Ewing Brandon (The Lawhead Press, 1944), 35–36.

12. Kennedy Kirkland, *Historic Camden: Nineteenth Century*, 68; the modern Lynches River.

13. *Southern Chronicle*, March 19, 1825, in Brandon, *A Pilgrimage of Liberty*, 45–46.

14. *Southern Chronicle*, March 19, 1825.

15. *Charleston Daily Courier*, March 19, 1825.

16. *Charleston Daily Courier*, March 30, 1825.

17. Auguste Levasseur, *Lafayette in America*, 312; *Southern Chronicle*, March 19 in Brandon, *A Pilgrimage of Liberty*, 51

18. *The Papers of Thomas Jefferson*, vol. 10, *22 June–31 December 1786*, ed. Julian P. Boyd (Princeton, NJ: Princeton University Press, 1954), 310–313.

19. Brandon, *A Pilgrimage of Liberty*, 90–91.

20. Autobiographical sketch of Maurice Moore in Brandon, *A Pilgrimage of Liberty*, 58–59.

21. Auguste Levasseur, *Lafayette in America*, 314–315.

22. Juliet Ravenel, *Charleston the Place and the People* (The MacMillan Company, 1906), 445–449.

23. Levasseur, *Lafayette in America*, 325; *Charleston Courier*, March 21, in Brandon, *A Pilgrimage of Liberty*, 87–88.

24. *Savannah Georgian*, March 16, 1825, in Brandon, *A Pilgrimage of Liberty*, 92.

25. Pension Application of John Shellman, Southern Campaigns American Revolution Pension Statements & Rosters, transcribed by Will Graves. January 20, 2015, 23.

26. *Savannah Georgian*, March 21, 1825, in Brandon, *A Pilgrimage of Liberty*, 94–97.

27. John Stevens Diary, March 19, 1825, transcription in Georgia Historical Society, Savannah, Georgia.

28. *Savannah Georgian*, March 14, 1825, in Brandon, *A Pilgrimage of Liberty*, 92.

29. *Troy Sentinel*, April 5, 1825; *Savannah Georgian*, March 24, 1825, in Brandon, *A Pilgrimage of Liberty*, 105–106.

30. Autobiographical sketch of Maurice Moore in Brandon, *A Pilgrimage of Liberty*, 60–61.

31. *Georgia Journal and Messenger*, April 27, 1825.

32. *Savannah Journal*, March 24, in Brandon, *A Pilgrimage of Liberty*, 107–114.

33. *Savannah Journal*, March 24.

34. *Savannah Journal*, March 24, in Brandon, *A Pilgrimage of Liberty*, 106.

35. The Marquis de Lafayette to George Bomford, March 22, 1825, Georgia Historical Society.

36. Hezekiah Niles, *Weekly Register*, May 14, 1825.

Chapter 14

1. The Marquis de Lafayette to George Bomford, March 22, 1825, Georgia Historical Society.
2. Auguste Levasseur, *Lafayette in America*, 337.
3. Brandon, *A Pilgrimage of Liberty*, 128–129.
4. The Marquis de Lafayette to Mes Chéres Amies, March 28, 1825, Dean Collection, Box 26, Folder 33.
5. Auguste Levasseur to Émilie de Lafayette, May 7, 1825, Dean Collection, Box 68, Folder 34.
6. George Lamplugh, *Rancorous Enmities and Blind Partialities, Factions and Parties in Georgia Politics, 1807–1845* (University Press of America, 2015), 117–119.
7. Andrew Frank, "The Rise and Fall of William McIntosh: Authority and Identity on the American Frontier," *Georgia Historical Quarterly*, vol. 86, no. 1, 18–48.
8. Christopher D. Haveman, *River of Sand: Creek Indian Emigration, Relocation & Ethnic Cleansing in the American South* (University of Nebraska Press), 11.
9. Auguste Levasseur to Émilie de Lafayette, May 7, 1825, Dean Collection, Box 68, Folder 34.
10. Auguste Levasseur to Émilie de Lafayette, May 7, 1825, Dean Collection, Box 68, Folder 34; Auguste Levasseur, *Lafayette in America*, 342–343.
11. Auguste Levasseur, *Lafayette in America*, 343–344.
12. Thomas Simpson Woodward, *Woodward's Reminiscences of the Creek, or Muscogee Indians, Contained in Letters to Friends in Georgia and Alabama* (Barrett & Wimbish, 1859), 67.
13. Thomas Simpson Woodward, *Woodward's Reminiscences of the Creek*, 67.
14. Auguste Levasseur, *Lafayette in America*, 345.
15. Auguste Levasseur to Émilie de Lafayette, May 7, 1825, Dean Collection, Box 68, Folder 34.
16. Chilly McIntosh to George M. Troup, March Telamon Cuyler, Hargrett Rare Book and Manuscript Library, The University of Georgia Libraries, March 9, 1825.
17. Thomas Simpson Woodward, *Woodward's Reminiscences of the Creek*, 68.
18. *Charleston Daily Courier*, April 21, 1825.
19. Auguste Levasseur to Émilie de Lafayette, May 10, 1825, Dean Collection, Box 68, Folder 35.
20. Thomas Simpson Woodward, *Woodward's Reminiscences of the Creek*, 68
21. J. B. Chambers to Israel Pickens, April 2, 1825, Administrative Files of Governor Israel Pickens Papers, Alabama Department of Archives and History.
22. Auguste Levasseur, *Lafayette in America*, 348.
23. Auguste Levasseur to Émilie de Lafayette, undated letter, Dean Collection, Box 68, Folder 26.
24. Ibid.
25. Auguste Levasseur to Émilie de Lafayette, June 20, 1825, Dean Collection, Box 68, Folder 38.
26. Ibid.
27. Ibid.
28. *Cahawba and Alabama State Gazette*, April 9, 1825, in Brandon, *A Pilgrimage of Liberty*, 147–148.
29. Ibid.
30. *Cahawba and Alabama State Gazette*, April 9, 1825.

31. J. B. Chambers to Israel Pickens, March 31, 1825, Administrative Files of Governor Israel Pickens Papers, Alabama Department of Archives and History.

32. Receipt for items bought from Jackson & Swift of Mobile by the Lafayette Committee in preparation for General Lafayette's visit to Alabama, March 21, 1825; Receipt for items bought from Richard Corrie and Company of Mobile by the Lafayette Committee in preparation for General Lafayette's visit to Alabama, March 21, 1825. Voucher for money owed to Philip Flanagan of Cahaba by the Lafayette Committee, April 1825. Voucher for money owed by the Lafayette Committee, for the burial expenses for Joseph Tousant, April 6, 1825. Voucher for money owed to Robert Travers of Cahaba by the Lafayette Committee, April 1, 1825. Alabama Department of Archives and History.

33. *Cahawba Press*, April 16, 1825, in Brandon, *A Pilgrimage of Liberty*, 155.

34. Auguste Levasseur to Émilie de Lafayette, Dean Collection, June 20, 1825, Box 68, Folder 38.

35. Report of the Select Committee of the House of Representatives, March 3, 1827, 400.

Chapter 15

1. Georges Washington de Lafayette to Eliza Custis, April 7, 1825, Maryland Historical Society.

2. Auguste Levasseur to Émilie de Lafayette, June 20, 1825, Dean Collection, Box 68, Folder 38.

3. Ibid.

4. *Louisiana State Gazette*, April 27, 1825.

5. *Louisiana Courier*, April 13, 1825, in Brandon, *A Pilgrimage of Liberty*, 171.

6. The Marquis de Lafayette to Jacques-Charles Dupont De L'Eure, April 22, 1825, *Memoires*, vol. 6, 201–202.

7. *Louisiana Courier*, April 13, 1825, in Brandon, *A Pilgrimage of Liberty*, 171.

8. Auguste Levasseur, *Lafayette in America*, 365–367.

9. Jason Berry, *City of a Million Dreams: A History of New Orleans at Year 300* (University of North Carolina Press, 2018), 122; Auguste Levasseur, *Lafayette in America*, 374.

10. Auguste Levasseur, *Lafayette in America*, 367–369.

11. *Louisiana State Gazette*, April 25, 1825.

12. *The Courier*, April 18, 1825, in Brandon, *A Pilgrimage of Liberty*, 180.

13. The Marquis de Lafayette to Mes Chéres Amies, April 15, 1825, *Memoires*, vol. 6, 199–200.

14. Karen T. Abbey, "The Land Ventures of General Lafayette in the Territory of Orleans and the State of Louisiana," *Louisiana Historical Quarterly*, vol. 16, no. 3, July 1933, 372.

15. Cecilia Payne-Gaposchkin, "The Nashoba Plan for Removing the Evil of Slavery."

16. *The Papers of James Madison*, Retirement Series, vol. 3, *1 March 1823–24 February 1826*, eds. David B. Mattern, J. C. A. Stagg, Mary Parke Johnson, and Katherine E. Harbury (Charlottesville: University of Virginia Press, 2016), 482.

17. *Painesville Telegraph*, April 30, 1825.

18. *Diary of William Owen*, Vol. Indiana Historical Society, ed. Joel W. Hiatt (Bobbs-Merrill Company, 1906), 128.

19. Owen Gwathmey to "William," May 17, 1825, typescript, Gwathmey Family Correspondence, Filson Historical Society, Louisville, Kentucky.

20. *Diary of William Owen, Indiana Historical Society*, ed. Joel W. Hiatt (Bobbs-Merrill Company) 1906, 128.

21. Cecilia Payne-Gaposchkin, "The Nashoba Plan for Removing the Evil of Slavery."

22. Bernhard, Duke of Saxe-Weimar Eisenach, *Travels Through North America During the Years 1825 and 1826*, 82.

23. Ibid.

24. Cecilia Payne-Gaposchkin, "The Nashoba Plan for Removing the Evil of Slavery."

25. Andrew Jackson to William Claiborne, September 21, 1814, in *Correspondence of Andrew Jackson*, vol. II, *1814–1819*, ed. John Spencer Bassett (Carnegie Institution of Washington, 1927), 56–57.

26. John U. Rees and Don Troiani, *Black Soldiers in America's Wars: 1754–1865* (Stackpole Books, 2025), 86.

27. Cecilia Payne-Gaposchkin, "The Nashoba Plan for Removing the Evil of Slavery."

28. The Marquis de Lafayette to unknown, Lilly Library, February 23, 1825.

29. *Louisiana Courier*, April 19, in Brandon, *A Pilgrimage of Liberty*, 181–182.

30. The Marquis de Lafayette to Mes Chéres Amies, *Memoires*, vol. 6, April 15, 1825, 199–200.

31. Cecilia Payne-Gaposchkin, "The Nashoba Plan for Removing the Evil of Slavery."

32. *Courier*, April 20, 1825.

33. Cecilia Payne-Gaposchkin, "The Nashoba Plan for Removing the Evil of Slavery."

Chapter 16

1. Nolte, *Fifty Years in Both Hemispheres*, 321.

2. Ibid.

3. *Mississippi Gazette*, April 23, 1825, Brandon, *A Pilgrimage of Liberty*, 203–205.

4. The Marquis de Lafayette to Jacques-Charles Dupont De L'Eure, April 22, 1825, *Memoires*, vol. 6, 200–201.

5. *Daily National Journal*, August 16, 1824.

6. Frances Trollope, *Domestic Manners of the Americans*, 34.

7. *Knoxville Register*, May 13, 1815.

8. Cecilia Payne-Gaposchkin, "The Nashoba Plan for Removing the Evil of Slavery," 237.

9. The Marquis de Lafayette to Virginie (Lafayette), April 21, 1825, Dean Collection, Box 26, Folder 25.

10. Levasseur, *Lafayette in America*, 386–387.

11. Levasseur, *Lafayette in America*, 388.

12. Levasseur, *Lafayette in America*, 388–389.

13. Levasseur, *Lafayette in America*, 389–390.

14. The Marquis de Lafayette to Joel Poinsett, April 24, 1824, Historical Society of Pennsylvania, copy in Lilly Library.

15. Auguste Levasseur, *Lafayette in America*, 390.

16. The Marquis de Lafayette to Edward Coles, April 12, 1825, Chicago History Museum.

17. Edward Coles to the Marquis de Lafayette, April 28, 1825, Chicago History Museum.

18. Hamilton apparently changed his middle name to his mother's maiden name, Schuyler, upon relocating West.

19. A. K. Fielding, *Rough Diamond: The Life of William Stephen Hamilton, Alexander Hamilton's Forgotten Son* (Indiana University Press, 2021), 18.

20. Nathan Morse, Louis T. Caire, to Frederick Bates, April 28, 1825, Bates Papers, Missouri Historical Society.

21. 1825 Rough draft, Bates Papers, Missouri Historical Society.

22. 1825 Rough draft, Bates Papers, Missouri Historical Society.

23. Auguste Levasseur, *Lafayette in America*, 393.

24. *Missouri Advocate and St. Louis Public Advertiser*, April 29, in Brandon, *A Pilgrimage of Liberty*, 215–216.

25. *Missouri Advocate and Missouri Public Advertiser*, May 6, 1825, in Brandon, *A Pilgrimage of Liberty*, 216.

26. Bernhard, Duke of Saxe-Weimar-Eisenach, *Travels in America*, 96–97.

27. Levasseur, *Lafayette in America*, 397.

28. Henry R. Schoolcraft, *Travels in the Central Portions of the Mississippi Valley* (Collins and Hannay, 1825), 293–294.

29. J. F. McDermott, "William Clark: Pioneer Museum Man," *Journal of the Washington Academy of Sciences*, vol. 44, no. 11 (1954), 370–373, http://www.jstor.org/stable/24533301.

30. Levasseur, *Lafayette in America*, 395.

31. Sophie Radford De Meissner, *Old Naval Days, Sketches from the Life of Rear Admiral William Radford* (Henry Holt and Company, 1920), 23.

32. *Missouri Advocate and Missouri Public Advertiser*, May 6, 1825, in Brandon, *A Pilgrimage of Liberty*, 217.

33. The Emancipation of the Slaves of Edward Coles, October 1827, Folder 21, Box 3, Coles Family Papers, Historical Society of Pennsylvania.

34. "The Emancipation of the Slaves of Edward Coles," October 1827.

35. Edward Coles to Thomas Jefferson, July 31, 1814, *Founders Online*, National Archives, https://founders.archives.gov/documents/Jefferson/03-07-02-0374. [Original source: *The Papers of Thomas Jefferson*, Retirement Series, vol. 7, *28 November 1813 to 30 September 1814*, ed. J. Jefferson Looney (Princeton, NJ: Princeton University Press, 2010), 503–504.]

36. Thomas Jefferson to Edward Coles, August 25, 1814, *Founders Online*, National Archives, https://founders.archives.gov/documents/Jefferson/03-07-02-0439. [Original source: *The Papers of Thomas Jefferson*, Retirement Series, vol. 7, *28 November 1813 to 30 September 1814*, ed. J. Jefferson Looney (Princeton, NJ: Princeton University Press, 2010), 603–605.]

37. The Emancipation of the Slaves of Edward Coles, October 1827.

38. The Emancipation of the Slaves of Edward Coles, October 1827.

39. *Transactions of the Illinois State Historical Society for the Year 1927* (State of Illinois, 1927), 65–71.

40. Levasseur, *Lafayette in America*, 403.

41. Levasseur, *Lafayette in America*, 411.

42. Levasseur, *Lafayette in America*, 407–417.

43. *Illinois Gazette*, May 21, 1825, in Brandon, *A Pilgrimage of Liberty*, 220–222.

Chapter 17

1. James Parton, *Life of Andrew Jackson*, vol. III (Mason Brothers, 1860), 80.

2. *Republican Banner*, April 23, 1825.

3. Andrew Jackson to Samuel Swartwout, May 16, 1825, in *Some Letters of Andrew Jackson*, ed. Henry F. DePuy (American Antiquarian Society, 1922), 20–21.

4. G. W. Featherstonhaugh, *Excursion Through the Slave States*, vol. I (John Murray, 1844), 193.

5. Auguste Levasseur, *Lafayette in America*, 421.

6. *Republican Banner*, April 23, 1825.

7. *Republican Banner*, October 11, 1824.

8. *Republican Banner*, April 23, 1825.

9. Andrew Jackson to Samuel Swartwout, May 16, 1825, in *Some Letters of Andrew Jackson*, 20–21.

10. *Mississippi Gazette*, April 23, 1825, in Brandon, *A Pilgrimage of Liberty*, 205.

11. The Marquis de Lafayette to George Bomford, March 22, 1825, Georgia Historical Society.

12. James Parton, *Life of Andrew Jackson*, vol. III, 64–65.

13. James Parton, *Life of Andrew Jackson*, vol. III, 72.

14. James Parton, *Life of Andrew Jackson*, vol. III, 73.

15. *Knoxville Register*, May 13, 1825.

16. *Republican Banner*, May 7, 1825.

17. Robert Baird, *View of the Valley of the Mississippi, or, The Emigrant's and Traveller's Guide to the West* (H. S. Tanner, 1834), 209.

18. Auguste Levasseur, *Lafayette in America*, 422.

19. Pension Application of John Hagey (Hagar) R4428, transcribed and annotated by C. Leon Harris, September 2015; *Knoxville Register*, May 27, 1825; Auguste Levasseur, *Lafayette in America*, 422.

20. "Personal Memoirs of James Norman Smith, 1871," University of Memphis Digital Commons (2022). Documents 3, 88.

21. *Philadelphia Columbian Observer*, quoted in the *Louisville Public Advertiser*, December 6, 1823; Robert Hay, "The American Revolution Twice Recalled: Lafayette's Visit and the Election of 1824," in *Indiana Magazine of History*, vol. 69, no. 1 (March 1973).

22. *Republican Banner*, May 7, 1825.

23. *Republican Banner*, May 7, 1825.

24. Nashville Whig May 7-14, 1825, in Brandon, Pilgrimage of Liberty, 244.

25. Charles Sydnor, *The Development of Southern Sectionalism, 1819–1848* (Louisiana State Press), 71.

26. *Republican Banner*, May 14, 1825.

27. *Republican Banner*, April 16, 1825; Auguste Levasseur, *Lafayette in America*, 426–427.

28. Auguste Levasseur, *Lafayette in America*, 427.

29. Augustus C. Buell, *History of Andrew Jackson*, vol. II (Charles Scribner's Sons, 1904), 178.

30. Levasseur, *Lafayette in America*, 428.

31. *Village Messenger*, originally printed in the *National Intelligencer*, February 11, 1824.

32. *Knoxville Register*, May 27, 1825.

33. Levasseur, *Lafayette in America*, 429.

Chapter 18

1. Thomas Jefferson, *Notes on Virginia*, 14.

2. Diary entry: October 22, 1770, *Founders Online*, National Archives, https://founders.archives.gov/documents/Washington/01-02-02-0005-0029-0018. [Original source: *The Diaries of George Washington*, vol. 2, *14 January 1766–31 December 1770*, ed. Donald Jackson (Charlottesville: University Press of Virginia, 1976), 295–297.]

3. "Sinking of the Mechanic, Captain Hall's Narrative, April 25, 1859," in *Ohio Archeological and Historical Publication*, XXIX (Ohio Arch and Historical Society, 1920), 250.

4. Auguste Levasseur to Émilie de Lafayette, May 10, 1825, Dean Collection, Box 68, Folders 34–37.

5. Levasseur to Émilie de Lafayette, May 10, 1825, Cornell University, Dean Collection, Box 68, Folder 34.

6. "Sinking of the Mechanic," 197.

7. "Sinking of the Mechanic," 197.

8. Auguste Levasseur to Émilie de Lafayette, May 10, 1825, Dean Collection, Box 68, Folders 34–37.

9. Auguste Levasseur to Émilie de Lafayette, May 10, 1825, Dean Collection, Cornell University, Folder 36.

10. Levasseur, *Lafayette in America*, 431.

11. Levasseur, *Lafayette in America*, 423.

12. Levasseur, *Lafayette in America*, 432.

13. Auguste Levasseur to Émilie de Lafayette, May 10, 1825, Dean Collection, Box 68, Folder 35.

14. Auguste Levasseur to Émilie de Lafayette, May 10, 1825, Dean Collection, Cornell University, Box 68, Folder 34.

15. Auguste Levasseur to Émilie de Lafayette, May 10, 1825.

16. C. N. Thompson, "General La Fayette in Indiana," *Indiana Magazine of History*, vol. 24, no. 2 (1928), 57–77.

17. Pension Application of Thomas Turnham, S36831, transcribed by Will Graves, January 2012.

18. *Illinois Gazette*, May 14, 1825, in Brandon, *A Pilgrimage of Liberty*, 255

19. Auguste Levasseur, *Lafayette in America*, 435.

20. Marquis de Lafayette to Peter Du Ponceau, May 10, 1825, Lilly Library.

21. *Louisville Public Advertiser*, May 18, 1825, in Brandon, *A Pilgrimage of Liberty*, 463.

22. E. E. Hume, "LA FAYETTE IN KENTUCKY (Continued)."

23. Marquis de Lafayette to Peter Du Ponceau, May 10, 1825, Lilly Library; *Evening Post*, May 27, 1825.

24. William Hurst to William Bodley, May 10, 1825, Filson Historical Society, Louisville, Kentucky.

25. E. E. Hume, "LA FAYETTE IN KENTUCKY (Continued)."

26. The Marquis de Lafayette to Mes Chéres Enfants, May 22, 1825, *Memoires*, vol. 6, 205.

27. *Eastern Argus*, July 14, 1825.

28. Samuel F. B. Morse, *His Letters and Journals*, 273.

Chapter 19

1. *Indiana Palladium*, vol. 1, no. 5, February 4, 1825.

2. From George Washington to Richard Henderson, June 19, 1788, *Founders Online*, National Archives, https://founders.archives.gov/documents/Washington/04-06 -02-0304. [Original source: *The Papers of George Washington*, Confederation Series, vol. 6, *1 January 1788–23 September 1788*, ed. W. W. Abbot (Charlottesville: University Press of Virginia, 1997), 339–342.]

3. The Marquis de Lafayette to M. Roche, April 24, 1825, Lilly Library.

4. *Western Sun and General Advertiser*, April 16, 1825.

5. *Indiana Palladium*, May 13, 1825.

6. *Indiana Palladium*, 1825, Messages and Papers of James Brown Ray, Indiana State Library, 46.

7. *Louisville Public Advertiser*, May 18, 1825, in Brandon, *A Pilgrimage of Liberty*, 259.

8. *Western Citizen*, October 30, 1824.

9. Ibid.

10. J. J. Weisert, "The Chief Competitor of Drake's City Theatre," *Register of the Kentucky Historical Society*, vol 66, no. 2 (1968), 159–167; *Republican Banner*, May 28, 1825.

11. John Thompson Gray, *A Kentucky Chronicle* (The Neale Publishing Company), 118–120.

12. *Louisville Public Advertiser*, May 18, in Brandon, *A Pilgrimage of Liberty*, 269.

13. Cecilia Payne-Gaposchkin, "The Nashoba Plan for Removing the Evil of Slavery," 239.

14. Ibid, 240.

15. Ibid, 243.

16. Ibid, 242.

17. *Argus of Western America*, May 18, 1825, in Brandon, *A Pilgrimage of Liberty*, 279.

18. Alice Elizabeth Trabue, *A Corner in Celebrities* (Geo. G Fetter Company, 1922), 24.

19. *Frankfort Argus*, May 18, 1825.

20. Auguste Levasseur, *Lafayette in America*, 440–441.

21. E. E. Hume, "LA FAYETTE IN KENTUCKY (Continued)."

22. *Kentucky Gazette*, April 28, 1825.

23. The Marquis de Lafayette to Nathalie de Lafayette, May 22, 1825, *Memoires*, vol. 6, 204–205.

24. Levasseur, *Lafayette in America*, 441.

25. *Lexington Weekly Press*, May 30, 1825.

26. *Reporter*, May 23, 1825, in Brandon, *A Pilgrimage of Liberty*, 304.

27. *Reporter*, May 23, 1825, in Brandon, *A Pilgrimage of Liberty*, 293.

28. E. E. Hume, "LA FAYETTE IN KENTUCKY (Continued)."

29. Edgar Erskine Hume, "LA FAYETTE IN KENTUCKY," *Register of Kentucky State Historical Society* vol. 33, no. 103 (1935), 131.

30. E. E. Hume, "LA FAYETTE IN KENTUCKY (Continued)."

31. Ebenezer Hiram Stedman, *Bluegrass Craftsman*, 75.

32. Ibid.

33. Frances Trollope, *Domestic Manners of the Americans*, 51.

34. Brandon, *A Pilgrimage of Liberty*, 319.

35. Joel J. Orosz, *Curators and Culture, The Museum Movement in America, 1740–1870* (University of Alabama Press, 1990), 127–128.

36. *Cincinnati Advertiser*, May 25, in Brandon, *A Pilgrimage of Liberty*, 332.

37. *Liberty Hall and Cincinnati Gazette*, May 21, 1825, Ibid, 338.

38. Auguste Levasseur, *Lafayette in America*, 452.

39. John James Dufour, *The American Vine Dresser's Guide* (S. J. Browne, 1825), 7–8.

40. To George Washington from Jean-Jacques Dufour, 19 December 1796, *Founders Online*, National Archives, https://founders.archives.gov/documents/Washington/05-21-02-0171. [Original source: *The Papers of George Washington*, Presidential Series, vol. 21, *22 September 1796–3 March 1797*, ed. Adrina Garbooshian-Huggins. Charlottesville: University of Virginia Press, 2020, pp. 397–399.]

41. To Thomas Jefferson from John James Dufour, January 15, 1802, *Founders Online*, National Archives, https://founders.archives.gov/documents/Jefferson/01-36-02-0227. [Original source: *The Papers of Thomas Jefferson*, vol. 36, *1 December 1801–3 March 1802*, ed. Barbara B. Oberg (Princeton, NJ: Princeton University Press, 2009), 373–376.]

42. Auguste Levasseur, *Lafayette in America*, 452–453.

43. Levasseur, *Lafayette in America*, 452.

44. Levasseur, *Lafayette in America*, 452–453.

45. Brandon, *A Pilgrimage of Liberty*, 350.
46. *Free Press*, in Brandon, *A Pilgrimage of Liberty*, 351–352.
47. *Genius of Liberty*, June 7, in Brandon, *A Pilgrimage of Liberty*, 366.
48. *Genius of Liberty*, June 7, in Brandon, *A Pilgrimage of Liberty*, 370.
49. *Pittsburg Dispatch*, May 5, 1889.

Chapter 20

1. Cecilia Payne-Gaposchkin, "The Nashoba Plan for Removing the Evil of Slavery."
2. *United States Gazette*, June 10, 1825.
3. Cecilia Payne-Gaposchkin, "The Nashoba Plan for Removing the Evil of Slavery."
4. Ibid.
5. Ibid.
6. Ibid.
7. Ibid.
8. Ibid.
9. *Pittsburg Gazette*, June 3, in Brandon, *A Pilgrimage of Liberty*, 380.
10. *Buffalo Emporium and General Advertiser*, June 11, 1825.
11. The Marquis de Lafayette to Elisha Ely, May 30, 1825, Lilly Library.
12. C. Hale Sipe, *History of Butler County, Pennsylvania* (Historical Publishing Company, 1927) 356–357.
13. *Crawford Messenger*, June 9, 1825, in Brandon, *A Pilgrimage of Liberty*, 389.
14. Andrew W. Young, *History of Chautauqua County* (Matthews and Warren, 1875), 125.
15. *Fredonia Censor*, June 9, 1825, in Brandon, *A Pilgrimage of Liberty*, 397.
16. Auguste Levasseur, *Lafayette in America*, 475.
17. Orsamus Turner, *Pioneer History of the Holland Purchase of Western New York* (Jewett Thomas, 1849), 305.
18. Auguste Levasseur, *Lafayette in America*, 475.
19. Auguste Levasseur, *Lafayette in America*, 477.
20. Peter L. Bernstein, *Wedding of the Waters, the Erie Canal and the Making of a Great Nation* (W. W. Norton, 2005) 279–281.
21. *Charleston Daily Courier*, July 23, 1825.
22. Auguste Levasseur, *Lafayette in America*, 479.
23. Auguste Levasseur, *Lafayette in America*, 480.
24. *Rochester Telegraph*, June 14, 1825, in Brandon, *A Pilgrimage of Liberty*, 407.
25. *Republican*, June 15, 1825, in Brandon, *A Pilgrimage of Liberty*, 410.
26. *Onondaga Register*, June 15, 1825, in Brandon, *A Pilgrimage of Liberty*, 417.
27. *Oneida Observer*, June 14, 1825, in Brandon, *A Pilgrimage of Liberty*, 421.
28. Auguste Levasseur, *Lafayette in America*, 482–483.
29. Auguste Levasseur, *Lafayette in America*, 483.
30. Upon leaving America in 1784, Lafayette had traveled back to France accompanied by a twelve-year-old Onondaga boy, Kayenlaha. Louis Gottschalk, *Lafayette Between the American & French Revolution, 1783–1789* (University of Chicago Press, 1950), 405, 433–434.
31. *The Magazine of American History with Notes and Queries*, vol. IV (A.S. Barnes and Company, 1880), 467.
32. Auguste Levasseur, *Lafayette in America*, 485.
33. The Marquis de Lafayette to Mes Chéres Amies, June 12, 1825, Dean Collection, Box 26, Folder 37.

34. The Marquis de Lafayette to Mes Chéres Filles, June 17, 1825, Dean Collection, Box 26, Folder 38.

Chapter 21

1. *Boston Patriot*, reprinted in the *Alexandria Gazette*, June 23, 1825.
2. Josiah Quincy, *Figures of the Past from Leaves of Old Journals*, 29.
3. Lafayette described himself as "being of a '76" since it was the year he enlisted; *Southern Chronicle*, March 19, 1825.
4. *Springfield Weekly Republican*, June 29, 1825.
5. The Marquis de Lafayette to Bunker Hill Monument Association, May 24, 1825, Lilly Library.
6. *Charleston Daily Courier*, January 25, 1825.
7. The History of the Bunker Hill Monument Association, 31–45.
8. The History of the Bunker Hill Monument Association, 31–45.
9. *Charleston Mercury*, February 1, 1825.
10. *Charleston Daily Courier*, January 25, 1825.
11. The History of the Bunker Hill Monument Association, 61–62.
12. The History of the Bunker Hill Monument Association, 80.
13. The History of the Bunker Hill Monument Association, 86.
14. The History of the Bunker Hill Monument Association, 102.
15. Kevin Butterfield, *The Making of Tocqueville's America* (University of Chicago Press, 2015), 173.
16. *Rhode Island Republican*, May 12, 1825.
17. Message from Bunker Hill Executive Committee, June 15, 1825, published in the *United States Gazette*, June 21, 1825.
18. Josiah Quincy, *Figures of the Past from Leaves of Old Journals*, 133.
19. *Lancaster Intelligencer*, July 26, 1825.
20. *Lancaster Intelligencer*, July 26, 1825.
21. Josiah Quincy, *Figures of the Past from Leaves of Old Journals*, 128–131.
22. Josiah Quincy, *Figures of the Past from Leaves of Old Journals*, 128–131.
23. *Eastern Argus*, June 23, 1825.
24. Sarah Harvey Porter, *The Life and Times of Anne Royall* (Torch Press Book Shop, 1909), 71.
25. *Lancaster Intelligencer*, July 26, 1825.
26. William Buell Sprague, *Annals of the American Unitarian Pulpit* (Robert Carter & Brothers, 1865), 84–87.
27. Josiah Quincy, *Figures of the Past from Leaves of Old Journals*, 137.
28. Auguste Levasseur, *Lafayette in America*, 491–506.
29. *Eastern Argus*, June 30, 1825.
30. The Marquis de Lafayette to Mes Chéres Filles, July 5, 1825, Dean Collection, Box 26, Folder 39.
31. The Marquis de Lafayette to Mes Chéres Filles, June 17, 1825, Dean Collection, Box 26, Folder 38.
32. Auguste Levasseur, *Lafayette in America*, 507–508.

Chapter 22

1. Josiah Quincy, *Figures of the Past from Leaves of Old Journals*, 143–145.

2. Lafayette to Mes Chéres Amies, March 5, 1825, *Memoires*, vol. 6, 196–197.

3. *Maryland Gazette*, July 28, 1825.

4. From John Adams to Charles Francis Adams, August 17, 1825, *Founders Online*, National Archives, https://founders.archives.gov/documents/Adams/99-03-02-4560.

5. Josiah Quincy, *Figures of the Past from Leaves of Old Journals*, 149.

6. Josiah Quincy, *Figures of the Past from Leaves of Old Journals*, 149.

7. (Concord) *Patriot*, June 27, 1825.

8. *Western Sun and General Advertiser*, October 30, 1824.

9. Jay Read Pember, *A Day with Lafayette in Vermont*.

10. (Concord) *Patriot*, June 27, 1825.

11. T. Wentworth to J. Burleigh, June 29, 1825, Lafayette College, Marquis de Lafayette Manuscripts Collection.

12. *Proceedings of the Massachusetts Historical Society, October 1908–June 1909*, Vol. XLII (Massachusetts Historical Society), 314–316.

13. *Commercial Advertiser*, July 6, 1825.

14. *Long Island Star*, July 7, 1825.

15. Walt Whitman, *Lafayette in Brooklyn*.

16. *Vermont Republican and Journal*, July 25, 1825.

17. *New-York Evening Post*, July 5, 1825.

18. *Philadelphia Inquirer*, July 26, 1825.

19. Samuel F. B. Morse; *His Letters and Journals*, 267.

20. Samuel F. B. Morse; *His Letters and Journals*, 267.

21. Cecilia Payne-Gaposchkin, "The Nashoba Plan for Removing the Evil of Slavery," 244.

22. Celia Morris Eckhardt, *Fanny Wright, Rebel in America*, 104–106.

23. From Thomas Jefferson to Frances Wright, August 7, 1825, *Founders Online*, National Archives, https://founders.archives.gov/documents/Jefferson/98-01-02-5449.

24. Cecilia Payne-Gaposchkin, "The Nashoba Plan for Removing the Evil of Slavery," 246.

25. Wright, Camilla to Julia Garnet, July 9, 1825, in Cecilia Helena Payne-Gaposchkin, "The Nashoba Plan for Removing the Evil of Slavery: Letters of Frances and Camilla Wright, 1820–1829," *Harvard Library Bulletin*, vol. XXIII, no. 3 (July 1975), 250.

26. Ibid.

27. *George Washington's Beautiful Nelly*, 167.

28. Hezekiah Niles, *Weekly Register*, July 23, 1825.

29. Auguste Levasseur, *Lafayette in America*, 528.

30. *Wyoming Herald*, June 29, 1825.

31. *The Aurora*, reprinted in the *Alexandria Gazette,* July 21, 1825.

32. *Charleston Daily Courier,* August 2, 1825

33. Lafayette's Visit to Germantown, July 20, 1825.

34. Ibid.

35. *Delaware Advertiser and Farmer's Journal*, July 21, 1825.

36. E.I. du Pont's daughter's album and scrapbook, Hagley Museum.

37. *Eastern Argus*, July 29, 1825.

38. Augustus Loucks, *History of the York Rifle Company, from 1775 to 1908* (Augustus Loucks, 1908), 23.

39. Louis Gottschalk, "Lafayette in America, First Bicentennial Edition," (University of Chicago, 1975), 44.

40. *Eastern Argus*, August 19, 1825; Auguste Levasseur, *Lafayette in America*, 540.

41. *Village Record*, quoted in the *Charleston Mercury*, August 15, 1825.

42. Friedrich List, *Writings, Speeches, Letters, Vol. 2: Outlines of a Political Economy and Other Contributions from the American Period 1825-1832*, ed. William Notz (Hobbing, 1931).

43. Ibid.

44. Auguste Levasseur, *Lafayette in America*, 547.

45. Auguste Levasseur, *Lafayette in America*, 548.

46. Sophie Radford De Meissner, *Old Naval Days*, 17.

47. Michael Shiner, *The Diary of Michael Shiner Relating to the History of the Washington Navy Yard, 1813–1869*, 17.

48. Reprinted in the *Evening Post*, June 20, 1825.

49. Charles Morris, *Autobiography of Charles Morris*. Proceedings of the U.S. Naval Institute, published by the U.S. Naval Institue, No 12, vol VI, 1880.

50. The Marquis de Lafayette to Mes Chéres Filles, July 5, 1825, Dean Collection, Box 26, Folder 39.

51. *Baltimore American*, reprinted in the *Charleston Daily Courier*, September 28, 1825.

52. Lafayette to Émilie de Lafayette, May 10, 1825, in Dean Collection, Cornell University. Box 26, Folder 36.

53. Levasseur, *Lafayette in America*, 549.

54. *Fredericksburg Herald*, quoted in *Richmond Enquirer*, August 23, 1825.

55. Lafayette to Andrew Jackson, August 21, Correspondence of Andrew Jackson, vol. III, 1820–1828, ed. John Spencer Bassett (Carnie Institute of Washington, 1928), 290–291.

56. The Marquis de Lafayette to "Mes Chéres Amies," August 28, 1825, Dean Collection. Box 26, Folder 41.

57. Ibid.

58. The Marquis de Lafayette to Émilie de Lafayette, May 10, 1825, Dean Collection. Box 26, Folder 36.

59. Eleanor Parke Custis Lewis to George Washington de Lafayette, September 6, 1825, Dean Collection, Box 69, Folder 24.

60. The Marquis de Lafayette to Richard Peters, August 14, 1825, copy in Lilly, original in Historical Society of Pennsylvania.

61. *The Diary of John Quincy Adams*, 352.

62. Levasseur, *Lafayette in America*, 554.

63. *William Winston Seaton of the "National Intelligencer,"* 182.

Chapter 23

1. The Marquis de Lafayette, *Memoires*, vol. 1, 90, 292.

2. Levasseur, *Lafayette in America*, 558.

3. Levasseur, *Lafayette in America*, 558–560

4. Ibid.

5. *Delaware Advertiser and Farmer's Journal*, September 15, 1825.

6. *United States Gazette*, September 13, 1825.

7. *National Gazette and Literary Register*, September 13, 1825.

8. *United States Gazette*, September 13, 1825.

9. *Edwardsville Spectator*, October 8, 1825.

10. Loyall Farragut, *The Life of David Glasgow Farragut, First Admiral of the United States* (D. Appleton, 1879), 103.

11. Charles Morris, *Autobiography of Charles Morris*.

12. Auguste Levasseur to Peter Du Ponceau, September 25, 1825, Library Company of Philadelphia.

13. Auguste Levasseur, *Lafayette in America*, 565.

14. Auguste Levasseur, *Lafayette in America*, 572.

15. James Brown to Henry Clay, October 13, 1825, in *The Papers of Henry Clay*, vol. IV, *Secretary of State*, edited by James F. Hopkins (University Press of Kentucky), 735–736.

16. Memorandum describing the release from prison and homecoming of General William Barton of Rhode Island, The American Revolution Institute of the Society of the Cincinnati, Washington, DC.

Epilogue

1. *Vermont Gazette*, July 29, 1834.

2. Achille de Vaulabelle, *Chute De L'Empire Histoire des deux Restorations Jusqu'a La Chute de Charles X*. 10 Vols. (Perrotin, 1850), 275–276

3. *Samuel F. B. Morse, His Letters and Journals*, 272.

4. Sara Bodley to unnamed recipient, January 14, 1864, Filson Historical Society, Bodley Family Papers, 1773–1939.

BIBLIOGRAPHY

Research for and archival materials and manuscripts cited through-
out this book were drawn from the Alabama Department of
Archives and History; the American Revolution Institute of the
Society of the Cincinnati; the Arthur H. and Mary Marden Dean
Lafayette Collection, Division of Rare and Manuscript Collections,
Cornell University Library; the Captain Francis Allyn Papers at the
University of Kentucky Special Collections Research Center; the
Chicago Historical Society; the Filson Historical Society; the Fred
W. Smith National Library for the Study of George Washington at
Mount Vernon; the Georgia Historical Society; the Gilder Lehrman
Institute of American History; the Historical Society of Pennsylvania;
the Indiana State Library; James Monroe Papers at the Library of
Congress; the Joseph Downs Collection of Manuscripts and Printed
Ephemera, Henry Francis du Pont Winterhur Museum, Garden &
Library; Lafayette Manuscripts at the Hanna Holborn Gray Special
Collections Research Center at the University of Chicago Library;
Lafayette Manuscripts at the Lilly Library at Indiana University;
Marquis de Lafayette Papers at the Library of Congress; the Missouri
Historical Society Library & Research Center; the Morgan Library
& Museum; the New York Historical Society; the New York Public
Library; the Special Collections and College Archives at Lafayette
College; the Reutlingen City Archives; the University of Virginia
Library; and the William H. Crawford Papers at the Library of
Congress.

Additional research came from contemporary publications
including but not limited to the *Charleston Daily Courier*, *Columbian*

Centinel (Boston), *Daily National Intelligencer* (Washington, DC), *Daily National Journal* (Washington, DC), *Evening Post* (New York), *Harrisburg Chronicle, London Courier, Louisiana Courier, Louisiana State Gazette, Louisville Public Advertiser, Mississippi Gazette, Nashville Whig, New York Daily Advertiser, Niles' Weekly Register, Richmond Enquirer,* and *Troy Sentinel.*

Selected Bibliography

Abbey, Kathryn T. "The Land Ventures of General Lafayette in the Territory of Orleans and the State of Louisiana." *The Louisiana Historical Quarterly* 16, no. 3 (July 1933): 372.

Abbey, Kathryn T. "The Story of the Lafayette Lands in Florida." *The Florida Historical Society Quarterly* 10, no. 3 (1932): 115–33.

Ames, William E. "*The National Intelligencer*: Washington's Leading Political Newspaper." *Records of the Columbia Historical Society, Washington, D.C.* 66/68 (1966/1968): 71–83.

Ammon, Harry. *James Monroe: The Quest for National Identity.* University Press of Virginia, 1990.

Armistead, Margaret Beauchamp. "Chief William McIntosh and the Indian Springs Treaties." *The Georgia Review* 11, no. 3 (1957): 306–16.

Auricchio, Laura. *The Marquis: Lafayette Reconsidered.* Vintage Books, 2014.

Bernhard, Duke of Saxe-Weimar-Eisenach. *Travels Through North America During the Years 1825 and 1826.* Vol I. Philadelphia: Carey, Lea & Carey, 1828.

Bernstein, Peter L. *Wedding of the Waters: The Erie Canal and the Making of a Great Nation.* W.W. Norton, 2005.

Brady, Patricia. "Carnival of Liberty: Lafayette in Louisiana." *Louisiana History: The Journal of the Louisiana Historical Association* 41, no. 1 (2000): 23–40.

Brady, Patricia. *George Washington's Beautiful Nelly: The Letters of Eleanor Parke Custis Lewis to Elizabeth Bordley Gibson, 1794–1851.* Expanded ed. University of South Carolina Press, 2006.

Brandon, Edgar Ewing. *Lafayette, Guest of the Nation: A Contemporary Account of the Triumphal Tour of General Lafayette Through the United States in 1824–1825 as Reported by the Local Newspapers.* Vol. I. Oxford Historical Press, 1950.

Brandon, Edgar Ewing. *Lafayette, Guest of the Nation: A Contemporary Account of the Triumphal Tour of General Lafayette Through the United States in 1824–1825 as Reported by the Local Newspapers.* Vol. II. Oxford Historical Press, 1954.

Brandon, Edgar Ewing. *A Pilgrimage of Liberty: A Contemporary Account of the Triumphal Tour of General Lafayette Through the Southern and Western States in 1825, as Reported by the Local Newspapers.* The Lawhead Press, 1944.

Broglie, Duc de. *Souvenirs, 1785–1870.* Paris: Calmann Lévy, 1886.

Brown, Everett Sommerville, ed. *The Missouri Compromises and Presidential Politics, 1820–1825: From the Letters of William Plummer Jr., Representative from New Hampshire.* Missouri Historical Society, 1926.

Brown, Stuart Gerry, ed. *The Autobiography of James Monroe.* Edited and introduced by Stuart Gerry Brown and with a foreword by William M. Ferraro. Syracuse University Press, 2017.

Browning, Andrew H. *The Panic of 1819: The First Great Depression*. University of Missouri Press, 2019.

Buell, Augustus. *History of Andrew Jackson: Pioneer, Patriot, Soldier, Politician, President*. Vol 2. Charles Scribner's Sons, 1904.

Burstein, Andrew. *America's Jubilee: How in 1826 a Generation Remembered Fifty Years of Independence*. Alfred A. Knopf, 2001.

Butterfield, Kevin. *The Making of Tocqueville's America: Law and Association in the Early United States*. University of Chicago Press, 2015.

Cappon, Lester J. "The First American Tribute to Lafayette in 1824." *Virginia Magazine of History and Biography* 47, no. 3 (1939): 230–33.

Chambers, Thomas A. *Memories of War: Visiting Battlegrounds and Bonefields in the Early American Republic*. Cornell University Press, 2018.

Chinard, Gilbert, ed. *The Letters of Lafayette and Jefferson*. The Johns Hopkins Press, 1929.

Chinard, Gilbert. *Thomas Jefferson: The Apostle of Americanism*. 2nd ed., rev. University of Michigan Press, 1975.

Clark, Charles S. *George Washington Parke Custis: A Rarefied Life in America's First Family*. McFarland, 2021.

Clary, David A. *Adopted Son: Washington, Lafayette, and the Friendship That Saved the Revolution*. Bantam, 2007.

Cloquet, M. Jules. *Recollections of the Private Life of General Lafayette*. London: Baldwin and Cradock, 1835.

Cooper, James Fenimore. *The Travelling Bachelor; or, Notions of the Americans*. New York: Stringer and Townsend, 1856.

Cornog, Evan. *The Birth of Empire: DeWitt Clinton and the American Experience, 1769–1828*. Oxford University Press, 1998.

Costello, Matthew. *The Property of the Nation: George Washington's Tomb, Mount Vernon, and the Memory of the First President*. University Press of Kansas, 2019.

Dangerfield, George. *The Era of Good Feelings*. Ivan R. Dee, 1989.

De Meissner, Sophie Radford. *Old Naval Days: Sketches from the Life of Rear Admiral William Radford, U.S.N.* Henry Holt, 1920.

Dufour, John James. *The American Vine-Dresser's Guide*. Cincinnati: S.J. Browne, 1825.

Dugan, Frances L. S., and Jacqueline P. Bull, eds. *Bluegrass Craftsman: Being the Reminiscences of Ebenezer Hiram Stedman Papermaker, 1808–1885*. University of Kentucky Press, 1959.

Duncan, Mike. *Hero of Two Worlds: The Marquis de Lafayette in the Age of Revolution*. PublicAffairs, 2021.

Eckhardt, Celia Morris. *Fanny Wright: Rebel in America*. Harvard University Press, 1984.

Elliott, Helen. "Frances Wright's Experiment with Negro Emancipation." *Indiana Magazine of History* 35, no. 2 (1939): 141–57.

Farmer, Lydia Hoyt. *The Life of La Fayette: The Knight of Liberty in Two Worlds and Two Centuries*. New York: Thomas Y. Crowell, 1888.

Farragut, Loyal. *The Life of David Glasgow Farragut, First Admiral of the United States Navy*. New York: D. Appleton, 1879.

Fielding, A. K. *Rough Diamond: The Life of Colonel William Stephen Hamilton, Alexander Hamilton's Forgotten Son*. Indiana University Press, 2021.

Frank, Andrew K. "The Rise and Fall of William McIntosh: Authority and Identity on the American Frontier." *Georgia Historical Quarterly* 86, no. 1 (2002): 18–48.

Franklin, Wayne. *James Fenimore Cooper: The Early Years*. Yale University Press, 2007.

French, Allen. *The Siege of Boston*. MacMillan, 1911.

Fuye, Maurice de la, and Émile Babeau. *The Apostle of Liberty: A Life of Lafayette*. Translated by Edward Hyams. Thomas Yoseloff, 1956.

Gallagher, H. M. Pierce. *Robert Mills: Architect of the Washington Monument, 1781–1855*. Columbia University Press, 1935.

Gerson, Noel B. *Statue in Search of a Pedestal: A Biography of the Marquis de Lafayette*. Dodd, Mead, 1976.

Gilbert, Amos. *Memoir of Frances Wright: The Pioneer Woman in the Cause of Human Rights*. Cincinnati: Longley Brothers, 1855.

Gilchrist, Agnes Addison. *William Strickland: Architect and Engineer, 1788–1854*. University of Pennsylvania Press, 1950.

Gilder, Roman. *The Battery*. Houghton Mifflin, 1936.

Gilje, Paul A. "The Rise of Capitalism in the Early Republic." *Journal of the Early Republic* 16, no. 2 (1996): 159–81.

Glatthaar, Joseph T., and James Kirby Martin. *Forgotten Allies: The Oneida Indians and the American Revolution*. Hill and Wang, 2007.

Gobel, David, and Daves Rossell. *Commemoration in America: Essays on Monuments, Memorialization, and Memory*. University of Virginia Press, 2013.

Gottschalk, Louis. *Lafayette Comes to America*. University of Chicago Press, 1935.

Gottschalk, Louis. *Lafayette Between the American and the French Revolution (1783–1789)*. University of Chicago Press, 1950.

Gross, Robert A. *The Minutemen and Their World*. Rev. and expanded ed. Picador, 2022.

Hall, John Elihu. *The Port Folio*. Vol. 18, *From July to December 1824*. Philadelphia: Harrison Hall, 1824.

Hamilton, Stanislaus Murray, ed. *The Writings of James Monroe: Including a Collection of His Public and Private Papers and Correspondence Now for the First Time Printed*. Vol. 5, *1807–1816*. G.P. Putnam's Sons, 1901.

Hamilton, Stanislaus Murray, ed. *The Writings of James Monroe*. Vol. 6, *1817–1823*. G.P. Putnam's Sons, 1902.

Hamilton, Stanislaus Murray, ed. *The Writings of James Monroe*. Vol. 7, *1824–1831*. G.P. Putnam's Sons, 1903.

Haveman, Christopher D. *Rivers of Sand: Creek Indian Emigration, Relocation, and Ethnic Cleansing in the American South*. University of Nebraska Press, 2016.

Hay, Robert P. "The American Revolution Twice Recalled: Lafayette's Visit and the Election of 1824." *Indiana Magazine of History* 69, no. 1 (March 1973): 43–62.

Hofstadter, Richard. *The American Political Tradition and the Men Who Made It*. Vintage Books, 1989.

Howard, Thomas W. "Indiana Newspapers and the Presidential Election of 1824." *Indiana Magazine of History* 63, no. 3 (1967): 177–206.

Howe, Daniel Walker. *What Hath God Wrought: The Transformation of America, 1815–1848*. Oxford University Press, 2007.

Hume, Edgar Erskine. "Lafayette in Kentucky." *The Register of Kentucky State Historical Society* 33, no. 103 (1935): 118–36.

Hunt, Gaillard, ed. *The First Forty Years of Washington Society, Portrayed by the Family Letters of Mrs. Samuel Harrison Smith (Margaret Bayard) from the Collection of Her Grandson, J. Henley Smith*. Charles Scribner's Sons, 1906.

Idzerda, Stanley J., Anne C. Loveland, and Marc H. Miller. *Lafayette, Hero of Two Worlds: The Art and Pageantry of His Farewell Tour of America, 1824–1825*. University Press of New England, 1989.

Jackson, Donald. "George Washington's Beautiful Nelly." *American Heritage* 28, no. 2 (February 1977). https://www.americanheritage.com/george-washingtons-beautiful -nelly.

Jackson, Joseph, and William Strickland. *The First Native American Architect and Engineer*. Alpha Editions, 2019.

Kite, Elizabeth S. "Lafayette and His Companions on the 'Victoire.'" *Records of the American Catholic Historical Society of Philadelphia* 45, no. 1 (1934): 1–32.

Klein, Philip Shriver. *Pennsylvania Politics, 1817–1832: A Game Without Rules*. Historical Society of Pennsylvania, 1940.

Kramer, Lloyd. *Lafayette in Two Worlds: Public Cultures and Personal Identities in an Age of Revolutions*. University of North Carolina Press, 1996.

Lafayette, Marie-Joseph Paul Yves Roch Gilbert Du Motier, Marquis de. *Memoirs, Correspondence and Manuscripts of General Lafayette*. Vol 1. London: Saunders and Otley, 1837.

Lafayette, Marie-Joseph Paul Yves Roch Gilbert Du Motier, Marquis de. *Memoirs, Correspondence and Manuscripts of General Lafayette*. Vol 2. London: Saunders and Otley, 1837.

Lafayette, Marie-Joseph Paul Yves Roch Gilbert Du Motier, Marquis de. *Mémoires, Correspondance et Manuscrits du Général Lafayette*. Vol. 6. Paris: H. Fournier Aîné, 1838.

Laffitte, Jacques. *Mémoires de Laffitte (1767–1844)* Edited by Paul Duchon. Firim-Didot, 1932.

Lamplugh, George R. *Rancorous Enmities and Blind Partialities: Factions and Parties in Georgia Politics, 1807–1845*. University Press of America, 2015.

Lane, Margaret. *Frances Wright and the "Great Experiment."* Manchester University Press, 1972.

Lefebvre, Georges. *The French Revolution*. Vol. 1, *From Its Origins to 1793*. Translated by Elizabeth Moss Evanson. Columbia University Press, 1962.

Lefebvre, Georges. *The French Revolution*. Vol. 2, *From 1793 to 1799*. Translated by John Hall Stewart and James Friguglietti. Columbia University Press, 1964.

Levasseur, Auguste. *Lafayette in America in 1824 and 1825*. Translated by Alan R. Hoffman. Lafayette Press, 2006.

Loveland, Anne C. *Emblem of Liberty: The Image of Lafayette in the American Mind*. Louisiana State University Press, 1971.

Mabee, Carleton. *The American Leonardo: A Life of Samuel F. B. Morse*. Rev. ed. Purple Mountain Press, 2000.

Maier, Pauline. *American Scripture: Making the Declaration of Independence*. Alfred A Knopf, 1997.

Malone, Dumas. *Jefferson and His Time: The Sage of Monticello*. Little, Brown, 1981.

Maurois, André. *Adrienne: The Life of the Marquise De La Fayette*. McGraw-Hill, 1961.

McDermott, John Francis. "William Clark: Pioneer Museum Man." *Journal of the Washington Academy of Sciences* 44, no. 11 (1954): 370–73.

Mires, Charlene. *Independence Hall in American Memory*. University of Pennsylvania Press, 2002.

Mooney, Chase C. *William H. Crawford: 1772–1834*. University Press of Kentucky, 1974.

Moore, Glover. *The Missouri Controversy, 1819–1821*. University of Kentucky Press, 1953.

Morris, Charles. *The Autobiography of Commodore Charles Morris*, U.S. Naval Institute Press, 2002.

Muldoon, Sylvan J. *Alexander Hamilton's Pioneer Son: The Life and Times of Colonel William Stephen Hamilton; 1797–1850.* The Aurand Press, 1930.

Nagel, Paul C. "The Election of 1824: A Reconsideration Based on Newspaper Opinion." *The Journal of Southern History* 26, no. 3 (1960): 315–29.

Neely, Sylvia. *Lafayette and the Liberal Ideal, 1814–1824: Politics and Conspiracy in an Age of Reaction.* Southern Illinois University Press, 1991.

Neely, Sylvia. "The Politics of Liberty in the Old World and the New: Lafayette's Return to America in 1824." *Journal of the Early Republic* 6, no. 2 (1986): 151–71.

Nevins, Allan, ed. *The Diary of John Quincy Adams, 1794–1845: American Political, Social, and Intellectual Life from Washington to Polk.* Longmans, Green, 1929.

Nolan, J. Bennett. *Lafayette in America Day by Day.* The Johns Hopkins Press, 1934.

Nolte, Vincent. *Fifty Years in Both Hemispheres; or, Reminiscences of the Life of a Former Merchant.* New York: Redfield, 1854.

Padgett, James A. "The Letters of Doctor Samuel Brown to President Jefferson and James Brown." *The Register of Kentucky State Historical Society* 35, no. III (1937): 99–130.

Payne-Gaposchkin, Cecilia Helena, ed. "The Nashoba Plan for Removing the Evils of Slavery: Letters of Frances and Camilla Wright, 1820–1829." *Harvard Library Bulletin* 23, no. 3 (July 1975): 221–51.

Perkins, A. J. G., and Theresa Wolfson. *Frances Wright, Free Enquirer: The Study of a Temperament.* Harper & Brothers, 1939.

Porter, Sarah Harvey. *The Life and Times of Anne Royall.* Torch Press, 1909.

Quertermous, Grant S. *A Georgetown Life: The Reminiscences of Britannia Wellington Peter Kennon of Tudor Place.* Georgetown University Press, 2020.

Quincy, Josiah. *Figures of the Past from the Leaves of Old Journals.* Boston: Roberts Brothers, 1884.

Quincy, Eliza Susan Morton. *Memoir of the Life of Eliza Susan Morton Quincy.* Boston: John Wilson and Son, 1861.

Ratcliffe, Donald. *The One-Party Presidential Contest: Adams, Jackson, and 1824's Five-Horse Race.* University Press of Kansas, 2015.

Remini, Robert V. *The Life of Andrew Jackson.* Perennial Classics, 2001.

Remini, Robert V. *Henry Clay: Statesman for the Union.* W. W. Norton, 1991.

Rémusat, Charles de. *Mémoires de Ma Vie.* Preface by Jean Lebrun. Perrin, 2017.

Rothbard, Murray Newton. *The Panic of 1819: Reactions and Policies.* Columbia University Press, 1962.

Schama, Simon. *Citizens: A Chronicle of the French Revolution.* Vintage Books, 1990.

Sheriff, Carol. *The Artificial River: The Erie Canal and the Paradox of Progress, 1817–1862,* Hill and Wang, 1996.

Silverman, Kenneth. *Lightning Man: The Accursed Life of Samuel F. B. Morse.* Da Capo, 2004.

Somkin, Fred. *Unquiet Eagle: Memory and Desire in the Idea of American Freedom, 1815–1860.* Cornell University Press, 1967.

Spitzer, Alan B. *Old Hatreds and Young Hopes.* Harvard University Press, 1971.

Stegeman, John F., and Janet A. Stegeman. *Caty: A Biography of Catherine Littlefield Greene.* University of Georgia Press, 1977.

Stendhal. *Memoirs of an Egotist.* Translated by David Ellis. Horizon Press, 1975.

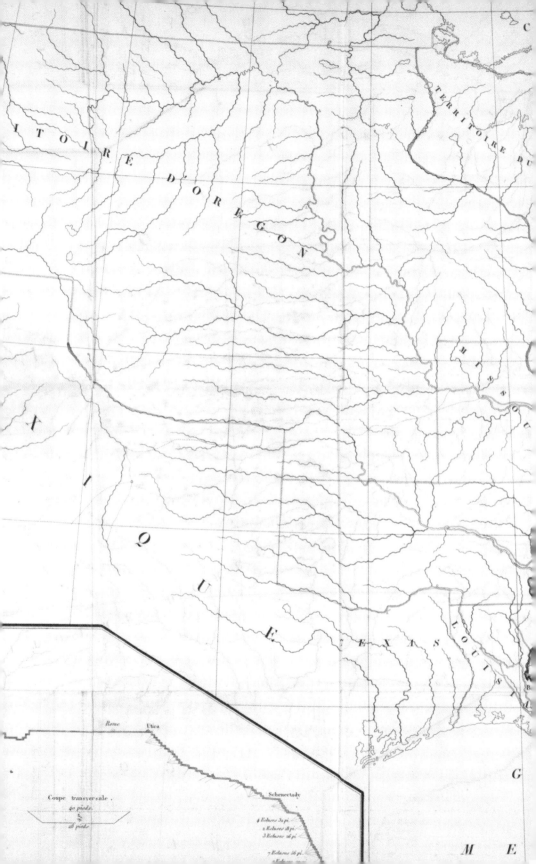